本书课题组成员

郭建晖　张祥志　李松杰

张广弘　卢　群　颜璐佳

IP与创意产业

景德镇故事

IP and Creative Industry

Jingdezhen Story

中国国家版权局
世界知识产权组织　编著

江西人民出版社
Jiangxi People's Publishing House
全国百佳出版社

序

　　我谨代表世界知识产权组织，祝贺各位作者成功完成《IP 与创意产业：景德镇故事》。本项目是世界知识产权组织与中国国家版权局的合作项目，由江西省版权局和景德镇市人民政府共同实施。

　　本项目展示了版权在促进和保护当地产业，特别是陶瓷产业方面发挥的重要作用。景德镇素有"瓷都"美誉，数百年来以其精湛的制瓷工艺和推动陶瓷艺术发展演变的卓越贡献闻名于世。

　　通过有效整合数字技术，如今的景德镇正受益于传统知识、创意作品与数字的融合。这种融合带来了新理念和新内容，进一步提升了陶瓷创意产业的竞争力，并推动了该行业的高质量发展。

　　在这一变革之旅中，版权保护是保护艺术家作品和支持品牌发展的关键要素。通过版权，陶瓷产业正助力年轻人构建他们的艺术天地，并将他们的创意和文化传播到世界各地。

　　本项目探讨了景德镇陶瓷行业利用版权推动产业进步的多元路径，包括提升产品价值、鼓励创业精神和促进可持续发展等。

创作者们越来越多地借助版权取得成功，让知识产权为新兴数字创作和传统艺术形式赋予文化和经济价值。

景德镇的发展历程展示了陶瓷产业所取得的成就，以及知识产权如何促进具有创新性、竞争力、文化活力和包容性的行业发展。

我们衷心感谢各位作者和研究人员以深刻的见解记录景德镇陶瓷产业的转型历程。他们的贡献不仅记录了一段文化保护与创新的非凡道路，还引发了人们对知识产权在经济、社会和文化发展中不断演变的作用的深刻思考。

世界知识产权组织

区域与国家发展部门副总干事

哈桑·克莱布

2025 年 6 月

FOREWORD

On behalf of the World Intellectual Property Organization (WIPO), I wish to congratulate the authors on the successful finalization of the report of the IP and Creative Industry: Jingdezhen Story, a collaborative initiative between WIPO and NCAC, implemented by the Jiangxi Provincial Copyright Administration and Jingdezhen Municipal People's Government.

The Project demonstrates the important role copyright can play in the promotion and protection of local industries, such as the ceramic industry. Often referred to as the "Porcelain Capital," Jingdezhen is world renowned for its centuries old expertise in porcelain production and for its role in the development and evolution of the ceramic arts.

Through the effective integration of digital technology, Jingdezhen is today benefiting from the fusion of traditional knowledge, creative works and digitalization. By bringing new ideas and content, this combination is further enhancing the competitiveness of the porcelain creative industry as well as promoting high-quality growth in the sector.

In this transformative journey, copyright protection is a key element to protect the work of the artists and to support brand development. Through copyright, the ceramic industry is helping the youth design their universe and spread their creativity and culture everywhere.

This Project explores the many ways in which Jingdezhen's porcelain sector is leveraging copyright to drive industrial progress—enhancing product value, encouraging entrepreneurship and promoting sustainable development.

Creators are increasingly leveraging copyright for success, allowing intellectual property to enrich both emerging digital creations and traditional art forms with cultural and economic value.

Jingdezhen's journey showcases the porcelain industry's accomplishments and how intellectual property can foster innovative, competitive, culturally vibrant and inclusive sectors.

We extend our sincere thanks to the authors and researchers for their insightful work in capturing the transformation of Jingdezhen's porcelain industry. Their contribution not only documents a remarkable journey of cultural preservation and innovation but also sparks meaningful reflection on the evolving role of intellectual property in economic, social and cultural development.

Hasan Kleib
Deputy Director General
Regional & National Development Sector
World Intellectual Property Organization (WIPO)
June 2025

目　录

版权创意产业：
景德镇故事

Contents

Chapter III   The Historical Evolution and Foundations of
            Jingdezhen's Ceramic Copyright Awareness   243

Chapter IV   Preserving Jingdezhen Ceramic Heritage: Copyright's Role in the New Era   269

项目概要和实施情况

千年不息的窑火积淀了深厚的陶瓷文化底蕴，历久弥新的制瓷技艺成就了世界瓷艺高峰，蓬勃发展的陶瓷创意文化产业催生了一座因瓷而盛的千年古城，无数个精彩绝伦的陶瓷艺术作品铸就了世界瓷都的金字招牌，景德镇陶瓷已经成为世界认识中国的典型代表，它是世界文明花园里璀璨夺目的中华文化符号。在长久的瓷业发展史中，景德镇已经摸索出独具特色的版权保护办法。近年来，随着陶瓷创意文化产业的迭代升级，景德镇在党和国家的领导下，不断优化司法保护体制机制，创新性地打造版权防护网，打通版权运用、保护、管理的全链条，为陶瓷创意文化产业创新发展提供了新的机遇，为全球版权治理贡献了中国智慧和中国方案。

第一节
项目的背景

一、产业发展背景

景德镇自唐宋以来，一直是享誉国内外的陶瓷产业中心；明清时期，景德镇不仅独领国内陶瓷产业的发展，而且产品出口到世界许多国家和地区，成为名副其实的"世界瓷都"。近年来，景德镇陶瓷产业发展迅速。2023 年，全市陶瓷工业总产值为 861.25 亿元人民币，同比增长 29.44%；陶瓷市场主体超过 2 万家，规上企业 258 家，陶瓷从业人员约 15 万人，陶瓷技能人才 4.5 万人，陶瓷专业技术人才 6600 多人。其中，70 多家陶瓷企业成立了研发中心，形成了集勘探、制造、设计、研究、教育、交流于一体的完备的陶瓷产业体系。景德镇在全国 13 个口岸、65 个国家实现常态化通关出口，真正实现了"买全球、卖全球"。

二、版权保护背景

自 20 世纪 90 年代以来，景德镇陶瓷产业经历了从公有陶瓷产业体系向个体、分散陶瓷生产体系的转变，出现了一些不正当竞争、产品侵权的现象。与此同时，景德镇肩负着陶瓷文化的传承创新、产业结构转型升级、营商环境进一步优化的历史使命。鉴于此，景德镇市高度重视版权保护，逐步探索形成了集民事、行政、司法保护于一体的版权保护体系。自21世纪以来，景德镇陶瓷产业快速发展，陶瓷创意作品大量涌现，陶瓷版权工作得到推进和加强。2014年修订发布的《景德镇陶瓷知识产权保护管理规定》，从保护机制、主要部门职责和保护措施等三个方面，开启了陶瓷知识产权保护，景德镇进入陶瓷产权保护的快速发展期。

自2019年以来，景德镇市着力建设国家陶瓷文化传承创新试验区，把版权工作作为陶瓷文化传承创新的核心要素，努力打造"全国版权示范城市"的景德镇样本。2019年，在国家版权局和江西省版权局的大力支持和精心指导下，景德镇正式获批创建版权示范资格。在两年的创建期内，景德镇在版权创造、运用、保护、管理、服务各个环节开展了卓有成效的工作，在版权登记、交易、保护等方面也取得了显著进步（其中版权登记数量增长情况参见下表1-1）。以景德镇国家陶瓷文化传承创新试验区建设为统领，景德镇市把版权作为陶瓷文化传承创新工作的核心要素，倾力打造版权工作新发展格局。2020年4月，景德镇市委、市政府把"推动中国景德镇（陶瓷）知识产权快速维权中心升级为中国（景德镇）知识产权保护中心"，列入景德镇国家陶瓷文化传承创新试验区建设重点任务。2020年9月，景德镇市人民政府发布《景德镇市创建全国版权示范城市实施方案》，从提升版权创造能力、提升版权保护能力、提升版权运用能力和提升版权管理能力等方面部署重点任务。2021年4月，景德镇设立全国第六家非省会城市的知识产权法庭。该法庭以陶瓷产业知识产权保护为重心，深耕陶瓷文化，推出"快速立案、简案快审、繁案精审"办案流程，创建"诉前快速保全、诉中多元调解、判后跟踪回访"工作机制，实行专业化、规范化、集约化办案模式。同时，加强对"景德镇制"地理标志、先进工业陶瓷、文化艺术陶瓷、高端日用瓷的司法保护。围绕陶瓷知识产权保护和版权意识提升，该法庭先后举办了2021中国景德镇国际陶瓷博览会陶瓷知识产权保护论坛、"景德镇"陶瓷地理标志司法保护座谈会、女陶艺家知识产权保护座谈会，推动形成强化陶瓷知识产权保护共识，共同致力于维护好"景德镇"金字招牌。

2021 年 7 月，景德镇国家陶瓷版权交易中心成立，这是全国第一家面向特定行业的国家级版权交易中心，也被江西省委、省政府列为打造赣鄱文化品牌的重点建设项目。在各方共同努力下，2021 年 10 月，景德镇正式荣获"全国版权示范城市"称号，成为中部地区首个、中国第 13 个全国版权示范城市。

表 1-1　景德镇市历年版权登记数量表

年份	版权登记总数 / 件	较上年增长率
2001	1	
2002	2	100.00%
2003	24	1100.00%
2004	104	333.33%
2005	113	8.65%
2006	76	−32.74%
2007	66	−13.16%
2008	128	93.94%
2009	182	42.19%
2010	190	4.40%
2011	223	17.37%
2012	151	−32.29%
2013	310	105.30%
2014	755	143.55%
2015	332	−56.03%
2016	446	34.34%
2017	444	−0.45%
2018	844	90.09%
2019	888	5.21%
2020	6633	646.96%
2021	5794	−12.65%
2022	19295	233.02%
2023	31563	63.58%
2024	41815	32.48%

数据来源：景德镇市文旅局

IP与特色产业：
景德镇故事

景德镇市版权局荣获"2022中国版权金奖·管理奖"（景德镇市版权局供图）

为巩固全国版权示范城市创建成果，深入推进版权事业与版权产业发展，进一步提升版权创造、保护、运用、管理水平，充分发挥版权工作在推动经济发展和文化繁荣中的重要作用，景德镇市持续推进陶瓷产业发展，先后启动实施了238个重点项目，建设了陶博城、陶阳里、陶溪川等一批标杆项目。2023年，景德镇市版权局获评2022中国版权金奖（管理奖）。2023年6月，景德镇市人民检察院成立陶瓷文化遗产和知识产权检察保护中心，集案件办理、专家咨询、便捷服务等功能于一体，实现相关业务事项"一中心通办"。2023年10月，景德镇市公安局成立陶瓷知识产权保护中心，创新条块结合、部门协同、综合治理的警务运行机制，建立公安与文化执法等部门快速联动机制，构建以公安机关为牵头和主导的举报受理、鉴定执法、打击犯罪等为一体的陶瓷版权维权体系，并出台知识产权专项保护机制，推动商标权保护、著作权登记、原产地保护、名人作品保护等"全面升级"。2024年3月，江西省第十四届人民代表大会常务委员会第七次会议审议通过《"景德镇制"陶瓷保护条例》。该条例为规范"景德镇制"陶瓷市场秩序、保证"景德镇制"陶瓷产品质量提供了切实可行的依据和保证。自 2021 年以来，景德镇先后创建全国版权示范基地 2 家、江西省版权示范基地 10 家，设立版权服务站 4 处。此外，景德镇市还建成"陶瓷艺术设计版权交易平台"，打造版权交易、转化、运营一体化产业链，实现诉讼与调解、仲裁、行政裁决、行政复议等非诉讼解纷方式间的相互配合与协调。

景德镇陶瓷产业的快速发展和版权登记数的迅速增加，引起了世界知识产权组织和国家版权局的关注和重视。2019 年，景德镇版权登记数为 888 件，2022 年已经增加到 19295 件。2022 年 11 月，在景德镇举办的 2022 国际版权论坛开幕式上，国家版权局、世界知识产权组织、江西省委宣传部（江西省版权局）、景德镇市人民政府，共同启动了世界知识产权组织版权保护优秀案例示范点调研项目。对以版权促进陶瓷产业传承创新进而实现城市高质量发展的经验做法，进行深入调研，进一步推动地方特色版权产业高质量发展。同时，该项目为讲好中国版权故事提供鲜活素材，也为全球版权治理贡献中国智慧和中国方案。2024 年 8 月，中宣部版权管理局的领导和专家到景德镇调度和指导案例示范点的研究工作，对调研项目进行指导。江西省委宣传部（江西省版权局）、景德镇市委宣传部和景德镇文旅局为课题顺利开展提供了便利的条件。

第二节
立项的目的和意义

本项目的目的在于揭示版权与促进创意产业发展、城市高质量发展的内在逻辑关系。在景德镇陶瓷版权发展的历史逻辑、当代版权保护工作的特色、版权运用工作的实践、版权工作对城市发展的助推作用等方面，从政府、社会和个体三个维度，围绕景德镇陶瓷产业发展中逐步形成的全链条版权保护模式，通过政府管理、市场竞争、资源配置和创新激励等视角，进行个案分析和总结，说明版权保护对促进陶瓷文化创意产业发展、促进市场规范有序运转、推动版权在地方经济社会发展和构建和谐社会竞争合作环境中起到的积极作用。

第一，简明论述景德镇陶瓷发展演变史，并在此基础上，进一步论证景德镇陶瓷版权的发展历程；提出景德镇陶瓷版权保护观念向法治嬗变的三个时期，归纳景德镇陶瓷版权保护意识的生成基础；阐明版权保护向法律规范优化的演进逻辑，证明景德镇以日臻完善的"版权制度"，推进"千年瓷业"生生不息；以多元共生的"版权保护"，助力"千年瓷都"蜚声中外。

第二，梳理总结景德镇市在陶瓷版权工作方面的举措与模式。通过对景德镇市版权地方政策、版权激励体系、版权保护机制、版权服务实践、版权运用实例和版权管理特色的梳理和总结，从版权创造、运用、保护、管理、服务五个维度提炼出景德镇市陶瓷版权工作的模式，总结出景德镇市陶瓷版权创造持续化、运用灵活化、保护专门化、管理特色化、服务常态化的鲜明特色与可推广经验。

第三，展示呈现景德镇陶瓷版权的精彩故事与典型个案。通过描述景德镇瑞牛公司、陶溪川文创街区、景德镇市知识产权法庭、景德镇陶瓷版权交易中心和景德镇国际瓷博会在版权工作方面的具体做法，让读者了解景德镇版权保护的具体细节与具象方案；立体化、全方位、多视角，为全球呈现景德镇的 IP 与创意产业。

第四，剖析解释版权在助力景德镇陶瓷文化创意产业发展和赋能城市高质量发展过程中的效用。通过大量的调研和数据，在理论上厘清 IP（含版权）与城市高质量发展间的关联，尝试构建版权赋能城市高质量发展的指标体系，并通过对景德镇市城市发展的法治、经济、产业、社会和文化等相关数据的分析，揭示政府积极有效的版权政策措施在促进城市发展方面的重要作用，以此论证版权有益于城市高质量发展。

第五，推广传播景德镇市版权保护的成功经验。通过提炼总结景德镇陶瓷版权保护的成功经验，提出版权保护在推进陶瓷文化传承发展、促进城市经济社会发展和激发个人创造力中发挥的作用，为中国其他地区和其他国家加强版权保护，提供可参考、可借鉴的经验。

项目内容

本项目以"IP 与创意产业：景德镇故事"为主线，在对景德镇陶瓷发展历史和传统知识产权保护经验体系梳理的基础上，分析当前景德镇陶瓷产业发展规模和发展类别，描述景德镇市场状况和产品种类。在此基础上，对景德镇陶瓷版权保护的生动实践进行解读，指出版权在构建公平竞争的市场秩序，促进城市经济发展、社会文化繁荣中起到的重要作用。调研报告主要分为以下六个部分。

第一部分，主要介绍调研项目的背景、意义、内容、方法和研究结论等。景德镇是闻名世界的"瓷都"，在数千年持续发展的陶瓷历程中留存了丰厚的陶瓷文化遗产，也是世界上为数不多的手工业"活态"传承的样板城市。厚重的历史、丰富多元的陶瓷版权元素和充满活力的文化创意产业让这座城市得到各方的关注和认可。

第二部分，主要分析景德镇陶瓷产业发展历史，尤其是侧重对景德镇陶瓷产业发展现状的分析。重点总结了景德镇在陶瓷产业体系、产业规模、产业类别和产品特色等方面的成就。

第三部分，基于景德镇不同时期的版权保护表现形式，以景德镇陶瓷创作主体、管理机构及其他社会主体之间因陶瓷作品创作、发表、传播与运用而产生的各项精神或财产关系，划分出景德镇陶瓷版权保护观念向法治嬗变的三个时期，归纳出景德镇陶瓷版权保护意识的生成基础，阐明版权保护向法律规范优化的演进逻辑，揭示景德镇陶瓷版权演进轨迹和发展历程。

第四部分，通过对景德镇在版权"创造、运用、保护、管理、服务"等方面的全链条保护个案和相对应的版权保护模式的分析，进一步对新时代版权保护现状进行阐述，侧重论述版权助推城市高质量发展的政策和举措，总结景德镇版权保护的经验。

第五部分，论述陶瓷版权助推景德镇高质量发展，主要从陶瓷版权助推城市制度体系构建、城市法治维权机制完善、城市经济结构优化、城市公共服务提升、城市人文环境打造等维度，揭示陶瓷版权在助推景德镇高质量发展中的作用。构建陶瓷版权助推景德镇高质量发展的评价体系，并通过陶瓷版权在评价体系中的相关数据呈现，客观地印证陶瓷版权在景德镇高质量发展过程中的助推作用。依据景德镇高质量发展的脉络，提出陶瓷版权在未来的助力方向。

第六部分，结合景德镇在陶瓷版权保护过程中的诸多启示，提出四点经验，用以宣传推广。

第四节
项目思路和方法

　　本项目综合运用定性分析和定量分析相结合、个案调研和抽样调查相结合、口述访谈和文献解读相结合等法学、社会学、经济学、历史学多学科交叉的研究方法，明确调研重点和难点，确定调研的方向和目标，形成调研大纲和任务分工。

　　一是定性分析法和定量分析法。通过对陶瓷资料、统计数据和实地调研、口述访谈等定性和定量相结合的方法，将主观和客观分析有机统一起来。

　　二是文献搜集和数据整理。搜集整理景德镇陶瓷发展史和版权保护的相关资料和数据，包括产业规模、产品特征、版权保护的法律法规、版权保护的文件、版权保护代表性的事件和案例等，掌握版权助力城市发展的相关资料。

　　三是口述访谈和个案分析法。通过对职能部门相关人员、企业人员、陶瓷从业者等的访谈，从实践主体上了解版权助力景德镇陶瓷产业发展的成就；通过对陶溪川、版权交易中心、知识产权法庭、瑞牛公司、国际瓷博会和"洋景漂"个案的分析，从实践客体了解景德镇在版权保护上的成就。

第五节

项目团队情况

国家版权局，江西省委、省政府，景德镇市人民政府对此项目高度重视，江西省委宣传部专门成立包括景德镇市委宣传部、景德镇市文化广电新闻出版旅游局相关职能部门领导在内的协调组，负责对项目进行总体协调。成立课题组，由时任江西省委宣传部常务副部长郭建晖同志总负责，统筹完成各项研究任务，并把课题分成景德镇陶瓷产业发展史中的版权保护意识研究和版权保护助力景德镇城市高质量发展两项子课题。由景德镇陶瓷大学中国陶瓷发展研究院研究团队完成子课题一的研究任务，由华东交通大学知识产权学院团队完成子课题二的研究任务。

第六节

研究结论概述

　　景德镇千年不息的窑火，累积了浩如烟海的陶瓷文化宝藏，不仅以陶瓷器物承载创新创意成果，也使思想观念上的版权保护得以产生并延续。千百年来，景德镇围绕陶瓷作品保护产生的牌记、官样、款识、禁例等相关措施，构建了源起于宋元、赓续于明清、嬗变于晚清民国的陶瓷版权发展历程。不同阶段的陶瓷版权表现形式，忠实记录了我国陶瓷版权保护活动与创新治理变迁的历史信息，生动展现出陶瓷版权保护观念在我国手工业发展中的重要价值。

　　版权保护助力景德镇陶瓷产业的传承发展。景德镇有着丰富多样的物质和非物质文化遗产资源。景德镇通过制定一系列版权保护的法规，加强对手工制瓷非物质文化遗产传承人队伍建设，调动传承人的积极性和主动性；景德镇还深度挖掘物质文化资源，通过设立古陶瓷基因库等形式，为陶瓷文化传承提供固定版权资源。比如，2021年，景德镇首款城市礼物"福如意"，其创作灵感来自中国陶瓷博物馆收藏的清乾隆青花葫芦纹葫芦瓶，集中展示了以"和合"文化为代表的中国优秀传统文化的传承和发展。

版权保护激发景德镇陶瓷产业的创新创造。景德镇陶瓷生产具有小型、分散、手工、从业者人数多等特点，这种特点导致产品易被仿冒、维权难的现象。经过实践探索，景德镇构建了"四中心一联盟"的陶瓷版权保护体系，重点保护重塑"景德镇制"区域品牌，完善"景德镇制"标准体系的制定、执行、监管机制，推广"标准制定＋检测认证＋溯源系统"认证模式；依托国家陶瓷版权交易中心，为陶瓷产品提供质量检测、产品溯源、防伪认证、鉴定拍卖等服务，发挥政府、平台方、陶瓷文化企业和创作者的积极性；为陶瓷创作者提供版权登记、维权、咨询和交易等最便捷的保护渠道，激发了创作者的热情，激活了陶瓷创意产业的发展。

版权赋能景德镇城市高质量发展。通过制定版权保护的法律政策和一系列的举措，实现了资源配置的优化，促进景德镇陶瓷产业的规范化、有序化。在陶瓷产业发展方面，持续做大日用陶瓷、做精艺术陶瓷、做强先进陶瓷，实现了陶瓷产业的快速发展；在文旅融合发展方面，以陶阳里、陶溪川、陶源谷、陶科园、陶博城"五陶"等为重点，构建起以陶瓷文化为核心要素的全域旅游发展新格局；在对外文化交流方面，坚持以瓷为媒、以瓷会友，全力做好"请进来、走出去"文章，加快构建陶瓷文化对外话语体系；在人才集聚方面，大力实施"候鸟计划"，吸引更多"景漂"和"洋景漂"创新创业、创意创造，推进景德镇成为陶瓷艺术创作者创业、生产和生活的理想之地。

千年瓷都景德镇的
历史与传统

一座景德镇，半部陶瓷史。景德镇以 2000 多年的冶陶史、1000 多年的官窑史、600 多年的御窑史见证了我国陶瓷业的创新与发展。在千余年不间断的制瓷业发展历程中，景德镇以特色鲜明、结构完善的手工制瓷工艺生产体系，创造出世界陶瓷史上辉煌灿烂的篇章；在千余年不间断的制瓷业发展历程中，景德镇以源远流长、博大精深、底蕴深厚的陶瓷历史积淀，形成了丰富多元的陶瓷文化；在千余年不间断的制瓷业发展历程中，景德镇以开放包容的城市文化，构建了集全国名窑之大成、天下窑器之所聚的世界瓷业中心。

第一节
景德镇古代制瓷史

2023年10月，习近平总书记在景德镇考察调研时指出，陶瓷是中华瑰宝，是中华文明的重要名片。[①]景德镇因制瓷而立，城因瓷业而兴，得益于得天独厚的自然优势、纯熟精湛的手工技艺与千年不息的窑火。景德镇留存了珍贵的陶瓷古迹，传承了精湛的制瓷技艺，制作了精美的陶瓷艺术作品。

景德镇制瓷历史始于汉，起于唐，兴于宋，盛于明清。大体而言，景德镇陶瓷发展的历史，可以归纳为以下几个主要阶段。

汉代（前206—220年）至五代（907—960年）是景德镇陶瓷生产的起步阶段。"新平治陶，始于汉世。大抵坚重朴茂，范土合渥，有古先遗制。"[②]至汉代，景德镇已经能烧制出瓷器，但此时的瓷器身粗体厚，釉色淡而糙，尚未达到较高的烧造水平。唐代（618—907年），约半数时间处于盛世。在此

---

① 《解放思想开拓进取扬长补短固本兴新　奋力谱写中国式现代化江西篇章》，《人民日报》2023年10月14日。

② 乔溎修、贺熙龄纂《浮梁县志》卷八《食货　陶政》，道光三年刻本，第44页。

期间，中国社会得以安定，政治较为清明，人口大量增加，经济稳步上升，唐代瓷器生产也迎来了发展高峰时期。景德镇多生产满足生活需要的日用品，如碗、盘、壶、罐之类。优质瓷胎质地细腻，釉层均匀，釉色莹润，具有较高的工艺水平。在唐代瓷业基础上，五代，景德镇瓷器生产规模进一步扩大，产品质量好、产品种类多，尤其以透光性好、白度高的白瓷著称。五代，景德镇的窑址主要分布在南河两岸和今市区范围，产品类别包括碗、盘、碟、壶、罐、钵等，在烧造方式上，采用支钉垫烧。

唐代白釉双龙耳壶（中国陶瓷博物馆供图）

宋代（960—1279 年）是景德镇陶瓷产业的发展时期。宋代，景德镇地区的窑址数量超过唐代，瓷器品种大为增加，制瓷技术较之唐和五代时期大幅提升，烧造技术和制作工艺日臻成熟；原料的选择、炼制更加专业，器物的成型制作分工更加明确。景德镇等地创烧的温润如玉的青白瓷深受宋真宗垂青，宋真宗命瓷器底部书"景德年制"四字，并于元丰五年（1082 年）八月，"置饶州景德镇瓷窑博易务"[1]。朝廷在景德镇设置税收机构，委派督陶官员，正式由政府直接实施征税、管制专卖等措施，即所谓"监镇"。根据考古发掘资料，证实目前 19 个省、自治区的 16 个县（市）、乡均有宋元青白瓷出土。[2]并通过"海上丝绸之路"出口到亚洲的日本、朝鲜、菲律宾和马来西亚等国家和地区，甚至远及欧洲、非洲。"宋末，欧人已多赞赏之者，荷兰人由福建商贩瓷器至欧洲，价值每与黄金重量相等，且有供不应求之

---

① 熊寥、熊微编注《中国陶瓷古籍集成》，上海文化出版社，2006，第 5 页。
② 中共景德镇市委宣传部编著《景德镇陶瓷简史》，江西教育出版社，2023，第 59 页。

势。粤人见荷商得利，遂到饶州贩载而去。"[1]

元代（1206—1368 年）是景德镇陶瓷完善和发展的突破阶段，此时景德镇的瓷器烧造技艺有了极大提升。1278 年，元朝政府在景德镇设立了全国唯一的瓷局——浮梁瓷局，据《元史·百官志·将作院》记载，"浮梁磁局，秩正九品。至元十五年立。掌烧造磁器，并漆造马尾棕藤笠帽等事。大使、副使各一员。"[2]元青花，在制瓷史上具有重要的地位。青花瓷是运用钴料进行绘画装饰的一种釉下彩瓷器，具有着色力强、发色鲜艳、呈色稳定等特点，引领景德镇制瓷业迎来了空前的繁荣。枢府瓷是元代枢密院在景德镇定烧的瓷器，胎体厚重，色白微青，恰似鹅蛋色泽，因此被称为卵白。一般印有"枢府""太禧"等字款，胎质、釉色上乘，制作工艺精湛。元代，景德镇瓷器所承载的文化取向发生了一定变化。蒙元文化有多重性质，既有中原汉文化的面貌，又有蒙古游牧民族的风格，同时还融合了包括伊斯兰文化在内的各种宗教文化。这种多元融合的文化特色，对景德镇瓷器的造型和装饰都产生了深刻影响。

明代（1368—1644 年）是景德镇陶瓷生产的繁盛阶段。明朝建立以后，政府在景德镇设立御器厂，专门生产皇家陶瓷产品，限制民窑烧制的瓷器品种。御器厂独占最好的原料和工匠，生产不计成本，质量追求精益求精，在景德镇陶瓷业发展过程中有特殊的贡献和地位。随着海内外市场的扩大，景德镇制瓷业得到了稳步发展，明中期产生了"官搭民烧"制度，使民窑得以迅猛发展，出现官民竞市局面。景德

元代青花牡丹纹梅瓶（中国陶瓷博物馆供图）

①　冯和法：《中国陶瓷业之现状及其贸易状况》，《国际贸易导报》1932 年第 3 卷第 2、3、4 号合刊。
②　宋濂：《元史》卷八十八，中华书局，1976，第 2227 页。

IP与创意产业：
景德镇故事

镇瓷器海外贸易进一步扩展。明永乐宣德时期，郑和七次出使西洋，将景德镇瓷器通过太平洋、印度洋，大量输出到中亚、西亚以及非洲的诸多国家和地区，提升了景德镇陶瓷的对外影响力。15世纪末16世纪初，通过欧洲各东印度公司，以景德镇瓷器为代表的中国产品大量出口到欧洲各国，瓷器成为全球性商品，对人类文明进程起到了积极的推动作用。

明代万历青花斗彩人物图盘（中国陶瓷博物馆供图）

清代（1616—1911年）前中期是景德镇陶瓷业发展的高峰阶段。清代前中期的御窑厂（明代御器厂更名），产品质

清代雍正青花折枝花果纹天球瓶（中国陶瓷博物馆供图）

清代乾隆粉彩九桃图瓶（中国陶瓷博物馆供图）

第二章
千年瓷都景德镇的历史与传统

量进一步提高,产品种类进一步丰富。清代御窑瓷器的生产受皇帝喜好的影响很大,康熙、雍正、乾隆三位皇帝十分重视技艺,甚至亲自关注瓷器的设计与生产。同时,民窑生产在产品类别、组织形式和陶瓷贸易等方面,亦有突飞猛进的发展,产品质量和生产规模远超前朝。清初,海禁政策的施行严重阻碍了陶瓷销往海外。清康熙二十三年(1684年),清政府开放海禁,以景德镇陶瓷为代表的中国瓷器大量出口到欧洲,对欧洲社会的许多领域产生了深刻的影响。对于欧洲王室贵族而言,精美的中国艺术瓷成为贵族之间竞相收藏且展示高贵身份的珍品。对于广大的欧洲市民而言,中国瓷器的到来,使他们在厨房里和餐桌上抛弃了昂贵的金银餐具和粗笨而且难以清洗的陶器餐具,由此引发了欧洲社会的"餐桌革命"。

第二节
景德镇近代制瓷史

　　清末至民国时期，在全国政局动荡的影响下，景德镇瓷业每况愈下，生产规模缩小，制瓷水平大为降低，传统瓷业生产体系遭遇重大危机和挑战。为了维系瓷业生产，景德镇社会各界采取多种模式，进行瓷业生产改良运动。一方面，改良群体学习新式制瓷业技术，成立公司、开办学校，开启了瓷业现代化的历程；另一方面，传统手工业者依托高超的传统手工制瓷技艺，进行艺术陈设瓷的生产。

　　成立新式陶瓷公司。1840 年鸦片战争后，包括瓷器在内的大量国外商品倾销到中国，景德镇陶瓷在国内的市场也日渐受到挤压。洋瓷畅销引起了景德镇瓷器生产者的关注，他们希望通过改革扭转制瓷业发展的被动局面。1903 年 7 月，江西巡抚提出创办瓷业公司，振兴景德镇陶瓷业。但受到各方面因素影响，直到 1910 年才最终成立官商合办的江西瓷业公司。公司分两厂，本厂在景德镇，用旧法生产；分厂设在饶州府所在地鄱阳，用新法制瓷，这标志着新型瓷业生产体系的初步确立。①1912 年，中华民国成立以后，江西瓷业公司陷入困境，在内外交困下，难以完成最初引领景德镇瓷业发展的目标。

创新陶瓷管理机构。清末民初，景德镇官员通过加强地方社会管理、制定瓷业生产规范，保证瓷业生产正常运转和社会秩序的稳定。国民政府成立以后，为了复兴景德镇瓷业，开启了一系列的瓷业改良举措。1929 年，江西省建设厅设立江西陶务局，进行陶瓷的改良，采取了包括新式煤窑建造、釉色及新式器型设计在内的技术研究，制定瓷器税率和调查陶瓷生产等在内的社会改良方案，对促进景德镇陶瓷发展起到了推进作用。1934 年，江西省政府在景德镇设立陶业管理局，围绕新型瓷器产品设计和生产、传统瓷业生产模式的改良和转型、陶瓷知识的普及和推广以及陶瓷产业工人训练等方面，开展瓷业改良活动。

创办新式陶瓷学校。1910 年，为了配合江西瓷业公司的发展，瓷业改良群体创办了中国陶业学堂，这是景德镇乃至中国第一所正规培养陶瓷人才的专门学校。学堂的宗旨是培养"明白学理、精进技术之人才"。1912 年，学校更名为江西省立饶州陶业学校，主要培养新式技术人才和饰瓷人才。1915 年，学校又更名为江西省立第二甲种工业学校。1925 年，学校再次更名为江西省立窑业学校，不久后更名为江西省立景德镇陶业学校。1926 年，更名为江西省立陶业学校，由邹俊章担任校长。1937 年底学校流亡靖安，后遵省陶业管理局令于1938 年 8 月迁至萍乡上埠镇。1944 年 10 月更名为江西省立陶瓷职业学校。同年底，浮梁县立陶瓷科职业学校并入。1946 年，更名为江西省立陶瓷专科学校。此外，在景德镇创办的各类学校，还包括浮梁私立国瓷艺术专修学校、景德镇私立东方艺术专科学校。尽管这些学校规模比较小，但依旧在培养陶瓷人才中发挥了积极作用。

探索陶瓷艺术新方向。清同治以后，官方对御窑厂内部工匠控制力下降，大量绘瓷名家流落民间，从事艺术创作，推动了陶瓷生产创作模式的转变。在

---

① 景德镇市地方志办公室编《中国瓷都·景德镇市瓷业志（市志·2 卷）》，方志出版社，2004，第 4 页。

传统粉彩创作技艺和中国文人画基础上，景德镇陶瓷艺人创作出浅绛彩艺术形式门类。浅绛彩创作的代表人物有王少维、金品卿、程门、汪友棠、潘匋宇等人。清光绪时期，国外新型瓷器釉料和生产工艺的引入，促使了洋彩创作技法的形成，洋彩也被称为"新彩"或"新粉彩"。民国时期，新粉彩创作以"珠山八友"为代表，作品以瓷板画为主，或者类似于平面的镶器和圆盘。这一独特的创新，促进了景德镇陶瓷工匠地位和影响力的提升，将陶瓷艺术进一步发扬光大。另外，景德镇曾多次承接制作生产定制瓷和国礼瓷的任务。1915年，袁世凯曾委派陶瓷专家到景德镇专门生产个人使用瓷器，后来这批瓷器被称为"洪宪瓷"。许多达官显贵也曾以自己的堂号在景德镇定烧瓷器。如曹锟以延庆楼、徐世昌以静远楼的名义烧造了专属瓷器。景德镇也定烧了赠送国外领导人和国际友人的瓷器，赠送给已故英国女王伊丽莎白二世的瓷器，便是其中的典型代表。

晚清浅绛彩瓷板画（中国陶瓷博物馆供图）

第三节

景德镇现代陶瓷产业

中华人民共和国成立至今，不断探索、改革与创新陶瓷产业体系，景德镇陶瓷生产技术不断革新，陶瓷装饰风格变化多元，陶瓷艺术繁荣发展，陶瓷文化交流日益频繁，陶瓷文化遗产保护成就突出，古老瓷都重现辉煌，续写了新的历史篇章。这一时期，景德镇陶瓷生产分为两个阶段：从新中国成立到党的十八大，是景德镇陶瓷产业恢复与转型发展时期；从2012年开始，景德镇陶瓷产业进入高质量建设时期。

一、景德镇现代陶瓷产业发展现状

新中国成立后，景德镇市政府大力推动陶瓷产业恢复和发展。在原有小作坊的基础上，景德镇市政府组建了建国、人民、艺术、光明、新华、景兴、红星、红旗、宇宙、为民、雕塑、曙光等大型国营瓷厂，通称"十大瓷厂"，传统制瓷工艺得到了恢复和传承。在计划经济年代，十大瓷厂生产的代表性瓷器，如人民瓷厂的青花瓷、光明瓷厂的玲珑瓷、建国瓷厂的颜色釉瓷、艺术瓷厂的粉彩瓷等，被誉为"景德镇四大传统名瓷"，其产品设计独特，制作精美，做工精细。景德镇生产的各类陶瓷不仅产量大，产值与利税高，而且是江西省出口创汇的重点产品，1990年，景德镇陶瓷出口创汇占江西省的50%。1992年，党的十四大确定我国经济体制改革的目标是建立社会主义市场经济体制，景德镇的陶瓷产业进入了转型发展期，形成了日用瓷、艺术瓷和仿古瓷生产于一体的产品体系，陶瓷产业逐步恢复和发展。2012年，景德镇陶瓷产业总产值近214.9亿元。其中，日用陶瓷产业67.83亿元，占比31.6%；艺术陈设瓷82.91亿元，占比38.6%；建筑卫生瓷28.91亿元，占比13.4%；高技术陶瓷30.4亿元，占比14.1%；陶瓷辅助材料4.95亿元，占比2.3%。基本形成了涵盖陶瓷原材料、陶瓷机械、日用陶瓷、建卫陶瓷、艺术陈设陶瓷、高技术陶瓷等在内的陶瓷产业体系。与此同时，与陶瓷生产相关的窑炉、包装、印花、物流、文博等产业快速发展，形成了较为完整的体系。景德镇还建立了景德镇陶瓷大学、江西省陶瓷工艺美术职业技术学院等陶瓷高等学府，国家日用及建筑陶瓷工程中心和国家、省、市三级陶瓷研究所等科研机构，成为陶瓷产业发展的重要支撑。

自2012年以来，尤其是自景德镇国家陶瓷文化传承创新试验区批复至今，景德镇陶瓷产业进入了高质量快速发展时期。目前，景德镇坚持做大日用陶瓷、做精艺术陶瓷、做强先进陶瓷，形成了以先进陶瓷为引领、以艺术陈设瓷和日用陶瓷为特色、以建卫陶瓷为补充、以创意陶瓷为后发优势的多元化融合发展格局。2023年，景德镇陶瓷工业总产值为861.25亿元，同比增长29.44%；规上陶瓷企业258家，同比增长27.09%，规上陶瓷工业产值为296.93亿元，同比增长5.29%；陶瓷海关出口为10.4亿元，同比增长100.7%；陶瓷产业的税收为10.06亿元，同比增长31.4%（见表2-1）。

表2-1 景德镇陶瓷产值情况

年份	工业产值（测算值）		产业税收		海关出口		规上企业		规上工业产值	
	数值/亿元	同比增长	数值/亿元	同比增长	数值/亿元	同比增长	数量/家	同比增长	数值/亿元	同比增长
2019	423	5.33%	4.45	68.15%	4.62	45.38%	103	3.88%	127	10.73%

第二章
千年瓷都景德镇的历史与传统

续表：

年份	工业产值（测算值）		产业税收		海关出口		规上企业		规上工业产值	
	数值/亿元	同比增长	数值/亿元	同比增长	数值/亿元	同比增长	数量/家	同比增长	数值/亿元	同比增长
2020	432	2.13%	3.75	−15.83%	2.45	−46.89%	121	17.48%	129	1.68%
2021	516	19.44%	5.2	38.67%	2.09	−14.81%	140	15.7%	185	19.67%
2022	665	28.9%	7.6	46%	5.2	147.9%	203	45%	282	52.4%
2023	861.25	29.44%	10.06	31.4%	10.4	100.7%	258	27.09%	296.93	5.29%

数据来源：景德镇市陶瓷产业发展局

二、景德镇陶瓷产业特色

厚重的陶瓷文化资源、得天独厚的发展条件、种类多样的陶瓷产品门类以及有力的政策支持，助力景德镇陶瓷产业高质量发展，形成了独具特色的产业发展模式。

产业集聚效应日益显著。经过多年的发展与整合，景德镇陶瓷的细分产业快速崛起，集聚效应明显。昌南新区已经成为以景陶集团、陶瓷智造工坊为代表的传统日用陶瓷产业聚集区，以名坊园为代表的高端手工制瓷聚集区，以江丰电子、晶达新材料、和川粉体为代表的先进陶瓷集聚区；珠山区陶溪川、三宝瓷谷、皇窑、雕塑创意园等陶瓷文化创意产业平台初具规模，呈现良好的发展态势；高新区、昌江区已经成为以航空陶瓷等军民融合发展为核心的先进陶瓷集聚区，同时也是陶瓷机械、窑炉、中高档泥釉料、色料等陶瓷产业链配套的专业化生产和销售中心；浮梁县形成了以湘湖工业园景华、景龙等企业为代表的先进陶瓷片区，以金意陶、乐华洁具为代表的建卫陶瓷集聚区。

陶瓷线上销售异军突起。电子商务兴起之后，陶瓷作为其中的一个品类，其销售量增长迅速。目前，景德镇从事陶瓷电商的企业近万家，陶瓷直播年交易额占全国的70%。在淘宝、天猫、京东等全国各第三方交易平台注册并产生交易的陶瓷网店有 5 万余家，昌江区新枫街道的三河村成为江西省上榜的四个淘宝村之一。景德镇着力打造的陶溪川直播基地已成为陶瓷电商的集中区，入驻电商达到 6000 家，陶瓷主播超过 1 万人，帮助众多的陶瓷商家实现了线上销售。从整体上分析，景德镇陶瓷产业正在向线下沉浸式体验、跨界融合与线上的品牌宣传、销售相结合的方向发展。

陶瓷人才队伍日益壮大。截至 2023 年末，景德镇陶瓷行业从业人员约 15 万人，有各类陶瓷技能人才约 4.4 万。其中，陶瓷行业专业技术人员有 6500 余名，陶瓷行业高技能人才有 4000 余名，各级非遗传承人有 874 名；截至 2022 年，景德镇有中国工艺美术大师 45 人（占全国总数的 41.7%）、中国陶瓷艺术大师 43 人（占全国总数的 19.6%）、中国陶瓷设计艺术大师 35 人、江西省工艺美术大师 120 人、江西省陶瓷艺术大师 60 人。景德镇在校大学生有 7.6 万人，预计 2025 年突破 10 万人；景德镇还引进江丰电子姚力军团队、上硅所曾宇平团队、清华大学李刚团队等一批陶瓷领域高端人才。近年来，3 万余名来自国内外的艺术家、设计师、创业者及陶瓷爱好者来到景德镇，学习和交流陶瓷文化，寻根创业，他们被当地人亲切地称为"景漂""景归"。其中，"洋景

王锡良新彩矾红井冈山图瓷板画（中国陶瓷博物馆供图）

漂"5000 余名，形成了一种独特的陶瓷文化现象。

景德镇陶瓷文化遗产保护和传承成就突出。作为享誉世界的千年瓷都，景德镇拥有数量众多、保存完好的陶瓷文化遗存。老窑址、老里弄、老街区遍布全城；御窑厂、高岭古矿等 30 多处陶瓷遗迹闻名遐迩，它们皆属于没有同构性的世界精品级文化资源。在古代陶瓷遗址保护方面，从 20 世纪 70 年代初至 21 世纪初，景德镇先后开展了三次文物普查，并根据普查结果，有针对性地开展文物保护。1972—2006 年，景德镇先后开展了 22 次考古调查与发掘，系统性地开展对陶瓷文化遗产的保护。2015 年，景德镇正式启动以明清御窑厂遗址为核心的世界文化遗产保护申报工作，将能反映景德镇千年制瓷历史的具有代表性的遗产类别，作为遗产构成要素进行整体申报。2017 年 1 月，国家文物局将景德镇御窑厂遗址列入中国世界文化遗产预备名单。至 2019 年，全市有国家级非物质文化遗产生产性保护示范基地 2 个、省级 27 个、市级 100 个；省级研究基地 2 个、传承基地 3 个、传播基地 2 个；市级研究基地 1 个、传承基地 7 个、传播基地 7 个。[①] 截至 2023 年，景德镇拥有全国重点文物保护单位 12 处，江西省文物保护单位 29 处，市、县级文物保护单位 205 处。[②] 打造了陶瓷文化遗产传承发展的新样板。

文旅产业融合高质量发展。景德镇政府发挥自身资源整合的优势，牵头推动传统景区的调整升级，积极探索工业遗产活化利用新路径。通过保留历史感、融入现代感，许多传统的陶瓷景区或废弃的瓷厂遗址被改造，焕发新生，吸引了大量游客。尤其是以陶瓷为核心的现代化景区（其代表有陶溪川文化创意园和景德镇陶瓷工业遗产博物馆），吸引了大量年轻游客。通过原汁原味保护修缮原有的老厂房、隧道窑、工业设施等，完整保留原有建筑肌理和风貌，同时新"嫁接"了博物馆、瓷器店、音乐室、咖啡吧等新元素，用新业态复活老工业遗迹，让老旧瓷厂蜕变为时尚创意街区。此外，景德镇还探索建设了一些新兴的

---

① 《在营造非遗新生态中增强文化新活力——景德镇市非遗保护工作亮点与成效》，《景德镇陶瓷》2022 年第 3 期，第 41 页。

② 中共景德镇市委宣传部编著《景德镇陶瓷简史》，江西教育出版社，2023，第 266 页。

景德镇御窑博物馆（景德镇市融媒体中心供图）

旅游吸引物，例如，高岭中国村和景德镇记忆《china》实景演出。近两年来，景德镇市文旅局围绕国家陶瓷文化传承创新试验区建设，坚持科学规划、项目引领，全力打造以御窑厂为核心的陶阳里历史街区、以陶溪川为主体的文创街区、以三宝国际瓷谷为依托的陶源谷艺术景区，以及陶大小镇科教区、陶科园产业园区等五大片区十余个集中呈现文化魅力的景区、景点，形成了以"陶瓷文化"为核心，以"历史文化""艺术创意""文艺治愈""田园生活"等为支撑的文旅融合新格局。

陶瓷文化交流与日俱增。景德镇不断扩大国际"朋友圈"，积极拓展友城交往的深度和广度，入选全球创意网络城市，加入联合国海陆丝绸之路城市联盟、国际友好城市旅游联盟，与 72 个国家、180 多个友好合作城市开展多层面、立体化的文化交流合作，为世界了解景德镇、景德镇走向世界，架起了一座宽广的桥梁。为了贯彻落实习近平总书记 2019 年作出的"建好景德镇国家陶瓷文化传承创新试验区，打造对外文化交流新平台"和 2023 年作出的"进一步把陶瓷产业做大做强，把'千年瓷都'这张靓丽的名片擦得更亮"等重要指示精神，景德镇深度融入"一带一路"倡议，积极参与"感知中国""今日中国""丝路瓷行""Z 世代瓷缘"等高端对外文化交流活动，立体化塑造与传播世界瓷都

景德镇陶溪川（景德镇市融媒体中心供图）

新形象，高水平承办第五届阿拉伯艺术节、2022 国际版权论坛、2023 战略传播论坛、景德镇国际陶瓷艺术双年展、全球先进陶瓷暨高科技产业发展大会、高技术陶瓷国际论坛等交流活动。《匠心冶陶》纪录片入选中宣部文化"走出去"重点项目，《用 china 讲 China——江西景德镇用陶瓷名片讲述中国故事》入选"2021 年度对外传播十大优秀案例"，《以中国瓷　交世界友——江西景德镇创新打造陶瓷文化国际"朋友圈"》入选"2023 年度对外传播十大优秀案例"。参加"丝绸之路旅游城市联盟专家论证会"和埃及"艺汇丝路——中阿知名艺术家采风作品展"暨中阿艺术家对话沙龙活动。成功创建全国首个"文艺两新"集聚区实践基地，吸引众多"景漂"，尤其是"洋景漂"创新创业。近年来，

景德镇加强与新华社、《人民日报》（海外版）、央视 CGTN、《中国日报》、中新社等中央媒体海外渠道合作，广泛开展网络国际传播。与新华网合作拍摄《"洋景漂"说 china》系列短视频；《人民日报》（海外版）刊发的《"洋景漂"爱上"镇生活"》，讲述一批"洋景漂"在景德镇市工作和生活的故事，引发网民热议。景德镇市融媒体中心作品《有朋远方来——法国艺术家爱玛》获国际短视频大赛优秀作品奖。《缠之恋》MV 作品入选"中国好故事"网络国际传播精品案例。陶瓷主题舞剧《唯我青白》选段《瓷影》亮相央视龙年春晚，通过中国国际电视台向全球 200 个国家和地区的 2100 多家媒体同步直播和报道，全球总阅读量突破 6.66 亿；《传承中国》景德镇篇在欧洲新闻台播出，累计观看 1.28 亿次，线上观众 5400 万以上；短视频《看见景德镇》发布在多个海外社交媒体平台上，被境外多家媒体采用，阅读量达 268 万；依托"Z 世代"国际青年来景德镇研学交流，举办"Z 世代"国际青年"话陶瓷"线上交流活动，吸引 50 多个国家（地区）3100 名青年艺术家参与，发布网络作品达 3560 个，成为传播中国文化的重要力量。[1] 积极开展国际陶瓷文化研学班、"一带一路"共建国家青年汉学班等活动，让更多国际友人深入了解景德镇深厚的陶瓷文化。

---

[1] 张龙：《江西景德镇：以瓷为媒 打好网络国际传播"组合拳"》，《中国网信》2024 年第 7 期，第 63 页。

三宝国际瓷谷（景德镇市融媒体中心供图）

景德镇陶瓷版权保护意识的
历史演进与生成基础

　　陶瓷文化是中华文明形成与发展的重要组成部分。早在造纸术与印刷术诞生前，陶瓷器物就承载了文化艺术可被客观感知的独创性表达，凝聚了创新创造的智力成果，开创了特色陶瓷美学。景德镇千年不息的窑火，累积了浩如烟海的陶瓷文化宝藏，使发端于文学、艺术和科学领域的版权不仅以有形陶瓷器物承载独创性智力成果，也使思想观念方面的版权保护得以产生与延续。千百年来，传承有序的景德镇陶瓷版权保护意识和实践，构筑了当代陶瓷创新与法治保护的根脉，滋养了景德镇陶瓷创新发展的沃土，提供了陶瓷版权保护的"中国特色方案"。

第一节

景德镇陶瓷版权保护意识的历史演进

景德镇两千余年窑火不熄的陶瓷文化发展与传播实践，建构了源起于古代、赓续嬗变于近代、优化完善于当代的陶瓷版权演进历程。不同历史阶段的陶瓷版权表现形式，忠实反映了我国陶瓷版权保护意识与创新治理变迁的历史信息，生动展现了陶瓷版权保护在我国手工业发展历程中的重要价值。

一、古代陶瓷版权保护意识的肇始与发展

宋元时期是景德镇陶瓷版权保护意识的肇始期。考古资料表明，景德镇最早的窑业遗存是晚唐五代时期生产青瓷和白瓷的窑址，此前窑业遗存不见报道。[①] 加之文献所提及的"陶

---

① 江西省文物考古研究所、乐平市博物馆、景德镇陶瓷考古研究所、景德镇民窑博物馆：《江西乐平南窑窑址调查报告》，《中国国家博物馆馆刊》2013年第 10 期。

窑"与"霍窑"①一直未见相关窑址及考古遗物,考古发现与文献资料尚显不足,存在争议。《浮梁县志》明确记载:"宋景德中,始置镇,因名。置监镇一员,以奉御董造。"②宋代景德镇窑业文献的《陶记》记载:"景德镇陶,昔三百余座。"③加之南市街遗址④、湖田窑址⑤与落马桥遗址⑥等宋元窑址出土的大量文物资料,表明宋元时期景德镇市镇街区已具有一定规模,陶瓷生产从农业中分离出来⑦,并逐渐向批量化商品制作转变。这一时期,景德镇陶瓷版权保护意识使陶瓷创新成果受到保护,体现出在版权法律规范产生前景德镇窑业已出现创新成果权益意识。

瓷器创作以精细分工形成天然防抄袭的版权保护意识。宋代,景德镇制瓷业生产过程已经有明确分工,蒋祈所著《陶记》是系统记录宋代景德镇窑业的文献,记载有:"陶工、匣工、土工之有其局,利坯、车坯、釉坯之有其法,印花、画花、雕花之有其技,秩然规制,各不相紊。"⑧这表明宋代景德镇已出现了明确分工,并产生印花复制技术。"宋代的瓷器生产不仅存在着明确的分工,而且生产过程还存在着系统性……宋代的窑户应与若干个坯户组成较固定的、互相配合的生产团体各生产专业户之间平等相处,体现了商品买卖的形式。"⑨发

① 所提及的"陶窑""霍窑"是依据《浮梁县志》所载"唐武德四年,里人陶玉献假玉器,于是置务"及"新平霍仲初,制瓷日就精巧,唐兴素瓷在天下,而仲初有名"。参见乔溎修、贺熙龄纂《浮梁县志》卷八《食货 陶政》,道光三年刻本,第6、44页。
② 乔溎修、贺熙龄纂《浮梁县志》卷八《食货 陶政》,道光三年刻本,第7页。
③ 蒋祈:《陶记》,转引自乔溎修、贺熙龄纂《浮梁县志》卷八《食货 陶政》,道光三年刻本,第25页。
④ 郭建晖:《文化遗存保护传承的当代价值与现实路径——基于景德镇青白瓷遗址群的调查》,《江西社会科学》2023年第43卷第1期。
⑤ 徐长青、余江安:《湖田窑考古新收获》,《故宫博物院院刊》2004年第2期。
⑥ 翁彦俊、江建新、秦大树、江小民:《江西景德镇落马桥窑址宋元遗存发掘简报》,《文物》2017年第5期。
⑦ 詹嘉、赵传玉、袁胜根:《历史时期景德镇陶瓷文化景观的演变》,《农业考古》2009年第6期。
⑧ 蒋祈:《陶记》,转引自乔溎修、贺熙龄纂《浮梁县志》卷八《食货 陶政》,道光三年刻本,第25页。
⑨ 陈朝云:《宋代瓷器制造技术的考古学观察》,《考古学报》2017年第4期。

展至元代，元人洪焱祖记载："一器成初售，争先样又新。低昂百工手，鼓舞四方人。雕刻知何极，渐磨岂易淳。光阴并红紫，衮衮付泥尘。"[1] 各个工序衔接紧密，有序的分工构成完整的生产流水线，不仅极大地提高了生产效率，而且确保工匠专事一项——画者画而不染，染者染而不画——使每一道工序都以极致的工艺形态形成创作的天然壁垒。

瓷器销售以标记署名的牌记款识彰显人身权利意识。《景德镇湖田窑址1988—1989年考古发掘报告》与相关纪年墓葬表明，在湖田窑北宋中后期的地层中，出土了一定数量的印花瓜棱形粉盒，且底部印有"詹""宋""陆""程九郎""李明"等姓名款识。[2] 这类粉盒在各地北宋后期的墓葬中也发现了一定数量，其中部分粉盒的型式上同吕氏家族墓园及包拯家族墓群出土的银质粉盒型式相近。宋代，景德镇大量私有化署名标记在陶瓷上的直接显现，不仅体现商品竞争下增强市场辨识度的意识，而且彰显了人们对陶瓷器物私有权利意识的萌发。元代，陶瓷器物的款识逐渐丰富扩展，带有铭款的卵白釉瓷"枢府""太禧""福禄""东卫""江夏"等大量出现。[3] 现藏于英国大英博物馆的元代瓷器"青花云龙纹象耳

"彭七"铭，北宋景德镇窑青白瓷标本，江西陶瓷工艺美院美术馆藏（杨洋摄）

"颜大"铭，北宋景德镇窑青白瓷标本，江西陶瓷工艺美院美术馆藏（杨洋摄）

① 洪焱祖撰、洪在编《杏庭摘稿》，四库全书本，第13页。
② 徐香玉：《宋景德镇青白瓷若干文字识记的分类及考证》，硕士学位论文，景德镇陶瓷大学，2022，第8—18页。
③ 张柏、姚嬴主编《大观·元末明初青花瓷海上巡礼论文集》，江西美术出版社，2017，第122页。

中写制瓷产业
瓷绝侨故事

瓶",瓶颈撰写有铭文"信州路玉山县顺城乡德教里荆塘社奉圣弟子张文进喜舍香炉花瓶一付祈保合家清吉子女平安至正十一年四月良辰谨记星源祖殿胡净一元帅打供"[1]。此瓶以年代、地区、人名、事件等内容的款识进一步体现了私权占有性与可视化区分的关系,以铭文或款识区别主体,不仅是早期质量责任意识的标记,而

元代"至正"铭文青花瓷片,景德镇陶瓷大学元青花博物馆藏(熊露摄)

且代表了封建生产关系下人身私有权利的觉醒。

明清时期是景德镇陶瓷版权保护意识的发展期,这一时期景德镇成为"天下窑器之所聚"的瓷业发展中心。明洪武期间,朝廷即在景德镇设立全国唯一瓷器官方生产与管理机构——御器厂。这一时期,御器厂不仅成为景德镇陶瓷管理机构,且直接参与陶瓷生产。皇权的直接介入促使景德镇陶瓷向生产规模化、产品优质化与分工精细化发展,为陶瓷创新试验与技术突破提供了强大的物质与人才保障。特别是明代中期随着"官搭民烧"的实施,官民技术流通联动,提高了民窑陶瓷的技术水平和产品质量,使景德镇民窑在机遇与挑战中稳步前行,至明代晚期形成了"官民竞市"的蓬勃发展态势。清代延续并完善了御窑制度,"官搭民烧"成为普遍的生产方式,陶瓷生产规模与品类达到顶峰。这一时期,景德镇陶瓷版权保护受到了技术发展与皇权干预的双重影响。随着景德镇陶瓷商帮与行会日趋活跃,陶瓷生产逐渐向中心市区集聚,官方与民间的陶瓷版权保护并非自上而下地单向链接,而是与"行业规约"一同形成景德镇陶瓷版权保

明代嘉靖御窑铭文瓷板(御窑博物院供图)

---

① 赵燕:《元至正十一年青花云龙纹象耳瓶铭文考辨》,《新美术》2013年第34卷第4期。

护发展中官方管理、社会组织与创新主体的多方权利联动体系。

在官窑瓷器生产创作过程中，景德镇制窑业通过"官颁样式"守护原创画面。"官样"是由画工为御用瓷器设计制定的供窑工依照生产的标准式样。自明初景德镇御器厂设立以来，便按官颁式样生产，《明会典》记载："凡烧造供用器皿等物，须要定夺样制，计算人工物料。"[1] 清代御窑厂承袭明代旧制，《大清会典事例》记载："凡上用瓷器，照内颁式样数目行江西饶州府烧造解。"[2] 清代官样数量达到顶峰，《浮梁县志》记载："……（嘉靖）十五年，降发瓷器样一十件……十八年，降发瓷器二样四十三件……十三年……又烧成桌器一千三百四十桌，每桌计二十七件：内案酒碟五、果碟五、菜碟五、碗五、盖碟三，茶钟、酒盏、渣斗、醋注各一。裹青双云龙等花样三百八十桌，暗龙紫金等花样一百六十桌，翠青色一百六十桌，鲜红改作矾红一百六十桌，翠绿一百六十桌……三十六年……各样桌器一百桌，每桌五十三件……"[3] "官样"使原创画面以官方禁令的形式在创作完成后于固定范围内传播，历来严禁外传，禁止流通。明中后期采取"官搭民烧"的方式生产，推进官民技术流通联动，民窑得以接触官样，使官样的"占有与回收"成为窑业制度重要内容，且常有御旨涉及，成为最高统治者直接关注的窑事内容之一。[4] 由此可见，在官民互动生产中，创新成果的

景德镇御窑厂"官"字匣钵（御窑博物院供图）

永乐时期"官用供器"款识（御窑博物院供图）

---

[1] 徐溥等撰、李东阳等重修《明会典》卷一百五十七，四库全书本，第 3 页。

[2] 铁源、溪明：《清代官窑瓷器史 2》，中国画报出版社，2012，第 286 页。

[3] 乔溎修、贺熙龄纂《浮梁县志》卷八《食货　陶政》，道光三年刻本，第 19—21 页。

[4] 王光尧：《从故宫藏清代制瓷官样看中国古代官样制度——清代御窑厂研究之二》，《故宫博物院院刊》2006 年第 6 期。

重要性被逐渐认知，促使陶瓷版权保护意识进一步发展完善。

官窑管理作品发表过程中通过"官方禁令"保护创新成果。根据《江西景德镇明清御窑遗址发掘简报》的记录，在珠山北麓发掘的明初官窑掩埋坑遗迹中，掩埋坑是有意识地挖掘而掩埋砸碎的瓷器的，从这些被摧毁的出土遗物看，有的是没有瑕疵的贡余品，有些是微有瑕疵次品。①说明明代前期，官窑陶瓷生产严格禁止对外公开，官府对于瓷器管理从瓷土到工匠进行集中垄断，除精品直接贡御外，次品、试制品和剩余品全部打碎掩埋，以官方禁令的方式禁止公开或随意处理，民众难以睹见御窑产品，更无从抄袭模仿。正统年间，官府对民窑烧造进行极严厉的限禁，《景德镇陶录》亦有"所贡者俱千中选十，百中选一"的记载。《明英宗实录》记载："正统三年十二月丙寅，命都察院出榜，禁江西瓷器窑场烧造官样青花白地瓷器于各处货卖及馈送官员之家。违者正犯处死，全家谪戍口外。"②"禁江西饶州府私造黄、紫、红、绿、青、蓝、白地青花等瓷器……首犯凌迟处死，籍其家资，丁男充军边卫，知而不以告者连坐。"③在

明代景德镇御窑厂掩埋坑（御窑博物院供图）

---

① 北京大学考古文博学院、江西省文物考古研究所、景德镇市陶瓷考古研究所：《江西景德镇明清御窑遗址发掘简报》，《文物》2007年第5期。
② 《明英宗实录》（卷四十九），转引自熊寥、熊微编注《中国陶瓷古籍集成》，上海文化出版社，2006，第16页。
③ 《明英宗实录》（卷一百六十一），转引自熊寥、熊微编注《中国陶瓷古籍集成》，上海文化出版社，2006，第17页。

瓷行（景德镇市档案馆供图）

东埠街码头瓷土装运告示碑（景德镇市档案馆供图）

技术手段和保护方式不成熟的早期版权控制阶段，禁止或限制公开发表的就打碎掩埋，此种方式是早期陶瓷版权保护意识形成的核心保护手段与重要历史形式。

民窑为了限制陶瓷核心工艺、技艺的传播，则通过"行规制度"的方式控制核心竞争。明清时期，景德镇民窑主要以行业帮会组织及其行规帮约等固定制度，维持景德镇庞大的瓷业生产、销售、流通体系。严格控制的传承方式与陶瓷商帮行会的规范惯习，有效防止核心创新外泄并防止抄袭作假，使陶瓷创新成果掌握在固定的群体手中。《景德镇陶业纪事》记载有"镇陶分工，人执一事，此疆彼界，各不相谋"[1]。景德镇制瓷各业收徒有严格的规定，部分行业三年收一次。此外，还有五年收一次。圆器等行业通常每二十年才开禁收徒。各行分工明确，徒弟之间不得跨行，只能招籍贯为五府十八帮的人。学徒要有中间人进行作保，并写明师徒合约，禁止中途毁约。[2]由于分工细致加之核心工艺与创新成果保密，制瓷技艺以师徒或家族内部形式传承，私权观念进一步完善。"各据一行，不传他人"与"其业之精者，且仅传其本帮，而世守其业"的行业控制思想深入

① 向焯：《景德镇陶业纪事》，转引自熊寥、熊微编注《中国陶瓷古籍集成》，上海文化出版社，2006，第669页。

② 景德镇市地方志办公室编《中国瓷都·景德镇市瓷业志（市志·2卷）》，方志出版社，2004，第778—779页。

人心，使得陶瓷技艺学习时间长、成本高，将其传播范围固定在一定的人群之中，该人群掌握核心创新竞争优势。《景德镇陶录》记载："结砌窑巢，昔不可考。自元、明来，镇土著魏姓世其业。"[①]

二、近代陶瓷版权保护意识的赓续与嬗变

晚清至民国是景德镇陶瓷版权保护意识的嬗变期。这一时期是中国飘零动荡的社会转型与改革时期，加之西方法治思想传入中国，景德镇版权保护在观念传承下受外部影响而不断嬗变。清政府于1910年颁布了中国历史上第一部成文版权法律——《大清著作权律》。这一时期，社会转型与文化变革并行，景德镇在瓷业转型下赓续版权保护并通过法规普及版权思想，反映了景德镇陶瓷版权文化在观念传承下受外部影响而不断嬗变的复杂过程。

在瓷业转型下赓续版权保护意识。鸦片战争以后，景德镇瓷业日渐式微，瓷窑数量减少，西方机械化陶瓷生产极大冲击了景德镇瓷业市场，创新竞争的核心动力受到极大冲击，景德镇传统陶瓷生产模式遭遇挑战。咸丰年间，景德镇御窑陶瓷数量与质量逐渐下降，民窑质量不及从前。在内部瓷业衰退与外部影响的双重挑战下，景德镇开始近代瓷业改良，宣统二年（1910年），正式成立江西瓷业公司，采取大量举措振兴瓷业，开启现代化转型。晚清时期颁布的《大清著作权律》，虽然开启了近代版权立法探索，但这一时期，版权发展总体较为粗疏，且法律衔接与配套设施不完备。我国本土版权法治观念仍处在嬗变与过渡阶段，景德镇基于血缘、地缘行业关系形成的复杂版权利益保护体系，仍存在较强依赖性与惯性，难以快速适应制度变化，所颁布的法规政策并未得到较好落实，陶瓷版权保护仍以私力救济与行业规范等方式为主。

通过规范性文件制定普及版权思想。1909年出版的《汉译日本法律经济辞典》和我国编辑发行的《法律名词通释》，均明确使用"版权（著作权）"一

---

① 蓝浦、郑廷桂著，余柱青编著《古典新读景德镇陶录》，黄山书社，2015，第102页。

词。[1]随着汉语法律辞书的解释的普及，"著作权""版权"等词语已经成为常用语被大众知悉。《大清著作权律》首次以成文法形式确立版权概念、版权客体的范围、作者的权利、登记版权的程序、版权期限和限制及侵犯版权的处罚等问题，使版权的保护范围从书籍、绘画、摄影等平面作品，扩张至雕刻、模型等立体作品，使陶瓷作品得到有效规制。1915 年，北洋政府在保持清代版权法律的制度框架基础上颁布《北洋政府著作权法》。1928 年，南京国民政府颁布《中华民国著作权法》，确定了版权法和版权法施行细则的结构体系。随着版权法律规范的日臻完善，景德镇版权观念亦随之普及发展。在近代景德镇出口瓷业中，烧造圣品瓷的江西临川人范乾生创办的范永盛瓷号，其产品都印有红彩中英文"中国景德镇范永盛瓷号出品"字样。瓷器经由上海教廷托运到罗马教廷，在国外畅销达数十年之久。直到 1980 年后，"中国景德镇范永盛瓷号出品"仍在国外具有极强的影响力。[2]这一时期，出口景德镇瓷器上的英文标识与版权法律术语的普及，均表明陶瓷版权保护意识获得一定发展。

三、当代陶瓷版权体系的建构与优化

新中国成立后是景德镇陶瓷版权事业奋楫笃行期。新中国成立后，景德镇陶瓷版权事业随着中国版权制度发展而有序推进。特别是改革开放后，中国逐步构建了以《中华人民共和国著作权法》为核心的特色版权法律制度体系，构建了以司法行政并行的版权保护体系，构建了围绕版权全链条服务的社会服务体系，构建了围绕多边合作的版权国际合作体系。这一时期，景德镇陶瓷版权体系在新中国特色版权体系的构建完善中不断优化。

改革开放促进版权法制体系完善。早在 1955 年中国就成立了著作权法起草小组。1957 年，完成《保障出版物著作权暂行规定（草案）》的起草工作。

① 　周林、李明山：《中国版权史研究文献》，中国方正出版社，1999，第 97 页。
② 　铁源、溪明：《民国瓷器鉴定——胎釉　彩绘　器型》，华龄出版社，2004，第 42 页。

1990年，颁布新中国第一部著作权法，并加入《保护文学和艺术作品伯尔尼公约》和《世界版权公约》，成为成员国，有效解决了我国对外版权关系问题。随着版权法治体系建构与完善，针对景德镇陶瓷等传统文化的保护与发展，我国颁布了系列加强文化法治环境建设与保障的政策措施，推进传统文化创新发展，使景德镇版权事业发展与传统陶瓷手工业创新进一步联动配合。版权法律法规体系与高效的执法司法体系及行政措施，使景德镇陶瓷版权保护进入发展新时期。

陶瓷复兴推进景德镇版权事业发展。新中国成立后，景德镇整合陶瓷生产资源，复兴陶瓷产业。通过组建设立人民、新华、宇宙、东风、光明、红星、红旗等大型瓷厂，形成以工艺美术瓷、日用瓷、工业用瓷和高技术陶瓷等多门类的陶瓷生产格局，创新活力被有效激发，陶瓷作品类型极大丰富。1952年底，日用陶瓷产量达9022万件，比1949年的6350万件增长42%。[1]改革开放以后，景德镇进一步创新了陶瓷工艺与材料，陶瓷产业步入新发展阶段。1976年至1983年，景德镇陶瓷荣获国家金质奖5项，银质奖3项，获轻工业部优质产品奖12项，江西省优质产品奖23项。[2]2010年，景德镇市新闻出版（版权）局以维护陶瓷艺人权益为中心，将陶瓷作品版权申报登记纳入创业服务年活动中，建立陶瓷作品版权申报登记的长效机制，取得明显效果。陶瓷艺术作品版权登记数量占全省版权登记总量的53%。[3]景德镇陶瓷版权事业逐步发展完善。

---

① 景德镇市志编纂委员会编纂《景德镇市志略》，汉语大词典出版社，1989，第45页。
② 景德镇市志编纂委员会编纂《景德镇市志略》，汉语大词典出版社，1989，第45页。
③ 《景德镇市大力保护陶瓷作品版权》，《江西日报》2010年3月22日。

第二节

景德镇陶瓷版权保护意识的生成基础

赓续千年的景德镇窑火，积蓄了不可胜数的陶瓷艺术精品，不仅以其独创性冠绝于世，而且以精益求精的陶瓷技术、通达四海的传播体系、创新包容的社会文化，共同构成了陶瓷版权保护意识生成的内在动力与实践基础。陶瓷版权保护意识的形成与发展，是景德镇陶瓷手工业社会发展中技术、文化与经济等要素合力作用的结果。

一、陶瓷技术发展培育版权保护物质基础

千百年来，景德镇陶瓷以釉色、纹饰与器型的创意表达，使文化艺术思想以客观外在形式固定并被公众感知欣赏，拓宽了早期版权保护内容，延展了以平面纸张为载体的作品类型。陶瓷生产的主要目的在于满足市场需求，市场需求增加，促使陶瓷生产复制技术改进发展。罗伯特·芬雷在《青花瓷的故事：中国瓷的时代》一书中指出："景德镇掌控了全球瓷器市场，不仅仅因为产品精良，也因为生产规模与组织先进；它代表了在蒸汽带动的机器年代来到之前，手工艺产业的最高峰，大规模集中制造生产最壮盛的成就。"①"用机械的手段大致成形，再以手工个别加工，这两种方法的结合一直是景德镇瓷器生产的典型特征"②。早在汉代，景德镇浮梁农户就采挖瓷石以水碓实现制料的半机械化加工。③唐代，南窑已出现模印装饰方法。④宋代，景德镇已大规模使用模具翻印出所需的图案。⑤发展至明清时期，景德镇已发展为"圆器之造，每一器必有

明正统青花龙纹大缸（御窑博物院供图）

一模，大小款式方能划一"⑥。1927 年的《瓷史》，记录了黄炎培调查景德镇的情况，详细记载了景德镇釉上与釉下瓷用贴花纸的情况。⑦新中国成立后，景德镇已经改手工拉坯为单刀压坯，改木棒搅车为机械电动皮带带动，减轻了工人劳动强度，提高了工效。单刀型发展到双刀和滚压成型，手工注浆发展到压力注浆和真空脱泡注浆等，还可以使用旋压、阴模滚压、阳模滚压、塑性挤压等多种成型方法。⑧标准化生产方式与精细化行业分工积淀出景德镇陶瓷生产的大量技术储备，形成了中国烧造时间最长、规模最大、数量最多、表现最丰富的陶瓷制造体系，使陶瓷器物承载无形的智力成果，而且在复制技术发展中培育完善陶瓷版权保护观念。

① （美）罗伯特·芬雷：《青花瓷的故事：中国瓷的时代》，郑明萱译，海南出版社，2015，第 32 页。
② （德）雷德侯：《万物：中国艺术中的模件化和规模化生产》，张总等译，生活·读书·新知三联书店，2005，第 123 页。
③ 《景德镇瓷业水碓营造技艺（2021 年第五批国家级非物质文化遗产代表性项目）》，《景德镇陶瓷》2022 年第 3 期。
④ 张文江：《景德镇南窑遗址考古发掘的重要收获》，《东方博物》2014 年第 2 期。
⑤ 程仁发：《宋代景德镇青白瓷装饰方法的研究》，《中国陶瓷》2015 年第 51 卷第 12 期。
⑥ 熊寥、熊微编注《中国陶瓷古籍集成》，上海文化出版社，2006，第 470 页。
⑦ 周觉民：《略谈我国陶瓷贴花纸的兴起》，《景德镇陶瓷》1982 年第 3 期。
⑧ 景德镇市志编纂委员会编纂《景德镇市志略》，汉语大词典出版社，1989，第 48 页。

二、陶瓷市场扩张凝聚版权保护核心优势

通达四海的陶瓷市场是景德镇陶瓷版权保护意识生成与发展的传播基础。景德镇四面环山，富产松柴，且周边的高岭、麻仓山及祁门等地蕴藏着丰富的制瓷原料，为陶瓷生产加工提供了优质原料来源与得天独厚的制作环境。昌江穿城而过，不仅为陶瓷原料加工提供水源动力，而且为陶瓷对外传播与贸易提供了高效便捷的运输条件，使景德镇成为海上丝绸之路的重要货源地。陶瓷器物传播范围之广、陶瓷文化影响之大，为中西方文化交融与互鉴作出不可磨灭的贡献。同时，广阔的市场带来巨额利益，陶瓷被欧洲王室贵族视为"白色金子"，使陶瓷抄袭与盗版变得有利可图，客观上推进了版权保护意识产生。

宋元时期，景德镇就已经拥有繁盛的内销与外销市场。据统计，除贵州、西藏、青海、宁夏和黑龙江等少数地区，全国大部分区域都有景德镇的青白瓷出土。[1]同时，在东北亚、东南亚、西亚至非洲，也有景德镇的瓷器出土。[2]明

高岭瓷土矿遗址（景德镇市文旅局供图）

---

[1] 李一平：《宋代的湖田窑》，《南方文物》2003 年第 1 期。
[2] 叶文程：《宋元时期景德镇青白瓷窑系的外销》，《景德镇陶瓷》1989 年第 3、4 期。

清时期,景德镇"自燕云而北,南交趾,东际海,西被蜀,无所不至"①。国际贸易市场主要有:东亚市场,如日本、朝鲜;东南亚市场,如越南、菲律宾、马六甲至印度尼西亚;南亚印度及斯里兰卡;西亚广大地区;东非市场;欧洲市场以及美洲市场等世界上极为广大的地区。这些形形色色的市场,是市场订制来样加工以及景德镇融汇世界样式及世界资源的主要途径。②在16—18世纪,景德镇瓷器外销规模合计约为26781万件。③《景德镇陶录》记载:"洋器,专售外洋者,有滑洋器、泥洋器之分,商多粤东人,贩去与鬼子互市,式样奇巧,岁无定样。"④景德镇陶工配合订单的要求,创新设计了一批图案性、装饰性强的瓷质西方生活用具。除传统花鸟、瑞兽及人物等纹饰图案外,还有西方国家的族徽、文字、罗盘、经书、喷水图及西洋风景画,边饰

三闾庙码头遗址(昌江区文管所供图)

景德镇里弄(陶阳里历史文化景区供图)

---

① 熊寥、熊微编注《中国陶瓷古籍集成》,上海文化出版社,2006,第46页。
② 周思中:《景德镇的历史文化特点、制瓷体系及发展战略》,《中国港口》2020年增刊第2期。
③ 翁彦俊:《景德镇16—18世纪陶瓷外销规模估略》,《中国陶瓷》2021年第57卷第10期。
④ 蓝浦、郑廷桂:《景德镇陶录》,转引自余家栋:《江西陶瓷史》,河南大学出版社,1997,第493页。

开光或镂雕，内绘枝花或硕果。[①]纹章瓷、克拉克瓷等原创订制瓷应运而生。在东印度公司文书记录中，也留存不少瓷器店铺查看瓷器样板、议价的记录。这种出于文化交流与商业利益需要，在瓷器造型、装饰创新上的原创表达，使"原创画面"或"二次创作"等定制图案和造型样式蕴含着丰厚的交易利润，保护定制画面的版权，成为保护交易的现实需求与核心竞争优势。版权观念在商品竞争与私营陶瓷手工业中不断完善。

三、社会环境滋养陶瓷版权保护意识转变

海纳百川的景德镇陶瓷文化，造就了千年不衰的瓷业繁荣。两宋时期，受战乱影响，大批北方工匠南下谋生，构成景德镇陶瓷创新结构的社会主体基础。元代，景德镇以兼收并蓄的社会环境融合多民族文化艺术，烧造的青花瓷器不

依河而建的瓷土加工碓棚（景德镇市档案馆供图）

---

① 张泽兵：《景德镇陶瓷文化传承创新的历史经验与当代实践》，《江西社会科学》2022 年第 12 期。

仅丰富了高温釉下彩的艺术表现形式，而且将"昭君出塞"与"三顾茅庐"等中国传统神话、小说、演义等文学题材转化为元青花创作主题，形成陶瓷"演绎作品"。明清时期，景德镇官民窑联动发展，形成综合装饰体系，并以行帮商会为依托，凭借地缘位置与血缘关系，形成"景德江右一巨镇也，隶于浮。业制陶器，利济天下，四方远近，挟其技能以食力者，莫不趋之若鹜"[①] 的陶瓷创新中心。不同时期，景德镇都以包容开放的社会环境滋养了陶瓷艺术创作的多元创新生态。大量聚集的陶瓷创新主体投入时间与智慧，使景德镇的陶瓷器物凝聚了丰富的创意构思，用极致与专注造就了历代陶瓷创新创作的源头活水与发展动力；高度的创新性与独创性，使版权保护意识在不断创新与融合间持续发展。

---

① 　熊寥、熊微编注《中国陶瓷古籍集成》，上海文化出版社，2006，第535页。

第三节

景德镇陶瓷版权保护的演进逻辑

景德镇陶瓷版权保护意识随着制度与技术发展，经历了漫长的蜕变与演进，由观念萌发到私力救济最终嬗变为法制保护的过程，形成版权保护向法律规范优化的演进逻辑。在不同历史时期，基于社会变迁、技术变革和经济发展，以不同表现形式介入版权建设与发展中，并呈现出不同的时代特征。

一、陶瓷版权保护形式由社会文化向法律规范优化

景德镇版权保护在成文法出现前，通过官方管控、商帮行会、技术限制等手段，形成官样、款识、禁例、行规等创新保护措施。但是，由于其运行缺乏稳定性与规范性，保护观念与思想不能长期促进陶瓷创新发展。随着社会制度变迁并融合外来法治思想，稳定的法律规范成为塑造版权保护规范性的优化路径。肇始于清末的版权法律规范，使西方版权保护思想与我国版权保护思想融合嫁接，首次以成文法的形式，开始探索与转变版权保护方式，明确了创作主体的中心地位，开启了尝试以较稳定的法律规则秩序规制景德镇陶瓷版权的发展。

二、陶瓷版权保护内容由局限零散向科学完备拓展

囿于我国立法进程与陶瓷技术发展等客观因素，宋元时期，景德镇陶瓷版权保护活动仅以署名形式萌发作品人身权利，私权观念尚不清晰完善。明清时期，陶瓷工匠人身依附关系逐渐松懈，加之商品经济发展使版权意识逐渐向财产权利扩展。王光尧指出，"工匠费用，在嘉靖以前并不存在，技术匠人系征用官匠，而人夫则从浮梁县和鄱阳县摊派上工夫在厂应役（后仅浮梁一县应役），嘉靖以后多有雇役，但其费用应来自官匠所纳班匠银"[①]。可见，创新主体开始因无形智力创作而产生财产关系。晚清时期，立法使版权保护范围从书籍、绘画、摄影等平面作品，扩张至雕刻、模型等立体作品，精神创作与财产权被纳入法律调整框架之中，顺应了版权发展的时代要求。

三、陶瓷版权保护思想由保守封闭向开放共享完善

宋元时期，陶瓷创作主体对创新智力成果的独占思想催生了陶瓷版权保护意识。明清时期，皇权介入，以封闭保守禁令等形式进行保护，加之陶瓷商帮行会以严格的行业规约与传承制度限制陶瓷创新成果与技艺外传，使创新成果无法共享甚至失传，私权也无法得到较全面保障。晚清《大清著作权律》规定，版权取得须在"专管文房物件注册之所"注册登记。[②] 注册登记版权成为法制保护的重要举措，版权律法使智力成果版权关联逐渐清晰。新中国成立后，不断完善版权登记渠道，构建版权社会服务体系，使版权不仅具备"个人独占"的私权属性，还具有"开放共享"的公权特征，向外扩展成为一种权利保护下的开放共享。

---

① 王光尧：《明代宫廷陶瓷史》，紫禁城出版社，2010，第 148 页。
② 周林、李明山主编《中国版权史研究文献》，中国方正出版社，1999，第 55 页。

第四节
小结

　　综上，景德镇不同历史阶段的版权保护形式，忠实记录了版权保护意识演进与创新治理变迁的信息，生动展现了版权保护思想在推动陶瓷行业发展中的重要价值。从景德镇版权生成基础来分析，陶瓷生产复制技术推动版权保护发展，活跃的国内外陶瓷市场加速版权保护完善，丰富的创意构思激励版权保护进步，景德镇以多元共生的"版权保护"助力"千年瓷都"蜚声中外。从景德镇版权制度演变来分析，版权保护形式由私力救济向法律规范优化，版权保护内容由局限零散向科学完备拓展，版权保护思想由保守封闭向开放共享完善。景德镇以日臻完善的"版权制度"，推进"千年瓷业"生生不息。

IP与创意产业：
景德镇故事

景德镇陶瓷版权的新时代担当

　　景德镇以"千年瓷都"的底蕴聚焦陶瓷文化传承创新，构建起以版权为核心的陶瓷文化创意产业发展新格局。景德镇通过建立集创造、运用、保护、管理、服务为一体的版权全链条发展机制，为实现陶瓷文化创意产业的更优质创造、更高效运用、更严格保护、更科学管理和更便民服务提供了根本保障。

第一节

景德镇陶瓷版权创造持续化

以瑞牛公司为代表的新兴陶瓷企业，证明了只有首先保障持续不断地创造高质量作品，版权的运用、保护、管理与服务才有意义。因此，景德镇陶瓷版权发展的基础，在于确保创造的持续化。得益于景德镇极其悠久的制瓷史，现阶段的版权创造活动，可以通过景德镇传统陶瓷文化的挖掘、传播与现代化转化，以实现创造资源获取的持续化。景德镇在采取政府与市场导向相结合的创造主体聚集模式的同时，也通过产业融合等方式，实现创造主体范围的扩大，二者共同确保了创造主体数量增长的持续化。而创造模式与时俱进的变革，最终也导致创造质量提升的持续化。

一、文创示范的瑞牛公司

在 2021 年瓷博会的开幕式上，景德镇向全球发布了首款城市礼物——"福如意"茶器，这款茶器是用创意设计讲述瓷都故事、用陶瓷文创引领美好生活、以文博 IP 激发城市文化动能的生动体现。"福如意"脱颖而出的背后，是瑞牛公司对陶瓷文化创意产业始终如一的坚持。它以持续化的版权创造驱动发展的经营理念，激励更多的陶瓷创作者致力于文化经典的传承与革新。

如日方升，瑞牛的创立初心

瑞牛公司在景德镇陶瓷文创领域已成为一颗闪耀的明珠，其发展历程也曾一路坎坷，但他们始终坚持创新。瑞牛公司的前身是"景德闲云居陶瓷文化发展有限公司"，当时它只是景德镇众多陶瓷企业中平平无奇的一员。公司中高端手工瓷器的定位，既不能使其产品进入日常生活，又不能使其在众多产品中拔得头筹。如何让文化创意融入陶瓷制造，让传统的陶瓷更贴近现代人的生活，让陶瓷文创从小作坊走向产业化的道路上不断提升企业创新能力，这是"闲云居"在当时面临的经营困境，也是众多景德镇陶瓷企业面临的发展难题。

经过大量的市场调研，他们发现景德镇陶瓷企业各有优势，但大多陷于"做不大""一大就倒"的怪圈。瑞牛公司深刻认识到，要探寻破局之道，必须重新定位企业发展方向、确立企业发展目标。"闲云居"董事长段建平认为，想要贯彻"原创设计、艺术生活"的理念，就必须在产品设计、工艺优化和生产模式上寻得新的突破，最终要让景德镇的千年技艺绝活创造出当代之美，使个性化的陶瓷文创产品从手工小作坊走向规模化和产业化。经过一年多的探索，2019年2月，一个崭新的创业项目——"瑞牛（Renew）文创"异军突起。

"瑞牛"取音于英文单词"Renew"，寓意重新出发、瑞牛开拓。他们创造性地把中国传统文化与千年陶瓷技艺融合在一起，把定制化与规模化结合在一起，用创意设计吸引市场关注，以生产能力支撑无限创意。"福如意"茶器的创意设计，就是瑞牛公司在探索新发展模式中最生动的实践。其创意设计灵感来源于景德镇中国陶瓷博物馆馆藏珍贵文物——清乾隆青花葫纹葫芦瓶，同时融入了中华文化"和合"思想。采用"葫芦"造型，谐音"福禄"，寓意多子多福；瓶形饱满圆润，开则为器，合则为艺，像"吉"字，寓意着吉祥如意，又寓意政通人和。整个作品映射出景德镇陶瓷产业守望传承、创新创造的非凡历程，呈现出当代生活美学的创新魅力和景德镇敞开怀抱、对话世界的崭新姿态。

突破瓶颈，实现定制量产化

"福如意"茶器的成功，更加坚定了瑞牛公司的创业初心，在推进产业化发

景德镇城市礼物——"福如意"茶器（瑞牛公司供图）

展过程中必须突破阻碍定制化、规模化的瓶颈问题。要突破定制化、规模化的瓶颈，就必须整合创意、设计、研发、制造等产业资源，以降低生产成本，提升生产力。

在定制化方面，实现定制与创新同轨。为解决艺术家、设计师与工匠三者之间衔接不畅的情况，把创意快速转化为作品，瑞牛公司通过合作的形式将艺术家、设计师与工匠融为一体，实现设计理念与制作技艺的完美结合，促使产品制作达到近乎完美的境地。首先，瑞牛公司让设计师深入了解艺术家的设计理念。通过与艺术家密切合作，设计师能更好地理解艺术家的创作灵感、审美追求和意图，从而将这些元素融入产品设计中。这样，产品不仅具备了设计师独特的视觉风格和创意，还能传达出艺术家深层次的文化内涵和情感表达。其次，瑞牛公司让设计师掌握工匠的制作技艺。通过对工匠技艺的深入研究和学习，设计师能掌握陶瓷制作工艺的要点和技巧，理解材料特性和工艺流程，从而在设计过程中考虑到产品的实操性。如此，产品的设计不仅具备了艺术性和创新性，还能在制作过程中充分体现出工匠的精湛技艺和品质。最后，设计师既了解艺术家的文化创新理念，又掌握工匠的传统制作技艺，使产品制作浑然天成。在生产制作过程中，瑞牛公司还聘请退休的陶瓷厂老职工负责陶瓷生产的监制，使产品质量始终在线。

在规模化方面，实现规模与效益同在。为解决生产过程中上下游产业链不顺畅、材料成本高等局限，瑞牛公司通过"设计＋研发＋供应链"模式，创新"陶瓷＋"产业生态，提升核心竞争力。即以陶瓷为抓手，融合"陶瓷＋非遗传承""陶瓷＋工匠精神""陶瓷＋版权""陶瓷＋艺术家""陶瓷＋设计师""陶瓷＋IP衍生""陶瓷＋跨界材料""陶瓷＋供应链""陶瓷＋数字化"等方式，精准对接客户的文创需求。为满足文创市场需求，实现设计与工艺研发转化为可落地的个性化陶瓷产品，瑞牛公司通过整合产业链资源，运用"柔性产业链"方式，实现产品类别差异化和规模化生产。规模化生产后，2020年，瑞牛文创实现盈利；2022年，瑞牛文创连续两年销售收入增长翻番。

无论是在定制化还是规模化方面，瑞牛公司始终将"创新"作为破局之道，模式创新、作品创新，在创新中自强、争先。其深谙保护知识产权就是保护创新之道，只有积极地保护自有知识产权，才能让企业具备持续的竞争力。截至2023年7月，瑞牛公司签约的艺术家有55名，签约的设计师有120名，自由设计师有16人。2022年版权登记数量为117项，2023年版权登记数量达989项。每一件作品，公司都会与设计师达成协议，明确作品的版权归属，便于后续公司统一维权。

创意革新，瑞牛一直在路上

瑞牛公司将"成为定制化陶瓷行业的顶流"作为企业的长期发展战略，矢

瑞牛公司生产线现场图（瑞牛公司供图）

志不渝做好文创领军示范企业，并以版权护航企业行稳致远。从成立至今，瑞牛公司先后获评"全国版权示范单位""江西省专精特新中小企业""江西省省级工业设计中心""高新技术企业"，其创新发展模式也成功入选第十三届"全国百篇优秀管理案例"。在文创设计方面，瑞牛公司更是大放异彩。2022年瑞牛公司与景德镇中国陶瓷博物馆、景德镇国家陶瓷版权交易中心联合发行景德镇市首款数字藏品——"青青子衿"。瑞牛公司旗下的"福瑞东方"数字文旅项目，荣获江西省工信厅第四批VR应用示范项目。瑞牛公司也先后为中国商飞、中国铁塔、阿里巴巴、VIVO、百度、雅诗兰黛、极氪汽车、蔚来汽车、招商银行、九江银行、北京大学、中国人民大学、江西师范大学等优秀品牌和单位研发陶瓷文创产品。除"福如意"茶器成为景德镇的城市礼物外，瑞牛公司研发的陶瓷文创产品"飞阁流丹"茶器，成为南昌的城市礼物。

站在新的历史起点上，瑞牛公司秉持"求实、求新、求质、求效"的企业精神，继续贯彻"设计优美""研发高效""供应链完备"的发展思路，时刻把握发展机遇，不断革新产品设计、提升制造能力。瑞牛公司为景德镇陶瓷文化创意产业发展注入新活力，展现出景德镇陶瓷企业在应对市场竞争和时代发展

瑞牛创研中心（瑞牛公司供图）

"青青子衿"数字藏品（瑞牛公司供图）

中不屈不挠、锐意进取的姿态，也展现出以版权为核心要素的陶瓷文化产业蓬勃的创新能力和无限的发展前景。

二、景德镇陶瓷版权创造的持续化模式

景德镇陶瓷版权创造资源的获取

景德镇陶瓷版权创造资源的持续获取是景德镇陶瓷版权创造的基础，是将景德镇传统文化资源向版权产品转化，进而形成版权产业，最终成为促进景德镇城市发展重要助推力的第一步。基于景德镇陶瓷版权资源同心圆扩散的事实①，景德镇陶瓷版权创造资源的获取则是一种同心圆逆向挖掘的模式。从繁荣的景德镇陶瓷文化资源中挖掘出陶瓷版权产品的创作方式，再从陶瓷版权产品的创作方式中倒推出版权产品的创作源头并加以挖掘与固定，这其中最典型的例子，就是景德镇市对御窑文化的深入挖掘与研究。景德镇通过开发"御窑厂

---

① 同心圆扩散：这种扩散路径既与产业化的地理范围有关，也与产业化的业务范围有关。是以发源地为基础，先扩散至第一轮扩散地，再逐渐扩散至第二轮扩散地的一种文化资源的扩散方式。参见王志标：《传统文化资源产业化的路径分析》，《河南大学学报（社会科学版）》2012年第52卷第2期。

遗址",对挖掘出的文物进行研究与保护,逐步模拟复原出已失传的陶瓷版权资源,为陶瓷版权创作提供了新的灵感。

景德镇拥有深厚的陶瓷文化历史,千年的制瓷历史贡献了不计其数的青花瓷、玲珑瓷、粉彩瓷和彩色釉,数以万计的花纹与图案印刻在这些精美的陶瓷之上。其中有些已然温柔地归于尘土,更多的则是以瓷瓶整体或是陶瓷残片的方式深埋地下。对文物的挖掘与保护,让这些凝聚着千百年艺术创作结晶的器物以陶瓷版权创造资源的形式重现荣光。

景德镇中国陶瓷博物馆作为新中国成立后建馆最早、藏瓷丰富的陶瓷艺术专业性博物馆,除了承担着中国陶瓷传统文化的展示任务之外,对于版权创作而言,它的重要意义在于能固定版权创造资源,提供陶瓷版权基因。正如景德镇首届城市礼物"福如意"的灵感来源于馆藏文物清乾隆青花葫纹葫芦瓶一样,越来越多的创作者发现,景德镇的陶瓷文化本身就是一汪取之不尽的灵感源泉。

景德镇获取陶瓷版权创造资源的信条是以景德镇的地理范围为核心,持续向内部挖掘,并将景德镇丰富多样的陶瓷传统文化确定为创造根基,因此并不需要过多依赖外部版本资源的借鉴。而景德镇"博物馆之城"的打造,也将固定陶瓷版权创造资源,并使其融入景德镇城市生活的愿景逐步变为现实。

景德镇陶瓷版权创造主体的聚集

随着景德镇文化经济贡献的增长、陶瓷版权产业规模的不断壮大以及陶瓷版权产业结构的日益合理,陶瓷版权产业的集群化发展是一个必然的趋势。景德镇陶瓷版权产业集群化发展的一大特征,是景德镇陶瓷版权创造主体的聚集。不同于较为单一的市场主导聚集模式或政府主导聚集模式,景德镇采取的是政府与市场导向结合的聚集模式,并且并不拘泥于传统陶瓷版权创造主体的聚集,而是实现了陶瓷版权创造主体范围的扩大。①

---

① 有学者研究发现,文化产业空间集聚的基本模式有三种:市场主导型、政府主导型、市场资源和政府导向型。由于集聚动力要素、集聚资源利用方式不同,三种基本集聚模式呈现出不同特征。参见戴钰:《文化产业空间集聚研究——以湖南地区为例》,博士学位论文,武汉理工大学产业经济学专业,2013,第71页。

陶溪川"文化游"（景德镇市融媒体中心供图）

　　景德镇市政府通过陶瓷版权资源的全新规划与原有陶瓷版权资源的提升、改造来吸引创造主体的聚集。陶瓷版权资源的全新规划，以从陶瓷版权相关制度的完善到陶瓷版权相关基础设施齐备的版权示范城市创建工作为代表。陶瓷版权资源的提升与改造，则在景德镇将老瓷厂旧址打造为规模仍在扩大的陶溪川街区、将陶瓷交易平台升级为陶博城国际交易中心等事件上，表现得淋漓尽致。拥有更明确的陶瓷版权资源规划和不断升级的陶瓷版权资源获取平台的城市，无疑会对该领域的创造主体更具有吸引力。在政府主导的资源保障下，包容与繁荣的市场环境，也吸引着拥有不同创造目的和创造风格的版权创造主体们的聚集。无论是致力于创意产业化发展的瑞牛公司，抑或是钻研独特图案和制作工艺的"碎纸图案陶瓷"创作者——"景德镇女孩"①，都能在这座城市中肆

① "景德镇女孩"名叫小芳墨墨，她的碎纸图案陶瓷作品，灵感来源于她对环保的关注，同时将传统的景德镇陶瓷工艺与现代艺术元素相结合，呈现出一种别样的美感。其作品自问世以来，便受到了业内人士和消费者的一致好评。许多人表示，她的作品既有传统文化的底蕴，又有现代艺术的创新，让人耳目一新。在景德镇的陶瓷市场上，墨墨的作品一度成为抢手货，甚至有人为了购买她的作品，特意从外地赶来。

景德镇陶瓷研学活动（景德镇市版权局供图）

意地将灵感转化为现实作品。

　　景德镇对于陶瓷版权创造主体的聚集，还体现在对主体本身的改造方面。景德镇主张融合发展文化与旅游，利用御窑遗址等文化资源，打造了以陶溪川为代表的"文化游"、以高岭中国村为代表的"沉浸游"、以瓷乐和瓷宴为代表的"夜珠山游"等文旅融合发展新模式。

　　同时，"文化＋教育"的发展模式，使得"研学游"活动频繁开展，利用陶瓷文化研学资源、陶艺教学资源，并结合国际化艺术思想和创作思维，为陶瓷版权创造提供了新的思路。在这个过程中，文化、旅游与教育三个行业进行融合，结果是行业主体之间的边界被打破。融合后的主体需要摒弃固有行业思维，开发具有文化价值的旅游项目，设计具有文化符号的研学课程，并使这些项目适应景德镇独特的市场规律。至此，他们也不再是传统意义上的旅游业或教育业从业者，而是成为景德镇陶瓷版权创造主体中不可或缺的一群人，并持续投入在陶瓷版权创造活动中。

景德镇陶瓷版权创造质量的提升

陶瓷版权创造资源的内部挖掘与获取，配合陶瓷版权创造主体的聚集与扩大，为陶瓷版权创造质量的最终提升提供了条件。而景德镇得以实现这一目标的原因，在于短时间内从大规模版权单向创造向大规模版权定制创造与大规模版权个性化创造的模式转变。"十大瓷厂"阶段是较为典型的大规模版权单向创造模式，制瓷企业是唯一的版权创造主体，客户仅仅是产品的接收者和使用者。这一阶段，尽管版权创造仍有突破，但是却受限于制瓷企业的创造习惯与较为保守的经营风格。这也直接导致了产品质量虽然有所维持，但创造质量却提升缓慢的结果。

在改革的浪潮中，国有制瓷企业在陶瓷产业中的主导地位逐渐弱化，加上本土自然资源逐渐枯竭的事实，景德镇自然无法沿袭之前的创造模式。此时，景德镇的做法是在秉持陶瓷传统文化精华的同时激发市场的活力，将陶瓷版权创造的重心，向定制创造与个性化创造移动。版权资源不断地被挖掘和创造主体的持续活动被解构成更小的单元，在创造阶段可以对其进行快速的重组与更新。最典型的例子在于，在传统陶瓷创造工艺中，只有一整套花纹图案严丝合缝地呈现在对应器物之上，这件器物才能被称为艺术品，这个过程才能被称为陶瓷创造。但在现今环境下，哪怕是一小块陶瓷残片中所搭载的图案都能经过创造主体的巧思而得以不断地变化表现形式，且能被市场所接纳。这种版权资源的结构与重构，为版权创造的定制与个性化提供了宝贵的财富。

定制创造与个性化创造的典型表现形式是服务型创造。不同于以往，顾客此时成为版权创造的主体之一。一方面，顾客的需求和偏好决定了企业的版权创造方向。在景德镇这个开放的环境中，顾客通过不断提出个性化需求，引导企业按照他们的要求进行创造。另一方面，顾客的需求多样化反哺版权创造过程。随着个性化需求的持续累积，企业甚至艺术家们开始重视并吸纳顾客所提出的诸多创造灵感，并结合专业技艺将其改造为版权产品。决定陶瓷版权创造质量的终归是市场，景德镇正是由于创造思路和创造模式的转变，才得以实现创造质量的提升。

第二节

景德镇陶瓷版权运用灵活化

陶溪川文创街区，作为景德镇陶瓷版权运用的璀璨典范，在短短十余载的光阴里，经历了从寂寂无闻到万众瞩目的华丽蜕变。它不仅承载着景德镇深厚的陶瓷文化底蕴，更因其独特的陶瓷版权运用模式而成为这座千年瓷都的一张耀眼名片。陶溪川的成功，说明景德镇正通过陶瓷版权运用体制的完善，强化各方主体在版权运用活动中的协同互动作用，通过陶瓷版权运用方式的拓创，实现了版权运用壁垒的打破与版权运用方式的共享；通过陶瓷版权运用产业的革新，突破了传统版权运用产业的限制，为版权运用产业发展渠道的持续拓宽提供了无限可能。

一、创意迸发的陶溪川街区

陶溪川是国家级文化产业示范园区、国家双创示范基地、全国创业孵化示范基地、全国版权示范园区、国家级夜间文化和旅游消费集聚区、国家旅游科技示范园区和全国非遗旅游街区，是一个国内外知名、无边无墙的文化艺术街区。对于艺术

陶溪川文创街区全貌图（陶溪川文创街区供图）

家、设计师、品牌商、游客而言，陶溪川是陶瓷文化交流和陶瓷艺术衍生的胜地。街区通过创新陶瓷版权创造激励机制和陶瓷版权服务制度，形成了创造与保护的集群效应。在这里，每个创意都能实现，每个创业者都能被发现，每件作品都可以通过版权制度得到保护。

妙手生花，打造陶瓷创意空间

"陶溪川"的名字，由何而来？陶是陶瓷，是景德镇之根本，也是陶溪川前身宇宙瓷厂的根本。"溪川"是自然的代表，是生命的象征，代表川流不息，连绵不绝的生命力。陶溪川背靠千年古瓷都，以瓷为源、集溪成川，因此取名"陶溪川"，有希望陶瓷文化创意如同小溪般汇聚成川之意。

2012 年，景德镇市政府决定对原国营宇宙瓷厂旧址进行改造、以原国营宇宙瓷厂旧址为核心区域启动"陶溪川国际陶瓷文化产业园"项目。该项目总投资 68 亿元，总建筑面积 150 万平方米，由北京清华同衡规划设计院携日本、韩国设计事务所进行规划设计。该项目通过贯彻可持续发展理念，整合陶瓷文化资源，"活化"保护和利用陶瓷工业遗存，发展文创、旅游和现代服务业，进而打造陶溪川文创街区。一是通过精巧设计，把锯齿形、人字形厂房，11 座高耸的烟囱、水塔，以及墙上的老标语、口号这些原生态的物件"变废为宝"般地融入街区每一个角落，让陶瓷人在这里找得到乡愁和记忆。二是对宇宙瓷厂 22 栋老厂房、煤烧隧道窑、圆窑包、工业设施等进行保护修缮，同时完全保留原有建筑的肌理和风貌，把原有的生产车间打造为陶瓷工业遗产博物馆、陶溪川美术馆、邑空间双创孵化基地、陶公塾教育研学基地、B&C 设计中心等空间。同时，为更好地推进陶溪川文化创意产业的发展，还引入中央美院、中国美院、人民网、唐英学社等知名文化机构，并吸纳功夫小瓷、陶瓷 3D 打印、欧洲陶艺中心、德国 DWH 木工坊等 170 余家知名文创品牌，将老瓷厂转型升级为具有"国际范"、跨界经营的文化创意街区。

陶溪川文化创意街区的打造，为文化创作提供了良好的平台。然而，在陶溪川开市之初，因抄袭而出现的作品同质化现象较为普遍。尽管当时的陶溪川已经聚集了上千名创客，但由于创客们较容易接触到他人创作的作品，加之当时侵权成本较低，抄袭事件经常发生。针对这一不良的市场现象，江西省和景德镇市版权管理部门、陶溪川管理者都意识到，只有在陶溪川建立系统、专业的版权保护体系，才能保障陶溪川文化创意产业的健康、可持续发展。因此，陶溪川围绕版权激励文化创新创造的作用机理，通过构建集创业资金、人才培育、平台服务、品牌宣传、版权激励机制为一体的全程式创新发展支撑体系，形成了陶瓷文化创意产业发展的新模式。

一是创业资金支持。陶溪川为入驻的陶瓷创客提供创业孵化基地运营费补贴、创业补助、贴息贷款、一次性创业补贴等创业资金支持，从资金层面帮助陶瓷创客缓解在创业不同阶段的资金压力。

二是人才培训支持。作为全国版权示范园区（基地），陶溪川着力加强知识产权保护意识的宣传，定期邀请版权行业专家为陶瓷创客开展知识产权公开讲座。不仅如此，还定期邀请国际级设计师、陶艺家开设论坛、讲座等进行人才专项辅导，帮助陶瓷创客管理和运营好版权资产。此外，陶溪川还借助"72 人青年艺术家"项目和国际交流活动，推动"洋景漂"与本土艺术家联动设计创作，激发更多国际化的原创作品。

三是平台服务支持。为陶瓷创客提供协助办理个体户或企业注册服务、工会服务、会计代理记账服务等支持。同时，结合陶溪川直播基地、供应链选货中心、仓储物流中心三大板块，为陶瓷创客打通线上销售渠道，提供"产、销、运"这一完备的商业运营渠道。

四是品牌宣传支持。陶溪川通过举办版权优秀作品展览、版权成果大赛等丰富多彩的主题活动，为陶瓷创客提供高质量、多样态的作品展示和产品交易平台。通过陶溪川官方合作媒体以及自媒体，为陶瓷创客提供全方位宣传服务。

五是版权准入和位阶晋升机制。陶溪川通过打造摊位市集和邑空间两个物理空间，推动版权准入和位阶晋升机制的实施。摊位市集分为传统区与创意区，合称为"普通市集"。普通市集主要由创客摆摊经营，售卖的商品基本为手工艺品，其中入驻创意区的创客需要至少获得一份作品登记证书。普通市集一周只能容纳1500个摊位，而实际上每月申请入驻摊位的总量却多达4000个，是实际容纳量的2~3倍，这也使得入驻摊位的创客们并不固定，且每周都会发生变

陶溪川文创街区夜间摊位市集（陶溪川文创街区供图）

第四章
景德镇陶瓷版权的新时代担当

动。创客们为了尽可能地在陶溪川充分展示自己的作品，需要申请到入驻摊位的资格。对此，陶溪川则要求创客的摆摊作品必须具有一定原创性，这样才会授予他们入驻资格。为了检验作品的原创性，陶溪川版权服务站建立了版权检索比对资源库，将普通市集的所有作品均收入资源库进行比对分析。当创客的作品与他人作品近似程度超过 60% 时，该作品将被认定为不具有原创性，其制作者也不能获得陶溪川摊位市集的入驻资格。

邑空间则是相对固定的摊位，进入邑空间的经营者可以长期展出作品。几乎所有陶瓷创作者都希望能入驻邑空间，只有入驻邑空间才能实现在陶溪川夜市的稳定经营。当然，邑空间相较于普通市集区而言，对准入资质有着更高要求。一是在普通市集摆摊时间不少于 3 个月，二是作品原创性较强，三是具有一定的产品量和销售量。在满足基本的准入条件下，最终能否入驻，需要经过专业设计师集的审批。陶溪川的设计师集由大约 70 人组成，采取自我管理的模式进行运作，即由设计师集原有设计师队伍自主投票，挑选出接任成员，整个过程没有其他组织介入。由于每个月都可能会有设计师退出原团队，所以普通市集的创客每个月都可以申请加入设计师集。设计师集除了承担自建邑空间的入驻申请筛选工作外，还承担普通市集摊位的进入退出决策工作，即每月由设计师集就摆摊人员的去留作出决策，评选出下个月具备摆摊经营资格的创客。借由设计师集的专业素养，陶溪川版权准入机制在保证作品原创性的同时，也激励了创作者不断创新，创作出更加优质的作品，从而向新的位阶晋升发起挑战。

百花齐放，营造陶瓷创作新生态

产业生态的核心是创新生态。[①] 陶溪川以陶瓷文化创意为核心产业，充分激发版权创造活力、拓展版权应用渠道、释放版权价值效应，打造出"生产配套服务＋销售渠道支持＋版权保护加持＋综合服务配套"的陶瓷文化创意产业生态链。基于该产业生态链，陶溪川已累计研发陶瓷产品近 20 万款，创立品牌2700 余个，注册小微企业 1000 多家。

一是提供完备的生产配套服务，促进创意转化。陶溪川为创客、艺术家等打造了 80 万平方米标准化厂房和全产业链的陶瓷智造工坊，引进德国、意大利关联公司的先进制造设备，集研发、设计、打样、生产于一体构建完备的陶瓷产业生态链。陶溪川还利用产业集群优势和通过提供"保姆式"服务，为陶溪川创客提供创业空间、原料精制、产品打样、个性生产、电商物流等配套服务，成为陶瓷创新创业的"加速器"。

二是打造数字化平台，拓宽陶瓷文化创意产品的销售渠道。为拓展销售渠道，陶溪川在持续优化线下产品销售渠道的同时，进一步拓宽线上销售市场，帮助商家精准触达用户群体。通过同抖音、快手、视频号、淘宝、京东等一线互联网平台合作，开设陶溪川文创线上旗舰店，打造陶溪川直播基地。当前，陶溪川成为抖音国内首个陶瓷直播基地、快手茶瓷直播江西唯一合作运营商。

---

① （美）布朗温·H.霍尔、内森·罗森伯格：《创新经济学手册（第一卷）》，上海市科学学研究所译，上海交通大学出版社，2017，第 735—791 页。

通过"主播＋电商＋直播"模式，实现资源整合，促成线上、线下联动销售。2020年，陶溪川直播基地的全年线上成交总额为3.5亿元人民币。随着电商纷纷落地陶溪川直播基地，2021年，直播基地的全年线上成交总额为30.7亿元人民币，2022年为57.6亿元人民币，2023年达到71.4亿元人民币。三年间，陶溪川直播基地全年线上成交总额增长近20倍。

三是建立健全版权服务体系，打出版权服务的"组合拳"。陶溪川

正在直播陶溪川夜集市的"网红主播"（张南摄）

陶溪川版权登记中心（陶溪川文创街区供图）

引入江西省陶瓷知识产权信息中心、江西省维权援助陶瓷工作站、景德镇陶瓷版权服务站、景德镇市陶瓷版权快速维权中心等版权服务机构，形成版权服务的矩阵。陶溪川通过"下沉式"版权登记服务，实现权利人足不出陶溪川就能获得版权登记证书，使得陶溪川创客的创新激情和版权登记热情异常高涨。陶溪川通过多元化版权咨询服务，从最初的版权讲座、咨询服务等活动，升级打造陶溪川陶然集等品牌活动，不断在陶瓷产品化、市场化中发挥版权的显性作用。陶溪川通过一站式维权服务，形成文化执法、公安、法院等部门间的快速联动机制，逐步构建起以司法保护为主导、行政保护为支撑的版权保护大格局，为陶瓷创客们提供良好的创作环境。

四是构建配套综合服务体系，优化创客、设计师和艺术家的创作和生活环境。陶溪川为优质创客免费提供入驻、培训、学习等全方位服务，营造优渥的创作环境和舒适的生活空间。陶溪川通过举办国际范、高品质的文化艺术展、春秋大集等活动，邀请世界各国陶艺家、设计师以及全国八大美院等知名艺术院校师生齐聚陶溪川，共同推动作品、理念和思维交流碰撞。创客们在这些活动的观摩学习中，不断汲取艺术营养、提升创作水平。陶溪川积极与街区内的艺术教育及培训机构开展合作，以每月定期邀请国内外知名艺术家、设计师及学者免费开展讲座教学的形式，为创客开办"邑讲堂"。大学生创新公开课、双创服务课、双创美学公开课等多项公开课等，为创客青年提供创业培训、艺术设计及营销指导，培育属于他们的自创品牌。此外，创客们在邑空间几乎"零花销"的运作模式，使得他们能安心创作、开心生活。入驻邑空间的创客在租金、水电费和税收上也会有一定的优惠。如果创客在景德镇没有休息的空间，陶溪川的兄弟产业"邑山制作工坊"还能为其提供一间环境幽雅的房间供其居住，创客每月缴纳 200 元即可。另外，居住在"邑山制作工坊"的创客，还能得到餐补。

花香四溢，提升陶瓷作品辐射力

陶溪川良好的版权环境，为广大陶瓷创作者提供了系统性的版权保护和服务，这些系统性的保护和服务不但有效激发了更多的陶瓷创意，也使得创客们

陶溪川版权优秀作品展上展览的作品（陶溪川文创街区供图）

期待自己的陶瓷作品得到更多的认可和推广。鉴于此，陶溪川不断通过品牌孵化、宣介展示、环境营造等方式，提升陶瓷作品的辐射力和影响力。

为提升陶瓷作品辐射力，陶溪川积极响应国家"大众创业、万众创新"的号召，以"年轻"和"原创"为核心，为陶瓷创客提供品牌孵化服务。从陶瓷创意、青年双创、人才培养、品牌塑造的方向出发，引导创客们打造具有原创、高品质、规模化的陶瓷品牌。目前，在陶溪川实现转化创业的实体已经超过3000家，接受服务的创客也已有2万余人，带动区域内10万余人就业。陶溪川通过举办版权优秀作品展览，增加创客年度优秀新作品曝光度；通过举办版权成果大赛，鼓励创客们相互学习交流，提升创作水平，增加创作新思想。

现阶段，陶溪川还在着力打造"邑空间"升级版——"社空间"，通过建设陶溪川直播基地、拓展国际驻场板块、建设"景漂"长租房等，为青年艺术家、设计师、手艺人构建一个更加开放共享的双创社区，持续培养陶瓷创作人才，解决人才的后顾之忧，使之专心投入陶瓷艺术创作。

IP与陶瓷产业：
景德镇故事

二、景德镇陶瓷版权运用的灵活化模式

景德镇陶瓷版权运用体制的完善

由于一般资源的不可再生与所有权的绝对，对资源的运用具有明显的排他性。尽管版权的无形性和可复制性相对弱化了版权运用过程中排他性所带来的负面影响，但市场竞争的残酷与行业主体间的相互掣肘，依然会消耗版权运用阶段所创造的各种资源。针对这样的潜在问题，景德镇打造了一套"主体合作—运用协同—价值共创"的陶瓷版权运用机理模式。[①] 通过强化各类参与主体的合作基础，充分发挥主体自身优势，强调陶瓷版权运用过程中的有效协同互动，最终实现"景德镇陶瓷版权运用共同体"的价值共创目标。

景德镇以陶瓷为核心文化元素，与区域产业优势、时代创新精神相结合，打造"千年瓷都景德镇"城市品牌。细言之，景德镇城市品牌是集"陶瓷文化遗址""企业陶瓷品牌""艺术大师作品""创客陶瓷作品"等诸多陶瓷版权元素于一体，结合景德镇旅游、教育的发展，从而衍生出来的具有强版权价值的城市形象。景德镇市政府引导鼓励陶瓷文化企业打造企业品牌 IP。青花故事等一批陶瓷文化企业着力开发陶瓷版权的经济效益；景德镇陶瓷"牡丹仙子"徐国琴大师继承了"青花大王"王步、王恩怀的风格，又独创了现代装饰结合传统用笔的画法，从而形成具有强烈个人风格的作品体系；电影《祭红》展示了景德镇市陶瓷艺术传承人，为保绝代祭红秘方而勇敢斗争的精神，带火了景德镇颜色釉祭红陶瓷。不同主体在进行陶瓷版权运用的活动中，都被深深地刻上了为景德镇城市品牌代言的烙印。景德镇通过激发运用主体们的文化认同感与归属感，强化了陶瓷版权运用过程中主体之间的责任意识、合作意识和文化构建意识，使共同维系景德镇城市品牌的使命凌驾于市场竞争之上。随之而来的是

---

① 封伟毅、李师萌：《基于知识产权运营视角的创新网络价值共创形成机理研究》，《情报科学》2023 年第 41 卷第 1 期。

同行业之间的资源共享和不同行业之间的产业融合，由于共同使命的赋予而提高了可能性。这也使得行业组织形成的行业保护规范、政府制定的区域保护政策以及立法机构颁布的相关领域的法律法规，并不完全需要强制力就能有效实施。"一荣俱荣，一损俱损"是景德镇陶瓷版权运用机理的核心，通过对这种观点的不断强化，城市品牌才得以树立，景德镇整体的价值共创效果才得以体现。

景德镇陶瓷版权运用方式的拓创

版权运用的方式，通常以多版权运营的方式呈现，即围绕作品的版权，通过多渠道的资源整合，将作品在合理的范围内进行多方位运作。多版权运营的最大难题在于不同产业间壁垒的打破。迪士尼就是一个很好的例子，它作为诸多知名 IP 的唯一控制者，无障碍地将最初动画中的版权元素，用于游乐项目开发、日常商品授权、游戏及真人电影改编以实现产业壁垒的突破。但景德镇则很难通过培育由单一主体掌控的大 IP，再将其进行全方位运作的方式复刻迪士尼的成功。它突破产业壁垒的方法，则是将陶瓷版权运用活动与频繁的交流展示活动紧密联系，以实现传播陶瓷文化、拓宽陶瓷版权交易市场（即"展出 + 交易"模式）、盘活陶瓷版权运用途径这三大目的。

"展出 + 交易"引导陶瓷版权运用的优势在于两点：其一，打通版权运用与产品交易的壁垒。版权运用的障碍之一，在于最终产品的市场价值是未知的，频繁的展会与交流活动能让版权运用方与潜在的市场购买者始终保持接触，引导版权运用方对运作范围进行理性判断。其二，使版权运用的方式透明化。版权运用的另一阻碍在于不同产业版权运用方式的不透明，展出活动将各个版权运用方齐聚一处，给予彼此相互学习借鉴的机会，丰富了陶瓷版权产业整体的运用方式，也为版权运用方式的进一步革新奠定基础。

景德镇陶瓷版权运用产业的革新

面对版权运用阶段易出现的时间、地域及行业限制，流程烦琐复杂，难以及时有效地对接供需双方等难题，景德镇顺应现代科技，充分开发信息网络传播权的运用途径，打造"平台经济 + 陶瓷版权运用"的产业模式。通过搭建适配景德镇陶瓷版权运用产业发展的互联网平台以及促成陶瓷企业与各大平台合作的方式，完成产业革新。

互联网平台有各种形态，用于服务产业经济中的不同领域。景德镇致力于打造信息咨询＋技术服务类平台，着手技术维度，创造版权交易条件。依托版权印、时间戳、数字签名、区块链等技术，为陶瓷版权数字经济的发展提供各类真实可靠信息的同时，也能进一步为版权归属的确认、权利人身份的证明、版权维权的举证，提供技术证明手段，保护版权交易主体和交易过程。景德镇国家陶瓷版权交易中心搭建的陶瓷工业互联网平台，以及与中国电信合作打造的陶瓷版权交易综合服务平台就是最好的例子。

在网络销售、社交娱乐、生活服务等版权运用中，更为核心的业务则是通过内部版权资源提供＋外部平台资源合作的方式开展。首先，抓住与电商平台合作的方式，拓展版权运用产业发展的新渠道。景德镇鼓励陶瓷企业与主流电商平台开展战略合作，将陶瓷技艺元素与非遗文化元素融合进电商平台的直播销售，实现推动陶瓷文化的保护传承、助力陶瓷作品版权价值再开发的双重目的。2022 年，全市网络零售达到 127.36 亿元（2012 年仅 8.06 亿元），年均增幅达 31.79%。全市在主要第三方交易平台上注册并产生交易的企业有 4756 家，网店有 32480 个，在扩大陶瓷商品交易市场的同时，也为陶瓷版权运用新样态的出现奠定基础。同年，国务院更是批复同意在景德镇设立跨境电子商务综合试验区，标志着景德镇市跨境电商发展已经进入快车道，陶瓷版权交易的国际市场取得新拓展。其次，利用新媒体发展突破陶瓷版权运用产业的限制。景德镇市抓住新媒体发展的"文化出圈"机遇，通过新媒体技术创造"二次传播和交易"的陶瓷版权发展机遇。例如，2023 年 5 月，景德镇中国陶瓷博物馆的"无语菩萨"出圈，火爆全网。博物馆借助其影响力，以此为原型创作了瓷画剧《瓷画怎讲》，打造出一个有趣出圈的卡通动漫 IP 形象的同时，也传播了中国优秀陶瓷文化。在该过程中，博物馆也突破了为社会单纯提供公共文化服务这一身份限制，实现了版权运用产业的革新。

第三节
景德镇陶瓷版权保护专门化

陶瓷版权的发展离不开版权保护在版权创造、版权运用乃至后续版权管理、版权服务过程中的护航作用。自版权制度诞生以来，如何平衡版权保护制度在维系权益与抑制创作中的作用始终是一大难题。针对此问题，我国采取了一项卓有成效的举措，即特别设立了具备高度集中管辖权限的知识产权法庭体系。景德镇知识产权法庭作为这一体系中的重要一环，发挥着不可或缺的作用。凭借此优势，景德镇结合陶瓷版权发展的特点，以陶瓷版权保护专门化的方式，首先专设景德镇陶瓷版权司法保护体系，通过专门保护机构的设置与统一保护模式的选择强化了司法保护的效率与专业性。其次，明确版权行政保护的路径，通过结合私益导向与公益导向这两种保护模式提升了行政保护的效果与影响力。最后，优化"版权行政保护＋版权司法保护"的衔接机制，通过确定景德镇市知识产权保护中心的中轴地位，带动了协同保护机制的高效运作。

一、陶瓷 IP 纠纷解决优选地——景德镇知识产权法庭

景德镇知识产权法庭是以陶瓷知识产权保护为重点的跨区域管辖的知识产权法庭，负责管辖九江、上饶、鹰潭、景德镇辖区内的版权、专利、技术秘密、驰名商标认定及垄断纠纷等一审知识产权民事和行政案件，是陶瓷知识产权纠纷解决的"优选地"。

因瓷制宜，立足陶瓷知识产权司法保护

作为举世闻名的陶瓷文化交流中心，景德镇汇聚了超十万的陶瓷从业者，如此庞大的从业群体，要想让自己创作的作品脱颖而出绝非易事。因此，一些创作者选择"剑走偏锋"，以抄袭方式来牟取利益。自 20 世纪 80 年代以来，肆意蔓延的陶瓷知识产权侵权现象，曾一度影响景德镇陶瓷产业的创新创造和健康发展。同时，陶瓷知识产权保护能力不足，维权时间长、维权成本高等问题，使得景德镇陶瓷版权纠纷的解决举步维艰，版权权利人的合法权益难以得到有效保障。为维持景德镇陶瓷版权市场交易秩序、提升版权保护力度，构建全方位、一体化的版权执法司法保护机制势在必行。

2012 年，最高人民法院批准景德镇市中级人民法院、景德镇市珠山区人民法院开展由知识产权审判庭统一受理知识产权民事、行政和刑事案件的试点工作。历经 8 年，景德镇陶瓷文化创意产业格局和司法保护的面向发生了新的变化。为了更好地给陶瓷文化创意产业发展护航，充分发挥司法保护功能，2020 年全国两会[①]上，代表们向全国人民代表大会提出了《关于设立景德镇知识产权法庭的建议》和《在景德镇设立陶瓷知识产权法庭的建议》提案。提案认为，景德镇已经形成了独具特色的陶瓷艺术业态，保护其生存发展环境十分重要，景德镇迫切需要设立专门的知识产权法庭，推动知识产权维权保护工作。最高人民法院在收到建议后，对在景德镇建立知识产权法庭的构想进行研究并开展

---

① 中华人民共和国全国人民代表大会和中国人民政治协商会议的统称。

景德镇知识产权法庭（景德镇知识产权法庭供图）

全面评估，认为在景德镇设立知识产权法庭符合法律规定，并具有现实意义。

最高人民法院通过多方考察和研究认为，景德镇知识产权法庭的建立有利于统一知识产权案件裁判尺度，提高知识产权审判的质量和效率；有利于陶瓷版权、商标、商业秘密等陶瓷知识产权的全方位司法保护，为建好景德镇国家陶瓷文化传承创新试验区提供有力的司法保障。2020 年 12 月，最高人民法院正式批复同意设立景德镇知识产权法庭。2021 年 4 月 26 日，以陶瓷知识产权保护为重点的跨区域管辖的知识产权法庭——景德镇知识产权法庭（全国第三家非省会城市的知识产权法庭），正式挂牌成立。

二纵三横，畅通全链条保护路径

为实现司法高效维权效能，景德镇知识产权法庭构建了"二纵三横"的知识产权立体式全链条保护体系。诉讼与调解、仲裁、行政裁决、行政复议等非诉讼方式之间的相互配合与协调，使各种纠纷解决方式有效互补。

一纵，即在九江、上饶、鹰潭及景德镇重点园区设立知识产权巡回审判点，践行司法为民的宗旨，进一步整合知识产权司法资源，提升知识产权司法保护水平与效能；实现知识产权司法保护一体化发展，方便当事人就近诉讼，并提升以案释法的针对性，增强法治宣传效果。

二纵，即在景德镇市昌南新区名坊园、浮梁工业园区、央视网·陶瓷数字产业文化基地三处设立知识产权司法服务点，为陶瓷从业者量身定制法律服务，积极回应企业对知识产权保护的新需求和新期待，提供一站式知识产权服务，实现司法服务"零距离"，确保企业能放心投资、安心经营、专心发展。自2022年以来，三个知识产权司法服务点先后提供法律咨询、法律"问诊"服务200余次，发放宣传资料、法律法规资料500余份。

一横，即司法保护与行政执法联动。景德镇市中级人民法院先后与景德镇市检察院、景德镇市公安局联合印发《知识产权协同保护合作框架协议》，建立知识产权刑事案件常态化联络机制，加大案件办理协作力度，提高知识产权违法犯罪行为的打击效率。

景德镇市中级人民法院还与景德镇市文旅局、市场监管局联合印发《景德镇市知识产权陶瓷技术调查官管理办法（试行）》《关于选任景德镇市知识产权陶瓷技术调查官的通知》，在全省首创知识产权陶瓷技术调查官制度。首批受聘的18名技术调查官，分别来自高校、科研院所、企事业单位、社会组织等单位，他们具备5年以上陶瓷领域工作经验以及副高以上专业职称，熟知陶瓷领域技术现状和发展趋势，能针对性地解决陶瓷知识产权纠纷认定难题。景德镇市中级人民法院还建立了集技术调查、技术咨询、技术鉴定于一体的多元技术事实查明机制，使技术思维和法律思维优势互补。景德镇市中级人民法院还与景德镇市市场监管局、文旅局等七家单位签订《知识产权纠纷合作备忘录》，构建知识产权纠纷调解多元化解渠道；与景德镇市知识产权保护中心签订《知识产权快速协同保护合作协议》，共同推进"司法确认＋行政调解"诉调对接机制。

二横，即司法保护与律师调解互促。景德镇成立全省首家知识产权律师调解中心，促进知识产权多元解纷驶入"快车道"，侧重在九江、上饶、鹰潭、景德镇四个设区市选定知识产权专业律师，轮流在调解中心值班，开展诉前调解工作。

三横，即司法保护与社会自治协同。与景德镇市妇联签署《关于共同推进对

知识产权律师调解中心揭牌（景德镇知识产权法庭供图）

女性知识产权保护的合作协议》，通过将妇联工作人员和人民调解员纳入知识产权调解体系，引导当事人依法解决纠纷，让纠纷化解实现情、理、法相结合，提升知识产权保护司法效能。还与景德镇市工商联进行联动，畅通质量投诉和消费者维权渠道，致力于共同打击假冒伪劣产品，为品牌营造良好法治环境。

加快布局，提升陶瓷法治保护水平

景德镇知识产权法庭通过不断创新陶瓷版权保护机制，实现陶瓷版权保护水平的快速提升，打造出一系列陶瓷版权司法保护"精品"和"典型"，为陶瓷版权保护营造良好法治氛围。

一是选树司法审判典型案例，为解决陶瓷版权纠纷提供示范指导。景德镇知识产权法庭审理的永丰源陶瓷版权纠纷案和传统"二方连续纹饰"陶瓷盖碗茶杯版权权属、侵权纠纷案，分别入选 2021 年和 2022 年中国法院 50 件典型知识产权案例；"珠山八友"陶瓷著作权纠纷案例，还入选最高人民法院《知识产权新规则案例适用》。另有多个涉陶瓷版权案件入选历年江西法院十大知识产权典型案例、江西法院数字经济知识产权司法保护典型案例和江西法院服务保障民营经济发展典型案例。

★永丰源陶瓷著作权纠纷案[①]

这是近年来发生的一起电子商务经营者侵犯含有通用元素陶瓷美术作品著作权的典型案例。在本案中，被告公司作为网店经营者，在其网店销售页面将涉诉产品标注为"夫人瓷"，经过比对发现，被告在网店上销售的产品与原告拥有著作权的产品在图案细节元素、颜色、立体层次以及整体布局等方面构成实质相似（见表4-1）。针对被告公司的行为是否构成著作权侵权，法院首先发现本案中的陶瓷美术作品含有通用元素，但随即明确了判决要旨。即使陶瓷美术作品含有通用元素，只要该作品并非简单复制、重复陶瓷行业沿袭下来的设计或样式，且具有独创性表达，同时在构成要素自主选择、编排、设计等方面具有审美意义，能使一般公众将其与现有其他作品相区分，就应给予著作权保护。而他人未经授权仿制该美术作品，应构成著作权侵权。法院的判决有力打击了电商平台上网店销售仿制陶瓷作品的侵权行为，较好地保护了著作权人的权益，

表 4-1　案涉侵权产品图案与原告著作权图片比对表

产品种类	侵权产品图片	原告作品
8寸汤盘（公证书附件第45页）		
花篮1个（公证书附件第16—17页）		粤作登字-2019-F-00009387 国作登字-2018-F-00595519

永丰源陶瓷"夫人瓷"图与侵权图片（景德镇知识产权法庭供图）

① 江西省景德镇市中级人民法院（2021）赣02知民初4号民事判决书。

有助于保护陶瓷作品的再创作，引领陶瓷行业的大繁荣大发展，也为规范瓷器市场经营秩序和网店经营者经营行为作出了指引，有利于优化法治化营商环境。

★传统"二方连续纹饰"陶瓷盖碗茶杯著作权权属、侵权纠纷案①

这是涉及传统元素陶瓷作品独创性判断、作品保护起始时间确定的一起典型案例。在本案中，原告公司向江西省版权保护中心登记了美术作品《绽放》，该作品为盖碗茶杯，杯身正面画有葫芦形线条，内有"吉"字图案标识，杯子底部、杯盖及杯托的图案均采用花朵、枝茎元素组成二方连续装饰图案。被告公司则是在淘宝网店销售"山音"陶瓷盖碗茶杯，杯身正面有葫芦形线条、内有"山音"字样。原告公司认为被告公司销售的茶杯侵害了其著作权，遂诉至法院。针对原告公司的诉求，法院经审理认为，设计者将传统二方连续装饰图案经过挑选、变换并配以相应色彩及变异的汉字造型融汇而成的图案具有审美意义，其思路虽来源于传统元素，但是整体构图展示出设计者自身的个性印记，体现设计者独特的智力选择与判断，达到了一定水准的智力创造高度，符合著作权法对作品独创性的要求。因此，首先肯定了原告公司的作品应受到法律保护这一事实。但随后认定现有证据难以确定涉案作品的创作形成时间，被告公司提供的证据可以证实其在淘宝店铺销售被诉侵权产品的时间早于案涉作品的登记时间。更重要的是，尽管原被告都在设计中运用了传统二方连续装饰图案，但被诉侵权产品上二方连续装饰图案中的缠枝纹、花朵均与原告公司作品上的缠枝纹、花朵在样式、形态上存在区别，不认为构成实质相似，不应认定被诉侵权产品构成侵权。法院认定的在传统元素的基础上进行创新运用，具备创作者独特的设计风格的作品具有独创性，应受到著作权法的保护的判决结果，有利于激发陶瓷从业者对传统陶瓷元素传承和创新的积极性，繁荣陶瓷市场，促进文化进步，对传统文化的知识产权保护和创新具有一定的导向作用。同时，法院在侵权判断标准上采用高标准、严要求，一定程度上能防止传统陶瓷元素和公有元素为他人所垄断，保障了陶瓷版权创造的宝贵资源。

① 江西省景德镇市中级人民法院（2022）赣02民终171号民事判决书。

二是审、宣并进，不断延展知识产权司法保护空间。2021 年，景德镇知识产权法庭被授牌为"江西省法治教育宣传基地"（江西省委宣传部、江西省司法厅、江西省法制办共同授牌），基于此，景德镇知识产权法庭每年以"世界知识产权日"为契机，在景德镇市人民广场设立普法点，分发知识产权宣传册，深入陶瓷企业进行法治宣传，大力开展知识产权宣传活动。此外，景德镇知识产权法庭还十分注重以案释法、以案普法，充分利用新媒体平台加大知识产权司法保护宣传力度。同时，景德镇知识产权法庭做到人才培养与法治宣传并重，在景德镇知识产权法庭设立景德镇陶瓷大学法学系实践教学基地[①]，以深入接触参与知识产权司法审判实务的教学模式培养法学系学生的知识产权司法实践能力，使得知识产权法治宣传工作更加全面。

三是与产、学、研紧密结合，推进司法保护深入化。2021 年 10 月，景德镇知识产权法庭承办了 2021 中国景德镇国际陶瓷博览会陶瓷知识产权保护论坛，广邀国内专家学者、资深知识产权法官、陶瓷大师、陶瓷企业从业人员、相关行政部门工作人员等 110 余人，共话陶瓷知识产权保护，首次为陶瓷知识产权学术界、产业界、艺术界搭建了重要交流平台。未来，景德镇知识产权法庭将继续完善"学、研、判"互补互促机制。通过定期组织内部培训、邀请专家学者进行授课、开展案例研讨等方式，不断提升法官的专业素养和审判能力。同时，法庭还将加强与国内外其他知识产权法庭的交流与合作，共同推动版权审判工作的创新与发展。

二、景德镇陶瓷版权保护的专门化模式

景德镇陶瓷版权司法保护体系的专设

我国知识产权司法保护体系的发展经历了两个阶段。首先是"三审分离"

---

① 胡志勇：《喜讯！景德镇知识产权法庭入选江西省法治宣传教育基地》（发布日期：2022 年 1 月 10 日），http://jdzzy.jxfy.gov.cn/article/detail/2022/01/id/6476936.shtml，访问日期：2023 年 12 月 11 日。

阶段。早在 20 世纪 90 年代，随着知识产权主要法律的出台，各个审判层级受理知识产权相关案件的频次开始增多。但是，技术性较强的知识产权一审案件的管辖权，仍然分布在众多中级人民法院和基层法院之中。传统的"三审分离"尽管具有便于当事人进行诉讼、便于案件的审理与执行以及平衡各级人民法院工作负担等优势，然而在专业性质更强的知识产权审判领域，"三审分离"则会导致管辖分散、管辖冲突、司法保护与行政保护脱节等问题的出现。其次是"大保护"阶段。自 2014 年开始，知识产权法院与知识产权法庭开始设立，知识产权案件类型不断被细化，审判法院层级也随之更加科学，并逐渐形成"知识产权法院案件审理 + 四级法院审判"的"大保护"体系。[①] 在知识产权"大保护"体系的基础上，知识产权"三审合一"[②] 保护模式的可行性开始被讨论并用于司法保护实践活动中（如 2020 年成立的海南自由贸易港知识产权法院）。"三审合一"保护模式的推行一方面需要该地区有较多知识产权案件的客观事实，需要审判机构跨区域对知识产权各类一审案件进行集中管辖。[③] 另一方面则需要完善该审判机构的人员配置，确保案件判决结果的专业性。[④]

陶瓷版权司法保护的难点在于：其一，一般法官并不具备陶瓷版权专业知识的事实会影响司法保护的质量；其二，相应刑事案件、民事案件、行政案件衔接困难的事实会影响司法保护的效率。面对这些问题，景德镇考虑到本区域内存在较多陶瓷版权纠纷的同时，也拥有充足的司法保护专业队伍这一事实。因此，选择通过设置两级知识产权审判机构加"三审合一"的模式，服务于陶瓷版权的司法保护。两级专门知识产权审判机构的设置，不仅发挥了级别管辖制度自带的明确法院分工、便于当事人进行诉讼、提高审判质量等优势，更重要

---

① 最高人民法院《关于第一审知识产权民事、行政案件管辖的若干规定》法释〔2022〕13 号。
② "三审合一"是指知识产权民事、刑事、行政案件统一集中审理的审判机制。其做法是将涉及知识产权的民事、刑事和行政案件全部集中到知识产权审判庭统一审理。
③ 何震、魏大海：《改革探索 积极创新——知识产权司法保护"三审合一"研讨会综述》，《法律适用》2010 年第 8 期，第 96—97 页。
④ 崔珊珊、张伟豪、汪亚楠：《知识产权司法保护与企业进口技术复杂度——基于知识产权案件"三审合一"的准自然实验》，《宏观经济研究》2023 年第 5 期，第 85—103 页。

景德镇知识产权法庭庭审现场（江西省景德镇市中级人民法院供图）

的是这种设置可以通过优化自主创新司法环境，激励陶瓷产业在版权领域的创造投入、减少陶瓷产业的版权运用收益损失[1]，进而促进整个景德镇陶瓷产业的创新。而"三审合一"的审判机制，则由于其具备的统一执法标准、降低当事人诉讼成本、提高审判效率等优势，进一步清扫了陶瓷版权产业主体的维权障碍，让主体能将更多的资源投入在版权的创造、管理与运用阶段。因此，"三审合一"的审判机制对陶瓷版权产业的创新能起到促进作用。此外，这种促进作用由于源自机制的革新，因而不存在时滞。尤其是对于没有更多维权资源，而是以版权创造为主要竞争力的小规模陶瓷企业、初创陶瓷企业甚至大量的"景漂"创客们的创新促进作用更为明显。正如前文所说，新时代景德镇的快速复

---

[1]　庄佳强、王浩、张文涛：《强化知识产权司法保护有助于企业创新吗——来自知识产权法院设立的证据》，《当代财经》2020年第9期，第16页。

第四章
景德镇陶瓷版权的新时代担当

兴更多依赖着版权创造的活力与版权运用的多样。专门审判机构配合"三审合一"的司法保护体系，则是更多地精准服务于版权创造与版权运用阶段的多方主体，通过更加有效的版权司法保护，为陶瓷版权创新提供更多空间。

景德镇陶瓷版权行政维权路径的开拓

在维护景德镇陶瓷版权发展的诸多因素中，版权司法保护对陶瓷版权创新的促进作用尽管较为突出，但是并不具有决定性。权利人大多并不希望以诉讼的方式解决陶瓷版权纠纷，而是更倾向于借助行政机关的力量开展版权保护工作。尤其是当景德镇市政府充分参与到陶瓷版权发展的全链条时，行政机关积极开展的版权维权工作，则更加体现政府在陶瓷版权保护过程中的引领作用。而行政机关直接执法的一大缺陷在于，由于版权维权仅仅是文化执法工作中的一部分，相较于专设的司法机关，行政机关的执法行为往往会缺乏针对性和专业性。因此，实现版权行政执法的专业化是中国版权行政执法的发展方向。景德镇市政府作为陶瓷版权创造主体聚集中的主导者、陶瓷版权运用体制的完善者、陶瓷版权运用平台的搭建者，充分参与陶瓷版权发展全链条的做法，正逐渐改变其作为单一行政执法者的事实。这样的优势在于行政机关也能全方位接收版权相关信息，并逐渐积累版权工作经验，实现版权行政执法阶段的专业能力提升。

更为重要的是，景德镇的行政维权路径正突破以私益导向型行政保护为主的限制，做到私益导向型与公益导向型相结合的模式。[①] 前者主要以文化执法为主，譬如 2022 年景德镇市版权局执法人员与市市场监督管理局、市公安局组成联合工作组，对景德镇某陶瓷厂和景德镇某陶瓷有限公司进行检查。发现了该公司电脑中存有北京冬奥会吉祥物"冰墩墩""雪容融"的花纸图案，而关联陶瓷厂生产的"冰墩墩""雪容融"造型陶瓷酒瓶的花纸是由该公司印刷的事实。最终对该公司作出没收侵权花纸，罚款人民币 2 万元的行政处罚，维护了北京

---

① 私益导向型行政保护是对知识产权人的法定权利的维护，公益导向型行政保护则是以维护和促进与知识产权有关的国家利益和社会利益为主要目的。参见戚建刚：《论我国知识产权行政保护模式之变革》，《武汉大学学报（哲学社会科学版）》2020 年第 2 期，第 154 页。

景德镇市知识产权保护中心现场（景德镇市知识产权保护中心供图）

冬奥会奥组委的法定权利。而后者则是兼顾私益与公益的保护，开拓了行政维权的新路径。2023年9月，景德镇市市场监管局、景德镇市知识产权保护中心，入驻第二十四届（唐山）中国陶瓷博览会，联合唐山市市场监管局开展知识产权保护及维权援助专项行动，并专设知识产权保护咨询工作站，提供版权相关服务。这种维权路径让行政部门主动深入市场，并将版权侵权假冒投诉处理、维权援助、法律咨询（私益保护）与公益教育、公益宣传（公益保护）相结合，提升行政维权的整体效果。

景德镇陶瓷版权协调保护机制的衔接

针对陶瓷版权司法保护与陶瓷版权行政保护的差异性，景德镇开辟了以景德镇市知识产权保护中心为中轴、联结版权行政执法机关、版权司法机关、版权社会管理机构建立"行政＋司法"衔接机制。旨在高效协助版权行政执法、版权司法裁决、版权维权援助和版权仲裁调解。中心的主要职责是快速授权和快速维权，"一站式"快速受理版权投诉和举报案件，受托处理行政裁决和调解案件，高效处理陶瓷版权纠纷，保障权利人利益的同时，也起到了分担版权保护工作。

保护中心与司法机关通过签订"合作备忘录"的方式，有效发挥了与版权司法保护的衔接作用，为权利人开辟出了一条具有可选择性的维权路径。2021年，保护中心与景德镇市珠山区人民法院竟成人民法庭签署合作备忘录，运用司法权对人民调解工作给予有力支持。保护中心与法院的合作，为人民调解制度提供了一条可供选择的纠纷解决路径，有效地突破了人民调解协议效力的局限性。换言之，保护中心作为组织协调方，协调司法机关赋予人民调解协议以强制力，保障协议的有效执行，创造了新的陶瓷版权维权途径。

此外，面对现阶段大量版权侵权案件发生在电商平台上的事实，保护中心链接了国家知识产权局电商全国执法体系，开展电商执法维权工作。保护中心成立了电商专案小组，确保每件电商案件在24小时内完成办理（通常以出具法律意见书等形式完成办理）。2021年，保护中心处理淘宝、天猫等国内外电商平台案件共计659件。通过快速维权机制，既帮助权利人快速维权并优化了网

知识产权快速协同保护合作协议签署现场（景德镇市知识产权保护中心供图）

印与创意产业：
景德镇故事

络营商环境，又为后续可能跟进的版权行政执法或版权司法保护工作提供了铺垫，这可谓一举两得。专设景德镇市知识产权保护中心作为版权协调保护主体的措施，彰显了版权保护观念由独立保护向协同互助保护、由封闭式保护转向开放式保护、由单一保护迈向多元保护的变革。这是景德镇在版权保护方面所采取的切实有效措施。

第四节
景德镇陶瓷版权管理特色化

　　陶瓷版权的持续化创造、灵活化运用与专门化保护，为景德镇陶瓷版权工作持续提供着动力与保障。为了进一步提升景德镇陶瓷版权工作的效率进而形成顺畅的体制机制，需要打造独具特色的陶瓷版权管理模式。景德镇通过在宏观层面上强化制度引领行政管理的作用，实现了陶瓷版权行政管理方式的创新。与此同时，景德镇还通过在微观层面上引导各陶瓷版权企业重视内部管理机制的制定，实现了陶瓷版权企业管理体系的构建。由外到内，由宏观到微观，景德镇用一套能连接各方主体的立体化管理网络，不断优化陶瓷版权工作的发展路径。景德镇国家陶瓷版权交易中心作为践行该模式的代表，融合行政资源与企业资源提供一系列陶瓷版权交易服务的同时，也实现了陶瓷版权管理在交易层面的特色化。

一、特定领域的版权交易中心

　　版权作为文化产业的核心资产，是推进文化创新创造的核心要素。景德镇国家陶瓷版权交易中心的成立，进一步夯实了陶瓷文化作品交易流转的基础，促进陶瓷文化创意产业快速发展。

首开先河，深耕陶瓷领域

为建好景德镇国家陶瓷文化传承创新试验区，打造对外文化交流新平台，努力走出一条具有世界意义、中国价值、新时代特征、景德镇特点的优秀传统文化传承创新发展新路径，景德镇密集考察国内各大文交所、版权交易中心等相关机构，为景德镇国家陶瓷版权交易中心的建设开展前期调查。通过广泛借鉴其他省市的先进经验，景德镇锚定陶瓷文化创意产业这一特色领域，在版权交易中心建设方面总结提炼出一套"景德镇模式"，即按照构建区域版权综合服务平台和打造以交易为核心的版权服务体系的思路，设立面向全国的版权质押与融资平台、区块链与大数据平台等功能平台，为全国的陶瓷企业和个人提供版权登记、交易、质押、融资等系列特色服务，不断激发陶瓷版权的强大活力，将交易中心建设成为覆盖全省、辐射全国、面向世界的知名陶瓷版权交易平台。

为加快推进陶瓷版权交易中心项目的落地，景德镇积极推进产学研结合，与江西省知识产权学院密切交流，利用科研平台的人才优势，共同谋划交易中心版权保护架构；组建版权经济研究院，借助国内外知名专家学者的力量，构建版权交易模块；建立完善的组织架构和管理制度，制定科学合理的工作流程和规范标准，促进版权交易的高效运作。同时，积极与国内外知名企业和机构建立合作关系，加强国际版权交流与合作。

2021年7月，景德镇国家陶瓷版权交易中心（以下简称"版权交易中心"）获国家版权局批准建设，于2022年8月28日正式启动运营。作为全国第五家国家级版权交易中心、国内首个特定领域及陶瓷行业唯一的国家级版权交易中心，为纵深推进景德镇国家陶瓷文化传承创新试验区建设凝聚新动能。

版权交易中心上线运营当天，即推出了三个版权运营业务并取得较好效果。一是利用由腾讯微盟集团构建的版权中心微信公众号程序，开通版权拍卖业务，可进行"版权＋实物、版权转让、部分版权授权许可"等多元组合拍卖。二是开通版权商城，当天推出的92份非遗传承人作品，全部都进行了版权登记，实现确权确真。三是开通数字文创平台业务，推出数字文创版权交易业务，将文

景德镇国家陶瓷版权交易中心全貌（胡燕飞摄）

化创意、数字创意和版权交易相互融合，按照合法合规路径，进一步丰富陶瓷数字版权资产交易模式。

聚沙成塔，探索运营方式

版权交易中心构建了陶瓷版权基础服务、运营服务、交易服务、金融服务四大板块业务，努力实现"版权＋区块链＋数字化＋金融"全链条综合版权开发的新业态、新格局，并取得阶段性成果。

版权基础服务。版权基础服务以版权登记、版权咨询等为核心业务。版权登记对维护著作权人合法权益，保障版权交易安全，促进版权有效运用，推进作品创作与传播，促进版权产业发展具有重要作用。版权交易中心主动投身版权登记工作当中，把登记的作品在版权交易平台进行公示，有助于保护权利人的权利和解决因版权归属造成的版权纠纷。为了搭建更为便捷的作品登记渠道，为版权交易中心积累原始资源，版权交易中心组建专职团队，主动出击、分类施策，实行点对点接洽。例如，集中与大学生、青年创客团队进行对接联系，上门为重点企业单位进行作品登记。同时，为提高作品登记效率、避免非本省艺术从业者版权资源流失，版权交易中心向江西省版权局（江西省版权保护中心）申请设立版权登记受理端口，并取得江西省跨区域版权作品登记试点资格，使得版权登记更加权威、受众更加广泛，促进作品登记量快速提升。截至2024年1月，景德镇市累计版权登记总数为40015件，其中版权交易中心累计版权登记总数为19144件。在中国景德镇国际陶瓷博览会期间，版权交易中心专门设立版权服务站，为各类陶瓷企业提供版权产业全方位服务。2023年，版权交易中心在景德镇国际陶瓷博览会上接受版权登记服务1000余人次，受理景德镇本土企业意向登记版权作品810余件。

版权运营服务。版权交易中心不断探索陶瓷产业创造性转化、创新性发展的新模式和新路径。版权交易中心与多家博物馆和版权企业合作，通过二次创作，盘活文物资源，实现文创产品产业化，实现版权与文化的巧妙结合。同时，版权交易中心抓住"优质作品版权控制力就是核心竞争力"这一关键，积极推进"陶瓷版权托管建库工程"，现与省内外200多家陶瓷企业签约，合力搭建优

景德镇国家陶瓷版权交易中心内部业务（景德镇国家陶瓷版权交易中心供图）

质版权数字化基础库。

版权交易服务。版权交易中心不断创新版权应用场景，与景德镇一大批老中青艺术家和非遗传承人签约，通过对艺术家原创作品进行二次创作，继而推进版权转让交易，使得版权交易不止于为原创者服务。为进一步确保线上交易的真实、可靠、顺利，景德镇市委、市政府对版权交易中心进行整体规划，初创期出资收购部分版权作品或获取相关授权，通过持有运营、引导交易的方式逐步培育市场认知及公众热度，市场交易稳定后转为轻资产运营模式，引领实体陶瓷产业。正在探索的"数字藏品发行＋陶瓷实物制造"、线上线下同步互动的商贸业务，依托版权交易中心的平台功能，能为前来参展的景德镇乃至全国的陶瓷企业提供更多的帮助以解决长期困扰陶瓷企业产品附加值不高、销路有限的问题。

版权金融服务。版权交易中心，正稳步推进申请金融机构经营许可证工作，为后续开展版权质押、债券、融资等金融服务做好准备。

专精特新，开辟 3+X 模式

版权交易中心以"3+X"模式构建主营业务范围。"3"包括版权综合服务业务、版权交易场所业务、版权产业园区运营业务，"X"包括所有其他促进版权交易和保护的业务。该模式致力于打造集版权保护、版权应用为载体，以数字化、金融化为内核，以区块链、大数据等为技术支撑，集作品确权、保护、交易、IP 开发与版权产业化服务等功能于一体的一站式版权交易与保护平台。

"3"的第一个业务是版权综合服务业务。构建一站式服务体系，包括登记、存证、确权、评估、保护、培训、咨询、宣传等基础服务，溯源鉴定、全网监测、代理维权、展览展示、衍生品开发、授权交易等增值服务。

"3"的第二个业务是版权交易场所业务。建立陶瓷版权资本体系、资产流通体系，开展文化要素配置、交易和融资服务，拟于粤港澳大湾区设立分支机构，构建"内地发行、香港交易"数字资产流通模式。

全国版权产业经济示范园区"名坊园"（景德镇市融媒体中心供图）

"3"的第三个业务是版权产业园区运营业务。以"大碗"[①]、品字楼为阵地，以"文化＋版权＋数字＋科技"为主题，打造版权特色小镇总部经济，落地博物馆集群、常年展、元宇宙、数字艺术、昌南"碗"集、版权设计大赛、培训研学、直播基地等业务，逐步构建全国版权产业经济示范园区。

"X"是指所有其他可以促进版权交易和保护的业务。交易中心通过积极主办或承办各类展览展示、赛事评选、论坛讲座等活动，推动知识产权市场培育，助力陶瓷文化传承创新，实现经济效益与社会价值相统一。其中，瓷博会配套活动"瓷漫来袭、集市行乐"昌南里陶瓷版权夜集，3天内吸引超过6万人次到场参观；阿拉伯艺术节配套活动"丝路瓷源、和光接物"陶瓷版权创意设计展，共征集到10个国家600多位艺术家的958件实物或数字版权作品，展出期间，多位中央部委领导及阿拉伯国家政要到访参观；首届全国陶瓷非遗版权作

---

① 景德镇昌南里文化艺术中心，"碗"型建筑，高80米，口部直径80米，底部直径40米，外型概念来源于宋代影青斗笠碗，庄重典雅，象征"万瓷之母"。

品大赛，征集到国内外各类艺术陶瓷作品 1132 件，并进行全国巡展。为给用户提供更加便捷的交易渠道，版权交易中心利用"版权中心"微信公众号和小程序，开通版权拍卖业务，可进行"版权＋实物""版权转让""部分版权授权许可"等多元组合拍卖活动。版权交易中心还在现有平台基础上，通过电商直播、研学活动、IP 文创开发等形式，拓宽业务范围和营收渠道，重点扶持 3000 名陶瓷艺术创造、技术开发及市场营销等方面的陶瓷人才，宣传推广代理 1000 家陶瓷企业版权作品。

未来，版权交易中心将继续坚持"数""实"结合、以"数"促"实"的理念，助推"实物＋数藏＋权益＋跨界"发展模式；不断优化业务内容，扩大业务范围，充分发挥版权交易中心在促进陶瓷文化创造性转化和陶瓷产业创新性发展中的坚实作用。

二、景德镇陶瓷版权管理的特色化模式

景德镇陶瓷版权行政管理方式的创新

景德镇以市场管理为最终目标，弱化版权微观管理，强化制度建设与体系化管理方式在宏观领域的作用。构建了在版权管理制度的牵引下，政府进行"行政监管＋政府推动企业"和行业协会管理的陶瓷版权多元组织管理模式。细言之，一方面，政府完善陶瓷版权管理制度，监管陶瓷版权产业发展；另一方面，政府通过版权行政管理战略化、版权行政管理网格化、版权行政管理智能化的方式，形成景德镇陶瓷版权特色管理模式。

景德镇加强版权管理顶层设计，完善陶瓷行业版权监管制度，优化陶瓷版权管理社会环境。在顶层设计方面，市委、市政府统筹和协调陶瓷产业整体管理，将陶瓷版权管理和发展纳入国民经济和社会发展规划。景德镇市文旅局负责具体陶瓷文化管理和发展工作，改革、财政、自然资源和规划、住房城乡建设、市场监督管理、陶瓷产业发展等部门各司其职、协力配合充分参与到陶瓷版权行政管理的全局工作中。这样的管理制度设计，意味着陶瓷版权管理已经

不是文旅部门日常行政管理中的一个小环节，而是关系到景德镇整体发展，需要联合各个行政部门协力完成的城市工作。

在版权行政管理方式的创新方面，首先，景德镇成立了高层次、综合性版权推进机构——由市长任组长的版权工作领导小组，开展版权保护、监管和宣传等工作，且实行常态化督查机制，将版权行政管理上升到了城市发展战略的高度。其次，设立覆盖市县两级，遍布各市辖区（如昌江区版权服务站）、版权产业园区（如景德镇陶邑文化发展产业园区版权服务站）及版权创造主体（如景德镇陶瓷大学版权服务站）的网格式版权服务站管理系统，并随时灵活增设新的版权服务站点，以满足陶瓷版权登记管理、陶瓷版权交易管理、陶瓷版权信息管理等多方面。最后，景德镇由行政机关牵头搭建了第三方陶瓷版权综合管理服务平台，推进智能版权管理系统的开发应用。标志性例子是 2022 年"景德镇昌南里陶瓷版权交易中心有限公司"的成立，公司采取国有控股、市场化运营模式，通过区块链、人工智能及大数据等技术推动陶瓷版权产业发展。行政机关通过操作平台技术管理系统，可以即刻监管陶瓷版权市场，保证行政管理的精确性和时效性，为陶瓷版权产业创造了良好的市场环境。

景德镇陶瓷版权企业管理模式的创建

景德镇通过以引导陶瓷版权企业建立内部管理机制为主，以设置行业协会与产业联盟作为版权管理社会化主体的外部管理机制为辅的模式，构建起陶瓷版权企业管理体系。

对于内部管理机制的建立，景德镇引导陶瓷企业打造全版权运营、全媒体营销、全自我服务的新型管理模式。首先，培养具备版权法律知识的管理人才，专注打造企业知名品牌，挖掘品牌商业价值。同时，推进贯彻《企业知识产权管理规范》国家标准的实施，助推陶瓷版权企业的内部规范管理。过程中，陶瓷企业能充分认识到陶瓷版权管理的重要性和版权作品的经济价值，故而成立专业的版权队伍负责企业陶瓷作品的版权登记、运营和保护等工作。其次，企业采取全媒体营销策略创造新的核心竞争力。新式企业的营销已不再是传统的商品销售模式，而是通过直播、自媒体广告、影视软广、纪录片等多种形式展示营销。全媒体营销策略不仅提高了陶瓷商品销售量，还扩展了作品版权的应用市场，企业文化和作品版权已成为企业的核心竞争力。最后，陶瓷企业构建了服务企业自身和客户的全链条管理体系，通过派专人参加市政府、省政府举办的版权知识培训，派专人负责版权登记，派法务专员负责版权维权，与版权专家建立长期合作关系，建成版权全链条自我服务模式。

对于外部社会管理机制的设置，景德镇陶瓷版权产业形成了行业协会加产业联盟的版权管理模式。版权管理社会化是版权产业的特性，因而需要发挥与版权相关的社会力量，凝聚版权利益群体，帮助企业实现版权利益最大化。一方面，景德镇市组建了"四中心一联盟"①，对陶瓷版权产业进行行业规范管理。联盟是联系政府、平台方、其他陶瓷文化企业、消费者等的桥梁，可承接企业陶瓷版权托管事项，协助企业对版权进行日常管理。企业通过联盟获得更多作品创意交流和版权交易的机会，活跃了陶瓷版权交易市场。另一方面，景德镇将非公有制维权服务领导小组、市版权协会、市陶瓷版权专家委员会等机构，纳入外部管理的主体序列中。通过社会组合管理的方式有效维护了权利人权益，使其能全身心投入到作品创作或企业运营中，同时更高效地打击侵权行为，维护着陶瓷版权交易市场秩序。

① "四中心一联盟"即全国唯一的中国陶瓷知识产权信息中心、国家陶瓷版权交易中心、知识产权保护中心、陶瓷版权快速维权中心和陶瓷知识产权联盟。

第五节
景德镇陶瓷版权服务常态化

　　景德镇陶瓷版权"China 模式"的最后一环是常态化的陶瓷版权服务。为了保证陶瓷版权服务的持续性和有效性，景德镇的陶瓷版权服务工作的重心，首先是版权服务体系的构建。清晰的任务设置与严谨的责任分配让景德镇的版权服务体系连续运作。在此基础上，市场主导的版权服务产业才可以不断被培育，同时形成能补充进版权服务体系的新模式，以实现景德镇陶瓷版权服务生态良性循环的常态化。在打造对外文化交流新平台的过程中，景德镇国际陶瓷博览会作为链接中外市场主体、展示陶瓷艺术与文化的重要窗口，其影响力日益扩大，成为推动景德镇陶瓷版权服务常态化的关键力量。

一、永不落幕的国际瓷博会

　　一年一度的景德镇国际陶瓷博览会（以下简称"瓷博会"）延续千年丝绸之路的盛景，汇聚八方来客共话陶瓷文化产业新"丝路"。景德镇将陶瓷交流交易作为瓷博会的核心业务，以多元化平台助推国际陶瓷文化和产业共融互鉴；将版权

夕阳下的陶博城（叶芳平摄）

作为瓷博会的重要支点，以多样化方式激活古老的陶瓷文化，谱写了与世界对话的陶瓷版权故事，探索出一条独具特色的优秀传统文化传承创新道路。

丝路千年，文化技艺绵延古今

景德镇瓷器从宋代开始就沿着陆上丝绸之路和海上丝绸之路源源不断地走向世界，创造了"匠从八方来，器成天下走"的繁荣景象。千百年来，一件件精美的瓷器从景德镇出发，穿越重洋，远播璀璨的中华文明。跨越千年，景德镇陶瓷文化和技艺仍对国内外陶瓷产业影响深远。在2004年之前，景德镇通过定期举办国际陶瓷节，吸引国内外众多陶瓷文化爱好者相聚景德镇，加强陶瓷文化和贸易交流。随着陶瓷产业发展格局的转变和景德镇日新月异的发展，单一的庆典型陶瓷节日已经无法体现会展经济的效应。因此，景德镇转变思路，致力于打造集陶瓷精品展示、陶瓷文化交流、陶瓷产品交易为一体的国际化陶瓷专业盛会。2004 年，适逢景德镇千年华诞，为促进景德镇陶瓷文化产业高质量发展和深度推进陶瓷文化和贸易的国际交流，再造景德镇陶瓷的千年盛况，景德镇国际陶瓷博览会应运而生。自此，瓷博会成为一个给陶瓷制造者、创作者、经销商、买家提供更大的展示、交流、交易的平台；一个集陶瓷信息沟通、贸易往来、技术合作与文化交流为一体的国际化、国家级、专业性的博览会。

2013 年 9 月和 10 月，中国国家主席习近平分别提出建设"新丝绸之路经济带"和"21 世纪海上丝绸之路"的合作倡议，标志着中国与"一带一路"共建国家之间的国家层面合作正式开启。2014 年，第十一届瓷博会开始通过举办与丝绸之路相关联的瓷茶展览和经贸活动，增进各相关国家和地区间的文化、商贸交流与合作，助推景德镇主动对接和融入"一带一路"倡议，拓展陶瓷企业接轨国际贸易渠道。之后，瓷博会通过举办与"一带一路"相关媒体活动、学术研讨会，与"一带一路"共建国家共同举办陶瓷艺术展、签订陶瓷文化传播文化战略协议等方式，不断增强景德镇在"一带一路"倡议中的城市担当，同时愈发提升了景德镇从古至今在丝绸之路上的城市影响力。

瓷博会的展会历程见证了陶瓷文化技艺的绵延与更迭，更展现出千年陶瓷文化传承发展的新面貌。瓷博会吸引大量陶瓷艺术精品汇聚于此，集中展示近年来陶瓷设计创新进步的丰硕成果和当代中国陶瓷艺术的全新风采，也展现出景德镇独有的文化魅力和独特的艺术造诣。人们能通过铺陈在瓷博会每个角落的陶瓷作品，感受到不同历史时期陶瓷文化与陶瓷贸易的辉煌成就。瓷博会的成功举办，为陶瓷文化产业的持续壮大带来了不竭动力，而版权引领陶瓷文化产业创新发展的举措，让古老的陶瓷文化、陶瓷技艺得以再放光彩。

一年一度，陶瓷盛会串联中外

瓷博会自 2004 年创办以来，已经连续举办了 20 届[①]，成为中国乃至世界陶瓷领域产业投资、展示交易、文化交流的重要平台，成为江西乃至中国深化与世界文化交流合作的桥梁纽带。景德镇以瓷博会为平台，以市场为导向，充分

———————

① 2004 年至 2023 年，共 20 届。

发挥陶瓷文化的经济价值，开拓陶瓷作品交易国际市场，形成"以活动传文化，以交流促交易"的景德镇陶瓷版权产业运营模式。瓷博会自举办以来，规模不断扩大，影响力与日俱增，国际性不断增强，累计有 49 个国家和地区的 2500 家境外企业参展。[①]线上、线下交易成交额逐年攀升，现已突破百亿；参展商、采购商覆盖了欧美、亚太、非洲、中东等地区，瓷博会的国际"交往圈""朋友圈""合作圈"越来越广。

近年来，瓷博会通过组织形式多样的陶瓷文化交流活动、构建多元的产品交易平台，促使陶瓷文化更好地融通中外、走向世界，推动陶瓷贸易更好地链接全球。瓷博会举办期间的陶瓷贸易成交额，呈现出逐年增长的趋势。在 2007 年举办的第四届瓷博会期间，内贸成交总额为 6.17 亿元人民币，外贸成交总额为 1 亿多美元，现场交易总额为 818.2 万元人民币，瓷博会带动陶瓷贸易的效

景德镇国际陶瓷博览会会展中心（陶博城供图）

① 唐莹：《"瓷行天下 贸连全球"2023 中国景德镇国际陶瓷博览会开幕》（发布日期：2023 年 10 月 18 日）https://jx.chinadaily.com.cn/a/202310/18/WS652fd0b1a310d5acd876aa7c.html，访问日期：2023 年 12 月 15 日。

IP与陶瓷产业：
景德镇故事

应已然初具规模。在十年后的第十四届瓷博会内，贸成交总额累计为 10.94 亿元人民币，外贸成交总额累计为 1.86 亿美元，现场交易总额累计为 7419.46 万元人民币（含拍卖 5059.1 万元人民币）。之后，陶瓷贸易形式与时俱进，线上交易的方式成为其主要组成部分。在 2021 年举办

管桂玲陶瓷作品《月光曲》（段新宇摄）

的第十八届瓷博会五天展会期间，陶瓷总交易额达到 91.45 亿元人民币，其中线上交易额达到 79.3 亿元人民币，线下交易额也保持在 12.15 亿元人民币。

2022 年，第十九届瓷博会通过更具国际影响力的合作项目，为陶瓷国际文化交流提供了更为广阔的平台。其中，包括市国际商会与深圳市西邮智仓科技有限公司签订合作共建海外仓项目、景德镇鸣海陶瓷有限公司与俄罗斯皇家陶瓷签订了贸易采购项目跨境电商买家和海外直采团与景德镇陶瓷企业开展现场对接洽谈等。同时，陶瓷文化交流与合作的深入持续带动着陶瓷贸易的增长。第十九届瓷博会的交易总额首次突破百亿大关，达到 102.8 亿元人民币，同比增长 12.4%。其中，线上实现交易额为 89.6 亿元人民币，同比增长 13%；线下实现交易额为 13.2 亿元人民币，同比增长 9%。2023 年，瓷博会进一步优化文化交流和贸易洽谈方式，把展陈分为会展中心和交易中心两部分，会展中心以文化展示为核心，重点呈现陶瓷文化交流、陶瓷文化传承、陶瓷文化创新三大板块，让中外来宾沉浸式体验景德镇"瓷越千年"的陶瓷文化底蕴和新时代的陶瓷文化盛况。为期 5 天的瓷博会，线下总人流量 20 万人次，达到历史之最。交易中心基于会展中心的平台集聚效应，实现的交易总额达到了 122.62 亿元人民币，在 2022 年百亿基础上依然增长了 19.28%。其中，线上实现交易额 107.52 亿元人民币，同比增长 20%；线下实现交易额 15.1 亿元人民币，同比增长 14%。

永不落幕，文明互鉴贯穿始终

瓷博会自举办以来，以"博览世界陶瓷精品、弘扬千年瓷都文明"为主题持续开展了 16 年。2019 年，景德镇国家陶瓷文化传承创新试验区获批，试验区建设的核心任务在于打造对外文化交流新平台，努力走出一条具有世界意义、中国价值、新时代特征、景德镇特点的优秀传统文化传承创新发展新路子。因此，2020 年，第十七届瓷博会确定以"加强国际化合作 助力产业链提升"为主题，落实试验区建设的核心任务，同时提出打造"永不落幕的瓷博会"的设想，促进瓷博会发挥在推进国际合作和产业提升方面的持续作用。通过"线下＋线上"的展会新模式，与天猫共同打造天猫"云瓷博会"直播中心，实现会展期间 24 小时直播不打烊。

2021 年，瓷博会通过在景德镇国际会展中心设立"中国景德镇国际陶瓷博览会常年展"主题展区的方式，保障特展商全部不撤展、不闭馆，365 天展览不停歇，延续瓷博盛筵，实现陶瓷展览"永不落幕"。以"展示＋市场"为导向

我在陶博城等你（危荣德摄）

构建"多商户 B2B 交易平台、云仓管理、供应链金融、仓储物流、直播运营、品牌建设"等系统，形成集"信息、交易、仓储、金融、营销"为一体的软件产品矩阵和平台服务，保障陶瓷交易常年有序开展，实现交易平台"永不落幕"。

2022 年，瓷博会以"瓷上世界 共享未来"为主题，进一步优化"云上瓷博会"。通过整合传统电商与抖音、快手、B 站等新媒体资源，加大网上营销精准靶向对接力度，不仅实现时间维度上的永不落幕，还在空间维度上实现了陶瓷展示和交易永不落幕。

2023 年，瓷博会以"瓷行天下 贸连全球"为主题，在往届基础上持续升级展销模式，采取"会展+交易"的市场化、常态化展出模式，通过招商方式入驻交易中心的 500 多家陶瓷商户将常态化运营。融合博览、交易、投资三大手段，打造"买全球、卖全球"的标杆性陶瓷大市场。[①]

纵观瓷博会举办史，蓬勃发展、体量庞大的陶瓷交流，贸易平台能长久持续运营的深层次动因在于，陶瓷文化传承创新从未停歇、中外文明互鉴共融贯穿始终。源远流长、赓续发展、创新创造的陶瓷文化和技艺，成为瓷博会"永不落幕"的内在机理。景德镇抓住这一历史发展脉络，深度把握陶瓷版权这一与世界对话的"通用语言"，深刻认识到版权是兼具文化属性和财富属性、产业属性、高价值属性的生产要素和资源且能成为全球陶瓷交流贸易的"通用货币"这一本质。自 2020 年的瓷博会起，景德镇将陶瓷版权融入瓷博会，激励创作者加强技术研发和专注创意转化，促进陶瓷文化创意产业推陈出新，同时也为陶瓷文化创意产业的持续繁荣保驾护航。

自 2020 年开始，瓷博会现场设立版权工作站，邀请省版权保护中心的工作人员和业界专家，现场就版权相关知识和法律法规等内容进行宣讲并答疑解惑。同时，现场还提供版权登记流程讲解、作品登记、审核等综合服务；行政执法人员进驻展会，对侵权问题开展现场执法。

在 2022 年举办的瓷博会期间，以"推动中华文化走向世界"为主题举办国际版权论坛，让全国乃至世界了解了中国版权事业，也充分展示了景德镇陶瓷文化、景德镇陶瓷版权工作成就。

在 2023 年举办的第二十届瓷博会期间，聚焦"文化传承发展、文明交流互鉴"主题，景德镇举办"文化创新发展论坛"，突出陶瓷贸易和陶瓷文化结合，挖掘陶瓷作品版权价值。同时，景德镇还举办了"版权助推城市高质量发展论坛"，开展版权国际学术论坛等系列交流活动。此外，景德镇还配套举办了世界

---

① 江西省人民政府公报：《2023 中国景德镇国际陶瓷博览会新闻发布会在南昌举行》（发布日期：2023 年 10 月 9 日）http://www.jiangxi.gov.cn/art/2023/10/9/art_5862_4616988.html，访问日期：2023 年 10 月 15 日。

知识产权组织版权保护优秀案例示范点、民间文艺版权保护、《马拉喀什条约》落地实施等主题展览。开展系列陶瓷版权活动方面，景德镇邀请海内外行业专家学者讲授版权相关知识和最新热点，来自世界知识产权组织、相关国家版权主管部门、境外著作权认证机构和国内相关部委、部分省（区、市）版权局、著作权集体管理组织以及业界、学界的数百名代表通过线上、线下参会，形成了浓郁的版权氛围，促进版权引领陶瓷文化创意产业高质量发展。

2024 年 9 月 8 日至 10 日，世界知识产权组织总干事邓鸿森一行，在江西调研版权工作，并出席了国家版权局和世界知识产权组织在景德镇举办的"2024 国际版权论坛"。

邓鸿森到访江西并出席在景德镇举办的 2024 国际版权论坛

2024 年 9 月 8 日至 10 日，世界知识产权组织总干事邓鸿森在江西调研版权工作。其间，邓鸿森出席了国家版权局和世界知识产权组织主办，江西省版权局和景德镇市人民政府承办的"2024 国际版权论坛"。这是继 2022 国际版权论坛之后国际版权论坛第二次落户景德镇，也是邓鸿森第一次亲临现场出席国际版权论坛。

9 月 9 日，在 2024 国际版权论坛开幕式上，来自世界知识产权组织等国际组织，40 余个国家的版权和文化官员及驻华使领馆知识产权参赞、文化参赞，部分国家和地区的版权相关协会、集体管理组织代表，来自我国部分省、自治区、直辖市版权管理相关部门的负责同志，以及国内外权利人、产业界、学术界代表等 300 余人参加论坛并在景德镇实地参观。本届论坛以"版权与创意产业推动可持续发展"为主题，旨在贯彻落实创新驱动发展战略，推动版权产业高质量发展，在新的历史起点上继续建设文化强国，以版权助力文明交流互鉴，推动全球文化繁荣。论坛内容丰富，包括"版权保护促进传统文化传承创新：政策与措施""人工智能在内容创作中的应用：机遇与挑战""版权制度保障文化获得感和参与度：保护与限制""知识经济时代的版权集体管理：现状与展望""版权在创意产业可持续发展中的作用：举措与成效"5 个主题。

参会外宾在会议期间还前往陶博城、景德镇国家陶瓷版权交易中心、三宝

国际瓷谷、皇窑等地调研景德镇版权和文化产业发展情况。来访外宾通过景德镇陶瓷（china）传承千年的魅力感受到中国（CHINA）文化创新创造的活力。

在景德镇期间，邓鸿森先后来到景德镇御窑博物院和陶阳里文化街区、浮梁古县衙、昌南新区名坊园邓希平颜色釉陶瓷艺术博物馆和赖德全大师工作室（美术馆）以及陶溪川文创街区调研传统文化和版权工作，参访了历史文化古迹，与陶瓷艺术大师亲切交流，亲身感受版权集市的活力与魅力。

在邓希平颜色釉陶瓷艺术博物馆，邓鸿森认真观赏一件件颜色釉作品，和邓希平老师亲切交谈，邓希平老师全方位、多角度、多形式地介绍了50余年来的创作心得和景德镇颜色釉瓷的历史发展、工艺特征、传承状态、创新成果和艺术魅力。在赖德全大师工作室（美术馆），邓鸿森仔细鉴赏赖德全老师的陶瓷作品，与赖德全老师深入探讨陶瓷艺术和版权保护，赖德全老师现场在瓷盘作画赠予邓鸿森，表达对邓鸿森来到江西和景德镇的热烈欢迎。邓鸿森对景德镇陶瓷文化给予高度赞扬，对景德镇版权工作给予充分肯定。

2024 国际版权论坛（景德镇市版权局供图）

邓鸿森指出，版权最有意义的方面之一是与文化和历史紧密联系。江西文化底蕴深厚，景德镇陶瓷是世界文化名片，江西致力于将文化创新与版权保护相结合，充分利用丰富的历史文化遗产，培育了传统与现代交织的繁荣的文化市场。开放和创新是景德镇这座千年瓷都仍然是国际交流中心的关键，而强有力的知识产权保护包括版权保护，对陶瓷行业的成功至关重要。2024年国际版权论坛在景德镇成功举办，展现了江西开放包容、勇于创新的精神，进一步巩固了江西在版权发展领域的国际声誉。

邓鸿森表示，世界知识产权组织将随时准备与所有人合作，使知识产权为所有国家的创作者、文化和遗产提供支持。世界知识产权组织将充分发挥版权促进创新创意可持续发展的作用，加深与江西在知识产权保护、专业人才交流、文化传承创新等领域合作，努力实现互利共赢、共同发展。

二、景德镇陶瓷版权服务的常态化模式

景德镇陶瓷版权服务体系的构建

景德镇通过划清主体边界、明确角色任务、完善责任机制的方式，基于政府、市场和社会三方主体协同的基础上进行战略性布局，形成整合性、协调性和实操性较高的版权服务"三元协同"体系。这既服务于不同类型的创新主体，也服务于版权运用、保护和管理全流程。

景德镇市政府作为版权服务的监督者和掌舵者，设计出相应的责任机制以回应结果绩效。其一，将版权服务供给绩效评估结果，作为评价和问责服务主体的依据。其二，将版权服务供给绩效评估结果，作为服务工作人员的考核依据。其三，利用版权服务供给绩效评估结果，优化服务资源和范围的配置。如此便能激励版权服务的提供，同时确保版权服务的质量。而对于具体的版权服务，则根据是否具有较强经营性及市场竞争性的区分，交由社会公益主体和市场经营主体具体完成。

景德镇陶瓷版权核心服务既包括陶瓷版权登记、陶瓷版权宣传教育、法律咨询等常态化服务，也包括陶瓷版权交易、陶瓷版权质押融资等专业化服务。在常态化服务方面，景德镇组建了集"政、企、学、研、司法"人员为一体的陶瓷版权专业服务队伍。服务队每年定期开展"版权五进"（进机关、进企业、进社区、进校园、进商场）活动，普及陶瓷版权基础法律知识，并深入瓷博会等大型陶瓷文化交流会，向参会各方普及陶瓷版权登记、保护等相关知识，解答创作者关于陶瓷版权的法律问题。另外，政府为了解决与企业、艺术家等有关的重大版权纠纷的疑难案件，会定期召开陶瓷版权座谈会，同时举办专家论证会，为景德镇陶瓷版权产业发展建言献策。由五十余家会员单位组成的景德镇市版权协会，也积极协助会员进行作品登记、版权交易，并配合市版权局开展版权宣传、举办版权论坛、承办版权作品展等活动。

这些常态化服务基本由政府发起并主导，由版权学者、司法审判专家、陶

瓷企业管理者、陶瓷研究专家等组成的社会服务队伍参与完成，最后再由政府评估服务效果并重新确定下一阶段的服务项目和相应服务主体。这样的做法，为景德镇持续提供高质量版权公益服务。在成熟的景德镇陶瓷版权服务体系下，专业化服务则会交由市场主导并形成版权服务产业，同时借助景德镇活跃陶瓷版权市场的力量，这些版权服务产业得以在这片土壤上蓬勃发展起来。

景德镇陶瓷版权服务产业的发展

景德镇通过"服务水平提升、服务平台赋能、服务模式创新、服务监管强化"的方式，建立了优质的景德镇陶瓷版权服务产业运营机制，推动陶瓷版权市场运营的有序发展。

一是提升版权服务机构的服务水平。景德镇市政府组织专家开展"版权进企业"的讲座活动，组织版权服务机构工作人员参加相关培训等，提高版权服务机构的代理、信息、咨询等服务水平，鼓励开展陶瓷作品版权价值评估、托管、转化等增值服务。二是打造数字化版权运营服务平台。景德镇市聚焦陶瓷作品交易，搭建了两个商业化交易平台，通过平台使供需市场信息畅通，还为陶瓷版权交易提供了专业化、国际化和法律化的服务。三是鼓励金融机构创新陶瓷版权融资新模式。景德镇市鼓励金融机构创建各类版权质押、贷款和保险业务，支持青年创客通过质押获得周转资金从而持续创作，促使高质量作品变现从而推动陶瓷版权产业进一步发展。四是加强版权服务业监管，形成激励与监管相协调的管理机制。运用区块链技术，实施动态监管、技术监管，营造公平清朗的版权服务业市场环境。

第六节
小结

　　景德镇打造了极具特色的"创造—运用—保护—管理—服务"陶瓷版权全链条发展体系。在版权创造方面，景德镇从传统的大规模生产逐步转向更加注重定制化与个性化的创造模式。这一转型不仅适应了市场日益多样化的需求，也推动了陶瓷艺术的创新和发展，使景德镇陶瓷在全球市场上展现出了独特的竞争优势。在版权运用方面，景德镇通过多样化和产业化的策略，大大拓宽了陶瓷版权的应用范围。陶溪川文创街区的成功建设，就是这一创新的典范。它将文化与产业紧密结合，不仅打破了传统的版权运用模式，还创造了新的商业路径，使陶瓷版权的价值得到了更为广泛的体现和推广。在版权保护方面，景德镇构建了完善的法律体系与监督机制，通过加大执法力度和广泛的社会宣传，切实保障了陶瓷作品的版权权益。这种全面的保护措施，不仅有效遏制了侵权行为的发生，还提高了公众对版权保护的认识和重视，为陶瓷艺术家的创作提供了更加安全的环境。在版权管理领域，景德镇通过推行科学化、系统化的管理模式，提升了版权管理的效率和规范性。通过建立标准化的管理流程和信息化的管理手段，景德镇成功优化了版权资源配置，确保了版权的公平分配与合理利用，为陶瓷产业的可持续发展奠定了坚实的管理基础。在版权服务方面，景德镇将政府、市场和社会的力量有机结合，形成了全方位的常态化版权服务体系。这一服务体系不仅提升了版权服务的专业化水平，还为版权创造、运用与保护提供了全方位支持，促进了景德镇陶瓷文化在全球范围内的传播与影响力的提升。总体而言，景德镇在版权创造、运用、保护、管理和服务这五个方面的综合创新，不仅推动了陶瓷文化的传承与发展，也为中国陶瓷产业的持续繁荣奠定了坚实基础，并展现了中国传统文化在现代化进程中的强大生命力与适应力。

陶瓷版权助推
景德镇高质量发展

　　景德镇，一座因瓷而生、因瓷而兴的城市，历史上的景德镇，其辉煌得益于制瓷业的繁荣，而如今其快速发展的关键在于陶瓷领域创新精神的涌现。短短十余年间，景德镇在陶瓷创新的推动下重焕生机，完成了一次华丽的蜕变。在这个过程中，版权起到了点石成金的作用，为景德镇的陶瓷创新注入源源不断的活力。景德镇深知，只有重视陶瓷版权的作用，才能让陶瓷创新熠熠生辉。因此，这座城市在陶瓷版权的各个领域进行充分挖掘，现已形成了一套独具特色且可复制推广的陶瓷版权发展模式。

　　展望未来，景德镇的高质量发展仍需要陶瓷版权的助推，助力这座城市攀升至新的历史高峰。在景德镇的未来发展征程中，需要更加明确版权助推城市高质量发展的理论基础，制定陶瓷版权助推景德镇城市高质量发展的评价体系，将城市发展的步伐精确化。在上述两项工作的支持下，同样需要规划好景德镇城市高质量发展的具体目标，为景德镇的未来发展指明方向。

景德镇城市全貌（景德镇市融媒体中心供图）

第一节
版权助推城市高质量发展的理论基础

　　版权在其 300 多年的发展历史中，已经由一项保护版权人合法权益的私法制度，转变为对城市高质量发展具有积极助推作用的综合制度。它在城市发展过程中扮演的角色早已不是最初用以保护图书出版商利益的"小规则"，而是演变成了在各个方面都能助推城市高质量发展的"大制度"。版权对城市发展的影响力逐渐被人们所感知的同时，关于版权助推城市发展的研究成果也接踵而至。各种研究成果表明，版权制度对城市产业转型、社会环境优化、城市竞争力提升等方面，均有着重要贡献。

一、版权助推城市产业转型

　　首先，版权能夯实文化产业基础。随着人类社会经济文化的不断发展，社会生产力的不断提高，物质财富的不断丰富，人们对美好生活的需要也日益增长。大家逐渐不满足于仅追求物质富足，而更加重视精神富有，尤其在知识经济时代表现为对知识产品、文化产品的巨大需求。这种需求进而反映出这些产品的巨大经济价值。因此，知识产品、文化产品已经成为当下社会财富的一个重要组成部分。在经济价值的引导下，人们源源不断地投身于相关产业的生产和经营活动中。[①]这种需求通过市场机制的作用，带动知识产品、文化产品的生产和流通，进而扩大产业范围，最终引领产业变革。

版权源于经济的必然性。从经济学的角度分析，版权制度的产生是由文化产品本身的经济价值和稀缺性促成的。文化产品的经济价值主要表现在三个方面。第一，文化产品能满足人们精神生活的需要，进而产生一定的社会效益；第二，将文化产品投入生产领域后能转化为有形的物质产品，满足人们物质生活的需要，进而产生一定的经济效益；第三，人们通过吸收文化产品中的知识元素提高自己的综合素质，进而增加在市场竞争中的实力。[②]文化产品的稀缺性主要源于产品生产的长期性、复杂性和高成本性，这些特性使文化产品的生产与获得并非易事。文化产品的经济价值和稀缺性使其具有了商品的价值，因此，为了维系这种价值，版权保护制度便应运而生。版权制度通过赋予作者以著作人身权和著作财产权，将未经权利人同意使用其作品的行为定义为侵权行为，以防止随意使用他人作品的情形发生，进而鼓励文学、艺术和科学领域的创作者创作出更多的优秀文化产品。只有在文化产品的创作、生产被制度保障的情况下，文化产业才有可能发展。因此，版权对文化产业而言是不可或缺的。

其次，版权能提升相关产业附加值。世界知识产权组织（WIPO）在 2015 年更新的《版权产业的经济贡献调研指南》中，依然将版权产业划分为核心版权产业、相互依存的版权产业、部分版权产业和非专用支持产业四个类型。[③]除了核心版权产业的版权因子固定为 100% 之外，其余三类版权相关产业（又称

---

① 吴学安：《优化调整产业结构 积极发展版权产业有利于消除经济 "软肋"》（发布日期：2015 年 2 月 9 日）http: //www.iprchn.com/Index_NewsContent.aspx？newsId=81793，访问日期：2023 年 9 月 14 日。

② 孙午生：《论版权保护制度与文化创意产业的发展》，《法学杂志》2016 年第 10 期，第 89 页。

③ World Intellectual Property Organization.Guide on Surveying the Economic Contribution of the Copyright-Based Industries［R/OL］.（2015）［2023-10-12］.https://www.wipo.int/edocs/pubdocs/en/copyright/893/wipo_pub_893.pdf.

为非核心版权产业）的版权因子需要进行测算，以体现版权对于该产业的贡献值或该产业对版权的依赖程度。其中，核心版权产业，包括新闻出版、广播影视、文艺创作表演等完全依赖版权的产业；相互依存的版权产业，包括电视机、计算机、复印机等版权相关设备的制造与销售产业；部分版权产业，包括纺织服装、珠宝手工艺品、陶瓷制品等具有艺术创作设计过程的产业；非专用支持产业，则是一般批发与零售、一般运输、电话和互联网等能支持其他版权产业发展的产业。

对于核心版权产业而言，由于该产业的发展完全依赖版权，因此版权对这类产业附加值提升的贡献是不言而喻的。对于非核心版权产业而言，首先，相互依存的版权产业生产的产品都需要凭借电视节目、电脑软件、音乐等作品的大量存在，才能体现相关产品的价值，因此，关联作品数量多少、质量优劣等因素会影响关联产品的产销量。譬如，索尼、微软等大型游戏主机制造厂商，会在新主机上市之初发布诸多主机独占游戏以带动新主机销量的行为已经成为行业惯例。[①] 其次，部分版权产业在产业发展转型期以"大文化发展观"为战略指导，愈发注重内容研发与载体融合以满足人们的个性化选择与文化需求。相比于传统部分版权产业致力于提升产品实用价值的做法，转型期的部分版权产业意识到产品实用价值提升瓶颈的存在，转而聚焦增添产品的创意元素，此过程对版权的依赖程度更高。因此，近年来版权对部分版权产业附加值的提升也愈发突出。[②] 最后，非专用支持产业在信息技术革命的影响下，同样进行着信息化变革。以景德镇陶瓷产业发展为例，传统意义上景德镇陶瓷产业规模扩大依靠的是人力资源的优化与产品制造能力的提升。如今，小至各陶瓷企业的内部管理需要依靠各类数字化办公软件，大至景德镇政府每年对陶瓷产业进行全局性盘点同样离不开以大数据为基础的计算机软件工具，都证明了与信息技术相关的作品开发与运用，已经与景德镇陶瓷产业的发展息息相关。

---

① 倪烽：《云游戏平台商业模式研究——以 OnLive 为例》，《质量与市场》2020 年第 16 期，第 83—85 页。
② 向勇：《转型期我国文化产业发展模式研究》，《东岳论丛》2016 年第 2 期，第 66 页。

二、版权助推社会环境优化

首先，版权能优化人才培养模式。版权助推社会就业主要体现在版权产业对就业的承载能力不断加强，一是版权维护原有的就业岗位，保持就业发展积极态势；二是版权助力新的就业岗位增加，繁殖就业机会。当今，知识经济和新科技革命的发展势不可挡，以智力成果为支撑、以知识创新为驱动力的版权产业迎来了发展的新机遇，版权产业由于具备高收益性、高成长性和高附加值等特征，对区域经济以及城市高质量发展贡献颇多。版权产业可以在区域经济体内部形成由众多独立又相互关联的版权企业以及相关支撑机构组成的专业化分工和协作关系，并在一定范围内集聚形成具有地区特色和符合区域发展实际的主导产业集群。① 源源不断涌向景德镇的"景漂"群体，以及景德镇陶瓷版权产业分支的持续蔓延便是该理论在这座城市落地的直接体现。所以，版权作为区域经济发展的重要引擎可以创造更多的就业机会。版权产业发展态势向好，版权产业的从业人数增加，致使版权产业对就业的承载能力不断加强，成为"惠民生"的重要力量。版权产业对社会就业的贡献，就是版权产业所带来的就业量对社会总就业量增长的促进作用。除却版权产业自身不断孵化更多的就业岗位外，在全民创作时代，短视频、直播等自媒体行业发展欣欣向荣，也为大众择业增添新的渠道，但是也衍生出诸多侵权问题。而版权保护制度也能充分发挥维护原创内容的功能，助力新兴产业蓬勃发展，使得版权促进就业常态化发展。

版权的发展能助力对更高水平版权人才培养模式的探索，而高素质的版权人才队伍，也是版权事业发展的根基。在全球经济模式转型大背景下，中国正在实施知识产权强国战略，社会对于复合应用型版权人才的需求愈发强烈，而传统的人才培养模式难以与企业需求耦合，版权人才供给侧与需求侧存在矛盾。

---

① 王行鹏：《版权产业：区域经济发展的新源泉》，《中国版权》2013 年第 4 期，第 30 页。

在市场需求的带动下，人才培养模式开始转型。艺术、理工、自然科学等专业在人才培养方面，除了向学生传授本专业知识，愈发倾向在教授学生创新中融入知识产权保护与管理的相关知识。而知识产权专业在以法学与管理学相结合的方式进行人才培养的基础上，也在持续探索与其他相关专业进行融合的可能。

其次，版权能助力女性多维度发展。女性在世界人口中占 49.6%，对全球社会经济发展作出了巨大贡献。尽管世界男女人口比例基本持平，但是数据显示全球性别差距依然非常明显。[①]性别差距体现在各种领域，在知识产权领域内，有研究表明，女性并不被鼓励进入需要进行创新创造的行业，她们也更少被告知知识产权领域的优势，以及更少被引入这个领域。此外，就职于知识产权立法和知识产权行政领域中的女性数量也明显少于男性数量。[②]因此，包括世界知识产权组织（WIPO）在内的诸多机构越来越意识到，在知识产权领域内，同样需要消除性别差距带来的负面影响。版权对于女性发展的助力主要体现在两方面。一方面，版权能为女性提供更多就业途径。一部分发展模式较为固化的传统行业，由于行业壁垒的长期存在，导致很难在短时间内进行行业人员结构的变革。相比之下，版权相关行业由于对创造性内容的依赖以及行业自身的多元化需求，使其对于女性从业者更加友好，也更容易消除性别差距。另一方面，版权能为女性提供更多表达机会。传统父权社会的教育方式决定了女性无法拥有与男性同等的教育机会。因此，她们也更少地具备进入文学、艺术、音乐等传统版权领域的条件。尽管人类文明的历史长河中诞生了无数经典作品，但是

---

① 根据世界经济论坛发布的《全球性别报告 2022》，2022 年在全球范围内只有 68.1% 的性别差距已经被消除，按照目前的发展水平仍需要 132 年才能够消除性别差距。World Economic Forum. Global Gender Gap Report 2022［R/OL］.（2022-06）［2023-10-18］.https：//www.weforum.org/docs/WEF_GGGR_2022.pdf.

② Jennifer Brant，Kaveri Marathe，Jaci McDole，Mark Schultz.Policy Approaches to Close the Intellectual Property Gender Gap－Practices to Support Access to the Intellectual Property System for Female Innovators，Creators and Entrepreneurs［R/OL］.（2019）［2023-10-18］.https://www.wipo.int/export/sites/www/ip-development/en/agenda/docs/policy_approaches_close_the_ip_gender_gap.pdf.

绝大多数作品依然是以男性视角进行叙述的剥夺女性话语权的产物。[1] 在女性主义表达需求强烈的今天，在景德镇，有越来越多的女性正在通过女性思维在陶瓷版权产业中进行创作与表达。江西省元青花非遗传承人蔡文娟，将女性思维融入青花故事品牌创立及后续企业管理过程中，她认为女性会多一些感性，在作品创作过程中更愿意结合生活，从而生产出兼具实用性和艺术性的作品；在企业管理过程中女性则能运用自身敏锐的洞察力和沟通力，在提升逻辑思维的同时，将理性与感性相结合，化解诸多发展中的困难。女性也能更多地进行换位思考，更多地体现互相尊重、互相鼓励、互相支持与互相关怀的企业管理精神。几年时间里，在蔡文娟创作、管理理念推动下，青花故事实现生产总值增长约4倍，并成为首批荣获"景德镇制"使用授权的企业。来自景德镇陶瓷大学的张婧婧女士，在创作其"风生水起"系列作品时，则将女性的柔美、优雅又不失张力的品性融入其中。这些作品融合了风和水的和谐与流畅，在追求极致线条美感的同时，又构建出了亦虚亦实、令人冥想的空间，成为景德镇前卫陶瓷艺术作品的代表。同时，作为国际学院院长的她认为，"交流"与"多元化"是景德镇陶瓷发展的关键词。陶瓷作为文化交流的中介，是文明交流互鉴的载体。随着景德镇陶瓷文化与外界交流的深入以及陶瓷发展多元化模式的持续，景德镇的创作环境会更加包容。不仅是陶瓷从业者，很多其他艺术门类相关人员也可以在景德镇待下来，让景德镇真正成为东亚文化之都。

三、版权助推城市竞争力提升

首先，版权能助力城市经济发展。版权制度通过创新激励功能，影响创新活动开展和智力成果积累，进而对城市经济发展和竞争力提升产生正向作用。这表现为三种实现路径。其一，版权制度以智力成果的产权界定和产权保护激

---

[1] 杜平、周维贵：《男性话语视野下的女性形象——莎士比亚笔下的维纳斯》，《海南大学学报（人文社会科学版）》2011年第6期，第96页。

励创新；其二，版权制度以智力成果公共领域保留、保护期等内部限制制度，限制了私人产权的无度行使，激励后续产出智力成果的创新活动持续开展；其三，版权使用制度协调了创造者、传播者与使用者之间的利益关系，保证智力成果在经济活动中的最大化利用，助推了城市经济高质量发展。

版权制度的设立是通过授予创新者一定的垄断权，从而激励创新。从本质上分析，智力创新成果的问世取决于私人利益相对于其投入成本的大小。如果私人利益与社会利益脱节，一些极有社会价值的智力创新成果就会迟迟不出现。[①]创新的结果是形成知识产品，版权制度能对知识产品的权属进行有效的安排。创新本身的激励作用在于创新者能获取预期的私人利益，版权制度授予创新者私人产权，使创新者获得较多收益，为权利人提供经济、有效和持久的创新激励，保证创新活动不断向前发展，进而促进经济增长。

其次，版权聚集城市创新资源。创新促进城市经济增长，是影响城市竞争力的重要因素。而创新活动离不开人才、资本、信息等资源要素的支持。因此，就城市经济而言，其竞争力就体现为市场化占有、配置和利用生产要素权利的大小。[②]城市竞争力源于城市对资源要素的吸引和转化能力，而版权制度通过产权确认削减产权交易成本，再通过对创新资源要素的流动导向作用发挥资源优化配置功能，进而对城市竞争力产生影响。

最后，城市版权保护制度的完善对资源尤其是创新资源的吸引，大致可分为两种作用路径。其一，版权保护影响城市对资源要素的集聚和配置能力。资源、资金和人才为了追求利益最大化在不同区域间流动。完善的产权制度使经济行为主体的财产安全得到保障，受利益驱使，国内外的资源要素就会向该城市聚集，该城市产业规模、专业化程度和市场的开放度将不断提高，从而增强城市的集聚效应，有利于城市竞争力的提升。资源要素显现"集聚效应"，有着

---

① 蒋玉宏、单晓光：《知识产权制度对城市竞争力的影响——基于创新激励的机理分析》，《知识产权》2007 年第 3 期，第 29 页。

② 周振华、陈维、汤静波、黄建富、沈开艳、靖学青、杨亚琴：《国内若干大城市综合竞争力比较研究》，《上海经济研究》2001 年第 1 期，第 17 页。

向少数的大企业和核心城市集中的明显趋势。如果一个城市的版权保护混乱，受预期收益的影响，不仅该城市之外的资源要素难以再流入该城市，而且该城市内部的资源要素将会大量流失。与此同时，知识产权侵权和滥用行为无法得到有效治理，那么智力成果创造者和版权权利人的利益将无法得到保证，创新人员的积极性就得不到充分发挥。这也会影响智力成果的开发以及转化，甚至导致人才和技术等资源要素进一步外流。即使在同一国家，不同城市之间也会因为地方立法和相关的公共政策，以及具体的行政管理、司法和执法方面的差异而具有不同的版权创造、运用、管理和保护的环境，从而影响技术、资金等资源要素在同一国家内的不同城市间进行流动。其二，版权保护影响资本的流动和积累。资本对版权保护的状况反应敏感，知识产权成果具有易被低成本复制的特点。因此，资本对知识产权领域的不正当竞争行为非常警惕。当一个城市竞争有序，维持经济安全的相关条件也同样保持良好时，城市拥有的资本将会快速增长，也能得到较好的使用。例如，有学者通过实证研究发现，地方加大知识产权保护执法力度，能有效促进外资流入，对服务业外资、技术密集型外资的正面影响更大。[①]而景德镇正是通过版权制度的完善与版权资源的积累从而实现城市竞争力提升、城市品牌打造的典范。

---

① 韩剑、许亚云：《知识产权保护与利用外资》，《经济管理》2021年第4期，第18页。

第五章
陶瓷版权助推景德镇高质量发展

第二节

版权助推景德镇高质量发展的评价体系

上述理论多角度地归纳了版权与城市高质量发展之间的关系，综合这些理论我们可以明确版权能助推城市高质量发展这一事实。在版权制度和版权资源的支持下，近年来，景德镇全面发展版权经济，在对陶瓷文创社区的打造、陶瓷艺术馆的完善、网络媒体上陶瓷文化的宣传、陶瓷艺术家创作全过程的支持等诸多方面着重发力，让景德镇这座城市彻底"火"了起来。未来若要实现"景德镇成为全国具有重要示范意义的新型人文城市和具有重要影响力的世界陶瓷文化中心城市"[①]这一目标，需要持续发挥版权助推经济社会发展质量变革、效率变革、动力变革的作用。然而，如何评估甚至量化版权对景德镇高质量发展的助推作用则需要进一步研究。考虑到版权作为一种制度，评估其作用的方式无法像评估某一类实体产业一样，能通过分析一系列直接的客观指标来显示该实体产业对某一城市的发展有着怎样的贡献。但是评估一项制度是否顺畅运行，

---

① 出自《景德镇国家陶瓷文化传承创新试验区实施方案》（2019 年 8 月印发）。

甚至评价一项制度如何影响城市发展的时候，都可以对该制度进一步概念化，再将更加具体的指标与城市发展的指标建立联系，通过数据搜集与比对得到较为客观的评价结果。因此，评价版权如何助推景德镇高质量发展，需要制定一套兼具定性指标和定量指标且符合景德镇发展基础和方向的评价体系，并在过程中通过综合相关指标的具体数值，量化版权对景德镇高质量发展的贡献，从而把握版权的赋能方向和效果。可以通过"评价体系框架的构建—评价体系指标的构建—评价体系内容的构建"的方式，为评价版权如何赋能景德镇高质量发展提供具有一定可行性的设想。

一、依托强国建设纲要打造评价体系框架

评价体系的框架构建需要以《知识产权强国建设纲要（2021—2035 年）》为依托。2021 年 9 月 22 日，中共中央、国务院印发了《知识产权强国建设纲要（2021—2035 年）》（下文简称《纲要》），该《纲要》以建设知识产权强国为目标，布局了未来十五年中国知识产权事业，一方面将知识产权事业提升到强国战略的高度，另一方面也为如何评估知识产权事业发展贡献了中国智慧。

总结《纲要》贡献的中国智慧，首先在于其将知识产权事业发展分为创造、运用、保护、管理和服务五个部分。其次，这五个部分可以反映在这六方面中。一、建设面向社会主义现代化的知识产权制度；二、建设支撑国际一流营商环境的知识产权保护体系；三、建设激励创新发展的知识产权市场运行机制；四、建设便民利民的知识产权公共服务体系；五、建设促进知识产权高质量发展的人文社会环境；六、深度参与全球知识产权治理。这种领域划分说明了知识产权事业发展需要在制度建设、保护体系建设、市场运行机制建设、公共服务体系建设、人文社会环境建设以及国际治理这六个方面进行评估，即知识产权事业发展能对上述六个方面产生正面影响。另一个角度，《纲要》从六个方面将"知识产权事业发展"这个相对模糊的词语概念化，当评估者需要评估知识产权对某一客体的影响时，可以通过评估上述六个方面对该客体的影响来达到评估

目的。同时会发现"制度""保护体系""市场运行机制""公共服务体系""人文社会环境"和"全球治理"这六个方面与评价城市高质量发展的一级指标关系密切。因此，《纲要》的一大重要意义在于为评估知识产权影响城市高质量发展的评价体系制定提供了理论框架。

由于版权是知识产权的一个重要类别，因此版权助推景德镇高质量发展的评价体系同样能以《纲要》为理论框架进行制定。最终参考《纲要》制定的理论框架，建议将版权助推景德镇高质量发展评价体系的一级指标拟定为：版权制度体系、版权维权机制、版权经济、版权与城市公共服务、版权与城市人文环境以及版权与国际影响力六项内容。[①]

二、依照四大相关标准锚定评价体系指标

评价体系的指标构建需要以城市发展相关评价体系的指标内容为参考。近年来已经有不少组织机构针对如何评价某一国家或者城市的创新发展、综合发展制定了科学的评价体系。在国家创新发展评价领域，世界知识产权组织每年制定的《全球创新指数》通过一套全面的指标体系对每个国家的创新能力进行评估。由于版权与创新能力提升紧密联系，《全球创新指数》对版权赋能景德镇高质量发展评价体系具体指标的确定能起到重要借鉴作用。在城市综合发展评价领域，较为权威的是国际标准化组织和国家标准化管理委员会制定的三种指标体系。一是，国际标准化组织（ISO）下属的城市可持续发展标准化技术委员会（ISO/TC 268）于2014年制定的 ISO 37120:2014，该标准已经于2018年修订为 ISO 37120:2018[②] 版本。二是，国家市场监督管理总局与国家标准化管理委员

---

① 考虑到只有上升到国家层面才会涉及参与全球版权治理的活动，同时，考虑到版权影响城市高质量发展的方式之一是通过版权这个"国际通用语言"来逐步提升城市的国际影响力。因此将评价体系中的最后一项设计为"版权与国际影响力"。

② 该国际标准的副标题是 Sustainable cities and communities—Indicators for city services and quality of life. 旨在通过具体指标体系来评估可持续发展的城市与社区。

会于 2020 年 11 月 19 日发布的《新型城镇化　品质城市评价指标体系》（GB/T 39497-2020）。三是，国家市场监督管理总局与国家标准化管理委员会于 2021 年 8 月 20 日发布的《城市发展质量评价指标》（GB/T 40482-2021）。

全球创新指数

该指标体系设立制度、人力资源与研究、基础设施、市场成熟度、商业成熟度、知识与技术产出以及创意产出 7 个一级指标，并下设 21 个二级指标和 80 个三级指标来评价一个国家的创新能力。相较于城市综合发展评价体系更注重经济、社会、生态、城建等因素，该指标体系将"制度"列为评价指标中的首要因素。考虑到《纲要》同样将"制度"和"保护体系"设定在框架的首要位置，所以在评估版权对景德镇高质量发展的助推作用时，版权政策制度的相关指标不可或缺。

ISO 37120:2018

该指标体系从经济、教育、能源、环境与气候变化、财政、治理、健康、住房、人口与社会条件、休闲、安全、固体废物、体育与文化、通讯、交通、城市/本地农业和食品安全、城市规划、废水、水等 19 个方面，共设立 104 项（其中核心指标 45 项，辅助指标 59 项）指标来评价城市发展。其中，版权与经济、教育、财政、治理、社会条件与文化等六大方面有着直接关联。

新型城镇化　品质城市评价指标体系（GB/T 39497-2020）

该指标体系设立经济发展、社会文化、生态环境、公共服务、居民生活等五大一级指标，包含 13 个二级指标，76 个三级指标（其中，包含 5 项拓展指标），来评价城市发展。其中，除生态环境之外的四大一级指标均与版权有直接联系。

城市发展质量评价指标（GB/T 40482-2021）

该指标体系设立经济发展、生态环境、城市建设、公共服务、居民生活等五大一级指标，包含 50 个二级指标来评价城市发展。同样，除生态环境与城市建设之外的三个一级指标与版权关系密切。

三、依据统计工作结果明确评价体系内容

在构建评价体系6个一级指标并参考借鉴相关指标体系的结构设置后，通过继续研究《纲要》的具体内容，并结合景德镇统计工作的实际数据结果，同时考虑到景德镇的版权发展基础，建议拟定15个二级指标和46个三级指标作为评价体系的具体内容。

一级指标"版权制度体系"是从地方立法与行政规范性文件等方面拟设的2个二级指标。二级指标"版权相关地方立法"，包括现行版权相关地方立法数量和近五年版权相关地方立法数量增长率等三级指标；二级指标"版权相关行政规范性文件"，包括现行版权相关行政规范性文件数量和近五年版权相关行政规范性文件数量增长率等三级指标。

一级指标"版权维权机制"，在司法保护、行政保护与协同保护等方面拟设

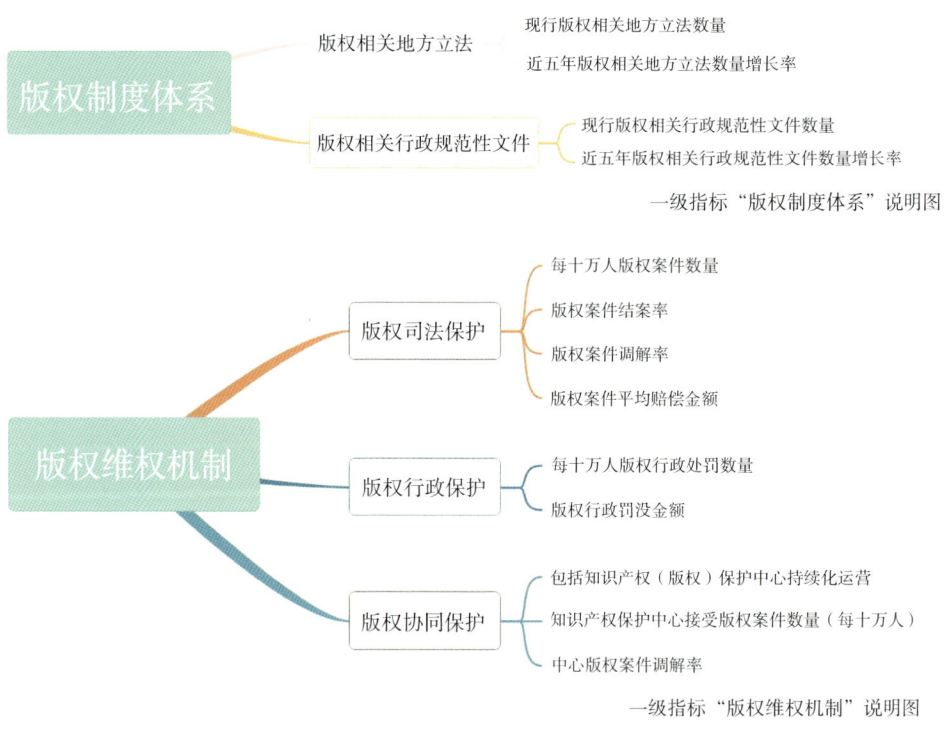

一级指标"版权制度体系"说明图

一级指标"版权维权机制"说明图

3个二级指标。二级指标"版权司法保护"，包括每十万人版权案件数量、版权案件结案率、版权案件调解率、版权案件平均赔偿金额等4个三级指标；二级指标"版权行政保护"，包括每十万人版权行政处罚数量与版权行政罚没金额等三级指标；二级指标"版权协同保护"，包括知识产权（版权）保护中心持续化运营、知识产权保护中心接受版权案件数量（每十万人）、中心版权案件调解率等3个三级指标。

一级指标"版权经济"，在产业、消费与金融服务等方面拟设3个二级指标。二级指标"版权产业"，包括规上版权相关工业企业数量、规上版权相关工业总产值、规上版权相关工业总产值占工业总产值比、规上版权相关服务业企业数量、规上版权相关服务业营业收入、规上版权相关服务业营业收入占服务业总营业收入比等6个三级指标；二级指标"版权消费"，包括版权相关消费品零售总额、版权相关消费品零售总额占社会消费品零售总额比、市民文娱消费支出、市民文娱消费支出占人均可支配收入比等4个三级指标；二级指标"版权金融服务"，包括版权交易中心持续化运营与每十万人版权融资金额等三级指

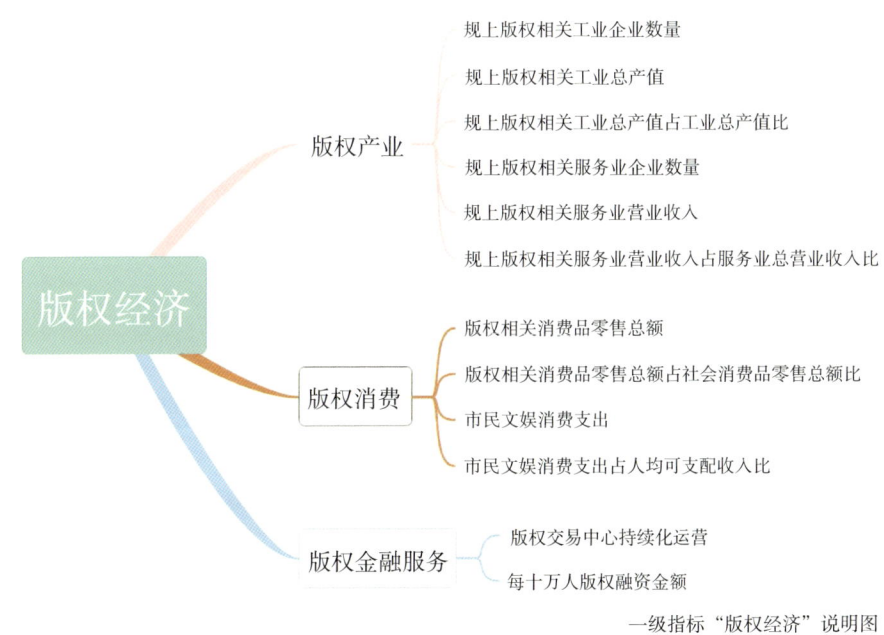

一级指标"版权经济"说明图

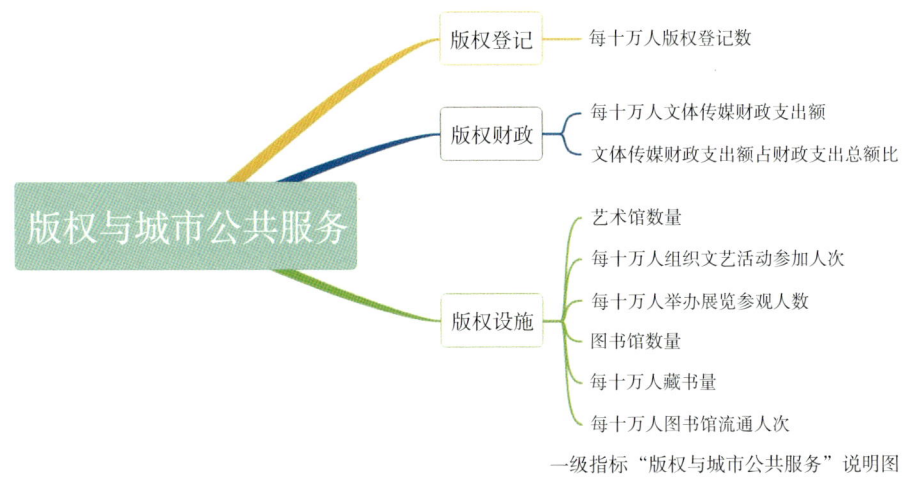

一级指标"版权与城市公共服务"说明图

标。

一级指标"版权与城市公共服务",在版权登记、版权财政、版权设施等方面拟设3个二级指标。二级指标"版权登记"下,设每十万人版权登记数作为三级指标;二级指标"版权财政",包括每十万人文体传媒财政支出额与文体传媒财政支出额占财政支出总额比等三级指标;二级指标"版权设施",包括艺术馆数量、每十万人组织文艺活动参加人次、每十万人举办展览参观人数、图书馆数量、每十万人藏书量以及每十万人图书馆流通人次等6个三级指标。

一级指标"版权与城市人文环境",从版权教育、旅游等方面拟设2个二级指标。二级指标"版权教育",包括政府举办版权普法宣传次数与中小学版权教

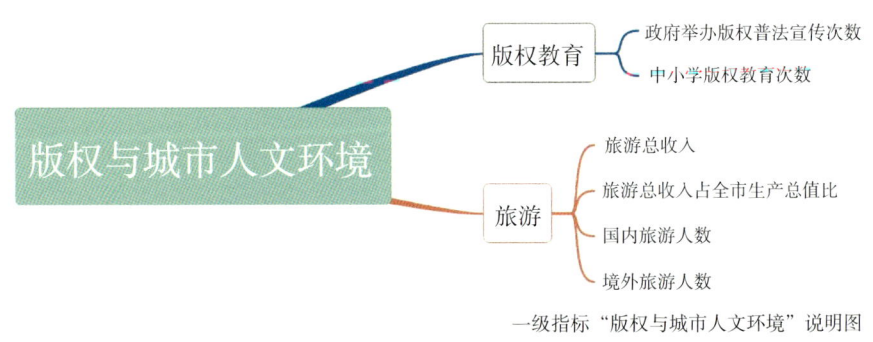

一级指标"版权与城市人文环境"说明图

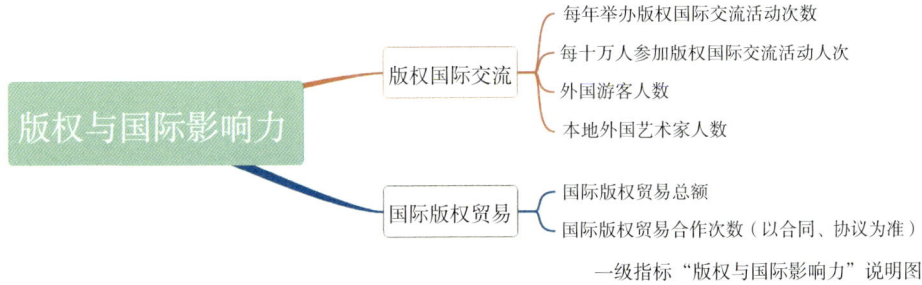

一级指标"版权与国际影响力"说明图

育次数等三级指标；二级指标"旅游"，包括旅游总收入、旅游总收入占全市生产总值比、国内旅游人数与境外旅游人数等4个三级指标。

一级指标"版权与国际影响力"，在版权国际交流与国际版权贸易等方面拟设2个二级指标。二级指标"版权国际交流"，包括每年举办版权国际交流活动次数、每十万人参加版权国际交流活动人次、外国游客人数、本地外国艺术家人数等4个三级指标；二级指标"国际版权贸易"，包括国际版权贸易总额与国际版权贸易合作次数（以合同、协议为准）等三级指标。

第三节

版权助推景德镇高质量发展的实际成效

通过整合并分析景德镇市文旅局、景德镇市统计局、景德镇知识产权法庭、景德镇市珠山区人民法院竟成人民法庭、景德镇市知识产权保护中心等单位提供的相关数据，可以从版权对制度的影响、版权对司法行政保护的影响、版权对市场经济的影响、版权对公共服务的影响以及版权对人文社会环境的影响五个方面，来呈现版权对景德镇高质量发展的助推结果。

一、版权助推景德镇制度体系构建

由于景德镇市较小的城市规模和人口数量以及大量上位法规的存在，使得景德镇市人民代表大会的立法工作并不需要那么活跃。自 2016 年以来，景德镇市人民政府官方网站上公开的地方性法规仅有 10 部，且大多为环境卫生管理或饮用水水源保护等与民生保障直接挂钩的地方性法规。在这 10 部地方性法规中，有两部法规属于版权相关地方性法规，包括 2018 年 5 月 1 日起施行的《景德镇市御窑厂遗址保护管理条例》和 2022 年 1 月 1 日起施行的《景德镇市陶瓷文化传承创新条例》。尽管样本量较小，自 2016 年以来新公布的版权相关地方性法规仅占所有地方性法规数量的 1/5，但这一事实也证明了版权相关法规已经成为景德镇地方性法规体系中的一个重要组成部分。

根据 2023 年 7 月公布的《景德镇市人民政府关于公布市政府行政规范性文件清理结果的通知》的内容可知，景德镇市现阶段继续有效的规范性文件有102 份，予以修改的规范性文件有 23 份，适时修改的规范性文件有 17 份，即全部规范性文件的数量有 142 份之多，构成了较为完备的政府规范性文件体系。其中，除《景德镇市人民政府办公室关于印发景德镇市艺术陶瓷从业主体税收征收管理试行办法的通知》（景府办发〔2015〕6 号发布，景府办字〔2018〕98号修改）之外并无其他版权相关规范性文件。尽管如此，景德镇市人民政府及相关部门于 2021 年发布了三份与版权直接相关的试行规范性文件[①]弥补了这一空缺，实现了从无到有的突破。

二、版权助推景德镇维权机制完善

版权对景德镇维权机制的影响体现在版权司法保护、版权行政保护和版权协同保护这三方面的成效上。

在版权司法保护方面，通过对 2016 年至今景德镇市珠山区人民法院版权案件处理情况进行分析，可以发现两种现象。[②]第一，版权案件数量显著增加。2016 年，法院受理的版权案件数量仍为 0 件，之后的 6 年时间数量分别增长至 1 件、2 件、6 件、25 件、42 件和 253 件，仅 2022 年受理的版权案件数量是之前 6 年受理数量总和的 3 倍多。第二，以调解方式结案成为主要结案方式。2016 年至 2021 年，法院共受理版权案件 76 件，其中以调解方式结案的仅有 3

---

① 分别为《景德镇市版权创新创造指导办法（试行）》《景德镇市版权产业扶持办法（试行）》和《景德镇市优秀版权作品评选办法（试行）》。

② 景德镇市的一审版权案件主要集中在景德镇市珠山区人民法院，因此选取该法院处理的版权案件情况作为分析研究的对象。

件，占比仅为 4% 左右。而在 2022 年，案件数量激增，法院也随之改变了纠纷解决机制，本年度通过调解方式解决纠纷的案件数量增至 156 件，占比超过了60%。以上数据显示了景德镇在版权司法保护方面的两点变化。其一，面对版权纠纷，权利人更愿意通过版权司法保护的方式进行维权，意味着社会公众对景德镇司法维权机制的信赖度越来越高。其二，面对日益增多的版权案件，法院更愿意通过调解去解决纠纷，意味着版权纠纷多元化解决机制已经逐渐发挥效力，平衡了当事人的权益与司法的效率。

在版权行政保护方面，2016 年至今，版权行政处罚案件数量呈波动状态，案件数量分别为 1 件、4 件、0 件、1 件、6 件、4 件、2 件和 14 件（截至 2023年 9 月）。版权行政处罚案件数量占文化市场综合执法案件数量的比例，也从最初的 5%~15% 升至 2023 年的 35% 左右。版权行政罚没总金额同样有对应提高的现象，自 2016 年以来分别为 1000 元、50400 元、0 元、3000 元、11050 元、26000 元、20000 元和 147020 元。同时，景德镇于 2021 年实行版权行政调解制度，近三年的版权行政调解案件数量分别为 3 件、13 件和 4 件。这些数据反映了景德镇在版权行政保护上做出的两点努力。一是，文化市场综合执法逐渐将执法重心放于版权类案件，以满足创作者的版权行政维权需求；二是，实施版权行政调解制度，并增加版权行政调解的次数，以降低版权行政维权的成本。

在版权协同保护方面，景德镇市知识产权保护中心已于 2022 年正式揭牌成立，现阶段保护中心的工作重点，依然放在专利协同保护与商标协同保护方面。接下来，保护中心计划把版权协同保护一并纳入工作任务当中，将积累的知识产权协同保护经验直接运用在版权协同保护工作上，探索出更为有效的版权协同保护机制。

三、版权助推景德镇经济结构优化

在经济结构转型期，版权对景德镇经济的影响，可以通过规模以上工业总产值、规模以上服务业营业收入与消费品零售额等方面的相关数据统计进行呈现。

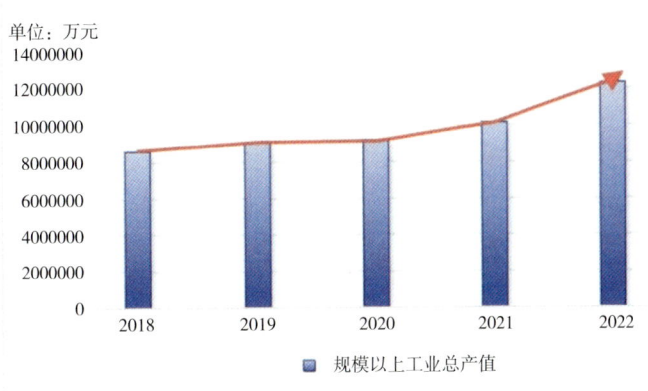

单位：万元

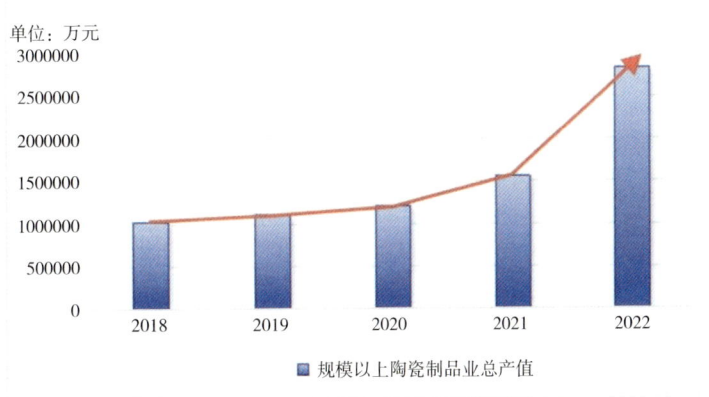

单位：万元

景德镇市规模以上工业总产值与规模以上陶瓷制品业总产值变化对比图

2018 年至 2022 年，五年间，景德镇市规模以上工业总产值从 861.17 亿元增长至 1229.95 亿元，增幅为 42.82%。同期，最能代表版权相关工业的景德镇市规模以上陶瓷制品业总产值从 103.06 亿元提升至 282.82 亿元，增幅高达 174.43%，增长数据为规模以上工业总产值的四倍。

版权相关工业的贡献度，可以通过版权相关工业总产值占工业总产值的比重变化更为直观地呈现。同样，2018 年至 2022 年，景德镇规模以上陶瓷制品总产值占规模以上工业总产值比从 11.97% 跃升至 22.99%，意味着版权相关工业对于景德镇市整体工业水平的影响在五年之间基本翻了一倍。同时，也呈现

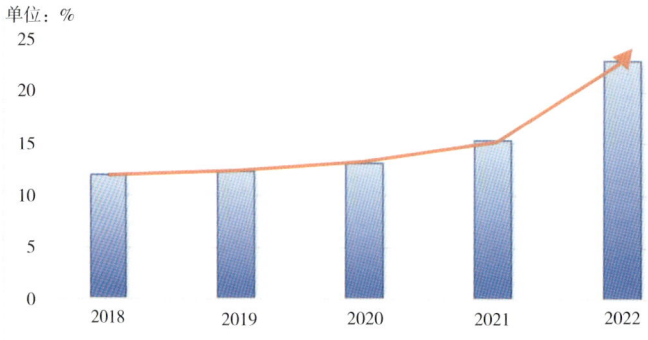

单位：%

景德镇市规模以上陶瓷制品业总产值占规模以上工业总产值比变化图

出该时期版权对景德镇市第二产业极强的产值带动作用与转型引领作用。

在作为第三产业代表的服务业领域，版权的影响也无法忽视。2018 年至 2022 年，尽管遭受新冠疫情等因素的影响，景德镇规模以上服务业营业收入依旧快速增长，从 69.64 亿元增长至 127.48 亿元左右，增幅达到 83.07%。相比之下，2018 年至 2021 年（2022 年数据暂未统计）的版权相关服务业 ① 的营业收入从 8709 万元提高至 39264 万元，增幅为 350.84%，尽管样本量较小，但依然能够呈现出版权相关服务业营业收入更为强劲的增长态势。

版权相关服务业营业收入占服务业整体营业收入的比重，是反映版权对服务业影响程度的重要依据。2018 年至 2021 年，景德镇市规模以上版权相关服务业营业收入占规模以上服务业营业收入比重从 12.5‰上涨至 31.5‰。尽管相关数据在 2020 年有所回落，但整体依然呈现出稳步提升的趋势。

民众对于版权相关产品、服务的消费情况变化，也能反映版权对整体经济结构的影响。以景德镇整体消费品零售为代表，2017 年至 2021 年的消费品零

① 按照景德镇市统计局每年发布的《景德镇统计年鉴》，版权相关服务业可以认定为软件和信息技术服务业，新闻和出版业，广播、电视、电影和录音制作业，文化艺术业与娱乐业这五类服务业的总和。

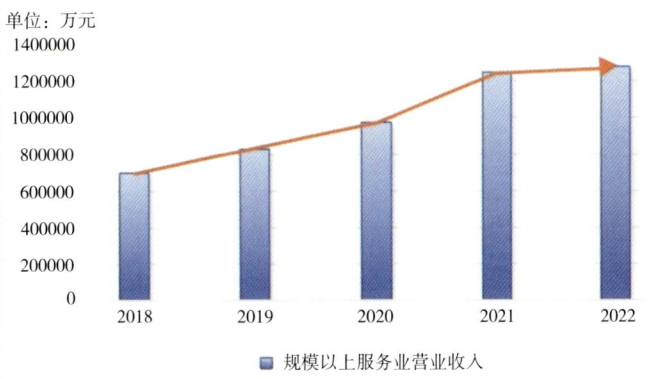

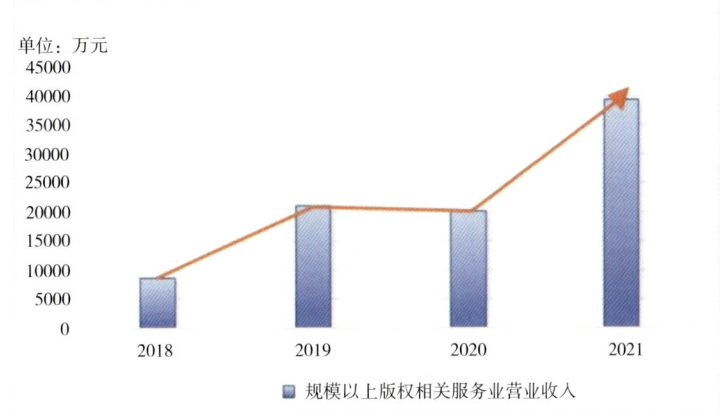

景德镇市规模以上服务业营业收入与规模以上版权相关服务业营业收入变化对比图

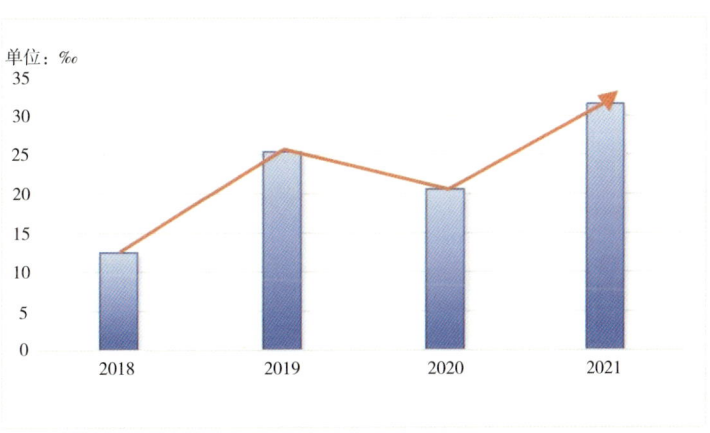

景德镇市规模以上版权相关服务业营业收入占规模以上服务业营业总收入比变化图

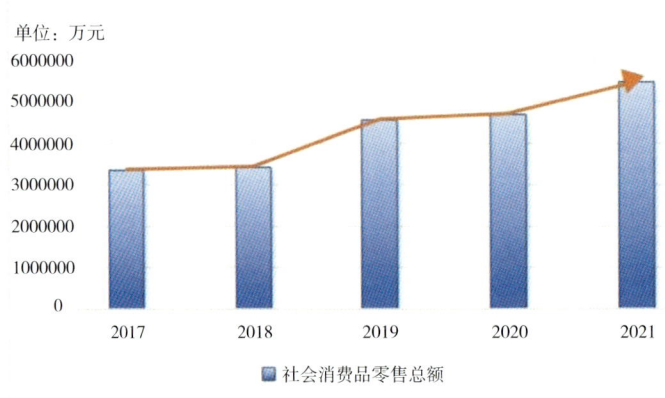

单位：万元

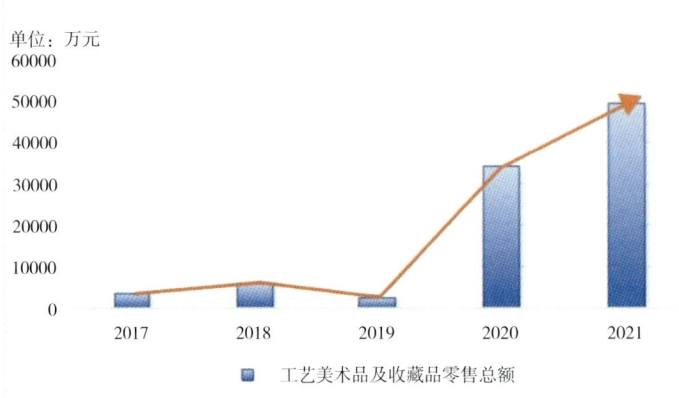

单位：万元

景德镇市社会消费品零售总额与工艺美术品及收藏品零售总额变化对比图

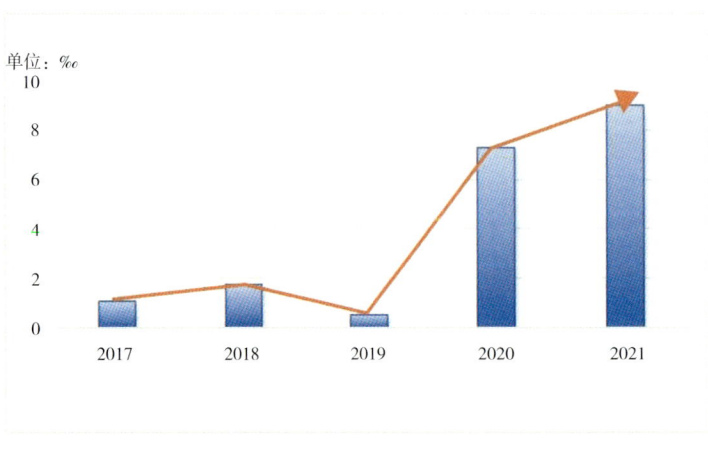

单位：‰

景德镇市工艺美术品及收藏品零售总额占社会消费品零售总额比变化图

售总额从 335.93 亿元增长至 548.17 亿元，尽管期间遭遇新冠疫情冲击，增幅依旧高达 63.18%。作为版权相关消费品的代表，同期的工艺美术品及收藏品零售总额从毫不起眼的 3565 万元激增至五年后的 49358 万元，涨幅达到惊人的1284.52%。得益于市场对版权相关消费品需求大增，工艺美术品及收藏品零售总额占全部消费品零售总额的比例也水涨船高：从 2017 年的 1.06‰迅速提高到2021 年的 9‰。

通过分析近年来版权对景德镇工业、景德镇服务业以及景德镇消费品市场的影响，可以发现三大事实。一、景德镇整体经济呈现出较为平稳的增长态势；[①]二、景德镇版权相关的经济指标爆发式提升；三、版权相关经济的占比越来越大。版权不仅对景德镇的经济增长起到助推作用，同时也在潜移默化地优化景德镇的经济结构，将景德镇从资源枯竭型城市的泥潭中拖出，是其成为转型为创新型城市的重要推手。

四、版权助推景德镇公共服务提升

公共服务提升可以体现在公共设施的建设、公共服务的提供等可视化方面，也可以表现为社会保险基金的填补、相关补助的发放等不可视化方面。然而，若需要以较为直观的数据体现政府对公共服务提升的投入，则可以对一般公共预算支出进行分析。一般情况下，公共预算支出与社会公共服务的质量呈现正相关关系。因此，比较分析 2017 年至 2021 年五年间的景德镇市一般公共预算支出可以发现：该支出额从 192.12 亿元小幅提升至 226.52 亿元，2019 年和 2020 年受新冠疫情影响，公共预算支出突破了 230 亿元大关，但是在 2021年又滑落至较为正常的水平。这期间该支出的增幅为 17.90%，属于平稳上升的

---

① 该事实也可以通过景德镇市地区生产总值的变化情况中得到印证，景德镇市地区生产总值从2016 年的 8495714 万元增长至 2022 年的 11921893 万元，经济呈现出平稳增长态势。

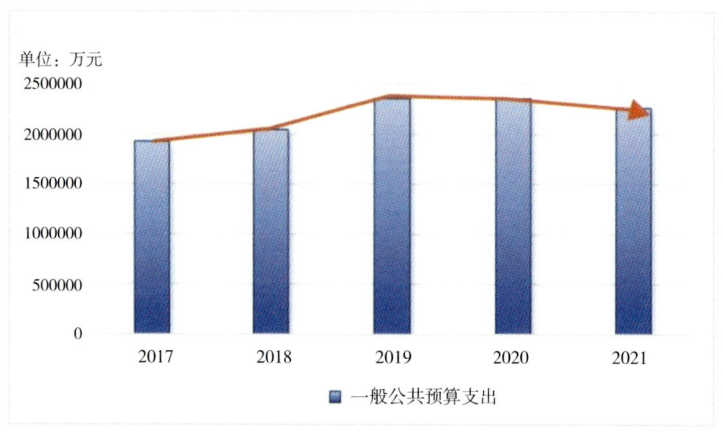

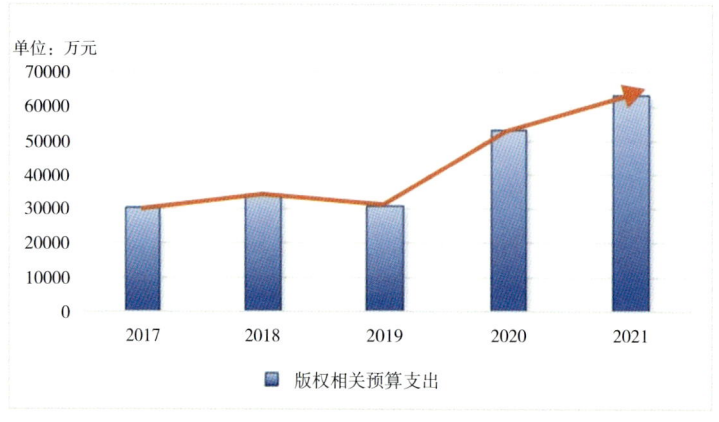

景德镇市一般公共预算支出与版权相关预算支出变化对比图

状态，也与国家整体公共预算支出增长水平保持一致。^①而同期的景德镇市版权相关公共预算支出（文化体育与传媒预算支出）从30217万元提升至53473万元，整体增幅达到76.96%，远高于城市一般公共预算支出的正常增幅，并且在2019年至2020年增幅明显。

版权相关公共预算支出的占比也从2017年的15.73‰提升至2021年的

---

① 全国一般公共预算支出从2017年的203330亿元增长至2021年的246322亿元，五年增幅为21.14%。考虑到国家公共预算支出项目与城市公共预算支出项目有所不同，可以认为该时期景德镇市一般公共预算支出的增幅与全国水平相当。

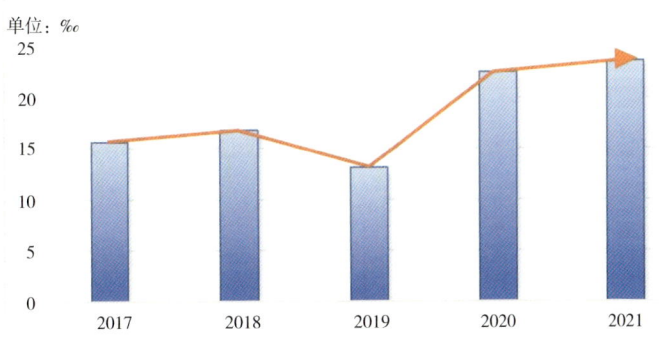

单位：‰

景德镇市版权相关预算支出占公共预算支出比变化图

23.61‰。尽管该项占比的变化并没有十分明显，但考虑到城市平稳发展期间各一般公共预算支出项目额度的增减并不会出现较大波动，景德镇近年持续增加版权相关公共预算支出比例的做法，尤其在整体支出额度略有下滑的趋势下，更能体现出景德镇市为了提升公共服务质量增加版权相关公共预算支出的决策价值。

五、版权助推景德镇人文环境打造

景德镇因"瓷都"闻名世界，吸引着国内外无数游客的到来。作为"中国优秀旅游城市"和"国家园林城市"的景德镇一直以陶瓷文化旅游为名片，持续打造城市人文环境。2018 年和 2019 年赴景德镇旅游总人次达到了峰值，分别为 4954.3 万人次和 5523.05 万人次，均超过了景德镇城市总人口的 30 倍。同期的旅游总收入也达到了 614.37 亿元和 718.57 亿元，占当年景德镇地区生产总值的比重分别为 71.71% 和 77.97%。受新冠疫情影响，尽管在 2020 年，赴景德镇旅游总人次跌落至 2247.45 万人次，但在接下来的两年，该数据又恢复至 4000 万 ~5000 万人次的正常规模（分别为 2021 年的 5531.65 万人次和 2022

年的 4466.69 万人次）。新冠疫情后的旅游总收入即使下滑至 2019 年一半左右，但依然能维持对地区生产总值贡献超过四成的水平。不同于省内其他优秀旅游城市更多以历史文化资源、自然资源、红色资源为基础打造城市的人文环境，景德镇持续以陶瓷文化资源为核心彰显独特的城市人文风貌。在此过程中，需要依靠陶瓷文化的传承，更需要依赖陶瓷文化的革新打造"千年瓷都"与"创意城市"相融合的人文环境。景德镇的陶瓷文化是鲜活的，人们对于这座城市的认同不仅来自景德镇悠久的陶瓷历史，还源于景德镇是一座能一直孕育出陶瓷艺术家和陶瓷作品的艺术之都。无论是彰显建筑美学的御窑博物馆还是陶溪川夜市里五花八门的陶瓷摆件，这些组成景德镇人文环境的各类元素，最终都需要版权予以支持。

第四节
版权助推景德镇高质量发展的未来展望

　　展望景德镇高质量发展的未来成果，版权将在产业的转型发展、新型人文城市的建成以及陶瓷文化中心的打造过程中发挥更大作用。首先，版权会持续为陶瓷产业的创新、多产业的融合提供动力；其次，版权能为城市规划的设计、城市精神的培育给予保障；最后，版权还可以为陶瓷文化生态的创建、陶瓷文化对外交流的开展注入能量。

一、版权助推景德镇落实产业转型示范

　　为了不断推动景德镇高质量发展的进程，产业转型必将持续。在《景德镇市国民经济和社会发展第十四个五年规划和二〇三五年远景目标纲要》（以下简称《景德镇市"十四五"规划》）中，把"发展景德镇特色现代产业体系"明确为景德镇未来发展的关键任务，其中诸多内容与产业转型息息相关，而版权在此过程中扮演的角色同样大有作为。

　　景德镇在未来会继续聚焦陶瓷产业，并将其打造为千亿级产业集群。除了发展日用陶瓷等传统陶瓷产业外，加快发

展高科技陶瓷产业和文化创意陶瓷产业以完善陶瓷产业链更是不可或缺的一步。版权不仅能助力日用陶瓷中创意元素的不断更新，为该产业增添附加值，而且作为高科技陶瓷产业和文化创意陶瓷产业的核心要素，直接关系着这两个产业的存亡兴衰。

景德镇将持续大力发展数字经济，推动数字经济与实体经济深度融合。无论是将大数据、人工智能、区块链等与陶瓷、文旅产业相融合，还是加快云计算、物联网、电子商务、数字视听等产业的技术研发，在此过程中相关产业发展所借助的"工具"（计算机软件作品）和最终开发出的"产品"（美术作品、视听作品等等）都与版权紧密相关。因此，版权在此过程中发挥着绝对保障作用。

景德镇需要将服务业扩容提质。进入新时代，对生产性服务业与生活性服务业的共同要求是信息平台的打造与信息云服务的提供，其本质同样是计算机软件作品的开发与通过无数个美术作品和视听作品为客户提供视听化服务，而这些作品的产生也都离不开版权保护。因此，版权同样能为新时代服务业的发展保驾护航。

二、版权助推景德镇建成新型人文城市

展望 2035 年，景德镇市的一项重要愿景是成为全国具有重要示范意义的新型人文城市。为此，在《景德镇市"十四五"规划》中提出了需要"提升城市功能品质，充分彰显'美景、厚德、镇生活'的独特韵味"的发展方向。

彰显美景需要精心搞好城市设计，强化对城市自然人文风貌的管控。在做好城市整体规划布局的基础上，景德镇需要进行一系列的设计、建设工作来提升城市的硬品质。除了加强新城区基础设施和公共服务设施的建设、推进老城的保护、加强近现代工业遗产的保护等完全依赖工程建筑的事宜之外。诸如对老厂区老厂房的改造利用、对近现代工业遗产的开发、对昌江百里风光带的建设、对整体生态景观的打造都要高度依赖艺术设计，都需要大量的建筑作品和

陶阳里文化街区（陶阳里供图）

美术作品去填充景德镇城市的每个角落，而这一切也都需要版权的支撑与保障。

彰显厚德则需要持续推进文明城市建设，让文明建设深入人心。其根本在于积极培育和践行社会主义核心价值观，深入挖掘优秀陶瓷历史文化蕴含的思想观念、人文精神和道德规范。越是深厚的思想就越需要丰富的表达方式。在挖掘、传递、栽培厚德的过程中，大至一批社会主义核心价值观主题街区、主题校园、主题广场的打造，小至一次精神文明创建活动的开展、一条精神文明宣传标语的撰写，也都离不开诸多承载着社会主义核心价值观和优秀陶瓷历史文化的作品的创作，而这些作品的背后推手依然是版权。

三、版权助推景德镇打造对外文化交流新平台

"打造对外文化交流新平台"是国家对景德镇发展的重要嘱托。在这一重要使命下，景德镇陶瓷文化深厚的历史底蕴和独特的艺术魅力具有显著的优势。为了进一步增强中华陶瓷文化的国际影响力，千年瓷都景德镇肩负着塑造全新对外文化交流阵地的重大责任。

因此，在《景德镇市"十四五"规划》中，景德镇制定的另一项重要目标，正是打造具有重要影响力的对外文化交流新平台。在此过程中，不仅要传承和弘扬景德镇陶瓷文化，而且要推动陶瓷文化创造性转化、创新性发展，进而走出一条具有世界意义、中国价值、新时代特征、景德镇特点的优秀传统文化传承创新发展的新路子。

通过完善陶瓷文物保护法规体系以及实施景德镇大遗址保护计划，陶瓷文化保护的基础得以夯实。为此，景德镇不仅要计划创建陶瓷文化生态保护区，加大手工制瓷非物质文化遗产代表性传承人队伍培养力度，还需要提升博物馆发展水平，创新博物馆展陈方式，规划建设数字化博物馆，开展线上博物馆活动，将景德镇打造为博物馆之城。另外，以一大批优秀文化创作成果为载体，实施陶瓷文化全媒体推广计划。在这个过程中，传承人需要不断以传统陶瓷文化为灵感，创造一个又一个崭新的陶瓷作品；博物馆需要不断以传统陶瓷文化

为纽带，打造一个又一个新颖的文化展示平台；景德镇也需要不断以传统陶瓷文化为素材，推广一个又一个震撼人心的文艺作品。而这一切的本质，还是版权的创造、运用、保护、管理和服务。

以瓷为媒，在与国外文化机构交流合作过程中，陶瓷文化无疑是最好的一张名片。景德镇的陶瓷艺术，无论是传统的精湛技艺，还是现代艺术家的创新之作，均凝聚了创作者的心血与智慧。这些作品不仅是艺术的展示，更是中国文化的传承与弘扬。在景德镇，文化交流通过一件件与陶瓷有关的作品的传播进行。在此过程中，版权的影响力毋庸置疑。景德镇对于外国友人而言，不仅是陶瓷艺术的朝圣地，亦是他们深入研习陶瓷技艺的殿堂，更是会成为承载着对外文化交流重大使命的平台。在此，他们得以领略中国文化的博大精深，在追求艺术创作与中外文化交流的同时，版权会对他们的作品创造、作品运用、作品保护、作品管理等方面产生深远影响。因此，进一步提升版权全链条发展质量以满足景德镇在打造对外文化交流新平台时的多方需求，将成为景德镇高质量发展进程中的重要任务。

版权制度在诸多国际公约与国内法律制度的斡旋之下逐渐发展，也反向影响着中国与国际的交流。中国在国际政治经济格局变革的浪潮中积累着国际声望，也反映着中国在版权国际博弈中话语权的提升。与此同时，来自中国江西省东北部的历史名城景德镇正在进行着城市转型，陶瓷文化在版权的守护下愈发光彩夺目。毫无疑问，版权也最终会在景德镇实现其愿景的历程中写下浓墨重彩的一笔。

第五节
小结

本章详尽剖析了景德镇陶瓷版权在多个维度所发挥的积极作用，深度覆盖了理论基础、评价体系、实际成效及未来展望四大板块，为景德镇的高质量发展路径铺设了坚实的理论与实践基石。

在理论基础层面，深刻揭示了版权制度在景德镇高质量发展历程中的战略要义。版权，这一法律利器，不仅为创作者构筑起权益的坚固防线，更成为点燃创新火花、驱动文化产业加速前行的核心引擎。通过为智力成果穿上法律铠甲，版权制度极大地激发了社会的创意潜能，引领景德镇在文化创意与高科技的浪潮中乘风破浪，稳固了其作为世界陶瓷之都的卓越地位。

评价体系的构建，则为景德镇的持续发展预设了科学的度量衡。本章创造性地构建了以版权制度为灵魂的城市发展评估框架，该体系广泛纳入版权制度的完备程度、版权经济的蓬勃态势、版权服务的深远影响等多重维度，为景德镇提供了精准衡量版权驱动效应的标尺。借助这一工具，景德镇能敏锐捕捉版权工作的成效与不足，灵活调整发展战略，进而在版权保护与提升城市综合竞争力方面迈出更加坚实的步伐。

实际成效的展示，则是景德镇版权制度实践成果的生动诠释。版权保护的强有力实施，不仅激发了陶瓷产业的创新活力，使得景德镇陶瓷产品在全球市场上独树一帜，而且带动了文化创意产业的全面繁荣。从传统的陶瓷艺术领域到新兴的文化旅游、文创产品等领域，景德镇均取得了令人瞩目的成就。这些重大成果充分证明了版权制度在推动景德镇经济转型升级中的不可或缺性。

展望未来，景德镇在版权保护与运用的征途上将持续探索与前行。面对新时代的挑战与机遇，景德镇将坚定不移地加强版权制度建设，以更加开放的姿态拥抱创新，加强版权与科技、文化、经济的深度融合，不断提升城市的国际知名度与影响力。以版权为引擎，景德镇将全力驱动全市高质量发展，确保其在全球陶瓷与文化创意产业的版图中始终保持领先地位，绘写更加辉煌的篇章。

综上所述，本章通过对理论基础、评价体系、实际成效及未来展望的深入剖析，全面展现了版权制度对景德镇全方位发展的深远影响。版权的有效运用，不仅为景德镇的经济文化繁荣注入了强劲动力，还为其在全球舞台上赢得了更高的赞誉，为其未来的可持续发展奠定了坚如磐石的基础。

结论：经验与启示

景德镇通过城市高质量发展过程中的系列规划、部署和举措，构建起来的全方位的版权制度、体制和机制，不断优化完善的版权创造、运用、保护、管理和服务体系，为全国甚至是全球其他城市探索如何通过版权助推城市高质量发展提供了可供参考的经验，形成了可复制、可推广、可借鉴的版权助推城市、文化和产业高质量发展的景德镇"时代样板"。

经验一　立破并举，构建完备的版权制度体系

当前，传统生产要素的比较优势逐渐减弱，制度供给成为重要的核心竞争力。景德镇围绕版权这一核心要素，在版权保护、创造、激励以及公共服务、产业等方面，构建了"地方性法规—政府规章—规范性文件"这一层次分明且实施有力的政策法规体系，不断推动版权制度精细化、时代化、特色化，优化版权保护环境，激发创新创造活力，推进版权治理体系和治理能力现代化。

出台系列地方性法规。景德镇于 2018 年 5 月起施行的《景德镇市御窑厂遗址保护管理条例》，是景德镇第一部历史文化保护类地方性法规，标志着御窑厂遗址保护管理工作走上法治轨道。2022 年 1 月起施行的《景德镇市陶瓷文化传承创新条例》，为试验区建设提供重要的法治保障，对保护好传承好利用好景德镇优秀陶瓷文化、发挥文化对产业转型升级的积极作用、协调推进区域高质量发展具有重要意义。2008 年 12 月施行的《景德镇陶瓷知识产权保护办法》即将修订，以适应新时代陶瓷知识产权保护的现实需求。

制定系列版权规章制度。出台《景德镇版权发展战略（2020—2025）》《景德镇市版权保护与运营三年行动计划（2021—2023）》等规章制度，旨在健全完善顶层设计、强化景德镇市知识产权保护力度、激发景德镇市各版权创造主体活力、完善景德镇市版权公共服务管理体系，让景德镇版权更有"亮度"，推动景德镇版权产业又好又快发展。出台《景德镇版权示范单位和示范园区认定办法》《景德镇市版权创新创造指导办法》《景德镇市优秀版权作品评选奖励制度》《景德镇市版权产业扶持办法》《景德镇市艺术陶瓷从业主体税收征收管理试行

办法》等，旨在创新知识产权管理与服务、提升知识产权创造质量、扩大知识产权运用效益、支持全面创新，让景德镇版权更有"温度"的"个性化"激励扶持制度，加强产业政策、金融政策等与版权相关产业有效对接，并促进版权创造与运用。出台《景德镇陶瓷知识产权保护办法》《景德镇市知识产权陶瓷技术调查官管理办法》，旨在推进版权保护工作，营造良好的版权保护政策环境，维护好景德镇陶瓷产业"金字招牌"，打造陶瓷版权司法保护"精品特色"，破解陶瓷侵权司法实践"现实困境"，让景德镇更有"力度"的版权保护制度切实解决权利人的维权困难。

制定系列版权规范性文件。景德镇国家陶瓷文化传承创新试验区建设领导小组办公室出台《景德镇国家陶瓷文化传承创新试验区建设工作要点》，扎实推进陶瓷文化传承创新，对版权护航陶瓷产业持续健康发展、陶瓷文化助推经济高质量发展和城市现代化建设发挥重要作用。景德镇市委、市政府制定《景德镇国家陶瓷文化传承创新试验区四年行动计划（2021—2025年）》，旨在突出保护传承、让文化活起来，突出创新升级、让产业强起来，突出融合发展、让旅游旺起来，突出引育用流、让人才聚起来。景德镇市文旅局于2021年发布的

昌南碗集活动（景德镇国家陶瓷版权交易中心供图　胡燕飞摄影）

《版权保护工作指南》，为陶瓷企业、艺术家、工作室和其他市场主体提供了详实清晰的版权保护行动指南和维权指导。

经验二　涤旧生新，版权助推产业结构转型升级

景德镇坚持以创建和建设"全国版权示范城市"为抓手，充分发挥版权示范企业、示范园区、示范基地的助推作用，通过版权研发、新业态培育、金融扶持等措施，推动版权产业高质量发展。

一是版权提升了陶瓷文化产业品质。版权示范城市建设过程中，全市70多家陶瓷企业成立了研发中心，加强陶瓷产品的研发能力，极大提升了陶瓷文化产业发展的核心竞争力。

二是版权助力了陶瓷文化业态创新。景德镇市商务局与抖音、京东、快手、淘宝、天猫等平台开展战略合作，取得陶瓷直播带货平台经营权，"短视频＋电商＋直播"等新业态发展迅猛，占比显著提升。此外，景德镇市还举办各类版权交易活动，促进版权成果的转化和运用，为版权产业的繁荣发展奠定了坚实基础。由景德镇市城投集团主办、景德镇国家陶瓷版权交易中心承办的"2023昌南碗集"活动，不仅为游客提供了一次丰富多彩的夜生活体验，更从"艺术＋音乐＋集市"角度，为推广版权意识、展示版权成果进行了一次有益尝试。景德镇国家陶瓷版权交易中心作为陶瓷产业和版权经济发展的助推者，始终致力于营造鼓励创新、保护版权的良好社会氛围，积极探索推动陶瓷产业创造性转化、创新性发展的新模式、新路径。

三是版权促进了陶瓷文化产业运营优化。2023年，中国人民银行景德镇市中心支行以版权为审贷依据，联合版权管理部门创新推出"产权质押贷"产品，为36户已具备一定经营规模的成长型"景漂"企业提供信贷支持5302万元；以陶瓷技术职称为审贷依据，创新"瓷都陶艺贷"产品，为73户拥有陶瓷艺术专业职称、荣誉称号或在高校艺术专业任职的成熟型"景漂"人才增加授信金额5675万元。自2020年起，景德镇农商行构建由"百福・陶瓷版权贷""百福・创客景漂贷""百福・小微流水信用贷"等30余款产品所组成的立体化陶瓷金融产品矩阵，满足各阶层客户多样融资需求；建立"5+2""白＋黑"快速

风险评估评审通道，开辟有速度的贷款申办渠道，缩短先进陶瓷企业贷款审批链条。此外，景德镇农商行还在景德镇国家陶瓷版权交易中心平台上，持续推进版权质押融资，为陶瓷企业和陶瓷从业人员量身定制"陶瓷版权贷"，以科技赋能为核心，打造"线上＋线下"双渠道发力的快捷便民版权金融服务生态链。

经验三　法护瓷兴，打造高效的版权维权机制

景德镇以陶瓷文化版权保护为突破口，创新版权保护方式方法，构建版权行政管理、司法审判、社会服务三位一体的版权全链条保护体系。在具体做法上，景德镇市成立知识产权法庭、知识产权保护中心、陶瓷版权快速维权中心、版权服务站等，通过文化执法、公安等部门的快速联动，建立版权确权登记、举报受理、鉴定执法、侵权处理等陶瓷版权维权体系。同时，通过加强多元主体的协同保护，进一步加大陶瓷版权保护力度，提高陶瓷版权维权水平。

一是版权行政保护持续推进，并有效落实行政调解司法确认机制和跨区域执法合作。在全国版权示范城市创建之初，景德镇市文化市场综合执法支队就高度重视侵权盗版类的版权执法案件，以满足陶瓷创作者的版权行政维权需求。景德镇持续开展的打击网络侵权盗版"剑网"行动、冬奥版权保护行动、青少年版权保护工作等专项行动成效显著。

2021 年至 2022 年，景德镇市在专项行动中检查各类场所 698 次，出动执法人员 1400 余人次，文化执法队伍行政调解版权纠纷 15 起，处罚 5 件、移送 3 件。2016 年至今，景德镇市文化综合执法支队持续强化对版权侵权案件的打击整治，不断加强文化综合执法中的版权执法力量，并采取有效措施提升版权行政执法的实效性和针对性。景德镇于 2022 年开始施行版权行政调解司法确认机制，通过"行政调解＋司法确认"，即以法院司法确认双方当事人行政调解协议的有效，来化解当事人之间的知识产权（版权）纠纷，体现了行政与司法工作的有效衔接，对完善知识产权纠纷多元调解机制和提升版权调解的实效性具有重要意义。此外，基于网络盗版侵权案件的跨区域性较强，景德镇市还与周边地区开展跨区域执法合作，共同打击侵权盗版行为，维护了良好的版权生态。

二是版权司法持续发力，立足陶瓷版权特色解决版权纠纷。2021 年至 2023

"景德镇制"地理标志（景德镇市市场监督管理局供图）

年，景德镇市有知识产权管辖权的景德镇知识产权法庭和珠山区人民法院受理的版权纠纷案件共分别为237件、276件和392件，为"景德镇制"地理标志，先进工业陶瓷、文化艺术陶瓷、高端日用瓷等瓷器产业提供了强有力的司法保护，形成了具有地方特色的陶瓷知识产权司法保护工作机制。

景德镇知识产权法庭立足景德镇实际，以陶瓷知识产权保护为重心，深耕陶瓷文化，积极推进涉陶瓷案件专业化、规范化、集约化审理，做到严保护、大保护、快保护、同保护。

三是版权多主体协同保护，营造良好社会氛围。景德镇做到了"保护不是将文化遗产束之高阁，不是把它们锁在保险箱里秘不示人，最好的保护是让文化走进人们的日常生活、浸润人们的精神世界"[1]。景德镇市版权协会从团体标准化工作视角，为版权服务体系建立了新标准；政企协同打造的陶溪川版权服务站以版权登记、管理服务推动企业孵化运营，为版权服务体系开创了新局面；景德镇皇窑陶瓷艺术博物馆等多个机构以青少年研学活动为载体，为版权服务体系谱写了新篇章；景德镇多位女性陶瓷企业家从女性视角宣讲版权，为版权服务体系注入了新灵魂。在景德镇，大到协会、公益组织等各个团体，小到企业、个人等各个市场主体，都在发挥自己的力量将版权保护融入各自的事业当中。此外，特别值得一提的是，景德镇市知识产权保护中心已经于2022年正式揭牌成立，现阶段保护中心的重点工作依然放在专利协同保护与商标协同保护方面，接下来保护中心计划把版权协同保护一并纳入工作任务当中，将积累的专利与商标协同保护经验直接运用在版权协同保护工作上，探索出更为有效的版权协同保护机制。

---

① 《将文化资源转化为发展优势（连线评论员·推动长江经济带高质量发展④）》，http://yn.people.com.cn/BIG5/n2/2023/1020/c372441-40609987.html，访问日期：2023年12月11日。

经验四　钟灵毓秀，版权优化人文社会环境氛围

景德镇持续打造良好版权生态。景德镇以陶瓷文化资源为核心，彰显独特的城市人文风貌。在此过程中，除了需要依靠陶瓷文化的传承，更需要依赖陶瓷文化的革新，才能实现"千年瓷都"与"创意城市"相融合的人文环境营造。景德镇的陶瓷文化是鲜活的，人们对于这座城市的认同不仅来自景德镇悠久的陶瓷历史，还源于景德镇是一座能一直孕育出陶瓷艺术家和陶瓷作品的艺术之都。应建立起全民接纳的版权生态系统，培育起全民版权意识。景德镇市连续多年以塑造尊重知识、崇尚创新、诚信守法、公平竞争的知识产权文化理念为目标，营造出了良好的创新氛围和创新生态，也逐渐激励起全民创新热潮，优秀的陶瓷创客、艺术家和"景漂"等人才源源不断涌入。

景德镇构建起内容新颖、形式多样、融合发展的版权传播矩阵。内容新颖、形式多样的大众传播，有利于知识产权文化的快速、准确传播，"细雨润无声"地让大众感受、接受。[①]景德镇充分利用公共宣传资源，增强版权宣传的创新性和针对性，打造面向不同群体的版权宣传品牌，使版权知识家喻户晓，形成人人关心、人人皆可参与版权工作的良好局面。一是景德镇通过多元形式宣传版

高校学生开展版权志愿服务（景德镇市版权局供图）

---

① 蔡莹：《建设促进高质量发展的人文社会环境》，《中国知识产权报》2021 年 12 月 15 日。

版权进校园活动（景德镇市版权局供图）

权知识，增强全社会的版权意识，营造良好的人文环境氛围。在"2022 景德镇版权宣传周"期间，全市范围内开展了形式多样的宣传活动。主办方不仅安排了 2022 版权作品展和版权集市供市民、嘉宾参观，还开展了"活力 激情 创新 发展"版权交流论坛及 NFT 数字推广演示活动。同时，景德镇市文化市场综合执法支队专门制作了版权知识宣传手册和宣传展板，将版权相关知识汇编成册向市民分发，并通过设置咨询服务台的形式，现场为市民答疑解惑。[①] 通过宣传工作下沉园区、企业、校园等场所，增强社会公众对版权的认知和理解。二是景德镇市以"中国国际版权博览会""瓷博会"等各种展会、版权微信公众号、版权征文和演讲等活动为平台，通过广播电视、报纸杂志、网站网页等传播途径，将版权宣传纳入创建"国家卫生城市""全国文明城市"的公益宣传当中，展现版权保护与产业发展成果。景德镇市还通过举办研讨会、拍摄有关版权工作成果的公益片等形式进行大力宣传，发动高校知识产权等相关专业学生作为版权宣传志愿者或形象大使，扩大版权宣传力度和受众面，提升版权社会影响。

---

① 《创建东亚文化之都——市文化市场综合执法支队参加"2022 景德镇版权宣传周"活动》。

中与特色产业：
景德镇故事

景德镇营造更加开放、更加积极、更有活力的版权人才发展环境。一是全方位、全覆盖培养培训版权人才。景德镇市积极组织版权管理人员进行业务培训、组织企业内部进行知识产权流动式讲座、组织执法人员进行执法业务专题培训，将版权教育纳入景德镇干部教育培训、公务员能力培训计划，使干部队伍成为尊重版权、保护版权的组织者和带头人。景德镇市还重点关注青少年版权教育工作，在青少年中开展版权宣讲，组织学生参与版权知识问答等教育活动，从小培养他们的版权保护意识。二是多举措、多渠道引进版权创造、运用、保护、服务和管理人才。景德镇市持续加大高层次人才引进力度，把版权人才引进纳入急需紧缺人才目录。引导支持版权优势企业面向省内外，以调动、岗位聘用、项目聘任、客座邀请、兼职、定期服务、项目合作等形式，引进或使用版权人才及其团队。充分发挥优势企业人才集聚功能，通过提供优惠的人才政策，在住房、医疗、子女教育等方面，开辟高层次人才绿色服务通道，打造版权人才高地。三是多层次、多方式建立人才激励机制。景德镇市采用开辟专题栏目等形式宣传先进典型，定期开展选拔评比，加大奖励力度，形成鼓励人才干事业、支持人才干事业、帮助人才干好事业的良好氛围。

景德镇在追求卓越、推动城市高质量发展的征途中，采取了诸多关键性策略，尤其聚焦于精心策划与不断优化的版权制度框架，以此促成陶瓷文化产业的创新浪潮与繁荣景象。通过一系列匠心独特的地方性法规的深入贯彻，以及多领域主体间高效协同的版权保护机制的稳固构建，景德镇不仅为陶瓷产业筑起了坚固的版权保护防线，更孕育了一个充满勃勃生机与无限创意的版权生态圈。

在这一保护与创新双轮驱动的发展模式下，景德镇的陶瓷产业被赋予了新生，绽放出前所未有的璀璨光芒，每一件作品都承载着文化的深厚底蕴与创新的独特灵魂。景德镇的这一成功实践，不仅为其自身的持续繁荣注入了不竭动力，更为全国乃至全球范围内的城市提供了一个可资借鉴的典范。这一宝贵经验，恰似历经时光洗礼的陶瓷艺术品，愈发光彩夺目。它不仅照亮了景德镇的发展之路，更以其独特的魅力，引领着未来文化产业发展的方向，绽放出引领时代潮流的万丈光芒。

附录一

调研陶瓷企业名录

景德镇陶文旅控股集团有限公司

景德镇陶邑文化发展有限公司

景德镇市瑞牛文化科技有限公司

景德镇红叶陶瓷股份有限公司

景德镇富玉青花玲珑陶瓷有限公司

深圳市国瓷永丰源瓷业有限公司景德镇分公司

景德镇玉柏瓷业有限公司

景德镇青花故事陶瓷文化发展有限公司

景德镇皇窑陶瓷有限公司

景德镇嘉加陶瓷有限公司

清和陶瓷（景德镇）有限公司

景德镇华德乐库陶瓷有限公司

景德镇雨秋陶瓷有限公司

景德镇常青家园工艺品有限公司

…………

调研实录（节选）

一、瑞牛公司调研实录

访谈时间：2023 年 8 月

访谈地点：瑞牛公司

访谈对象：瑞牛公司负责人段建平

（1）问：您有着十余年的媒体从业经验，且已经在传媒行业有了一定的影响力，为什么选择改变人生职业呢？您创建陶瓷公司的契机和想法是什么？

答：景德镇有着两千多年的陶瓷历史，这是一座陶瓷之城，这座城市里的每个人都与陶瓷有着不解之缘。我以前是景德镇《瓷都晚报》总编辑，在工作过程中，我常与艺术家、设计师、陶瓷工匠交流。在景德镇从事传媒行业最主要的是讲好陶瓷的故事。当决定要来创业的时候，自然而然地选择陶瓷，陶瓷相当于景德镇的基因，在我心中留下深刻烙印。

（2）问：景德镇陶瓷行业竞争压力极大，如何在众多陶瓷公司当中脱颖而出，并做大做强？

答：景德镇的企业＋作坊式的工作室超过 1 万，那么在这个行业竞争如此激烈的时候，该走哪条路是我们的选择之路。其实，在 2015 年创业期间，我们注册了景德镇市景德闲云居陶瓷有限公司。2015—2019 年，闲云居做的行业也是手工制瓷，中高端、精致的瓷器。品牌理念是"原创设计，艺术生活"，希望艺术走进生活，将设计融入生活。想要把景德镇陶瓷做得更加亲民，更多的人够分享到精致的瓷器（窑口），我们制作的茶具具有文人雅气，均价4000多元。实话说，在2015—2019年，我们闲云居有限公司与其他同行的经营方式撞车了，并未打造强大的设计团队，做的产品特色也并没有凸显出来。所以我们在2019年决定再出发，成立了子公司瑞牛文化科技有限公司（以下简称：瑞牛）。瑞牛的主要任务是定制化产品，要通过景德镇里面的各个元素，艺术家、设计师、陶瓷工匠都融入进来。艺术家有审美高度，对艺术有理解（瑞牛品牌的审美标准）；我们要通过设计师来实现定制化，我们现在拥有自由设计师16名（占企业总人员的1/3），我们也有签约设计师，还即将签约一名英国皇家设计师。这些设计师需要深入了解景德镇的制瓷工艺；陶瓷工匠把东西做到极致（"非遗"），是技艺的理念。我们专注创新与创意设计，快速了解客户需求，形成创意型、服务型（服务型制造）企业。最后，设计要强大，研发要高效，供应链（管理）要多而密。文化创业公司的核心竞争力是柔性供应链，立足景德镇，辐射产业区，面向全中国。各个类别都有专业化的供应链管理模式，供应链的管理模式更加高效、非常迅速，营造了很好良性循环的生态。瑞牛与景德镇多家企业有合作，为这些企业提供了很多合作的机会。其中，有一个专注出口的陶瓷贸易公司实现合作转型，从完全出口到部分出口、部分内销的转型，我们定制化的服务，让这个专注外贸的企业想要在国内市场立足提供了更好的靶向和机会。最后，我们瑞牛公司的企业理念是专注于创意设计，真正形成创意型、服务型（服务型制造）企业。

（3）问："城市礼物"创意迸发的灵感来源是什么？"城市礼物"享有盛名，发生过侵权抄袭案件吗？贵公司的解决方案是什么？或者说，贵公司是否遇到过侵权案件？如何维权？以及是否有相关的部门负责？

答："城市礼物"是我们2021年向全球发出的征集令，也是当年瓷博会的一大创新亮点。通过城市礼物这个创意，让更多人更好地了解景德镇。我们的企业能胜出，代表了我们企业、产品和创意对城市的独特理解和贡献。其实，在"城市礼物"征集的前半年，我们已经设计了"福如意"这一大特色产品。当福如意遇到城市礼物，是我们企业的机遇和机会。"福如意"是中华传统文化传承创新发展在陶瓷上的展现，能让中国馆藏博物馆以及藏品再创造、再出发、再开发，真正把握住了"守正创新、赓续传承"的理念，把握住了现代理念的潮流，设计创新、研发创新，让文物活起来。

现如今，我们还没有打过一场知识产权官司，我们没有精力去耗费大量时间去打持久战。我们一直在发展创新，只有发展创新才是我们企业发展的核心竞争力。只有在侵权影响到了我们生存发展时，我们才会拿起法律的武器保护自己。我们现在有专门的法务，还签约了广东的版权律师来负责知识产权，尤其是版权这一块儿的布局和保护。目前，我们公司有版权1000多件、专利100多件。

（4）问：贵公司被评为全国版权示范单位，你们的版权管理经验是什么？

答：我们公司是2021年省级版权示范单位、2022年全国版权示范单位。首先，需要感谢行政主管部门的慧眼识珠。其次，我们企业其实每天都在做版权管理。版权与企业的发展理念和管理方向非常契合。因为有版权的保护，版权的标杆，让企业如虎添翼。现如今，国家倡导的主流方向与企业发展的方向高度契合，不谋而合。

（5）问：贵公司以创意研发为主，在发展过程中，是否遇到过瓶颈期？贵公司是如何度过这一尴尬期的？

答：经济发展的不确定性，经济下行的趋势，让实体经济面临了严峻的考验，肯定会碰到一定的阻力。我们更担心和关心我们的合作商供应链的生态平衡，希望合作的供应链都能安稳发展，才能更好地互利合作，才能实现我们公司的差异化竞争目标，真正做到定制规模化。我们瑞牛的理念是"传千年艺，创当代美"。陶瓷文创的定制化，真正做到了用中国文化符号服务全球知名品牌。例如，现在已经达成合作的有海蓝之谜、雅诗兰黛、百度、阿里、吉利、极氪等知名品牌。

二、陶溪川文创街区调研实录

1. 大学生创业群

调研时间：2022 年 11 月

调研地点：陶溪川

调研对象：大学生创业群

（1）问：所有的作品都是自己原创设计的吗？

答：是的，全部都是自己设计的，包括陶瓷上的文字也都是自己写的。

（2）问：是否了解版权？是从什么渠道了解的？

答：了解，之前有作品投展了前段时间的阿拉伯知识展。

（3）问：现有作品是否做了版权登记？未来是否会考虑？

答：我们目前没有做登记，这也是我们第一次来陶溪川出摊，未来会考虑，这是对自己的一种保护。

（4）问：身边有发生过版权侵权的事件吗？如何维护自身权益？

答：有的，他们会做一些简单的改变，量产也很快投入销售了。目前，主要采取社交平台、媒体方式进行声讨，比如，小红书等。一般不会考虑到诉讼，相对而言，时间战线太长，性价比也不太高。

（5）问：通过媒体这类方式维护自身权益，问题得到解决了吗？

答：不算得到解决，只是通过宣传的方式，让公众感受到"清者自清"。

（6）问：对景德镇的印象如何呢？（受采者是外地人）

答：景德镇是一座年轻人很多的城市，很有发展空间。陶瓷其实很吸引年轻人，陶瓷现在的形式多样化，创作发挥空间很大，可以有很多不一样的想法，不再拘泥于以前古朴的风格。即便是同一种器型号，哪怕是一个普通的盖碗，都会有很多不同的创意，这都会给我们带来了很多灵感和启发。

2. "景德想器"经营者

调研时间：2022 年 11 月

调研地点：陶溪川

调研对象："景德恕器"经营者

（1）问：所有的作品都是自己原创设计的吗？

答：有一些是仿古器型。比如，这一套古窑，就是按照1：1定制的，虽然没有任何装饰，但一点也不逊色于同类产品，有的虽然做得非常富丽堂皇，但没有这种单色釉的器具经典好看。越质朴的东西反而越美。古窑的生产周期非常短，记载在案的只有67件。其他的都是我们自己设计的。

（2）问：现有作品是否申请版权登记了？

答：这幅作品我们申请了外观设计专利，版权暂时没有。

（3）问：市场上是否有人仿冒您的作品？

答：我不太管这个事情，没有这个概念，抄袭肯定是有的，这个也不可避免。

（4）问：后续是否会考虑将自己的作品申报版权呢？

答：更倾向于申请外观设计专利。

3. 工作室创客赵女士

调研时间：2023年8月

调研地点：陶溪川

调研对象：陶溪川工作室创客赵女士

（1）问：您是景德镇人吗？为什么会选择来到景德镇？

答：不是，我是外地人。大学是在这边上的，陶大陶艺专业，个人也比较喜欢陶瓷，就留在了这里创业。

（2）问：为什么没有选择像德化这样的其他陶瓷城市？

答：个人比较熟悉景德镇，创业成本相对较低，景德镇名声很大，优势较大。

（3）问：您目前有没有版权登记的证书？您是把所有的作品都进行了申请吗？

答：这些都是有证书的。但是没有全部申请，因为太多了。登记了自己比较喜欢的部分作品。

（4）问：为什么会选择陶瓷专业，是因为家里有人从事这份工作吗？

答：没有。自己选择的，因为热爱。我的朋友有一部分留在景德镇创业了，因为大家都是喜欢陶瓷也只会做陶瓷，也有从事其他行业的。

（5）问：那您这些创意是有什么灵感来源吗？

答：每个都来源于生活。比如，夏天到了，就会根据今年流行的颜色之类的进行设计。

（6）问：你们都是自己设计、自己烧制作品吗？

答：对。

（7）问：在景德镇，如果您有了自己的创意，是可以找专人帮忙制作陶瓷的，对吗？

答：对，景德镇这边分工很明确，你只要会其中一个环节就可以完成创作。例如，只会画画，可以成为画工，可以把设计图案交给他人。

（8）问：版权登记工作是您自己主动去做的，还是陶瓷工作站要求您去做的？您了解工作站平时的服务内容吗？

答：版权服务站工作人员会过来进行版权宣传，会指导和帮助我们完成版权登记，所以我就在他们的引导下登记了。如果想要进行版权登记，可以把图片发在群里面联系他们，版权服务站的工作人员看到以后就会指导你怎么去做、需要提供什么，最后他们会帮我们提交材料。从提交材料到最后拿到证书，大概一个月不到就能完成。

（9）问：版权服务站的工作人员平时会来巡查，做一些管理性的活动吗？每一个摊位都会管吗？

答：会有。主要是来了解情况，询问我们是否需要帮助，或帮我们进行版权登记，也会帮你进行一些宣传。他们的工作性质类似于巡检。比如，过来了看到你没有（登记），他就会过来和你说一下。我是从外边的摊位来到邑空间的，来邑空间需要提供的材料比摆摊的要多。首先，先需要证明自己是35周岁以下大学生，其次是工作室的性质、登记证书，（说明你的作品是）原创，他们会现场审核。如果只是申请外边摊位，就只用提交一下产品图、毕业证的照片，主要还是看产品。

（10）问：您之前在摆摊的时候除了摊位就是待在工作室吗？您的工作室开了几年了？从外边的摊位到邑空间，您花费了多少时间？

答：工作室是从2020年开始运作的。从外边的摊位到邑空间我没有花费很长时间，一年多，这个时间算比较快的。前期除了摆摊，其余的时间都在工作室做工艺品，得更新。当我有了稳定客户，就主动申报了邑空间，都是主动申报的。版权服务站如果觉得你的产品很好，卖得很好，就会进行一定程度的客观介入，询问你是否入驻店铺。

（11）问：您认为入驻陶溪川之后对您的创业生涯有没有什么影响？

答：收入增加，客源增加。

（12）问：您原创的这些耳环目前有没有侵权问题存在？

答：目前没有，我不太会去刻意寻找侵权，但是作为原创会很在意，有人告知的话就会去关注侵权。目前并没有去维权，因为担心用法律介入时间会很长，成本比较高，浪费时间精力。目前没有了解快维中心。我认为别人的抄袭速度跟不上作品的更新速度。目前经历过好几起，但是都没有去维权。一是很麻烦；二是我不是很在意，我认为自己有更新的能力。

（13）问：您如何看待您的竞争力？您这边有什么筛选机制吗？

答：竞争确实激烈。看情况，有时候一个月也会筛选一次。是这边的负责人，管理陶溪川这边的人来筛选，根据营业额、对店铺上心程度和产品更新速度，因为是创业，一定会有更新，人员流动很大，如果不提升很容易被筛掉。我们会有60%的补助，也没有其他额外的费用。主要是运营费上的补助，店铺是1000元一个月，补助60%，每个月只交400元。三个月会换一个位置，费用是400元，水电费还有优惠，补助很好。

（14）问：在您拿到版权登记证之后，他们会不会给什么补助或者奖励？提交材料的过程是否会很烦琐？

答：没有。在办理登记过程中，不收受理费。提交材料也不是很烦琐，他们都会提前说明具体需要什么材料。刚起步的时候，将材料给服务站工作人员，他们会帮忙线上操控，后面量大了，就变成咨询式解决了。

（15）问：您一开始提到的景德镇这座城市创业成本比较低，您是在比较之后得出的结论吗？

答：我曾经也在北京待过，也在其他地方工作过一段时间。从生产成本而言，景德镇的成本就很低，因为它是很多原材料的生产地，我在其他城市还涉及运输成本，这边产业链很全。再加上房租很低，生活成本低，很方便。当我这边出画面，可以直接找工厂，还有卖颜料的画工，我可能就是一张图纸给对方，他就能给我做出来，沟通成本很低。

4. 陶溪川创客赖先生

调研时间：2023 年 8 月

调研地点：陶溪川邑空间

调研对象：陶溪川创客赖先生

（1）问：这些都是你们做的？

答：对。从泥巴到成品，都是我们亲力亲为，源头都是从图纸画起的。

（2）问：您为什么来景德镇？

答：我比较喜欢陶瓷，觉得陶瓷的可能性很多，既可以画画、雕塑，也可以做日用瓷，做纯摆件，纯做传统艺术、当代艺术，景德镇的魅力就是因为这座城市的可能性很多。

（3）问：景德镇的创业成本会低一些吗？

答：直接创作的成本很高，很多人觉得泥巴很便宜，但是在制作过程之中还有很多道工序，耗费过大；而且作为年轻人，审美不到也不会了解陶瓷。但是生活成本低，并且景德镇陶瓷制作已经形成了产业化。

（4）问：现在是有了自己的工作室吗？作品登记您是自己主动申请的吗？

答：有。我是有自己的工作室。作品登记是我自己主动申请的。

（5）问：您是担心被侵权吗？

答：不全是。我主动进行作品登记有很多原因，我是明确要成为设计师的，因此，我需要通过作品来实现知名度的积累。况且，申请作品登记的数据可以帮助大家形成原创性保护的意识，我个人是赞成作品登记制度的，很方便我们做事情；登记可以鼓励创作、激励创作，也方便我们用法律保护自己的版权。

（6）问：这几年您的创作一直以猫为主题吗？

答：也不算，它只是我其中的小门类而已。我会的东西不止这些，所以我的版权证书很多。

（7）问：拥有工作室之前您是在外边摆摊吗？

答：是的，入驻独立工作室之前是要先摆摊的，我摆了两年摊，这个审核流程还是蛮长的。

（8）问：入驻前和入驻后，您觉得有什么区别？

答：当然是有区别的，在这里和在外边摆摊，相当于就是换了种思维。在这里摆，一个是要有作品看，就是我会要求自己把做好的作品带到这里，至少做到有真作品可以看吧，因为这就代表着你跟别人不一样了。不一样也就代表你才能申请版权。如果你的作品跟别人的作品一样，也申请不了版权，或者随意抄袭拼接，也过不了审核的。

（9）问：版权工作站的工作人员，平时会和你们有工作上的对接吗？

答：我在申请的时候（会）去。他是这样，就是任何一个作者有需求，找到版权工作站的人，他们都会一笔一笔按流程教你怎么去做。你知道流程之后，自己直接拍照上传就可以了，而且他们现在审核很快。有一次我上午上传作品，中午就审核完了，效率还蛮高的。现在也有很多年纪很大的大师也开始申请版权了，开始重视版权了。

（10）问：那您这几年在创作过程中，有从别人的作品那里获得灵感吗？灵感来源是什么？

答：创作和我们的生活是断不开的，就比如我朋友有猫，我做的第一只猫作品，就是以他养的那几只猫为原型。在那之后我就不用看那些猫了，自己在这儿就可以凭空捏出来。所以每个作品都不一样，创作灵感都跟我的生活是分不开的。

（11）问：您认为在您的事业上，陶瓷、景德镇对于您而言，意味着什么？

答：我每个时期对它的看法是不一样的。每个时期关注的点也是不一样的。比如，某个时期我想画画，就会关注画画；这段时间我研究材料，就会关注材料。可以理解为学习还有很大的进步空间，瓷器有材料科学和艺术科学两个门类，艺术它不仅有古代的还有当代的，还有未来的；在材料科学方面，景德镇古陶瓷到现在融合了全国各地的工艺、材料科学在其中。（艺术科学）材料科学都够你研究一辈子，而陶瓷就是二者相结合的。所以为什么瓷器是最贵的。但是也会出现一个问题——陶瓷贵是因为它材料贵还是因为它艺术价值高？它的研究空间是很大的。我们这代人会面临两个问题，任务很重，艺术、材料兼具，才是真正的陶艺家。

（12）问：我们在外边采访摊主的时候，他们就会觉得自己有创作瓶颈。您有没有什么建议给他们？

答：这是很多创客都会遇到的问题，但是这个问题给不了答案，只能自己摸索，这与自己的知识储备、眼界，包括学习艺术的追求有很大的关系。每个人的追求不一样，就会导致他们的高度不一样。

三、景德镇知识产权法庭调研实录

访谈时间：2023 年 8 月

访谈地点：景德镇市知识产权法庭

访谈对象：知识产权法庭林庭长、知识产权法庭但法官

（1）问：从知识产权法庭成立至今的知识产权案件数据、涉瓷知识产权案件数据、涉瓷版权案件数据有多少？

答：知识产权案件数据、涉瓷知识产权案件数据、涉瓷版权案件数据随后发送电子版。但其实我们这边涉瓷案例并不是特别多。因为，首先，景德镇人民维权意识还不算特别强；其次，由于管辖规则为原告就被告住所地、侵权行为发生地，基本上都是别人起诉景德镇市人的案件才在景德镇市知识产权法庭。

其实，这表明了景德镇市人民的原创意识比较强，以原创为主。

（2）问：从司法保护与行政执法协同保护，从快速维护中心视角，法院承担什么样的职责？

答：法院与知识产权保护中心共同协作，法院管辖专利、商标、软件著作权等类型有技术壁垒，法官只靠法律思维是很难解决纠纷的。这个时候，需要借助技术调查官的职能来架起法律与技术之间的桥梁。有关技术类的案子，我们法院就会委托知识产权保护中心出具技术报告（法院参考）。知识产权保护中心也属于调解组织的范畴，知识产权保护中心可以就案件进行调解，知识产权法庭可以就其进行司法确认，达到高效的保护。法庭与市场监督管理局、文旅局开展联席会议，各机关组织就知识产权事项相互学习交流；且每个知识产权宣传周都是联合起来共同举办活动，以扩大影响力。

（3）问：司法与行政衔接上的优势做法有哪些？

答：我们主要邀请了技术调查官。这些技术调查官主要来自大学、机关单位、陶瓷研究所。首批技术调查官主要是陶瓷类的技术调查官。想要以陶瓷为精品品牌（主要是保护本土品牌）。我们每年在大走访、大调研司法活动调研当中，会发现有恶意诉讼的问题，我们一般会给予相应的对策和知识普及。

（4）问：请谈谈知识产权法庭单独成立的优势与展望。

答：以陶瓷为切入点，打造全国示范的知识产权法庭，建设以陶瓷为主体的司法保护示范高地。

四、陶溪川版权服务站调研实录

访谈时间：2023 年 8 月

访谈地点：陶溪川版权服务站

访谈对象：版权服务站工作人员徐女士、袁女士

（1）问：请问您可以介绍一下陶溪川服务站的基本情况吗？

答：陶溪川版权服务站于 2019 年成立，由陶溪川管理机构推动，2019 年

收到市里指令，与市里版权中心对接，给创客进行版权的申请注册，起协助作用。版权中心提供绿色通道，其场所和人员均是陶文旅自己的，由省委宣传部批准。陶溪川版权服务站管理范围是陶然集＋邑空间＋邑画廊＋创意集市，景德镇其他地区的版权服务站并非陶文旅在做。

陶溪川版权服务站从 2015 年开始筹备，2016 年开始正式有创客入驻。2016—2019 年，还没有挂牌服务站的时候，我们就已经开始了版权服务工作；2019 年以后，我们才具备中介服务资质。在 2019 年之前一直没有绿色通道，相关的工作一直在开展，但速度比较慢，省里审核相关资料大概要 1 个月；现在陶溪川基本上当天就可以审核完成，最慢一周也可以完成。

（2）问：您认为为什么要在陶溪川设立版权服务站呢？

答：有自身需求的原因，也有完成上级指令的意思。我们的集市分为传统区和创意区，市场流动快，希望可以保护好创意产品，给创意孵化青年提供好的平台及更好的服务。

（3）问：版权服务中心工作重点具体有哪些？

答：版权咨询＋登记、登记申请（版权服务站进行初审，省局进行复审）、维权（版权争议时还有维权通道，这是快维中心的一部分，快速维护中心在陶溪川设置了一个点，有线索会提供到文化执法队）、宣传（座谈会）；入驻企业也被纳入版权服务站的管理范畴，一般附近入驻企业都会来此申请版权登记（常态化，辐射范围）。版权服务站的出勤、营收量可见，申请数量较大。因此，设立前期，工作量大。

（4）问：入驻陶溪川夜市有什么标准吗？

答：针对的均是手工艺、年轻态的孵化基地，提交申请入驻的人必须满足 35 周岁以下＋手工艺。

（5）问：您能介绍一下陶溪川夜市的基本情况吗？

答：陶溪川夜市大概分为三个部分：摊位集市、邑空间与邑画廊、工作室。从摊位到邑空间、邑画廊采用晋级制度，在集市摆摊至少要有 3 个月，质量较高有一定的销量、产量才可以入驻邑空间。具体情况如下。

首先，摊位集市分为传统区+创意区。一个月筛选一次，一周大概有1500个摊位容量，每周摊位人员会发生变动。每个月要大概审核通过4000多个摊位的申请，筛选出1500个摊位。之前申请过的没有快捷通道，2019年之前为线下纸质，现在为线上。设计师审核相关申请的审核量大概是2~3倍。其一，传统区。传统类的必须手作，大多创作品以模仿再现为主，相似度超60%，就不能申请（版权有自身检索比对库，江西省自己的比对库）。除此之外，还会通过淘宝电商平台自行比对。其二，创意区。创意类的要有自己的作品，从未申请过的，第一个月可以试摆，但是之后至少要有一份版权证书，审核质量再获批，普通集挂红伞、黄伞，用以区分。其三，创意区进阶版——设计师集。设计师队伍大概有70人，一个月筛选一次设计师队伍。被换掉的设计师可能会选择不继续申请。筛选方式大概是（创意区进阶版）约70位设计师进行自主投票。（设计师集摊位用白伞，且比普通集大很多）还有邑空间，入驻邑空间的数量是固定的。邑空间一楼入驻106家，每3个月淘汰一部分，进行筛选，具有流动性，请设计师队伍自主管理，自主投票。

（6）问：可以再深入介绍一下您刚刚提到的自治模式吗？

答：版权服务站，本身是带有行政管理意味的，因此不会自己审，否则有失公平；交给设计师集，专业水平达标，且可以相互学习交流，创客也非常乐意。设计师也是申请来的，普通集每经过1个月就可以申请来到设计师集，申请量也是2~3倍；对于邑空间而言，他们会建立管理委员会，3个月轮换一次。

（7）问：那维权工作进展如何呢？

答：维权我们做得比较少，频率较低。摊主投诉，与摊主之间线下协商，基本上能达到线下调解。接摊主举报，如真的存在抄袭情况，直接勒令下架。要求赔偿的情况目前较少，赔偿要通过执法大队。

（8）问：您方便透露一下咨询登记的流程和数量吗？

答：可以。一般传统类少有咨询登记；在创意类管理委员会管理人员或版权服务站工作人员询摊时，如遇还不错的会主动提出登记事宜，建议申报版权证明。上个月（7月）版权登记量有4000多份。

（9）问：开展的研学活动的受众群体和活动开展模式是什么呢？

答：受众群体一般是陶大等高校学生。开展模式一般是实习、讲座、春秋大集（每年7月份、10月份，国内外艺术家，八大美院，本地的），附近的学院都会派志愿者协助开展活动。我们还有一个国外驻厂项目——国际工作室，负责邀请国外艺术家，每个阶段都会有固定的国外艺术家入驻，通常3个月、6个月为一个周期，会给补助；产品研发、开设讲座、中外交流，都有自己专门的工作室。

五、洋景漂调研实录

访谈时间：2023年8月

访谈地点：陶溪川邑空间

访谈对象：新加坡陶艺家 Nelson Lim Sang Choon 林善春

（1）问：景德镇陶瓷对您意味着什么？

答：意味着历史的传承、整个中国的文化。对中国的哲学（如老子等）感兴趣，略有研究。

（2）问：您那么多著名的作品，有遭受过版权侵权吗？

答：没有，我做的作品类型很少有人涉及，现有的作品也并未申请版权保护。但是也会有人抄袭，但作为艺术家，作品完成后会公开展览，他人仿制，圈内人都会知道。考虑过以后为作品进行版权登记。

（3）问：您去了那么多国家，有没有感觉到中国（景德镇）与其他国家的区别？

答：景德镇的瓷文化氛围十分浓厚，与陶瓷息息相关，驻场氛围不像其他国家那样，（其他国家）只是驻场而没有与创作相关太多的元素。希望自己闲下心去多逛逛景德镇。

（4）问：您对景德镇烧瓷文化有所了解吗？您为什么会选择陶瓷这个行业呢？

答：我买了一本介绍景德镇民俗的书，有所了解。我读艺术学院时主修多媒体，大一时期需要修艺术学院的所有课程。在陶瓷课过程中，希望老师留多些时间来完成作品，与启蒙老师接触逐渐变多，对陶瓷的兴趣越发浓厚，在大二期间把主修专业换成陶瓷，毕业后也一直在从事陶瓷教学工作。

（5）问：您觉得景德镇或景德镇陶瓷未来发展走向是什么？

答：保持传统，不断创新，要有更高的包容度，去了解外来文化的输入，同时要守住自身的文化。传统瓷业应该一直会有市场，但是要看陶瓷的整体效果。自身的创作方向还在不断摸索。

（6）问：您对景德镇师傅带徒弟或子承父业这种技艺的传承有什么看法？

答：技艺公开和"留一手"两者有很大区别。如外国对于各种釉色的配比，网上会有配方，可以使更多的人不断进步。保守不利于创新，更希望存在一个开放包容的态度。

（7）问：对于年轻人对陶瓷文化不了解，对传统技艺文化不感兴趣，您有什么看法？

答：对于传统技艺要不断记录保存，老师的引导十分重要。尽量鼓励，以自身经历来激励年轻人。

附录三

景德镇建设全国版权示范城市大事记

2019 年 11 月，景德镇市获国家版权局批复同意创建全国版权示范城市；

2020 年 4 月，成立景德镇市陶瓷版权快速维权中心；

2020 年 9 月，国家版权局在景德镇市举办 2020 年全国版权示范工作培训班；

2020 年 11 月，景德镇陶溪川文创街区荣获"中国版权金奖·推广应用奖"；

2021 年 4 月，成立景德镇市版权协会；

2021 年 7 月，获批设立"景德镇国家陶瓷版权交易中心"；

2021 年 9 月，荣获"全国版权示范城市"称号，实现中部地区"全国版权示范城市"零的突破；

2022 年 1 月，景德镇传媒集团获批成为全国"区块链 + 版权"特色领域试点单位；

2022 年 6 月，景德镇昌南里陶瓷版权交易中心有限公司揭牌；

2022 年 7 月，举办"丝路瓷源　和光接物"陶瓷版权创意设计大赛；

2022 年 10 月，景德镇市获批开展世界知识产权组织版权保护优秀案例示范点调研项目"IP 与创意产业：景德镇故事"；

2022 年 11 月，国家版权局、世界知识产权组织在景德镇市举办 2022 国际版权论坛、版权产业国际风险防控培训班；

2022 年 12 月，第五届"阿拉伯艺术节"在景德镇市举办；

2023 年 4 月，景德镇陶邑文化发展有限公司荣获"2022 年度十大著作权人"称号；

2023 年 4 月，景德镇市版权局荣获"中国版权金奖·管理奖"；

2023 年 10 月，在中国景德镇国际陶瓷博览会期间举办 2023 景德镇文化创新发展论坛、版权助推城市高质量发展论坛；

2023 年 12 月，举办"瓷的旅程"——2023 景德镇国际陶瓷艺术双年展。

版权保护对景德镇陶瓷产业发展影响的调查问卷

尊敬的女士/先生：

您好！

您现在参加的是世界知识产权组织版权保护优秀案例示范建设项目"IP与创意产业：景德镇故事"的调查问卷。该调研对了解版权保护对景德镇陶瓷产业发展的影响，持续推进景德镇陶瓷版权保护体系完善，以及向全球推广景德镇陶瓷版权保护的有益经验有着深远意义。本调查不是专门针对企业的具体调查。感谢您的支持！

填表说明：

1. 本次调查获取的所有信息仅供专项科研之用，我们将对您所填写的信息严格保密。

2. 请您根据实际情况选择对应选项（可在选项上打"√"或直接填写序号）；回答问题请按要求填写相应的文字或数字。

一、基本信息

企业名称：＿＿＿＿＿＿　　注册资本：＿＿＿＿＿＿

1. 填写问卷人身份

   A. 独立创客

   B. 研究人员

   C. 管理人员

D. 企业负责人

2. 您的年龄是？［单选题］

A.18 岁以下

B.18~35 岁

C.36~45 岁

D.46 岁以上

3. 您从事陶瓷产业的时间是？［单选题］

A.1 年以下

B.1~5 年

C.6~10 年

D.10 年以上

4. 您从事陶瓷产业相关工作的企业组织形式是？［单选题］

（备注："工作室"不是法律上的概念，只是一种运营模式，"工作室"可以是个体工商户，也可以公司的形式存在，请根据实际选择。）

A. 股份有限公司（a. 上市公司；b. 非上市公司）

B. 有限责任公司

C. 个人独资企业

D. 合伙企业

E. 个体工商户

F. 其他：_____

5. 您所在的陶瓷企业规模是？［单选题］

A.10 人以下

B.10~50 人

C.51~100 人

D.100 人以上

二、陶瓷版权创造、保护情况

6.您是否参加过陶瓷版权创造活动？［单选题］

    A.是

    B.否

7.近 5 年您所在企业陶瓷产品版权登记数量分别为？［填空题］

    A.2023 年：＿＿＿＿＿＿＿＿＿＿＿＿

    B.2022 年：＿＿＿＿＿＿＿＿＿＿＿＿

    C.2021 年：＿＿＿＿＿＿＿＿＿＿＿＿

    D.2020 年：＿＿＿＿＿＿＿＿＿＿＿＿

    E.2019 年：＿＿＿＿＿＿＿＿＿＿＿＿

8.您所在企业是否有陶瓷版权创造的专项奖励机制？［单选题］

    A.有

    B.没有

9.您认为版权保护对陶瓷产品创新有何影响？［单选题］

    A.促进创新

    B.无影响

    C.阻碍创新

10.您所在企业是否曾因陶瓷版权问题发生法律纠纷？［单选题］

    A.是，发生过国际侵权纠纷（发生过＿＿＿＿次）

    B.是，发生过国内侵权纠纷（最大涉案金额＿＿＿元）

    C.否

11.在遭受陶瓷版权侵权时，您所在企业采取过什么途径解决？［不定项选择］

    A.由第三方调解解决

    B.自行与侵权人协商解决

C. 请求仲裁解决

D. 提起诉讼

E. 请求政府保护

F. 听之任之

G. 其他（请注明）：_____

12. 您认为哪些因素会导致陶瓷产品版权侵权行为发生？［多选题］

A. 法律意识薄弱

B. 市场监管不力

C. 市场竞争激烈

D. 维权成本高

E. 利益驱动

13. 您认为陶瓷企业在版权保护方面面临的主要挑战是什么？［多选题］

A. 版权保护意识不足

B. 维权成本高，资金不足

C. 缺少专门技术人员，侵权行为难以取证

D. 市场监管不力

E. 其他

14. 您认为哪些部门应参与陶瓷产业的版权保护？［多选题］

A. 政府

B. 企业

C. 行业协会

D. 法律机构

E. 教育机构

15. 您认为陶瓷企业在版权保护方面应采取哪些具体措施？［多选题］

A. 版权登记

B. 加强内部管理

C. 增强员工版权意识

D. 积极维权

E. 其他

16. 您认为哪些措施可以提高陶瓷产业的版权保护水平？［多选题］

    A. 完善法律法规

    B. 增强企业版权意识

    C. 增加版权保护培训

    D. 强化市场监管

    E. 提高侵权处罚力度

    F. 构建多样化版权纠纷解决机制

17. 您是否支持行政机关加大对陶瓷产业版权保护的政策力度？［单选题］

    A. 是

    B. 否

18. 在陶瓷版权保护方面，您希望有关部门今后在哪些方面加强？［不定项选择］

    A. 牵头建立陶瓷版权保护基金，提供维权补贴

    B. 构建陶瓷版权"行政＋司法"保护机制

    C. 加强陶瓷版权保护咨询、人才培养

    D. 加大对侵权行为的处罚力度

    E. 其他（请注明）：_____

19. 您认为版权保护对陶瓷产品的市场竞争力有何影响？［单选题］

    A. 增强

    B. 无影响

    C. 减弱

20. 您认为版权保护对陶瓷产品的品牌价值有何影响？［单选题］

    A. 增加品牌价值，增强企业竞争力

    B. 无影响

    C. 减少品牌价值，妨碍企业发展

21. 您认为陶瓷产业的版权保护对国际市场有何影响？［多选题］

A. 提高国际竞争力

B. 促进出口

C. 增加企业负担

D. 无明显影响

三、陶瓷版权运用、管理情况

22. 您所在企业是否请专业机构评估过陶瓷作品的版权价值？［不定项选择］

A. 是（a. 无形资产价值已入账；b. 无形资产价值未入账）

B. 否，且暂无此打算

23. 与没有进行版权登记的产品相比，有版权登记的产品价格是否更高一些？销售数量是否多一些？［单选题］

A. 都是

B. 都不是

C. 价格更高但销售数量没有更多

D. 销售数量更多但价格没有更高

E. 不一定（请说明原因）：＿＿＿＿＿＿＿＿＿＿＿＿＿＿＿＿＿

24. 目前，您所在企业尝试过的陶瓷版权运营方式有哪些？［多选题］

A. 陶瓷版权授权交易

B. 陶瓷版权转让许可交易

C. 陶瓷版权质押、贷款和保险业务等（该项请注明作品名称及金额：＿＿＿＿＿＿＿＿＿＿＿＿＿＿＿＿＿＿＿＿＿＿＿＿＿＿）

25. 您认为目前陶瓷产业版权运用面临的问题有哪些？［多选题］

A. 交易信息不畅

B. 市场监管不力

C. 交易方式守旧

D. 高质作品缺少

E. 其他（请注明）：＿＿＿＿＿＿＿＿＿＿＿＿＿＿＿＿＿＿＿＿

26. 近 5 年来，您所在企业陶瓷作品的版权交易金额曾最高达多少？〔单选题〕

A.10 万元以下

B.10 万元以上，50 万元以下

C.50 万元以上，100 万元以下

D. 超过 100 万元（该项请注明作品名称及具体金额：＿＿＿＿＿＿＿＿
＿＿＿＿＿＿＿＿＿＿＿）

27. 近 5 年来，您所在企业陶瓷作品的版权交易金额占企业年营业收入的比例平均是多少？〔单选题〕

A.5% 及以下

B.6%~10%

C.11%~15%

D.15% 以上

28. 您认为版权运用过程中的重要因素有哪些？〔不定项选择〕

A. 充足的资金支持

B. 高素质的知识产权人才队伍

C. 优惠政策的扶持

D. 畅通的信息渠道

E. 单位内部有效的激励措施

F. 完善的陶瓷版权管理制度

G. 其他（请注明）：＿＿＿＿＿＿＿＿＿＿＿＿＿＿＿＿＿＿＿＿

29. 您所在企业是否有专门的陶瓷版权管理部门或专业人员？您认为有必要实行陶瓷版权"专业化管理"吗？〔单选题〕

A. 有，已专业化管理

B. 没有，有必要实行

30. 您是否参加过陶瓷版权相关的专业培训？［单选题］

    A. 是

    B. 否

31. 您所在企业是否有成文知识产权管理制度？［单选题］

    A. 没有书面规程

    B. 有书面规程，其内容为（多选）：a. 陶瓷知识产权权利归属制度；
b. 知识产权管理办法；c. 知识产权专业培训制度；d. 知识产权考核制度

32. 您认为应从哪些方面提升陶瓷产业版权管理水平？［多选题］

    A. 政府加强版权管理顶层设计，完善陶瓷行业版权监管制度

    B. 引导陶瓷版权企业建立内部管理机制，建立健全企业内部知识产权
规章制度

    C. 发挥行业协会和产业联盟的外部管理作用

    D. 加大知识产权管理资金投入

33. 您认为目前哪种模式更能发挥版权管理的作用？［多选题］

    A. 只由行政管理部门主管

    B. 加强陶瓷版权企业自我管理

    C. 政府进行行政监管＋政府推动企业和行业协会管理

    D. 放任市场自由发展

四、完善版权服务意见

34. 您认为陶瓷产业中哪些环节最容易出现版权纠纷？［多选题］

    A. 设计

    B. 生产

    C. 销售

    D. 宣传

    E. 物流

35.您认为以下版权服务有利于陶瓷产业发展的有哪些？［多选题］

A.陶瓷版权基础服务（如版权登记、咨询等）

B.陶瓷版权运营服务（如陶瓷版权托管等）

C.陶瓷版权交易服务（如线下交易中心、线上交易平台等）

D.陶瓷版权金融服务（如陶瓷作品版权质押、债券、融资等）

36.您认为现有的陶瓷版权政策是否足够？［单选题］

A.足够

B.不足够，需完善以下方面的政策（可多选）：a.创造；b.运营；c.保护

37.您对版权推动陶瓷产业发展方面的建议和意见是什么？［填空题］

_____

答卷完成！再次感谢您的参与！祝您生活愉快、工作顺利！

附录五

版权保护对景德镇城市高质量发展影响的调查问卷

尊敬的女士 / 先生：

　　您好！

　　您现在参加的是世界知识产权组织（WIPO）版权保护优秀案例示范建设项目"IP 与创意产业：景德镇故事"的调查问卷。该调研对了解版权保护对景德镇城市高质量发展的影响，持续推进景德镇版权创造、运用、保护、管理、服务全链条体系完善，以及向全球推广版权助力城市高质量发展的景德镇经验有着深远意义。感谢您的支持！

填表说明：

　　1. 本次调查获取的所有信息仅供专项科研之用，我们将对您所填写的信息严格保密。

　　2. 请您根据实际情况选择对应选项（可在选项上打"√"或直接填写序号）；回答问题请按要求填写相应的文字或数字。

一、基本信息

　　1. 您的年龄在？［单选题］

　　　A.18 周岁以下

　　　B.18~35 周岁

　　　C.36~45 周岁

　　　D.46 周岁以上

2.您在景德镇生活了多久？［单选题］

    A.不到 1 年

    B.1~3 年

    C.4~10 年

    D.10 年以上

3.您所从事的职业属于？［单选题］

    A.陶瓷相关行业

    B.非陶瓷相关行业

    C.行政、司法或事业单位

    D.其他

二、版权制度层面

4.您所从事的职业会接触"版权"吗？［单选题］

    A.会，经常接触

    B.会，但接触得比较少

    C.不会接触

    D.不清楚

5.您或您所在单位曾经将自己的作品登记过版权吗？［单选题］

    A.登记过

    B.没有登记过

    C.不清楚

6.在您或您所在单位申请版权登记的过程中，是否曾收到官方提供的相关服务（例如申请版权的相关宣传、培训或平台支持等）？［单选题］

    A.收到过

    B.没有收到过

    C.不清楚

7. 您或您所在单位登记的版权作品有过被假冒仿制的经历吗？如有，一般是用什么方式解决呢？〔单选题〕

    A. 有过，但不知道如何处理

    B. 有过，选择私下联系和解

    C. 有过，选择通过官方的调解、执法或诉讼方式解决

    D. 没有

    E. 其他（请说明）：_____

8. 您或您所在单位有过侵犯他人版权作品的行为吗？如有，一般是用什么方式解决呢？〔单选题〕

    A. 有过，通过私下联系和解的方式

    B. 有过，通过官方调解、执法或诉讼的方式

    C. 没有

    D. 其他（请说明）：_____

9. 您或您所在单位在日常生活或生产经营中，会和官方的版权部门〔例如文旅局（版权局）、知识产权法庭、知识产权保护中心、文化执法队等〕有接触吗？〔单选题〕

    A. 频繁接触

    B. 有接触，但不多

    C. 没有接触

    D. 不清楚

10. 您或您所在单位在日常生活或生产经营中，是否收到过官方的版权相关支持（例如官方提供的版权扶助资金、知识培训、销售平台等公共服务）？〔单选题〕

    A. 收到过

    B. 没有收到过

    C. 不清楚

11. 您听说过所在区域的版权服务站或接受过版权服务站提供的版权相关服

务（例如版权知识宣讲、版权登记指导等）吗？〔单选题〕

    A. 听说过，并接受过版权相关服务

    B. 听说过，但没有接受过版权相关服务

    C. 没有听说过

    D. 不清楚

12. 您认为官方的版权相关行动（如提供的版权登记绿色通道服务、版权知识宣传、版权执法等）对您的具体生活或您所在单位的生产经营是否有影响呢？〔单选题〕

    A. 有影响，能明显感受到

    B. 有一定影响，但并不明显

    C. 没有影响

    D. 不清楚

13. 您对于景德镇当下的版权服务体系的满意度如何？〔单选题〕

    A. 比较满意，能够满足文化产品市场经营需要

    B. 基本满意，但还有一些地方需要改进

    C. 不太满意，还有很多地方需要改进

    D. 不清楚

14. 您认为景德镇还可以从哪些方面进一步完善版权相关服务体系？〔填空题〕

_____

三、社会经济层面

15. 从您个人体验而言，您认为将作品版权进行登记是否有经济价值呢？〔单选题〕

    A. 有，可以增强消费者的认可度，或增加作品的附加值

    B. 有一定价值，但影响不大

C. 没有，不会带来直观变化

D. 不清楚

16. 从您个人体验而言，您认为将作品版权进行登记是否能抑制市场上的侵权盗版现象呢？［单选题］

A. 能，例如可以凭借登记证书要求侵权者停止侵权或索赔

B. 不能，例如登记了版权也很难及时发现侵权行为

C. 不清楚

17. 您或您所在单位曾经进行过版权作品的转化运用（例如版权质押融资、版权作价入股等）吗？［单选题］

A. 经常有

B. 偶尔有

C. 没有

18. 您对于版权的具体态度是？［单选题］

A. 非常认可版权的作用，每件作品都会积极对版权进行登记

B. 无所谓，偶尔会选择将作品进行版权登记

C. 不认可版权的作用，从不进行版权登记

D. 其他（请说明）：＿＿＿＿＿＿＿＿＿＿＿＿＿＿＿＿＿＿

19. 在过去的五年间，您的年收入是否有增长呢？［单选题］

A. 保持平稳增长

B. 总体保持增长

C. 没有增长

D. 有所下降

20. 在过去的五年间，您所在企业的年营收是否有增长呢？［单选题］

A. 保持平稳增长

B. 总体保持增长

C. 没有增长

D. 有所下降

21. 相比过去，您认为如今景德镇陶瓷市场的假冒仿制情况如何？［单选题］

    A. 情况好转很多，市场上正版意识有较大增强

    B. 情况有所好转，但假冒仿制现象还是比较严重

    C. 情况基本没有变化

    D. 假冒仿制情况变得更加严重

    E. 不清楚

22. 您认为如今景德镇本地的市场竞争环境是否能支撑企业发展呢？［单选题］

    A. 有充分的公平竞争市场环境，能够支撑企业发展

    B. 市场竞争环境相对公平，但还有需要改进之处

    C. 市场竞争环境比较一般，有很多地方需要改进

    D. 不清楚

23. 相比过去，您认为如今的景德镇陶瓷市场总体发展情况如何？［单选题］

    A. 比过去更有活力，更有发展动力

    B. 比过去基本没有变化

    C. 发展活力和动力都不如过去

    D. 不清楚

24. 您对景德镇的营商环境优化有哪些建议？［填空题］

四、创新氛围层面

25. 您认为在如今的景德镇市场上，产品最需要依靠下列哪种手段取得竞争优势？［单选题］

    A. 具有新颖性、美观度的创意设计，"质量为王"

    B. 发达的上下游营销网络，"渠道为王"

    C. 周到便捷的售后服务，"服务为王"

D. 产品价格低廉，"价格为王"

26.您认为近些年来，景德镇的创意设计人员在企业中是否得到了重视（可以从相对普通员工的薪资水平、在企业中的职级地位等角度判断）？〔单选题〕

A. 得到了高度重视，在企业中处于较高地位

B. 得到了一定重视，在企业中处于中游地位

C. 并没有得到重视，在企业中处于一般地位

D. 被轻视，在企业中地位低下

E. 不清楚

27.您或您所在单位在生产经营活动中，是否会采取一定手段（例如与客户合同约定版权事项等）以避免侵犯他人版权？〔单选题〕

A. 会积极采取各种方式避免侵犯他人版权

B. 偶尔会采取有限手段避免侵犯他人版权

C. 不太重视是否会侵犯他人版权

28.您或您所在单位在生产经营活动中，是否会注重保护自身版权？〔单选题〕

A. 会在事前积极防范，并在侵权发生后积极采取包括法律手段在内的各种措施维护自身合法权益

B. 会在事前积极防范，但侵权发生后不会或不能进行有效维权

C. 不会在事前积极防范，但侵权发生后会积极维权

D. 不重视保护自身版权

29.您认为如今的景德镇形成了"尊重创新，崇尚创新"的社会风尚吗？〔单选题〕

A.已经形成，各行各业都非常重视创新发展

B.基本形成，但还有部分侵权盗版的行业乱象

C.没有形成，还有很长的一段路要走

五、可持续发展层面

30. 您或您所在单位，是否尝试过在城市建筑、陶瓷生产等方面使用绿色环保的创意设计？［单选题］

    A. 尝试过

    B. 没有

31. 您或您所在单位在陶瓷工业生产活动中，是否尝试过使用环保型的新型材料或研发能耗污染较小的新生产工艺？［单选题］

    A. 二者都尝试过

    B. 在陶瓷生产中使用过环保型新型材料

    C. 在陶瓷生产中研发过能耗污染较小的新生产工艺

    D. 没有

32. 您或您所在单位烧制瓷器后产生的工业废料是如何处理的呢？［单选题］

    A. 直接作为垃圾扔掉

    B. 使用专业设备进行无害化处理

    C. 二次回收利用

    D. 其他（请说明）：＿＿＿＿＿＿＿＿＿＿＿＿＿＿＿＿＿＿＿＿

六、社会文化层面

33. 您在景德镇经营企业或生活期间，体验到的公共服务（例如公共服务设施等硬件建设、企业登记注册等软件因素）是否便利？［单选题］

    A. 企业经营和个人生活都比较便利

    B. 企业经营比较便利，但个人生活体验一般

    C. 个人生活体验比较舒适，但企业经营服务比较一般

    D. 企业经营和个人生活都比较一般

E. 不清楚

34. 相比过去，您认为如今的景德镇市容市貌变化如何？〔单选题〕

A. 变化很大，生活体验更加良好

B. 有一定变化，但生活体验较为一般

C. 基本没有变化

D. 不清楚

35. 您认为如今的景德镇是个宜居城市吗？〔单选题〕

A. 是，很适宜居住和生活

B. 基本是，但还有需要改进之处

C. 不是，有很多需要改进之处

D. 不清楚

36. 您认为现在的景德镇能有助于发挥个人的创造力和天赋吗？〔单选题〕

A. 能够充分支撑个人创造力和天赋发挥

B. 基本能够，但还有部分需要改进之处

C. 不能，城市软硬件都有很多需要改进之处

D. 不清楚

37. 您认为如今的景德镇在传统文化保存和传承方面做得如何？〔单选题〕

A. 保存和传承状况很好，传统文化氛围浓厚，能够时常感受到传统文化的熏陶

B. 保存和传承状况一般，偶尔能够感受到传统文化的存在

C. 保存和传承状况较差，传统文化几乎被现代文明取代

D. 不清楚

38. 从您个人体验而言，景德镇如今的对外经济文化交流情况如何？〔单选题〕

A. 更加开放包容，国内外游客数量保持增长，文化交流增多

B. 比之前基本没有变化

C. 外来游客减少，文化交流减少

D. 不清楚

39. 您此后是否有长留景德镇的打算？〔单选题〕

A. 有

B. 没有

C. 不清楚

40. 您认为吸引人留在景德镇的主要因素可能有哪些？〔多选题〕

A. 气候、地理等自然因素

B. 市场公平竞争环境、产业集聚等经济因素

C. 人文艺术氛围浓厚等文化因素

D. 公共服务便利、基础设施完善等城建因素

41. 您认为如今的景德镇哪些地方还需要改进？〔填空题〕

_____

答卷完成！再次感谢您的参与，祝您生活愉快、工作顺利！

参考文献

第二章

图书

乔溎修、贺熙龄纂《浮梁县志》卷八《食货　陶政》，道光三年刻本。

熊寥、熊微编注《中国陶瓷古籍集成》，上海文化出版社，2006。

中共景德镇市委宣传部编著《景德镇陶瓷简史》，江西教育出版社，2023。

宋濂：《元史》卷八十八，中华书局，1976。

景德镇市地方志办公室编《中国瓷都·景德镇市瓷业志（市志·2卷）》，方志出版社，2004。

报刊文章

《解放思想开拓进取扬长补短固本兴新　奋力谱写中国式现代化江西篇章》，《人民日报》2023年10月14日。

冯和法：《中国陶瓷业之现状及其贸易状况》，《国际贸易导报》1932年第3卷第2、3、4号合刊。

《在营造非遗新生态中增强文化新活力——景德镇市非遗保护工作亮点与成效》，《景德镇陶瓷》2022年第3期。

张龙：《江西景德镇：以瓷为媒　打好网络国际传播"组合拳"》，《中国网信》2024年第7期。

第三章

图书

乔溎修、贺熙龄纂《浮梁县志》卷八《食货　陶政》，道光三年刻本。

洪焱祖撰、洪在编《杏庭摘稿》，四库全书本。

张柏、姚競主编《大观·元末明初青花瓷海上巡礼论文集》，江西美术出版社，2017。

徐溥等撰、李东阳等重修《明会典》卷一百五十七，四库全书本。

铁源、溪明:《清代官窑瓷器史2》，中国画报出版社，2012。

熊寥、熊微编注《中国陶瓷古籍集成》，上海文化出版社，2006。

景德镇市地方志办公室编《中国瓷都·景德镇市瓷业志（市志·2卷）》，方志出版社，2004。

蓝浦、郑廷桂著，余柱青编著《古典新读景德镇陶录》，黄山书社，2015。

周林、李明山主编《中国版权史研究文献》，中国方正出版社，1999。

铁源、溪明:《民国瓷器鉴定——胎釉　彩绘　器型》，华龄出版社，2004。

景德镇市志编纂委员会编纂《景德镇市志略》，汉语大词典出版社，1989。

（美）罗伯特·芬雷:《青花瓷的故事：中国瓷的时代》，郑明萱译，海南出版社，2015。

（德）雷德侯:《万物：中国艺术中的模件化和规模化生产》，张总等译，生活·读书·新知三联书店，2005。

余家栋:《江西陶瓷史》，河南大学出版社，1997。

干光尧:《明代宫廷陶瓷史》，紫禁城出版社，2010。

报刊文章

江西省文物考古研究所、乐平市博物馆、景德镇陶瓷考古研究所、景德镇民窑博物馆:《江西乐平南窑窑址调查报告》，《中国国家博物馆馆刊》2013

年第 10 期。

郭建晖:《文化遗存保护传承的当代价值与现实路径——基于景德镇青白瓷遗址群的调查》,《江西社会科学》2023 年第 43 卷第 1 期。

徐长青、余江安:《湖田窑考古新收获》,《故宫博物院院刊》2004 年第 2 期。

翁彦俊、江建新、秦大树、江小民:《江西景德镇落马桥窑址宋元遗存发掘简报》,《文物》2017 年第 5 期。

詹嘉、赵传玉、袁胜根:《历史时期景德镇陶瓷文化景观的演变》,《农业考古》2009 年第 6 期。

陈朝云:《宋代瓷器制造技术的考古学观察》,《考古学报》2017 年第 4 期。

徐香玉:《宋景德镇青白瓷若干文字识记的分类及考证》,硕士学位论文,景德镇陶瓷大学,2022。

赵燕:《元至正十一年青花云龙纹象耳瓶铭文考辨》,《新美术》2013 年第 34 卷第 4 期。

王光尧:《从故宫藏清代制瓷官样看中国古代官样制度——清代御窑厂研究之二》,《故宫博物院院刊》2006 年第 6 期。

北京大学考古文博学院、江西省文物考古研究所、景德镇市陶瓷考古研究所:《江西景德镇明清御窑遗址发掘简报》,《文物》2007 年第 5 期。

《景德镇市大力保护陶瓷作品版权》,《江西日报》2010 年 3 月 22 日。

《景德镇瓷业水碓营造技艺（2021 年第五批国家级非物质文化遗产代表性项目）》,《景德镇陶瓷》2022 年第 3 期。

张文江:《景德镇南窑遗址考古发掘的重要收获》,《东方博物》2014 年第 2 期。

程仁发:《宋代景德镇青白瓷装饰方法的研究》,《中国陶瓷》2015 年第 51 卷第 12 期。

周觉民:《略谈我国陶瓷贴花纸的兴起》,《景德镇陶瓷》1982 年第 3 期。

李一平:《宋代的湖田窑》,《南方文物》2003 年第 1 期。

叶文程:《宋元时期景德镇青白瓷窑系的外销》,《景德镇陶瓷》1989 年第 3、4 期。

周思中:《景德镇的历史文化特点、制瓷体系及发展战略》,《中国港口》

2020 年增刊第 2 期。

翁彦俊:《景德镇 16—18 世纪陶瓷外销规模估略》,《中国陶瓷》2021 年第 57 卷第 10 期。

张泽兵:《景德镇陶瓷文化传承创新的历史经验与当代实践》,《江西社会科学》2022 年第 12 期。

第四章

图书

(美)布朗温·H. 霍尔、内森·罗森伯格:《创新经济学手册(第一卷)》,上海市科学学研究所译,上海交通大学出版社,2017。

报刊文章

王志标:《传统文化资源产业化的路径分析》,《河南大学学报(社会科学版)》2012 年第 52 卷第 2 期。

戴钰:《文化产业空间集聚研究——以湖南地区为例》,博士学位论文,武汉理工大学产业经济学专业,2013。

封伟毅、李师萌:《基于知识产权运营视角的创新网络价值共创形成机理研究》,《情报科学》2023 年第 41 卷第 1 期。

何震、魏大海:《改革探索 积极创新——知识产权司法保护"三审合一"研讨会综述》,《法律适用》2010 年第 8 期。

崔珊珊、张伟豪、汪亚楠:《知识产权司法保护与企业进口技术复杂度——基于知识产权案件"三审合一"的准自然实验》,《宏观经济研究》2023 年第 5 期。

庄佳强、王浩、张文涛:《强化知识产权司法保护有助于企业创新吗——来自知识产权法院设立的证据》,《当代财经》2020 年第 9 期。

戚建刚:《论我国知识产权行政保护模式之变革》,《武汉大学学报(哲学社会科学版)》2020 年第 2 期。

第五章

报刊文章

孙午生:《论版权保护制度与文化创意产业的发展》,《法学杂志》2016年第10期。

倪烽:《云游戏平台商业模式研究——以OnLive为例》,《质量与市场》2020年第16期。

向勇:《转型期我国文化产业发展模式研究》,《东岳论丛》2016年第2期。

王行鹏:《版权产业:区域经济发展的新源泉》,《中国版权》2013年第4期。

杜平、周维贵:《男性话语视野下的女性形象——莎士比亚笔下的维纳斯》,《海南大学学报(人文社会科学版)》2011年第6期。

蒋玉宏、单晓光:《知识产权制度对城市竞争力的影响——基于创新激励的机理分析》,《知识产权》2007年第3期。

周振华、陈维、汤静波、黄建富、沈开艳、靖学青、杨亚琴:《国内若干大城市综合竞争力比较研究》,《上海经济研究》2001年第1期。

韩剑、许亚云:《知识产权保护与利用外资》,《经济管理》2021年第4期。

第六章

报刊文章

蔡莹:《建设促进高质量发展的人文社会环境》,《中国知识产权报》2021年12月15日。

Project Overview and Implementation Status

The millennia-old kilns of Jingdezhen have shaped a rich and enduring ceramic culture. The time-honored porcelain-making craft has reached the pinnacle of global ceramic artistry. The thriving ceramic creative and cultural industry has transformed Jingdezhen into a city that flourishes due to its porcelain legacy. Countless stunning ceramic artworks have forged Jingdezhen as the world's porcelain capital. Jingdezhen ceramics have become a symbol of China to the world, a brilliant emblem of Chinese culture in the global civilization landscape. Through its long history in the ceramic industry, Jingdezhen has developed its own distinctive approach to copyright protection. In recent years, with the evolution of the ceramic creative and cultural industry, and under the leadership of the Communist Party of China and the government, Jingdezhen has been refining its judicial protection system. It has built a network for copyright protection, paving the way for a comprehensive approach to copyright utilization, protection, and management, offering new opportunities for the innovative development of the ceramic creative industry and contributing Chinese wisdom and solutions to global copyright governance.

Section I

Background

(1) About Industrial Development

Since the Tang and Song dynasties, Jingdezhen, a prefecture-level city in eastern Jiangxi Province, has been renowned as a major center for ceramic production, both domestically and internationally. During the Ming and Qing dynasties, Jingdezhen not only dominated China's ceramics industry but also exported its products to numerous countries and regions around the world, earning its reputation as the "Porcelain Capital" of the world. In recent years, the ceramics industry in Jingdezhen has experienced rapid growth. In 2023, the city's total ceramic industry output value reached 86.125 billion yuan, a year-on-year increase of 29.44%. The number of market entities now has exceeded 20,000, including 258 large enterprises, employing approximately 150,000 people, with about 45,000 skilled workers and more than 6,600 ceramic technical experts. Notably, over 70 ceramics companies have established research and development centers, creating a fully integrated ceramics industry system that covers exploration, manufacturing, design, research, education, and communication. Jingdezhen has achieved regular customs clearance and exports through 13 national ports to 65 countries, truly embodying the concept of "buying globally and selling globally."

IP and Creative Industry:
Jingdezhen Story

(2) About Copyright Protection

Since the 1990s, Jingdezhen's ceramics industry has transitioned from the public ownership model to the private and decentralized model, which has led to challenges such as unfair competition and product infringement. At the same time, Jingdezhen has shouldered the historical mission to preserve and innovate its ceramic culture, upgrade its industrial structure, and further improve the business environment. In response, Jingdezhen has prioritized copyright protection, gradually developing a comprehensive framework that integrates civil, administrative, and judicial measures. Since the beginning of the 21st century, with the rapid expansion of Jingdezhen's ceramics industry, ceramic products with cultural creativity have sprung up. Efforts to protect copyright have, thus, been strengthened and advanced. In 2014, the revised version of the *Regulations for the Protection and Management of Jingdezhen Ceramic Intellectual Property Rights* was issued, which opened the protection of intellectual property rights of ceramics fom protection mechanisms, responsibilities of key departments, and specific protective measures. From then on, the protection of intellectual property rights for Jingdezhen ceramics has entered a period of rapid development.

Since 2019, Jingdezhen has focused on establishing itself as a ceramic culture inheritance and innovation pilot zone, positioning the copyright work as a core element of this cultural endeavor and striving to create a model for "National Copyright Demonstration Cities." With strong support and careful guidance from the National Copyright Administration and the Jiangxi Provincial Copyright Administration, Jingdezhen officially received approval to establish its copyright demonstration status in 2019. During the two-year preparation phase, the city made significant progress across all aspects of creation of copyrighted works, copyright utilization, protection, management, and services, along with notable advancements in copyright registration, transaction, and protection (see Table 1-1 for growth in copyright registrations). Under the framework of establishing the ceramic culture inheritance and innovation pilot zone, Jingdezhen has made copyright a core element of its efforts to preserve and innovate its ceramic culture, striving to develop a new landscape for copyright work. In April 2020, the Jingdezhen Municipal Committee of the Communist Party of China (CPC) and the Jingdezhen Municipal People's Government prioritized the upgrade of the "Jingdezhen (Ceramic) Intellectual Property Right Rapid Aid Center" to the "China Intellectual Property Protection Center (Jingdezhen)" as a key task in advancing the Pilot Zone endeavor. In September 2020, the Jingdezhen Municipal People's Government released the *Implementation Plan for Creating a National Copyright Demonstration City*, outlining key tasks aimed at enhancing copyright creation, protection, utilization, and management capabilities. In April 2021, Jingdezhen established the country's sixth Intellectual Property Court located in a non-provincial capital city, which focuses on protecting intellectual property rights within the ceramics industry, emphasizes a deep understanding of ceramics culture and has implemented streamlined case processes including "rapid filing, quick review for simple cases, and careful examination for complex cases." It has also created mechanisms for "rapid pre-trial preservation, diversified mediation during litigation, and follow-up visits post-judgment," all while promoting a specialized, standardized, and centralized approach to handling cases. Additionally, the court enhances judicial protection for geographical indications related to "Made in Jingdezhen" products, advanced industrial ceramics, cultural and artistic ceramics, and high-end daily-use porcelain. Focusing on the protection of ceramic intellectual property and the enhancement of copyright awareness, the court has hosted several important events on intellectual property protection, including the 2021 China Jingdezhen International Ceramic Expo Intellectual Property Protection Forum, discussions on the judicial protection of the "Jingdezhen" geographical indication, and seminars on protecting the intellectual property rights of female ceramic artists. These initiatives have fostered a consensus on strengthening ceramic intellectual property protection and a collective commitment to safeguarding the prestigious "Jingdezhen" brand. In July 2021, the Jingdezhen National Ceramic Copyright Trading Center was established, which is the first national-level copyright trading center for specific industries in the country. It has been recognized by the Jiangxi Provincial Committee of CPC and the Jiangxi Provincial People's Government as a key project in building the Gan-Po cultural brand. Thanks to the collaborative efforts of various stakeholders, Jingdezhen officially received the title of "National Copyright Demonstration City" in October 2021, becoming the first such city in Central China and the 13th nationwide.

Table 1-1: Annual Copyright Registrations in Jingdezhen City

Year	Total Number of Copyright Registrations (Items)	Year-on-Year Growth Rate
2001	1	
2002	2	100.00%
2003	24	1100.00%
2004	104	333.33%
2005	113	8.65%
2006	76	-32.74%
2007	66	-13.16%
2008	128	93.94%
2009	182	42.19%
2010	190	4.40%
2011	223	17.37%
2012	151	-32.29%
2013	310	105.30%
2014	755	143.55%
2015	332	-56.03%
2016	446	34.34%
2017	444	-0.45%
2018	844	90.09%
2019	888	5.21%
2020	6633	646.96%
2021	5794	-12.65%
2022	19295	233.02%
2023	31563	63.58%
2024	41815	32.48%

Data Source: Jingdezhen Municipal Bureau of Culture, Broadcasting, Television, Press and Publication

To consolidate the achievements of becoming a National Copyright Demonstration City and further advance the development of copyright initiatives and related industries, Jingdezhen is committed to enhancing its capabilities in copyright creation, protection, utilization, and management. The city aims to fully leverage the significant role that copyright plays in driving economic growth and cultural prosperity. As part of this effort, Jingdezhen has continued to foster the growth of its ceramics industry by launching 238 key projects, including benchmark projects like Ceramic Expo City, Taoyang Alley, and Taoxichuan Ceramic Art Avenue. In 2023, the Jingdezhen Municipal Copyright Bureau received the 2022 WIPO-NCAC Copyright Award for Copyright Administration & Management. In June 2023, the Jingdezhen People's Procuratorate established the Ceramic Cultural Heritage and Intellectual Property Prosecutorial Protection Center, combining functions such as case handling, expert consultation, and convenient services into a united hub for managing related business matters. In October 2023, the Jingdezhen Municipal Public Security Bureau set up the Ceramic Intellectual Property Protection Center, pioneering a comprehensive police operation mechanism that integrates central-regional departmental coordination and comprehensive governance. This center establishes a rapid response mechanism between public security and cultural law enforcement agencies, creating a unified framework for reporting, identification, law enforcement, and criminal prosecution in ceramic copyright protection. It has also introduced special measures for intellectual property protection, facilitating overall upgrades in trademark protection, copyright registration, origin protection, and the safeguarding of original works by prominent figures. In March 2024, the seventh meeting of the Standing Committee of the 14th Jiangxi Provincial People's Congress approved the *Regulations on the Protection of "Made in Jingdezhen" Ceramics*, providing practical guidelines and guarantees to regulate the market order for "Made in Jingdezhen" ceramics and ensure the quality of these products. Since 2021, Jingdezhen has established two national copyright demonstration bases, ten provincial copyright demonstration bases, and four copyright service stations. Moreover, the city has established the "Ceramic Art Design Copyright Trading Platform," which creates an integrated industrial chain for copyright trading, transformation, and operations. This platform facilitates the coordination of dispute resolution among litigation and non-litigation methods, which include mediation, arbitration, as well as administrative decisions and reconsiderations.

The rapid growth of Jingdezhen's ceramics industry and the significant increase in the number of its copyright registrations have garnered the attention of the World Intellectual Property Organization (WIPO) and the National Copyright

Administration of China (NCAC). In 2019, the number of copyright registrations reached 888, skyrocketing to 19,295 by 2022. In November 2022, during the opening ceremony of the 2022 International Copyright Forum held in Jingdezhen, WIPO, NCAC the Publicity Department of the CPC Jiangxi Provincial Committee (Jiangxi Provincial Copyright Administration), and the Jingdezhen Municipal People's Government jointly launched a Research Project on the Case Study of Best Practice in Copyright Utilization and Protection by WIPO. This project aims to conduct in-depth studies on how copyright can promote the inheritance and innovation of the ceramics industry, ultimately contributing to high-quality urban development. It seeks to further advance the high-quality development of copyright industries with local features while providing vibrant materials to showcase China's copyright commitment and contributing Chinese wisdom and solutions to global copyright governance. In August 2024, leaders and experts from the Copyright Management Bureau of the Publicity Department of the CPC Central Committee visited Jingdezhen to oversee and guide the research work on this case demonstration project. Besides, the Publicity Department of the CPC Jiangxi Provincial Committee(Jiangxi Provincial Copyright Administration), the Publicity Department of the CPC Jingdezhen Municipal Committee, and Jingdezhen Municipal Bureau of Culture, Broadcasting, Television, Press and Publication have created favorable conditions for the smooth implementation of this research project.

Section II

Purpose and Significance

The purpose of this research is to reveal the intrinsic logical relationship between copyright and the promotion of creative industry, as well as the high-quality urban growth. With a focus on various aspects of the Jingdezhen ceramics industry, this study examines the historical evolution of copyright, the unique features of contemporary copyright protection efforts, practical applications of copyright, and its role in facilitating urban development. The research will examine the all-encompassing copyright protection model that has gradually developed within the context of Jingdezhen's ceramics industry from three perspectives: government, society, and individuals. By exploring government management, market competition, resource allocation, and innovation incentives, the research will engage in case analyses and draw conclusions that demonstrate the positive impact of copyright protection. This includes promoting the development of the ceramic cultural and creative industry, ensuring orderly market operations, and enhancing the role of copyright in local economic and social development, as well as in creating a fair competitive environment.

First, a brief overview of the historical evolution of Jingdezhen's ceramics industry will be presented. Building on this foundation, the research will further discuss the development path of copyright in Jingdezhen ceramics, identifying three phases in the transformation of Jingdezhen's ceramic copyright protection concept towards a law-based framework. This discussion will summarize the foundational elements that shaped Jingdezhen's ceramic copyright awareness, elucidate the evolutionary logic by which copyright awareness has gradually been optimized into legal norms. Furthermore, the research will demonstrate how Jingdezhen has sustained its millennia-old ceramics industry through an increasingly refined "copyright system," and how its diverse and co-existing "copyright awareness" has bolstered its global reputation as a "ceramic capital."

Second, the initiatives and models that Jingdezhen has implemented in ceramic copyright will be reviewed and summarized. By analyzing and summarzing local copyright policies, incentive systems, protection mechanisms, service practices, application examples, and unique management characteristics in Jingdezhen, the research will distill a comprehensive model for the city's ceramic copyright efforts across five dimensions: creation, application, protection, management, and service. This analysis will highlight Jingdezhen's distinct features in ceramic copyright, including sustainable creation, flexible application, specialized protection, distinctive management, and normalized service, offering replicable experiences for broader application.

Third, the inspiring stories and exemplary cases about Jingdezhen's ceramic copyright will be displayed. By detailing the specific practices of entities such as Jingdezhen Renew Cultural Technology Co., Ltd., Taoxichuan Ceramic Art Avenue, Jingdezhen Intellectual Property Court, Jingdezhen National Ceramic Copyright Trading Center, and the International Ceramic Expo, readers will gain insights into the concrete details and tangible solutions for copyright protection in Jingdezhen. This multi-faceted and comprehensive presentation aims to offer the global audience a diverse perspective on Jingdezhen's intellectual property (IP) landscape and creative industry.

Fourth, the role of copyright in driving the development of Jingdezhen's ceramic cultural and creative industry while empowering the city's high-quality growth will be examined and elucidated. Through extensive research and data collection, the research will clarify the theoretical connections between IP (including copyright) and high-quality urban development, with the aim to build an indicator system that reflects how copyright contributes to urban progress. By analyzing data involving law-based governance, economy, industries, society, and culture in Jingdezhen, the research aims at revealing the pivotal role of proactive and effective government copyright policies in fostering urban development, thereby demonstrating the benefits of copyright on high-quality urban growth.

Fifth, successful experiences of copyright protection in Jingdezhen will be disseminated and promoted. By sorting out and summarizing the city's successful strategies in ceramic copyright protection, the research will highlight the role of copyright in preserving and advancing ceramic culture, fostering urban economic and social progress, and inspiring individual creativity. This effort will offer valuable references and insights for other regions in China and other countries worldwide for enhancing their copyright protection initiatives.

Section III

About the Project

The research report is centered around the theme "IP and Creative Industry: Jingdezhen Story." Based on the initial examination of the historical development of Jingdezhen's ceramics and its traditional intellectual property protection experiences, the report analyzes the current scale and categories within the Jingdezhen's ceramics industry, providing insights into the market conditions and the variety of ceramic products available. Building on this foundation, the report interprets the vibrant practices of copyright protection specific to Jingdezhen ceramics, highlighting the significant role that copyright plays in establishing a fair competitive market order and promoting economic growth, as well as social and cultural prosperity in the city. The report is structured into six main sections for detailed analysis.

The first section introduces the research project's background, significance, content, methodology, and findings. Jingdezhen, globally renowned as the "Porcelain Capital," has preserved a rich cultural heritage over thousands of years of continuous ceramic development. It stands as one of the few model cities worldwide that exemplifies a living tradition of handicraft. The city's profound history, diverse elements of ceramic copyright, and dynamic cultural and creative industries have garnered attention and recognition from various quarters.

The second section analyzes the historical development of Jingdezhen's ceramics industry, with a particular focus on its status quo. It summarizes Jingdezhen's achievements across various aspects, including its ceramics industry system, scale, categories, and distinctive product features.

The third section categorizes the evolution of concept of copyright protection towards law-based management in Jingdezhen ceramics into three distinct periods, based on the various expressions of copyright awareness throughout different times. This categorization reviews the relationships—both spiritual and property-related—among creation subjects, management institutions, and other societal entities involved in the creation, publication, dissemination, and use of ceramic works. It identifies the foundational elements of Jingdezhen's ceramic copyright awareness clarifies the logic of optimizing copyright protection through legal regulations, and reveals the developmental path of copyright in Jingdezhen ceramics.

The fourth section focuses on case studies of Jingdezhen's copyright protection and corresponding models across the entire chain of "creation, application, protection, management, and service," further elaborating on the current state of copyright protection in the new era. It highlights discussing policies and initiatives exemplifying copyright's role in promoting high-quality urban development and summarizing the city's copyright protection experiences.

The fifth section explores how ceramic copyright drives Jingdezhen's high-quality development. It reveals the role of ceramic copyright in driving advancements in various aspects, including establishing urban institutional framework, improving legal mechanisms for rights protection, optimizing urban economic structure, enhancing public services, and cultivating cultural-ethical environment. Moreover, it develops an evaluation system to assess the impact of ceramic copyright on Jingdezhen's high-quality development. By presenting relevant data within this evaluation framework, it objectively demonstrates the facilitating role of ceramic copyright in Jingdezhen's pursuit for high-quality development. Finally, based on the trajectory of the city's high-quality development, it proposes future directions for leveraging ceramic copyright to further support this growth.

The concluding section offers various insights drawn from the copyright protection process in Jingdezhen and puts forth four key recommendations to effectively promote and disseminate these findings.

Section IV

Approach and Methodology

This project employs a multi-disciplinary approach that integrates qualitative and quantitative analysis, case studies and sampling surveys, as well as oral interviews and document interpretation across fields such as law, sociology, economics, and history. The aim is to clarify the research focus and challenges, set the research direction and objectives, and develop a research outline with assigned tasks.

First, qualitative and quantitative analyses. By combining qualitative methods (such as field research and oral interviews) with quantitative approaches (including ceramic statistical data), this research seeks to organically merge subjective and objective perspectives.

Second, literature collection and data organization. The project involves collecting and organizing relevant materials and data on Jingdezhen's ceramic development and copyright protection. This includes information on industry scale, product features, copyright laws and regulations, associated documents, as well as notable events and typical cases, all aimed at understanding how copyright supports urban development.

Third, oral interviews and case analysis. Through interviews with personnel from relevant government departments, businesses, and practitioners in the ceramics industry, the research aims to gain insights into the achievements of copyright in advancing Jingdezhen's ceramics industry. Besides, by analyzing specific cases such as Taoxichuan Ceramic Art Avenue, the Copyright Trading Center, the Intellectual Property Court, Jingdezhen Renew Cultural Technology Co., Ltd. the International Ceramic Expo, and "Yang Jing Piao" (foreign potters in Jingdezhen), the study will provide practical insights into the successes of copyright protection in Jingdezhen.

217

Section V

About the Team

The National Copyright Administration, along with the Jiangxi Provincial Committee of CPC, the Jiangxi Provincial People's Government and the Jingdezhen Municipal People's Government, attaches great importance to this research initiative. In response, the Publicity Department of the CPC Jiangxi Provincial Committee has established a coordination team, including leaders from the Publicity Department of the CPC Jingdezhen Municipal Committee and relevant departments of the Jingdezhen Municipal Bureau of Culture, Broadcasting, Television, Press and Publication, to oversee the overall coordination of the research. The research task force has been established, led by Professor Guo Jianhui, who was the Executive Deputy Minister of the Publicity Department of the CPC Jiangxi Provincial Committee at the time, to ensure the successful completion of all research tasks. The project is divided into two subtopics: the first focusing on the study of copyright awareness within the historical development of Jingdezhen's ceramics industry, and the second on how copyright protection contributes to the high-quality urban development in Jingdezhen. The research team from the Chinese Ceramic Development Research Institute at Jingdezhen Ceramic University will handle the first subtopic, while the team from the School of Intellectual Property at East China Jiaotong University will take charge of the second subtopic.

Section VI

Summary of Conclusions

The millennia-old kilns of Jingdezhen have accumulated a vast treasure trove of ceramic culture, which not only embodies innovative and creative achievements through ceramic artifacts but also fosters and sustains copyright protection legacy originating from ideas. Over the centuries, measures related to the protection of ceramic works, such as inscriptions, official patterns, ceramic marks, and prohibitions, have gradually evolved and matured from the Song Dynasty through the Ming and Qing dynasties. This advancement has shaped a developmental trajectory of ceramic copyright that originated in the Song and Yuan dynasties and continued through the Ming and Qing dynasties, extending into the late Qing and early Republican periods. The varying expressions of ceramic copyright at different historical stages faithfully document the historical transformations of China's ceramic copyright protection activities and innovation governance, vividly showcasing the crucial value of copyright protection concept in the development of the handicraft industry in China.

Copyright protection supports the inheritance and development of Jingdezhen's ceramics industry. Jingdezhen boasts a rich array of both tangible and intangible cultural heritage resources. The city has been enlarging the team of its intangible cultural heritage inheritors in handcrafted porcelain by establishing a series of copyright protection laws and regulations aimed at encouraging the enthusiasm and proactivity of inheritors. Furthermore, Jingdezhen has deeply explored its material cultural resources through initiatives like the establishment of a gene bank of ancient ceramics, providing fixed copyright resources for the transmission of ceramic culture. For instance, the inspiration for Jingdezhen's first city gift, "Fu Ruyi,"[①] launched in 2021, was drawn from a Qing Dynasty Blue-and-White Gourd-Shaped Vase with Gourd Motif housed in the Jingdezhen China Ceramics Museum. This item serves as a crystallization of the inheritance and development of fine traditional Chinese culture, epitomized by the principle of harmony.

Copyright fuels innovation in Jingdezhen's ceramics industry. Jingdezhen's ceramics production is characterized by small-scale, decentralized, and handcrafted processes, with a large number of practitioners involved. These features make the industry susceptible to counterfeiting and pose challenges for rights protection. To address this challenge, Jingdezhen has, through practical exploration, established a ceramic copyright protection system called the "Four Centers and One Alliance." This system is focused on protecting and revitalizing the regional brand of "Made in Jingdezhen," while improving the formulation, implementation, and supervision mechanisms of the associated standards. It promotes a certification model that integrates standard formulation, testing and certification, and a traceability system. Relying on the National Ceramic Copyright Trading Center, this system provides services such as quality testing, product traceability, anti-counterfeiting certification, and appraisal auctions for ceramic products. It encourages government entities, platform providers, cultural enterprises, and creators alike, offering potters accessible channels for copyright registration, rights protection, consultation, and trading. This initiative has invigorated potters' passion and spurred the growth of the ceramic creative industry.

Copyright is empowering Jingdezhen's high-quality urban development. By formulating legal policies for copyright protection and implementing a series of initiatives, Jingdezhen has optimized resource allocation and fostered the normalized and orderly growth of its ceramics industry. In terms of industrial development, the city has focused on expanding daily-use ceramics, refining artistic ceramics, and strengthening advanced ceramics production, resulting in rapid growth of the ceramic sector. Regarding cultural and tourism integration, Jingdezhen has developed a new holistic tourism model centered around

---

① It conveys a heartfelt wish for someone to receive abundant blessings and have all their wishes and aspirations fulfilled.

ceramic culture, emphasizing ceramic cultural and creative areas like Taoyang Alley, Taoxichuan Ceramic Art Avenue, Taoyuan Valley, Taokeyuan Park, and Ceramic Expo City (also Taobocheng), collectively referred to as the "Five Taos." The character "Tao" (陶) in Chinese signifies ceramics. In international cultural exchanges, Jingdezhen uses porcelain as a medium for building friendships, with initiatives that encourage both inbound and outbound cultural interactions, thereby accelerating the creation of a narrative system for ceramic culture. Regarding talent attraction, the city has implemented the "Birds of Passage" program to attract more innovators and entrepreneurs, both domestic and foreign—often referred to as "Jing Piao" (Jingdezhen migrants) and "Yang Jing Piao"—encouraging them to create and thrive in Jingdezhen, making it an ideal place for ceramic artists to start their businesses, produce, and live.

Chapter II

Jingdezhen: A Millennium of Porcelain History and Tradition

Jingdezhen embodies half of the history of ceramics. With over 2,000 years of pottery-making legacy, more than 1,000 years of official kiln operations, and 600 years of imperial kiln craftsmanship, Jingdezhen has borne witness to the innovation and evolution of China's ceramics industry. Over a long and uninterrupted history of porcelain production, the city has established a distinctive and well-structured handmade porcelain craft system, contributing a splendid chapter in global ceramic history. Over the centuries, Jingdezhen has cultivated a diverse and vibrant ceramic culture, enriched by its extensive and profound heritage. With its open and inclusive ethos, the city has positioned itself as a global hub for ceramics, attracting renowned kilns from across the nation and showcasing ceramic wares from around the world.

Section Ⅰ

The History of Ancient Porcelain Making in Jingdezhen

In October 2023, during an inspection tour to Jingdezhen, General Secretary Xi Jinping emphasized that ceramics is the treasure of China and an important emblem of Chinese civilization.[①] Jingdezhen was founded on porcelain production and rose from its ceramics industry. Thanks to its exceptional natural resources, masterful craftsmanship, and millennia-long tradition of kiln operations, the city has preserved precious ancient ceramic relics, transmitted remarkable porcelain-making techniques, and created exquisite pieces of ceramic art.

The history of porcelain making in Jingdezhen traces its origins back to the Han Dynasty, gained prominence in the Tang Dynasty, flourished during the Song Dynasty, and reached its peak during the Ming and Qing dynasties. Overall, the development of ceramics in ancient Jingdezhen can be divided into the following key stages.

The period from the Han Dynasty (206 BCE-220 CE) to the Five Dynasties (907-960) marks the initial stage of ceramic production in Jingdezhen. "Ceramic production in Xinping (the former name of Jingdezhen) began during the Han Dynasty, characterized by thick, solid, simple, and natural qualities. These early ceramics were crafted from mixed molding clay and employed techniques handed

---

① "Embrace Innovation, Make Strides, Leverage Strengths, Address Weaknesses, Strengthen the Foundation, Promote Renewal, and Strive to Write a New Chapter of Chinese-style Modernization in Jiangxi," *People's Daily*, October 14, 2023.

down from previous generations."[1]

By the Han Dynasty, Jingdezhen had been capable of producing porcelain featuring broad, solid bodies and pale, coarse glaze, though the craftsmanship had not yet reached a high level. Well into the Tang Dynasty (618-907), about half of this era, China enjoyed prosperity and stability, characterized by effective governance, population growth, and steadily growing economy. Porcelain production also reached a peak, with Jingdezhen primarily manufacturing everyday items such as bowls, plates, pots, and jars. The porcelain from this era was notable for its fine and delicate body, even glaze layers and lustrous colors, reflecting a remarkable advancement in craftsmanship.

Building on the foundation of the Tang Dynasty, the Five Dynasties saw an expansion in the scale of porcelain production in Jingdezhen, with product quality enhanced and the range of items diversified. White porcelain, known for its translucency and brightness, gained particular acclaim. Kiln sites from this period were mainly distributed along both banks of the Nan River and within the present-day urban area, producing a variety of objects—including bowls, plates, dishes, pots, jars, and basins—and employing support pins for the firing process.

The Song Dynasty (960-1279) heralded a flourishing period for the ceramics industry in Jingdezhen. During this period, the number of kiln sites surpassed that of the Tang, along with a substantial increase in the variety of porcelain items. The techniques for porcelain-making also advanced beyond those of the Tang and Five Dynasties periods. Firing technologies and manufacturing processes matured, with a more specialized selection and refinement of raw materials, while the division of labor in shaping and crafting became clearer. Notably, the exquisite greenish- white porcelain, celebrated for its jade-like quality, gained favor with Emperor Zhenzong of the Song, who ordered the inscription of the phrase "Jingde[2] Nian Zhi" (Made in the Jingde period) on the bottom of these pieces.

---

[1]   Qiao Yanxiu and He Xiling, eds., *Fuliang County Annals: Food, Goods and Pottery Administration*, Volume Eight, Engraved Edition from the Third Year of the Emperor Daoguang's Reign of the Qing Dynasty, 44.

[2]   Jingde (1004-1007) was the era name used by Emperor Zhenzong of the Song Dynasty, lasting for a total of four years during the Northern Song Dynasty. The famous porcelain city Jingdezhen derives its name from this period.

Yingqing Glazed Gourd-shaped Box with Lid, Song Dynasty (Photo courtesy of the Jingdezhen China Ceramics Museum)

In August of the fifth year of the Yuanfeng period (1082), the Song court established the "Raozhou Jingdezhen Porcelain Trading Bureau[1]."[2] The court also set up a taxation bureau in Jingdezhen, delegating officials to oversee production, implement taxation, and regulate trade—known as the "Jianzhen" (supervision system). Archaeological findings have confirmed that Song and Yuan dynasties blue-and-white porcelain has been unearthed in 16 counties (cities) and towns across 19 provinces and autonomous regions.[3] They were exported via the Maritime Silk Road to various countries and regions in Asia, including Japan, Korea, the Philippines, and Malaysia, and even extending as far as Europe and Africa. "By the end of the Song Dynasty, Europeans had begun to highly appreciate Chinese porcelain. The Dutch traded porcelain from Fujian to Europe, where it was valued equal to gold by weight and was in high demand. Seeing the profits made by Dutch traders, merchants from Guangdong began to venture to Raozhou to trade and ship porcelain."[4]

The Yuan Dynasty (1271-1368) represented a pivotal stage in the optimization and development of Jingdezhen porcelain, marked by significant advancements in porcelain-making techniques. In 1278, the Yuan court established the only national porcelain bureau in Jingdezhen—the Fuliang Porcelain Bureau. According to the

[1] A trading management institution for the Jingdezhen porcelain kilns, established in Raozhou (present-day Poyang region, Jiangxi Province, which includes Jingdezhen within its jurisdiction).

[2] Xiong Liao and Xiong Wei, eds., *Collection of Ancient Chinese Ceramic Texts* (Shanghai: Shanghai Culture Publishing House, 2006), 5.

[3] The Publicity Department of the CPC Jingdezhen Municipal Committee, ed., *A Brief History of Jingdezhen Ceramics* (Nanchang:Jiangxi Education Publishing House, 2023), 59.

[4] Feng Hefa, "Current Status and Trade Conditions of China's Ceramics Industry," *International Trade Newspaper*, 1932(03):93.

History of the Yuan: Hundred State Offices: Ministry of Works, "in the 15th year of the Zhiyuan period, the Fuliang Porcelain Bureau was established (with a rank equivalent to the eighth grade), responsible for producing ceramics as well as lacquerware items such as horsetail, palm rattan, straw hats, and more. The bureau was equipped with a chief officer (ranked as the eighth grade) and one deputy (ranked as the ninth grade)."[1] Yuan blue-and-white porcelain holds a prominent position in the history of ceramics. This type of underglaze colored pottery, which utilizes cobalt for painting, is known for its strong coloring ability, vibrant hues, and stable colors, which led to an unprecedented boom in Jingdezhen's porcelain industry. Shufu porcelain wares, ordered by the Commission of Military Affairs in Jingdezhen during the Yuan Dynasty, are characterized by their thick body and slightly bluish-white color, resembling the hue of goose eggs, hence called "egg white." They typically bear inscriptions like *Shufu* (枢府) and *Taixi* (太禧),[2] exhibiting exquisite craftsmanship in terms of body quality, glaze color, and production techniques. The cultural orientation embodied in Jingdezhen porcelain during the Yuan Dynasty underwent notable transformations. The multifaceted Mongol culture blended elements of Han Chinese traditions from the central plains, influences

Blue-glazed Piled Dragon Pattern Celestial Sphere Vase, Wanli Period, Ming Dynasty (Photo courtesy of the Jingdezhen China Ceramics Museum)

---

[1]   Song Lian, *The History of the Yuan*, Volume 88 (Beijing:Zhonghua Book Company, 1976), 2227.

[2]   It also refers to imperial officials.

from the nomadic Mongolians, as well as various religious cultures, including Islamic traditions. This rich cultural confluence profoundly impacted the shapes and decorations of Jingdezhen porcelain, resulting in unique designs that echoed the diverse cultural influences of the time.

The Ming Dynasty (1368-1644) marked a golden era for porcelain production in Jingdezhen. Following the establishment of the dynasty, the court set up the Imperial Kiln Factory in Jingdezhen, dedicated to producing ceramics exclusively for the royal families, which consequently limited the types of porcelain that could be crafted by private kilns. The Imperial Kiln Factory enjoyed exclusive access to the finest raw materials and craftsmen, allowing it to prioritize quality without concern for costs. This made the factory integral to the development of Jingdezhen's ceramics industry. As domestic and international markets expanded, the porcelain industry in Jingdezhen experienced steady progress. By the mid-Ming period, the "government-supported, private-produced" system came into effect, fostering rapid development among private kilns and sparking competition between government and private producers. The trade of Jingdezhen porcelain also expanded overseas during this time. During the Yongle and Xuande periods, Zheng He undertook seven voyages to the "Western oceans," exporting large quantities of Jingdezhen porcelain through the Pacific and the Indian Ocean to Central Asia, West Asia, and various countries and regions in Africa. This greatly enhanced the global influence of Jingdezhen ceramics. By the late 15th and early 16th centuries, through the efforts of various European East India companies, Chinese products—particularly Jingdezhen porcelain—were exported in large quantities to European countries. Porcelain emerged as a global commodity, playing a positive role in advancing human civilization.

The early and the middle periods of the Qing Dynasty (1616-1911) marked the peak of Jingdezhen's ceramic industry. During this period, the porcelain quality has been enhanced, and the variety has grown. The imperial porcelain of the Qing Dynasty was heavily influenced by the tastes of emperors, with Emperors Kangxi, Yongzheng, and Qianlong placing a high value on craftsmanship, even personally overseeing the design and production of ceramics. Meanwhile, private kilns experienced sustained advancements in areas such as product diversity, organizational structures, and ceramic trade. Their output in terms of both quality and production scale far exceeded that of earlier dynasties. However, the imposition of maritime trade restrictions during the early Qing period severely hindered the export of ceramics to overseas markets.

In the 23rd year of the kangxi period (1684), the Qing court lifted the maritime trade ban, leading to the extensive export of Chinese porcelain, particularly Jingdezhen ceramics, to Europe. This influx had a profound impact on various areas of European society. For European royal and noble classes, the finely crafted Chinese porcelain became a highly prized collectible symbolizing their refined taste and elite status. For the broader public, the introduction of Chinese porcelain allowed them to replace their costly silver and gold tableware, as well as the heavy, hard-to-clean ceramic dishes, sparking what became known as the "dining table revolution" in Europe.

Section II

The History of Modern Porcelain
Making in Jingdezhen

During the late Qing to early Republican periods, the porcelain industry in Jingdezhen experienced a sharp decline due to national political turmoil. Production scale shrank, and the quality of porcelain considerably deteriorated, leading to the traditional porcelain manufacturing system in crisis. In response, various sectors in Jingdezhen implemented diverse approaches to reform the industry. On the one hand, reform groups embraced modern porcelain-making techniques, established companies, and opened schools, initiating the industry's modernization. On the other hand, traditional craftsmen leveraged their exceptional handmade porcelain techniques to produce artistic display pieces.

Establishing modern ceramic companies. After the Opium War in 1840, a flood of foreign goods, including porcelain, flowed into China, leading to a significant decline in the domestic market for Jingdezhen ceramics. The widespread popularity of foreign porcelain drew the attention of local producers, who sought to reform the industry to reverse its downturn. In July 1903, the Governor of Jiangxi Province, proposed founding a porcelain company to revitalize Jingdezhen's ceramics industry. However, due to various challenges, the Jiangxi Ceramics Company was officially established by until 1910 and jointly run by the government and businesses. This company operated two factories: the main factory in Jingdezhen, which adhered to traditional methods, and a branch factory located in Poyang, which adopted modern techniques. This marked the initial

IP and Creative Industry:
Jingdezhen Story

formation of a new porcelain production system.[①] After the Republic of China (ROC) was founded in 1912, the Jiangxi Ceramics Company fell into difficulties and was unable to fulfill its original mission of leading the revitalization of Jingdezhen's porcelain industry, facing both internal and external pressures.

Innovating ceramic management institutions. During the late Qing and early Republican periods, officials in Jingdezhen strengthened local governance and established production standards for the porcelain industry to ensure its smooth operation and maintain social order. Following the establishment of the Republican government, a series of reform initiatives were launched to revitalize Jingdezhen's ceramics industry. In 1929, the Jiangxi Provincial Construction Department established the Jiangxi Bureau of Ceramic Affairs, spearheading improvements in the ceramic sector. These efforts included technical research on building new coal kilns, innovating glazes, and designing modern ceramic forms. The Bureau also set ceramic tax rates and conducted surveys on production, which contributed to the advancement of Jingdezhen ceramics. By 1934, the Jiangxi provincial government set up a Ceramic Management Bureau in Jingdezhen, dedicated to reforming the ceramics industry. This initiative included various efforts, such as the design and production of innovative ceramic products, the improvement and transformation of traditional production methods, the promotion and dissemination of ceramic knowledge, and the training of workers in the ceramics industry. Through these comprehensive measures, the Bureau aimed to elevate the quality and competitiveness of Jingdezhen ceramics.

Establishing modern ceramic schools. In 1910, to support the development of the Jiangxi Ceramics Company, a group dedicated to ceramic reform established the China Ceramic School, which was the first formal institution in Jingdezhen and even in China dedicated to training ceramic professionals. The school aimed to cultivate talents who were "knowledgeable in theory and skilled in technology." In 1912, the school was renamed Jiangxi Provincial Raozhou Ceramic School, focusing on training skilled technicians and decorative porcelain artisans. By 1915, it was further renamed Jiangxi Provincial No. 2 Type A Industrial School. In 1925, the name changed again to Jiangxi Provincial Kiln School, and shortly thereafter,

---

① Jingdezhen Municipal Local Chronicles Office, ed., *The Porcelain Capital of China: Jingdezhen Ceramics Chronicle, Volume II* (Beijing: China Local Records Publishing House, 2004), 4.

it became known as Jiangxi Provincial Jingdezhen Ceramic School. In 1926, the school was renamed Jiangxi Provincial Ceramic School, with Zou Junzhang serving as the principal. At the end of 1937, the school temporarily relocated to Jing'an, and later, following the order of the Ceramic Management Bureau, it moved to Shangbu Town in Pingxiang in August 1938.In October 1944, it was renamed Jiangxi Provincial Ceramic Vocational School. At the end of the same year, the vocational school merged with the Fuliang Ceramic Vocational School. In 1946, it was renamed Jiangxi Provincial Ceramic College. In addition, several other schools were established in Jingdezhen, including the Fuliang Private National Porcelain Arts School and the Jingdezhen Private Oriental Arts College. Despite their smaller scale, they played a significant role in nurturing talent in the ceramics field.

Exploring new directions in ceramic art. After the Tongzhi era, the Qing court's control over artisans within the Imperial Porcelain Factory weakened, allowing many renowned porcelain painters to enter the public sphere in their relentless pursuit of artistic creation, leading to a shift in the model of ceramic creation.

Eight Friends of Zhushan Porcelain Plate Painting, Republic of China Period (Image courtesy of the Jingdezhen China Ceramic Museum)

Drawing inspiration from traditional famille-rose techniques and the aesthetics of Chinese literati painting, Jingdezhen ceramic artists developed the shallow-colored art form. Notable figures in this artistic movement included Wang Shaowei, Jin Pinqing, Cheng Men, Wang Youtang, and Pan Taoyu. During the Guangxu era, the introduction of new glazes and production techniques from abroad facilitated the emergence of Western-style decorative techniques, commonly referred to as "new color" or "new famille rose." In the Republican period, the innovative famille rose works produced by the "Eight Friends of Zhushan" primarily focused on porcelain plaques, or similar flat-mounted pieces and round plates. This unique innovation not only elevated the status and influence of Jingdezhen's ceramic artisans but also further enriched the ceramic art. Moreover, Jingdezhen frequently undertook the production of custom porcelain and tribute ceramics. In 1915, then provisional president of the Republic of China (ROC), Yuan Shikai, commissioned ceramic experts to Jingdezhen to create personal-use porcelain, which later became known as "Hongxian Porcelain," based on his reign title. Many ROC high-ranking officials and dignitaries also ordered bespoke porcelain under their own hall names. For instance, Cao Kun produced exclusive pieces in the name of Yanqing Lou, while Xu Shichang created his own in the name of Jingyuan Lou. Jingdezhen also crafted porcelain gifts for foreign leaders and international friends, with the porcelain presented to the late Queen Elizabeth II of the United Kingdom serving as a notable example.

Section III

Modern Ceramics Industry in Jingdezhen

Since the founding of the People's Republic of China (PRC) in 1949, Jingdezhen has transformed its ceramics industry system through continuous exploration, reform, and innovation efforts. Production techniques have continually evolved, decorative styles have diversified, ceramic art has thrived, and cultural exchanges have intensified, all while significant progress has been made in preserving ceramic heritage. This ancient porcelain capital has regained its brilliance and is now writing a new chapter in history. This journey can be divided into two stages: the first, from 1949 when the PRC was founded to 2012 when the 18th National Congress of the Communist Party of China (CPC) was held, marked by the restoration and transformation of the ceramics industry; and the second, from 2012, heralding a period of high-quality development in Jingdezhen's ceramics industry.

(1) The Profile of Jingdezhen's Modern Ceramics Industry

Following the founding of New China, the Jingdezhen Municipal People's Government made great efforts to restore and revitalize the ceramics industry. Building on the foundation of small local workshops, the government established a number of large state-owned porcelain factories, collectively known as the "Ten Great Porcelain Factories," including Jianguo, Renmin, Yishu, Guangming, Xinhua, Jingxing, Hongxing, Hongqi, Yuzhou, Weimin, and Shuguang. This initiative helped to preserve and revive traditional ceramic-making craftsmanship. During the planned economy era (1949-1978), these factories produced iconic ceramics that came to be known as the "Four Famous Jingdezhen Porcelains," including blue-and-white porcelain from the Renmin Porcelain Factory, delicate Linglong porcelain from the Guangming Porcelain Factory, color-glazed porcelain from the Jianguo Porcelain Factory, and exquisite famille rose porcelain from the Yishu Porcelain Factory. These pieces were celebrated for their unique designs, fine craftsmanship, and high-quality production. Jingdezhen's ceramics industry not only achieved high output but also contributed significantly to the province's economic growth through value creation and tax revenue. These ceramics also served as key products for export and were vital for generating foreign exchange in Jiangxi Province. By 1990, ceramic exports from Jingdezhen accounted for 50% of the province's total export earnings. In 1992, the 14th National Congress of the CPC determined that the goal of China's economic system reform was to establish a socialist market economy, ushering in a period of transformation for Jingdezhen's ceramics industry. This led to the development of a diversified product system that integrated daily-use porcelain, artistic ceramics, and antique-style ceramics, allowing the industry to recover and expand. By 2012, Jingdezhen's ceramics industry had grown to generate a total output value of nearly 21.49 billion yuan, with daily-use ceramics valued at 6.783 billion yuan (31.6%), artistic display ceramics at 8.291 billion yuan (38.6%), sanitary ceramics at 2.891 billion yuan (13.4%), high-tech ceramics at 3.04 billion yuan (14.1%), and auxiliary ceramic materials at 495 million yuan (2.3%). This established a comprehensive ceramic industry system that included raw materials, machinery, daily-use ceramics, sanitary ceramics, artistic display ceramics, and high-tech ceramics. At the same time, industries related to ceramics, including kilns, packaging, printing, logistics, and cultural heritage, developed rapidly, creating a more integrated system. Jingdezhen has also established higher education institutions focused on ceramics, such as Jingdezhen Ceramic University and the Jiangxi Arts & Ceramics Technology Institute, and research centers, including the National Engineering Research Center for Domestic and Building Ceramics and various national, provincial, and municipal ceramic research institutes, all of which provided vital support for the development of the ceramics industry.

Since 2012, particularly following the approval of the Jingdezhen Ceramic Culture Inheritance and Innovation Pilot Zone, the ceramics industry in Jingdezhen has entered a period of rapid high-quality development, focusing on expanding its daily-use ceramics, refining its artistic ceramics, and strengthening its advanced ceramics. This approach has led to a diversified and integrated development model, where advanced ceramics take the lead, artistic display and daily-use ceramics are key features, sanitary ceramics provide supplementary support, and creative ceramics serve as an emerging advantage. By 2023, the total output value of Jingdezhen's ceramics industry reached 86.125 billion yuan, marking a 29.44% year-on-year growth. There were 258 ceramic enterprises above the designated size, marking an increase of 27.09%, with a combined output value of 29.693 billion yuan, up 5.29% from the previous year. Ceramic exports through customs reached 1.04 billion yuan, reflecting a staggering year-on-year growth of 100.7%. The tax revenue from the ceramics industry also doubled to 1.006 billion yuan, a 31.4% increase year-on-year (see Table 2-1).

Table 2-1: Ceramic Output Value in Jingdezhen

Year	Industrial output value (estimated value)		Industry tax revenue		Customs export		Enterprises above designated size		Industrial output value of enterprises above designated size	
	Value (in billion yuan)	Year-on-year growth	Value (in billion yuan)	Year-on-year growth	Value (in billion yuan)	Year-on-year growth	Quantity (number of enterprises)	Year-on-year growth	Value (in billion yuan)	Year-on-year growth
2019	423	5.33%	4.45	68.15%	4.62	45.38%	103	3.88%	127	10.73%
2020	432	2.13%	3.75	-15.83%	2.45	-46.89%	121	17.48%	129	1.68%
2021	516	19.44%	5.2	38.67%	2.09	-14.81%	140	15.7%	185	19.67%
2022	665	28.9%	7.6	46%	5.2	147.9%	203	45%	282	52.4%
2023	861.25	29.44%	10.06	31.4%	10.4	100.7%	258	27.09%	296.93	5.29%

Data Source: Jingdezhen Ceramic Industry Development Bureau

(2) Characteristics of the Jingdezhen's Ceramics Industry

The high-quality development of the Jingdezhen's ceramics industry has been driven by its deep-rooted ceramic culture, favorable development environment, diverse range of products, and strong policy backing, resulting in a uniquely distinctive development model.

The agglomeration effect of the ceramics industry has become increasingly pronounced. After years of development and integration, Jingdezhen's ceramics industry has rapidly evolved into distinct sectors, showing strong clustering benefits. The Changnan New District has become a hub for traditional daily-use ceramic manufacturers, represented by the Jingdezhen Redleaf Ceramics Co., Ltd. and the Jingdezhen Intelligent Ceramic Manufacturing Workshop. The high-end handcrafted ceramics cluster is led by Mingfang Park, while the advanced ceramics cluster is anchored by companies such as Konfoong Materials International Co., Ltd., Jingdezhen Jingda New Material Co., Ltd., and Jingdezhen Hechuan Powder Technology Co., Ltd. In the Zhushan District, platforms for ceramic cultural and creative sectors, such as Taoxichuan, Sanbao International Ceramic Valley, Jingdezhen Imperial Kiln Ceramic Art Museum, and the Sculpture Creative Park, have taken shape, showing promising developmental potential. The High-tech Zone and Changjiang District have emerged as centers for advanced ceramics, with a particular focus on military-civil integration, especially in aerospace ceramics. These areas also serve as specialized production and sales hubs for the broader ceramic supply chain, covering ceramic machinery, kilns, mid-to-high-grade clay bodies, glazes, and pigments. Meanwhile, Fuliang County has developed into an advanced ceramics area led by enterprises like Xianghu Industrial Park, Jinghua Special Ceramics Co., Ltd., and Jinglong Special Ceramics Co., Ltd., along with a sanitary ceramics cluster represented by Guangdong KITO Ceramics Group Co., Ltd. and Lehua Ceramic Sanitary Ware.

The online sales of ceramics have surged dramatically. With the rise of e-commerce, ceramics has emerged as a rapidly growing category, experiencing significant increases in sales volume. As of now, there are nearly 10,000 enterprises engaged in ceramic e-commerce in Jingdezhen, with live-streamed ceramic sales accounting for 70% of the national total. Over 50,000 ceramic shops have registered and conducted transactions on major third-party online platforms such as Taobao, Tmall, and Jingdong. Notably, Sanhe Village in Xinfeng Subdistrict, Changjiang District has grown into one of the four recognized "Taobao Villages" in Jiangxi Province. The Taoxichuan Live-Streaming Base, developed by Jingdezhen, has emerged as a hub for ceramic e-commerce, housing around 6,000 e-commerce businesses and over 10,000 ceramic live-streamers, enabling numerous ceramic

Famille Rose Lushan Landscape Porcelain Plate Painting by Zhang Songmao (Photo courtesy of Jingdezhen China Ceramics Museum)

merchants to achieve online sales. Overall, Jingdezhen's ceramics industry is evolving towards an integrated model characterized by immersive offline experiences, cross-sector integration, and online brand promotion and sales.

The talent pool in ceramics is expanding. By the end of 2023, approximately 150,000 people were employed in Jingdezhen's ceramics industry, including about 44,000 skilled professionals. This group comprises over 6,500 technical specialists in ceramics, more than 4,000 high-skilled workers, and 874 inheritors of intangible cultural heritage at various levels. As of 2022, Jingdezhen boasted 45 Chinese arts and crafts masters (accounting for 41.7% of the national total), 43 Chinese ceramic art masters (19.6%), and 35 Chinese ceramic design art masters, along with 120 masters of arts and crafts and 60 ceramic art masters from Jiangxi Province. Furthermore, Jingdezhen is home to around 76,000 university students, with expectations to exceed 100,000 by 2025. The city has also attracted high-end ceramic talents, including teams led by Yao Lijun from Konfoong Materials International Co., Ltd., Zeng Yuping from the Shanghai Institute of Ceramics, and Li Gang from Tsinghua University.

In recent years, more than 30,000 artists, designers, entrepreneurs, and ceramic enthusiasts from both domestic and international backgrounds have come to Jingdezhen to study and exchange ideas on ceramic culture while seeking entrepreneurial opportunities. They are by locals affectionately called "Jing Piao" and "Jing Gui" (Jingdezhen returnees), with more than 5,000 recognized as "Yang Jing Piao," contributing to a unique cultural phenomenon in ceramics.

Jingdezhen has achieved remarkable success in preserving and developing its ceramic cultural heritage. As a world-renowned, millennia-old porcelain capital, the city boasts a wealth of well-preserved ceramic relics dotted with ancient kiln sites, old alleys, and historic neighborhoods. Over 30 prominent ceramic relic sites, such as the Imperial Porcelain Factory and the Gaoling Ancient Mine Ruins, are recognized worldwide as unique, top-tier cultural resources with no direct parallels elsewhere. In terms of preserving ancient ceramic sites, Jingdezhen has undertaken three archaeological surveys between the early 1970s and the early 21st century, implementing targeted preservation measures based on the survey results. From 1972 to 2006, the city carried out 22 archaeological investigations and excavations aimed at systematically safeguarding its ceramic heritage. In 2015, Jingdezhen officially initiated the application for World Heritage status, centering on the Ming and Qing Imperial Porcelain Factory ruins as its core, aiming to collectively submit representative heritage categories that reflect Jingdezhen's millennia-long porcelain-making legacy. In January 2017, the National Cultural Heritage Administration included the Imperial Porcelain Factory site on China's Tentative List for World Heritage nominations. As of 2019, the city had 2 national-level demonstration bases for the production protection of intangible cultural heritage, 27 provincial-level bases, and 100 municipal-level bases. It also had 2 provincial-level research bases, 3 inheritance bases, and 2 dissemination bases, along with 1 municipal-level research base, 7 inheritance bases, and 7 dissemination bases.[1] As of 2023, Jingdezhen is home to 12 national key protected cultural relic units, 29 provincial-level similar units, and 205 municipal and county-level ones.[2] The city has set a new benchmark for the preservation, transmission, and development of ceramic heritage.

The integration of culture and tourism in Jingdezhen showcases high-quality development. The local government has capitalized on its strength in resource integration to lead the revitalization and upgrading of traditional scenic areas while actively exploring new pathways to repurpose industrial heritage. By blending historical preservation with modern aesthetics, many traditional ceramic sites and abandoned porcelain factories have been rejuvenated, drawing new interest and attracting tourists, especially younger visitors, to these modernized

---

[1] "Fostering Cultural Vitality Through a New Intangible Cultural Heritage Ecosystem: Highlights and Achievements of Jingdezhen's Intangible Cultural Heritage Protection Work," *Jingdezhen Ceramics*, 2022(03): 41.

[2] The Publicity Department of the CPC Jingdezhen Municipal Committee, ed., *A Brief History of Jingdezhen Ceramics* (Nanchang: Jiangxi Education Publishing House, 2023), 266.

ceramic venues. Notable examples include those modern tourist attractions centered around ceramics, like the Taoxichuan Ceramic Art Avenue and the Jingdezhen Industrial Heritage Museum, which have drawn a large number of young visitors. Through authentic preservation and restoration of old factory buildings, tunnel kilns, and industrial facilities, the original architectural texture and style have been retained. Simultaneously, new features such as museums, pottery shops, music rooms, and coffee bars have been incorporated, breathing new life into old industrial relics. These outdated porcelain factories have been transformed into trendy, creative districts. Jingdezhen has also introduced new tourist attractions, such as The Gaoling·China Village and the live performance *Jingdezhen Memory: China*. Over the past two years, the Jingdezhen Municipal Bureau of Culture, Broadcasting, Television, Press and Publication has focused on establishing a ceramic culture inheritance and innovation pilot zone. Guided by scientific planning and project-driven development, it aims to create several key areas, including Taoyangli Historic District centered around the Imperial Porcelain Factory, Taoxichuan Ceramic Art Avenue, Taoyuangu Artistic Scenic Area based on the Sanbao International Ceramic Valley, as well as educational and industrial zones like the Taodaxiao Town Science and Education District and the Taokeyuan Park. Altogether, these efforts have resulted in over ten cultural attractions that showcase the unique charm of ceramics, forming a new model for integrating culture and tourism, centered on ceramic culture and supported by themes like historical heritage, artistic creativity, therapeutic arts, and pastoral living.

The exchange of ceramic culture in Jingdezhen continues to grow rapidly, with its international "circle of friends" steadily expanding and its interactions with sister cities worldwide deepening. It has been selected as a member of the UNESCO Creative Cities Network and has joined both the Maritime-Continental Silk Road Cities Alliance and the International Sister Cities Tourism Alliance. The city has engaged in multi-dimensional cultural exchanges and collaborations with 72 countries and more than 180 sister cities, building a broad bridge for the world to understand Jingdezhen and for Jingdezhen to connect more closely with the global community. In response to President Xi Jinping's important directives from 2019, which called for the establishment of the Jingdezhen Ceramic Culture Inheritance and Innovation Pilot Zone as a new platform for international cultural exchanges, and his 2023 instruction to further enhance the ceramics industry and enhance the reputation of Jingdezhen as the "Millennia-old Porcelain Capital," the city has deepened its integration into the Belt and Road Initiative (BRI). It actively participates in prominent international cultural exchange events, such as "Experience China," "China Today," "Porcelain Journey Along the Silk Road," and "Porcelain Fate with Generation Z," all while working to craft and promote a fresh global image of Jingdezhen as the world's porcelain capital. Jingdezhen has successfully hosted numerous high-level events, including the Fifth Arabic Arts Festival, the 2022 International Copyright Forum, the 2023 Strategic Communication Forum, the Jingdezhen International Ceramic Art Biennale, the Global Advanced Ceramics Industry and High-Tech Industry Development Conference, and China Jingdezhen International Forum on High-Tech Ceramics. The documentary *Porcelain: Clay and Fire* was recognized as a key project under the Ministry of Culture's "Going Global" initiative, while the project "Telling China Stories with Jingdezhen Ceramics" was selected as one of the top ten outstanding national cases in international communication. The project "Using china to Tell China—Telling China's Story through Jingdezhen Ceramics" was selected as one of the "Top 10 Outstanding National Cases in International Communication in 2021." The project "Connecting the world through Chinese porcelain— Using Chinese Porcelain to Foster Global Friendships" was selected as one of the "Top 10 Outstanding National Cases in International Communication in 2023." The city has participated in the "Expert Review Meeting on International Tourism Alliance of Silk Road Cities" and the "Silk Road Artists 'Rendezvous' exhibition," which included dialogues among artists from China and Arab countries. Jingdezhen successfully established the country's first practical base for "emerging literary and artistic organizations and groups," attracting numerous artists from both domestic and international backgrounds to innovate and start their businesses there. In recent years, Jingdezhen has strengthened its collaboration with overseas channels of major central media outlets, such as Xinhua News Agency, *People's Daily* (Overseas Edition), CCTV CGTN, *China Daily*, and China News Service, to expand its international online presence. It partnered with Xinhuanet to produce the short video series "Foreign Potters in Jingdezhen Talk About China;" *People's Daily* (Overseas Edition) published an article titled "Foreign Potters Fall in Love with Life in Jingdezhen," telling the stories of a group of foreign potters working and living in the city, which sparked a lively discussion among netizens. The Jingdezhen Municipal Integrated Media Center's production "Friends from afar—French artist Aima" won the Outstanding Work Award at an international short video competition. The MV "The Love of Twists (Chan Zhi Lian)" was selected as one of the top cases for international online communication in the "China's Good Stories" category. The ceramic-themed dance drama "Only Blue and White" featured the segment "Porcelain Shadows," which was performed at CCTV's 2023 Lunar New Year Gala and broadcast live to over 2,100 media outlets in more than 200 countries and regions through China Global Television Network, reaching a global audience of over 666 million. The program "Inheritors-Jingdezhen" aired on European news channels, accumulating 128 million views, with over 54 million online viewers. The short video "Seeing Jingdezhen" was shared on multiple overseas social media platforms and adopted by various international media outlets, garnering 2.68 million views. Leveraging the Gen-Z International Youth Study and Exchange program, Jingdezhen held an online exchange event titled "Talking Ceramics," attracting 3,100 young artists from more than 50 countries (regions). A total of 3,560 online works were published, making it an important force in promoting Chinese culture.[1] Moreover, international research programs on ceramic culture and youth Sinology classes for co-building Belt and Road countries are actively conducted, allowing more international friends to gain an in-depth understanding of Jingdezhen's rich ceramic heritage.

---

[1] Zhang Long, "Jingdezhen, Jiangxi: Using Porcelain as a Medium to Strike a Strong Punch in Online International Communication," *China Cybersecurity Review*, 2024(07): 63.

IP and Creative Industry:
Jingdezhen Story

The Historical Evolution and Foundations of Jingdezhen's Ceramic Copyright Awareness

Ceramic culture is an integral part of the formation and development of Chinese civilization. Long before the inventions of papermaking and printing, ceramics served as a tangible medium for the original expression of cultural art, embodying the intellectual achievements of creativity and introducing a distinct ceramic aesthetic. The unbroken tradition of kiln firing in Jingdezhen, spanning over a thousand years, has amassed an immense cultural heritage of ceramics. This legacy has allowed copyright—originating in literature, art, and science—to preserve not only the tangible original ceramic objects but also the ideas and concepts behind them. For centuries, the well-preserved copyright awareness and practices in Jingdezhen ceramics have laid the foundation for contemporary ceramic innovation and legal protection, thus nurturing a fertile environment for ongoing creative development and providing a uniquely Chinese solution for the protection of ceramic copyright.

Section I

The Historical Evolution of Jingdezhen's Ceramic Copyright Awareness

For over two millennia, the uninterrupted kiln firing in Jingdezhen has fostered the development and dissemination of its rich ceramic culture, shaping an evolutionary path for ceramic copyright. This journey, which began in ancient times, continued to evolve through modern periods, and has been refined in contemporary era. The various forms of ceramic copyright expression at different historical stages faithfully reflect the shifts in ceramic copyright awareness and innovation governance throughout China. These forms also vividly illustrate the vital role that ceramic copyright awareness has played in advancing the development history of handicrafts.

(1) The Origins and Evolution of Ancient Ceramic Copyright Awareness

The Song and Yuan dynasties mark the origin of ceramic copyright awareness in Jingdezhen. Archaeological evidence reveals that the earliest kiln remains in this area date back to the late Tang and Five Dynasties periods when celadon and white porcelain were produced. Prior to this, no kiln sites had been reported.[1]

---

[1] Jiangxi Provincial Institute of Cultural Relics and Archaeology, Leping Museum, Jingdezhen Ceramic Archaeological Institute, Jingdezhen Folk Kiln Museum, "Report on the Survey of the Nanyao Kiln Site in Leping, Jiangxi," *Journal of National Museum of China*, 2013 (10).

Moreover, historical references to "Tao Kilns" and "Huo Kilns"[1] lack corresponding archaeological findings or artifacts, leading to debate due to insufficient evidence from both archaeological findings and written records. It wasn't until the Song Dynasty that the *Fuliang County Annals* clearly stated: "During the reign of Emperor Jingde of the Song, a town was established here, named after the reign title. A supervisor was appointed to oversee the production."[2] *Records of Pottery (Tao Ji)*, a comprehensive record of Song Dynasty kilns, noted, "Jingdezhen had over three hundred kilns producing ceramics."[3] Substantial archaeological findings at sites like Nanshi Street[4], Hutian Kiln[5], and Luomaqiao site[6] further indicate that by the Song and Yuan periods, Jingdezhen had developed into a significant urban center. During this time, ceramic production had become distinct from agriculture[7] and gradually shifted towards mass production. This era also saw the emergence of a ceramic copyright awareness in Jingdezhen, which helped protect innovative achievements in ceramics and reflected an early awareness of intellectual property rights, even before the formal establishment of copyright

---

[1] The mentioned "Tao Kilns" and "Huo Kilns" are based on the records in *Fuliang County Annals* which states, "During the Wude period of the Tang Dynasty, a place named Taoyu transported porcelain into Guanzhong, referred to as fake jade artifacts, and paid tribute to the court, thereby making Changnan Town's porcelain famous the world over." See Qiao Yanxiu and He Xiling, eds., *Fuliang County Annals: Food, Goods and Pottery Administration*, Volume Eight, Engraved Edition of the Third Year of the Emperor Daoguang's Reign of the Qing Dynasty, 6, 44.

[2] Qiao Yanxiu and He Xiling, eds., *Fuliang County Annals: Food, Goods and Pottery Administration*, Volume Eight, Engraved Edition of the Third Year of the Emperor Daoguang's Reign of the Qing Dynasty, 7.

[3] Jiang Qi, *Records of Pottery*, Quoted from Qiao Yanxiu and He Xiling, eds., *Fuliang County Annals: Food, Goods and Pottery Administration*, Volume Eight, Engraved Edition of the Third Year of the Emperor Daoguang's Reign of the Qing Dynasty, 25.

[4] Guo Jianhui, "The Contemporary Value and Practical Path of Cultural Heritage Protection and Transmission—Based on the Investigation of the Jingdezhen Qingbai Porcelain Site Cluster," *Jiangxi Social Sciences*, 2023, 43 (01).

[5] Xu Changqing and Yu Jiang'an, "New Archaeological Discoveries at Hutian Kiln," *Palace Museum Journal*, 2004 (02).

[6] Weng Yanjun, Jiang Jianxin, Qin Dashu, and Jiang Xiaomin, "Excavation Brief Report of the Song-Yuan Remains at Luomaqiao Kiln Site in Jingdezhen, Jiangxi," *Cultural Relics*, 2017 (05).

[7] Zhan Jia, Zhao Chuanyu, and Yuan Shenggen, "The Evolution of Ceramic Culture Landscape in Jingdezhen Throughout Historical Periods," *Agricultural Archaeology*, 2009 (06).

laws.

During the Song Dynasty, the creation of porcelain, through meticulous division of labor, naturally fosters an awareness of copyright protection to prevent plagiarism, with distinct roles assigned throughout the porcelain-making process. In *Records of Pottery (Tao Ji)*, authored by Jiang Qi from the Song Dynasty, which systematically documents the kiln industry in Song-era Jingdezhen, it is noted that"Potters, mold makers, and clay workers each attend to their own duties. Trimming, shaping, and coloring clay have specific methods. Printing, painting, and carving have their techniques. All follow a well-structured system without confusion."[1] This implies that by the Song Dynasty, Jingdezhen had developed a clear division of labor, along with techniques like printing designs onto the ceramic. The text further noted that "not only was there a clear division of labor in porcelain production, but the production process was also highly systematic, with kiln owners collaborating with individual pottery makers to form stable, coordinated production teams."[2] By the time of the Yuan Dynasty, the craftsman Hong Yanzu recorded: "Once a piece is completed and ready for sale, new samples quickly follow. Craftsmen of all levels contribute, inspiring people far and wide. How far can carving go? Refining it is no easy task. Time moves forward, bringing vibrant reds and purples, while dust and mud swirl around."[3] Each step in the production process was tightly interlinked, creating a seamless workflow, which not only greatly boosted efficiency but also allowed artisans to focus solely on their specialized tasks—painters only painted, dyers only dyed—ensuring that every stage of production achieved the highest level of craftsmanship, thus establishing natural barriers to creativity.

The emergence of marked signatures and inscriptions on porcelain items reflect a growing awareness of individual rights. According to the *Excavation Report of the Hutian Kiln in 1988-1989* and associated studies of dated tombs, a

---

① Jiang Qi, *Records of Pottery*, Quoted from Qiao Yanxiu and He Xiling, eds., *Fuliang County Annals: Food, Goods and Pottery Administration*, Volume Eight, Engraved Edition of the Third Year of the Emperor Daoguang's Reign of the Qing Dynasty, 25.

② Chen Chaoyun, "Archaeological Observations on Porcelain Manufacturing Techniques during the Song Dynasty," *Acta Archaeologica Sinica*, 2017 (04).

③ Hong Yanzu, wrote, Hong Zai, ed., *Excerpts from the Apricot Garden*, Siku Quanshu Edition, 13.

notable number of stamped gourd-shaped powder boxes were unearthed from mid-to-late North Song strata at the Hutian kiln site, with family names such as "Zhan," "Song," and "Lu," or full names "Cheng Jiulang," and "Li Ming" inscribed on their bases as ceramic marks.[1] Similar powder boxes have also been found in late North Song tombs, with some closely resembling silver powder boxes excavated from cemeteries from Lyu family and Bao Zheng family. The widespread appearance of privatized signature markings on Song ceramics not only reflected an enhanced awareness of market differentiation amid increasing competition but also indicated an emerging consciousness around private ownership of goods. During the Yuan Dynasty, the ceramic markings grew even more diverse, with white-glazed porcelain pieces bearing inscriptions such as "Shufu," "Taixi," "Fulu," "Dongwei," and "Jiangxia"[2] becoming common. One example is the famous Yuan porcelain piece housed in the British Museum, the "Yuan Blue-and-White Dragon Pattern Vase with Elephant Ears(One of the 'David Vases')." Its neck is inscribed the following inscription: "Zhang Wenjin, from Jingtang Community, Dejiao Village, Shuncheng Township, Yushan County, Xinzhou Circuit, a disciple of the Holy Gods, is pleased to offer a set comprising one incense burner and a pair of flower vases to General Hu Jingyi at the Original Palace in Xingyuan, as a prayer for the protection and blessing of the whole family and for the peace of his sons and daughters. Carefully recorded in a good moment in the 4th month, 11th Year of the Zhizheng reign."[3] This inscription, detailing the date, location, names, and events, further illustrates the relationship between private ownership and visual distinction. Inscriptions or ceramic marks served not only to differentiate ownership but also as early marks of quality accountability, representing the awakening of personal property rights within the context of feudal production relations.

The Ming and Qing dynasties mark a significant period in the development of

① Xu Xiangyu, "Classification and Verification of Some Textual Records on Song Jingdezhen Qingbai Porcelain," Master's Thesis, Jingdezhen Ceramic University, 2022,8-18.

② Zhang Bai and Yao Jing, eds., *The Grand View: A Collection of Essays on the Blue-and-White Porcelain Pilgrimage during the Late Yuan and Early Ming Dynasties* (Nanchang: Jiangxi Fine Arts Publishing House, 2017), 122.

③ Zhao Yan, "Examination of the Inscription on the Blue-and-White Cloud Dragon Pattern Elephant Ear Vase from the 11th Year of Zhizheng Reign of the Yuan Dynasty," *New Arts*, 2013, 34 (04).

Jingdezhen's ceramic copyright awareness. During this time, Jingdezhen emerged as the center of porcelain production, often referred to as the "gathering place for kiln wares." During the Hongwu period of the Ming Dynasty, the Imperial Kiln Factory—the only official porcelain production and management agency in the country—was established in Jingdezhen, which, beyond its management role, directly engaged in manufacturing. The approach with imperial authority involved spurred Jingdezhen ceramics towards large-scale production, high-quality outputs, and refined specialization, providing substantial material and talent support for technological innovations. Particularly during the mid-Ming period, the implementation of the "government-supported, private-produced" policy facilitated the circulation of techniques between official and private sectors, enhancing the technological standards and product quality of privately-produced ceramics. This allowed Jingdezhen private kilns to advance steadily amid opportunities and challenges, culminating in a vibrant, competitive market between official and private producers by the late Ming period. During the Qing Dynasty, the Imperial Kiln System was continued and refined, with the "government-supported, private-produced" method becoming widespread. The scale and variety of ceramic production peaked during this time. The copyright protection of Jingdezhen ceramics was shaped by both technological advancement and imperial intervention. As the ceramic merchant guilds and associations became increasingly active, production gradually concentrated in urban centers. Thus, the relationship between official and civil ceramic copyright protection was not simply a top-down link; rather, it reflected a complex system of rights interaction involving official management, social organizations, and innovative entities within the evolving copyright protection of Jingdezhen ceramics.

In the production and creation of porcelain, Jingdezhen porcelain industry issued official patterns to protect original designs. The term "official pattern" refers to standard designs crafted by artisans specifically for imperial porcelain, which kiln workers use as templates for production. Since the establishment of the Imperial Kiln Factory in Jingdezhen during the early Ming Dynasty, porcelain has been produced according to these official standards. The *Collected Statutes of the Ming Dynasty* records: "All utensils and items produced were required to follow defined samples, with labor and material calculated."[1] The Qing Dynasty's Imperial Porcelain Factory continued this practice. The *Precedent Cases of Collected Statutes of the Qing Dynasty* states that "for all imperial porcelain, production was required to follow the samples and quantities issued internally, manufactured and sent by Raozhou Prefecture of Jiangxi."[2] The number of official samples peaked during the Qing Dynasty. The *Fuliang County Annals* notes: "In the 15th year of the Jiajing era, 10 porcelain samples were issued... In the 18th year, 43 samples were issued... In the 13th year... 1,340 sets of tableware were produced, each set consisting of 27 pieces: five wine saucers, five fruit dishes, five vegetable plates, five bowls, three lid plates, one tea cup, one wine cup, one waste pot, and one vinegar bottle. There were 380 sets with the 'Blue Cloud Dragon' pattern, 160 sets with the 'Dark Dragon and Purple Gold' pattern, 160 sets in turquoise blue, 160 sets in bright red altered to alum red, and 160 sets in emerald green... In the 36th year... 100 sets of each type of tableware, with each set containing 53 pieces..."[3] The "official sample" allowed original designs to be disseminated within specified boundaries sanctioned by official sanction upon completion, with strict prohibitions against unauthorized distribution or circulation. During the mid-to-late Ming Dynasty, a system known as "goverment-supported, private-produced" was adopted, facilitating technical exchanges between official and private sectors. This enabled private kilns access to official samples, making the "possession and recovery" of these samples a significant aspect of kiln industry regulations, often under direct imperial decree, thus becoming a matter of high importance to the ruling authority.[4] It evidently showed that official-private interaction, innovative outcomes were gradually recognized, promoting the advancement and refinement

---

[1] Xu Pu et al. wrote, and Li Dongyang et al. Revised the "*Ming Hui Dian*" (*The Ming Code*), Volume 157, in the Siku Quanshu edition, 3.

[2] Tie Yuan, Xi Ming, *A History of Qing Dynasty Imperial Kiln Porcelain* (Beijing: China Pictorial Press, 2012), 286.

[3] Qiao Yanxiu and He Xiling, eds., *Fuliang County Annals: Food, Goods and Pottery Administration*, Volume Eight, Engraved Edition from the Third Year of the Emperor Daoguang's Reign of the Qing Dynasty, 19-21.

[4] Wang Guangyao, "Observations on the Ancient Official Sample System in China from the Palace Museum's Collection of Qing Dynasty Porcelain Samples: A Study of the Qing Imperial Kiln Factory, Part Two," *Palace Museum Journal*, 2006 (06): 6-28, 155.

of ceramic copyright awareness.

The publications of artworks from official kilns were safeguarded by "government prohibitions" to protect innovative achievements. The act of publication determined whether innovations could be made public. The *Excavation Bulletin of the Ming and Qing Imperial Kiln Site in Jingdezhen* records: "In the burial pit excavated at the northern foothills of Zhushan Mountain, deliberately buried and smashed porcelain items were found. The artifacts recovered from these fragments included flawless tribute pieces, as well as some with minor defects."[①] This indicates that during the early Ming period, the production of ceramics in official kilns was strictly prohibited from being publicly displayed, with the government enforcing a centralized monopoly over all elements from clay to craftsmen. Apart from high-quality pieces offered as tributes, all inferior, trial, or surplus items were smashed and buried. This official prohibition effectively prevented public access or casual handling, making it difficult for the commoners to see imperial kiln products, let alone replicate them. During the Zhengtong period, the imperial court imposed severe restrictions on the production of private kilns. The *Records of Jingdezhen Ceramics* also notes that: "of those offered as tributes, ten were selected from a thousand pieces, and one from a hundred." Furthermore, records from the *Veritable Records of Emperor Yingzong of Ming*

Burial Pit of the Jingdezhen Imperial Kiln Factory from the Ming Dynasty (Image courtesy of the Imperial Kiln Institute)

---

① Peking University School of Archaeology and Museology, Jiangxi Provincial Institute of Cultural Relics and Archaeology, Jingdezhen Ceramic Archaeological Research Institute, "Excavation Report on the Ming and Qing Imperial Kiln Site in Jingdezhen, Jiangxi," *Cultural Relics*, 2007 (05).

state: "In December of the third year of the Zhengtong era, an edict was issued by the Censorate prohibiting kilns in Jiangxi from producing and selling official-style blue-and-white porcelain or gifting them to officials' homes. Violators would face the death penalty, and their entire families would be exiled."[1] The document further prescribes, "Prohibit the private production of yellow, purple, red, green, blue, and white blue-and-white porcelain in Raozhou Prefecture... First offenders face execution by slicing, and their families are punished by being sent to the military borders; those who know but do not report face collective punishment."[2] In this early stage of copyright control, where technical means and protective methods were still in their infancy, the practice of destroying and burying pieces to prevent or limit public exposure became a core protective measure and an important historical form in the formation of early ceramic copyright awareness.

To restrict the dissemination of core ceramic techniques and craftsmanship, private kilns established control over competitive practices through a system of "guild regulations." During the Ming and Qing dynasties, Jingdezhen's private kilns primarily relied on organized trade guilds and their customary regulations to maintain a mass production-sales-and-distribution network for ceramics. The strictly controlled methods of transmission and the normative practices within the ceramic merchant guilds effectively prevented the leakage of key innovations and deterred counterfeiting, ensuring that ceramic advancements remained confined to specific groups. As recorded in the *Chronicle of the Jingdezhen Ceramics Industry*: "The division of labor in ceramic production is strict: each person is responsible for a specific task, with clear boundaries separating their duties, and no one interferes with another's work."[3] There were strict rules governing apprenticeship in Jingdezhen's ceramics industry. Some sectors accepted apprentices every three years, others every five years, while certain fields, such as roundware-making, only allowed new apprentices once every 20

---

① *Veritable Records of Emperor Yingzong of Ming*, Volume 49, Quoted in Xiong Liao and Xiong Wei,eds., *Collection of Ancient Chinese Ceramics* (Shanghai: Shanghai Culture *Publishing House*, 2006), 16.

② *Veritable Records of Emperor Yingzong of Ming*, Volume 161, Quoted in Xiong Liao and Xiong Wei,eds., *Collection of Ancient Chinese Ceramics* (Shanghai: Shanghai Culture Publishing House, 2006), 17.

③ Xiang Zhuo (Chronicle), *Chronicle of the Jingdezhen Ceramics Industry: General Principles*, Quoted in Xiong Liao and Xiong Wei, eds.,*Collection of Ancient Chinese Ceramics* (Shanghai: Shanghai Culture Publishing House, 2006), 669.

years. Each sector had clearly defined roles, and apprentices were banned to switch trades. Recruitment was restricted to individuals from the designated "Five Guilds and Eighteen Associations." Apprentices needed a guarantor, and formal contracts between the master and apprentice were mandatory, with any breach of agreement strictly forbidden.[1] Due to the meticulous division of labor and the confidentiality surrounding core techniques and innovations, the porcelain-making craft was predominantly transmitted through mentor-apprentice relationships or familial lines, further solidifying the concept of personal rights. The industry's guiding principles—"Each specializes in their own craft, without passing it on to outsiders" and "Those highly skilled in their craft pass down their expertise only within their guild, preserving the trade for generations"—became deeply ingrained in the culture. As noted in the *Records of Jingdezhen Ceramics*: "The origins of kiln construction are untraceable, but since the Yuan and Ming dynasties, the Wei family has continued this tradition."[2] This lengthy and costly learning process confined the transmission of ceramic techniques to a limited group, allowing them to maintain a competitive advantage by holding exclusive control over core innovations.

(2) The Continuation and Transformation of Modern Ceramic Copyright Awareness

The late Qing and early Republican period—characterized by great social shift and reform, along with the introduction of Western rule-of-law thought—marked a transformative era for Jingdezhen's ceramic copyright awareness. Copyright protection evolved continuously under external influences while maintaining its traditional roots. In 1910, the Qing court enacted China's first codified copyright law—the *Copyright Code of the Great Qing Dynasty*. During this period, the intertwining of social transition and cultural changes prompted Jingdezhen to

---

[1]   Jingdezhen Municipal Local Chronicles Office, *The Porcelain Capital of China: Jingdezhen Ceramics Chronicle Volume II* (Beijing: China Local Records Publishing House, 2004), 778-779.

[2]   Lan Pu and Zheng Tinggui, wrote, Yu Zhuqing, ed., *A New Reading of Classical Jingdezhen Porcelain Records* (Hefei: Huangshan Publishing House, 2015), 102.

restructure its ceramics industry by incorporating novel copyright ideas and formulating related regulations. This evolution reflects the complex process of transformation in Jingdezhen's ceramic copyright protection as it adapted to external influences while preserving its foundational concepts.

The copyright awareness was carried forward amid the transition of ceramics industry. Following the Opium Wars, Jingdezhen's ceramics industry began to decline, evidenced by a decrease in the number of kilns. The advent of Western mechanized ceramic production profoundly impacted the market for Jingdezhen ceramics, severely undermining the core driving force of innovative competition and leaving traditional production models in crisis. By the reign of Qing Emperor Xianfeng (r. 1850-1861), both the quantity and quality of ceramics produced by imperial kilns in Jingdezhen had gradually diminished, while products from private kilns also fell short of previous standards. Faced with internal reductions and external pressures, Jingdezhen initiated modern improvements for its ceramics industry, formally establishing the Jiangxi Ceramics Company in 1910, which implemented various measures to revitalize the industry and embark on the process of modernization. Although the enactment of the *Copyright Code of the Great Qing Dynasty* during the late Qing marked the beginning of modern exploration of copyright legislations, overall development in this area remained rudimentary, lacking comprehensive legal frameworks and supporting infrastructure. Moreover, the understanding of copyright law in China was still in a transitional phase. The complex system for protecting copyright interests in Jingdezhen, rooted in familial and geographic industry ties, remained highly dependent and reluctant to change, making it challenging to adapt timely to institutional shifts. Consequently, established regulations and policies failed to be effectively implemented, and the ceramic copyright protection continued to rely primarily on private remedies and industry norms.

The concept of copyright was popularized through the issuance of normative documents. Both the *Chinese Translation of Japanese Law and Economics Dictionary* published in 1909 and the domestically compiled *Glossary of Legal Terms* both explicitly used the term "copyright."[1] As law dictionaries in Chinese

---

[1]　Zhou Lin and Li Mingshan, eds., *Research Literature on the History of Copyright in China* (Beijing: China Fangzheng Press, 1999), 97.

became more widely circulated, terms like "author's rights" and "copyright" became familiar and widely understood among the public. The *Copyright Code of the Great Qing Dynasty* was the first codified law to formally establish the concept of copyright, including the scope of copyrightable works, authors' rights, the procedures for registering copyrights, the duration and limitations of copyright, and penalties for infringement. This law expanded copyright protection from two-dimensional works such as books, paintings, and photographs to include three-dimensional works such as sculptures and models, thereby extending regulation to ceramic works. In 1915, the Beiyang Government issued the *Beiyang Government Copyright Law*, which largely maintained the institutional framework established during the Qing Dynasty. In 1928, the Nanjing Nationalist Government promulgated the *Copyright Law of the People's Republic of China*, which solidified the structure of copyright laws and implementation regulations. With the ongoing refinement of copyright legal norms, awareness of copyright in Jingdezhen grew and spread. During this period, in the export ceramics industry of Jingdezhen, Fan Qiansheng from Linchuan, Jiangxi, founded the Fan Yongsheng Porcelain Company, which stamped its products with the red inscription "Produced by Fan Yongsheng Porcelain Company, Jingdezhen, China" in both Chinese and English. These ceramics were shipped via the Diocese of Shanghai to the Roman Vatican and enjoyed great popularity abroad for several decades. Even after 1980, the label "Produced by Fan Yongsheng Porcelain Company, Jingdezhen, China" retained strong influence overseas.[①] This era marked a notable advancement of ceramic copyright awareness, reflected by the proliferation of English markings on exported Jingdezhen porcelain alongside the growing awareness of copyright legal terminology.

(3) The Establishment and Optimization of the Contemporary Ceramic Copyright System

After the founding of the PRC in 1949, Jingdezhen's ceramic copyright

---

① Tie Yuan and Xi Ming, *Identification of Republican Era Porcelain: Body Glaze, Colored Decoration, and Shape* (Beijing: Hualing Publishing House, 2004), 42.

industry experiences vigorous growth, progressing in tandem with the evolution of China's copyright law. Especially since the reform and opening-up period from 1978, China has gradually established a distinctive copyright law framework centered on the *Copyright Law of the People's Republic of China*. This framework includes a copyright protection system alongside judicial administration, a social service system that covers the entire copyright value chain, and an international cooperation system focused on multilateral collaboration. During this time, Jingdezhen's ceramic copyright system continuously optimized itself within China's unique copyright landscape.

The reform and opening-up have helped improve the copyright legal system. As early as 1955, China established a copyright law drafting group led by Director Hu Yuzhi, and by 1957, the drafting of the *Interim Regulations on the Copyright Protection of Publications* was completed. In 1990, China enacted its first copyright law, and became a member of the *Berne Convention for the Protection of Literary and Artistic Works* and the *Universal Copyright Convention*, effectively addressing the country's international copyright relations. With the enhancement of China's copyright law, a series of policies were introduced to strengthen the legal environment for cultural protection, particularly for traditional cultures like Jingdezhen ceramics. These measures aimed to revitalize traditional culture while promoting innovations, fostering closer integration between Jingdezhen's copyright initiatives and advancements in traditional ceramic craftsmanship. Rooted in the rich foundations of traditional copyright culture, the robust copyright legal framework, combined with effective law enforcement and administrative measures, has propelled Jingdezhen's ceramic copyright protection into a new era of development.

The revitalization of the ceramics industry boosted the development of Jingdezhen's copyright industry. After the PRC's founding, Jingdezhen integrated its ceramic production resources to rejuvenate the industry. By establishing major porcelain factories such as Renmin, Xinhua, Yuzhou, Dongfeng, Guangming, Hongxing, and Hongqi, the city created a diverse production landscape, offering ceramics for decoration, daily-use, industrial applications, and high-tech purposes. The resulting surge in creativity greatly enriched the variety of ceramic pieces produced, with the daily-use ceramics output reaching 90.22

million by the end of 1952, a 42% increase from 63.5 million in 1949.[1] Following the reform and opening-up, Jingdezhen further innovated its ceramic techniques and materials, elevating the industry to new heights. Between 1976 and 1983, Jingdezhen ceramics won five national gold awards, three silver awards, 12 quality product awards from the Ministry of Light Industry, and 23 quality product awards from Jiangxi Province.[2] In 2010, the Jingdezhen Municipal Bureau of Press and Publication (Copyright) focused on protecting the rights of ceramic artists by incorporating copyright registration for ceramic works into its annual entrepreneurship service activities. This initiative established a long-term mechanism for registering copyrights for ceramic works, yielding noticeable achievements. Copyright registrations for ceramic artworks accounted for 53% of the province's total copyright registrations,[3] leading to the gradual development and improvement of Jingdezhen's ceramic copyright industry.

---

[1] Jingdezhen City Chronicles Compilation Committee, ed., *Outline of Jingdezhen City Chronicles* (Shanghai: Chinese Dictionary Publishing House, 1989), 45.

[2] Jingdezhen City Chronicles Compilation Committee, ed., *Outline of Jingdezhen City Chronicles* (Shanghai: Chinese Dictionary Publishing House, 1989), 45.

[3] "Jingdezhen City Strengthens Protection of Copyright for Ceramic Works," *Jiangxi Daily*, Mar. 22, 2010.

Section II

The Foundations of Jingdezhen's Ceramic Copyright Awareness

For over a thousand years, the kilns of Jingdezhen have continuously produced ceramic masterpieces, renowned for their originality. Beyond the artistry, their exceptional ceramic techniques, extensive distribution networks, and innovative and inclusive social culture have collectively provided the intrinsic driving force and practical foundation for the rise of ceramic copyright awareness. The formation and evolution of copyright awareness are the result of the synergistic interplay of technological, cultural, and economic factors within the social context that shaped Jingdezhen's ceramic craftsmanship.

(1) The Development of Ceramic Technology Lays the Material Foundation for Copyright Protection

For centuries, Jingdezhen ceramics have conveyed cultural and artistic ideas through the innovative use of glazes, patterns, and forms, allowing these concepts to be appreciated by the public in tangible forms. This broadened the scope of early copyright protection, extending beyond works typically confined to flat mediums like paper. In addition, since the primary purpose of ceramic production was to meet market demand, growing consumer needs drove advancements in replication technologies. In *The Pilgrim Art: Cultures of Porcelain in World History*, American scholar Robert Finlay notes: "Jingdezhen dominated the global porcelain

257

market not only because of the quality of its products but also due to its advanced scale of production and organizational sophistication. It represented the peak of the craft industry before the steam-powered machine era, achieving remarkable success in large-scale, concentrated manufacturing."[1] He also highlights that, "The combination of roughly shaping mechanics using mechanical means, followed by detailed hand finishing, has long been a hallmark of Jingdezhen porcelain production."[2] As early as the Han Dynasty, farmers in Fuliang, near Jingdezhen, were extracting porcelain stone and using water-powered mills to achieve semi-mechanized processing.[3] By the Tang Dynasty, decorative moulding techniques had emerged at southern kiln sites,[4] and during the Song Dynasty, Jingdezhen widely employed moulds to reproduce desired patterns on a large scale.[5] By the Ming and Qing dynasties, Jingdezhen had developed a system where "every round vessel has its own mould, ensuring uniformity in size and style."[6] *The Ceramic History*, published in 1927, documented Huang Yanpei's investigation into Jingdezhen, detailing the use of paper decals for underglaze and overglaze porcelain in Jingdezhen[7]. After the establishment of the PRC, Jingdezhen transitioned from manual wheel-throwing to single-head pressing, and wooden stirring rods were replaced with mechanized electric belt drives. These innovations lightened the workload for craftsmen and boosted productivity. The single-blade method evolved into double-blade and rolling-forming techniques, while hand-

---

[1]   Robert Finley, *The Pilgrim Art: Cultures of Porcelain in World History*, Trans. Zheng Mingxuan (Haikou: Hainan Publishing House, 2015), 32.

[2]   Lothar Ledderose, *Ten Thousand Things: Module and Mass Production in Chinese Art*, Trans. Zhang Zong (Beijing: SDX Joint Publishing Company, 2005), 123.

[3]   "The Water Mill Construction Technique of Jingdezhen Ceramics (Fifth Batch of National Intangible Cultural Heritage Representative Projects in 2021)," *Jingdezhen Ceramics*, 2022 (03).

[4]   Zhang Wenjiang, "Significant Discoveries from the Archaeological Excavation of the Nanyao Site in Jingdezhen," *Cultural Relics of the East*, 2014 (02).

[5]   Cheng Renfa, "A Study on the Decorative Techniques of Qingbai Porcelain in Jingdezhen during the Song Dynasty," *China Ceramic*, 2015, 51 (12).

[6]   Xiong Liao and Xiong Wei, eds., *Collection of Ancient Chinese Ceramic Texts* (Shanghai: Shanghai Culture Publishing House, 2006), 470.

[7]   Zhou Juemin, "A Brief Discussion on the Rise of Ceramic Decal Paper in China," *Jingdezhen Ceramics*, 1982 (03): 36-37.

pouring was replaced by pressure pouring and vacuum de-airing pouring. A variety of shaping methods, such as centrifugal casting, inner and outer mould rolling, and plastic extrusion, were also adopted.[1] These standardized production methods, along with a highly specialized industry structure, have built up a vast reserve of technical knowledge in Jingdezhen's ceramic production, creating the most extensive, longest-standing, and most diverse ceramic manufacturing system in China. This system not only imbues ceramic objects with the fruits of intellectual innovation but has also fostered and refined a concept of ceramic copyright protection, thanks to the continuous advancements in replication technologies.

(2) The Expansion of the Ceramic Market Consolidates Core Strengths in Copyright Protection

The expansive reach of the ceramic market has been the foundation for the creation and development of Jingdezhen's ceramic copyright awareness. Surrounded by mountains rich in pinewood, Jingdezhen also benefits from abundant porcelain-making materials from nearby regions like Gaoling, Macang Mountain, and Qimen, providing high-quality raw materials and an exceptional environment for ceramic manufacturing. The Chang River, flowing through the city, not only supplied water power for processing but also facilitated efficient and convenient transportation for the trade and dissemination of ceramics. This made Jingdezhen a key hub along the Maritime Silk Road, allowing its ceramics to spread far and wide. The far-reaching influence of Jingdezhen's ceramic products and culture has made indelible contributions to the blending and mutual appreciation of Eastern and Western cultures. As the vast market brought enormous profits, European royalty and nobility prized ceramics as "white gold." This high demand made ceramic counterfeiting and piracy lucrative, which in turn, played a role in fostering the emergence of ceramic copyright awareness.

By the Song and Yuan dynasties, Jingdezhen had already established a thriving domestic and export market for its ceramics. Evidence shows that Jingdezhen

---

[1] Jingdezhen City Chronicles Compilation Committee, ed., *Outline of Jingdezhen City Chronicles* (Shanghai: Chinese Dictionary Publishing House, 1989), 48.

Chapter III
The Historical Evolution and Foundations of Jingdezhen's Ceramic Copyright Awareness

Dongbu Wharf (Image courtesy of the Jingdezhen Municipal Bureau of Culture, Broadcasting, Television, Press and Publication)

blue-and-white porcelain has been unearthed throughout most of China, except for a few regions such as Guizhou, Xizang, Qinghai, Ningxia, and Heilongjiang.[1] Jingdezhen ceramics have also been found in foreign regions, including Northeast Asia, Southeast Asia, West Asia, and even Africa.[2]

During the Ming and Qing dynasties, Jingdezhen ceramics were widely distributed, reaching "from Yan-Yun Sixteen Prefectures[3] in the north, to Giao Chỉ[4] in the south; eastward to the sea, and westward to Sichuan."[5] The international trade primarily focused on East Asia (Japan and Korea), Southeast Asia (Vietnam, the Philippines, and Indonesia), South Asia (India and Sri Lanka), West Asia,

[1]   Li Yiping, "The Hutian Kiln during the Song Dynasty," *Southern Cultural Relics*, 2003 (01).

[2]   Ye Wencheng, "Export of Qingbai Porcelain Kiln System in Jingdezhen during the Song and Yuan Dynasties," *Jingdezhen Ceramics*, 1989 (03,04): 50-54.

[3]   The Yan-Yun Sixteen Prefectures, also known as the "Sixteen Prefectures of Yan and Yun," were a group of strategic territories in northern China that were of significant military and political importance during different historical periods, particularly during the Five Dynasties and Ten Kingdoms period (907-979) and later during the Liao Dynasty.

[4]   Giao Chỉ (交趾) was an ancient administrative region in what is now northern Vietnam. It was part of the larger area of Nam Việt during the Han Dynasty and became significant during various periods of Chinese history.

[5]   Xiong Liao and Xiong Wei, eds., *Collection of Ancient Chinese Ceramics* (Shanghai: Shanghai Culture Publishing House, 2006), 46.

IP and Creative Industry:
Jingdezhen Story

East Africa, and both Europe and America , which were among the largest areas worldwide. These diverse markets not only provided vital channels for customized processing based on demand but also allowed Jingdezhen to integrate global styles and resources.[1] It is estimated that from the 16th to the 18th centuries, Jingdezhen exported approximately 267.81 million pieces of porcelain.[2] According to the *Records of Jingdezhen Ceramics*, "Foreign goods, specifically for overseas sale, can be divided into smooth foreign wares and clay foreign wares. Many merchants from eastern Guangdong trade with foreigners. The styles are intricate, changing each year without a fixed pattern."[3] In response to these orders, Jingdezhen artisans creatively designed a range of decorative and patterned porcelain items tailored for Western consumers' daily use.

In addition to traditional motifs such as flowers, birds, auspicious beasts, and figures, decorative elements on Jingdezhen porcelain began to include Western clan emblems, foreign scripts, compasses, scriptures, fountains, and Western landscape paintings. Borders featured panel motifs or carved designs, while interiors were adorned with branches or fruits.[4] Original custom-made porcelains, such as Armorial Porcelain and Kraak porcelain, emerged in response to these demands. Records from the East India Company document numerous instances where porcelain samples were inspected, and prices were negotiated. This blend of cultural exchange and commercial interests fostered innovative expressions in both porcelain shapes and decorations. Custom designs, whether original creations or adaptations, proved highly profitable, making copyright protection crucial for safeguarding business interests and maintaining a competitive edge. As private ceramic manufacturers vied for market share, the concept of copyright steadily matured.

---

[1] Zhou Sizhong, "The Historical and Cultural Characteristics, Porcelain Production System, and Development Strategy of Jingdezhen," *China Ports*, 2020(S2).

[2] Weng Yanjun, "Estimation of the Scale of Ceramic Exports from Jingdezhen in the 16th to 18th Centuries," *China Ceramics*, 2021,57(10).

[3] Lan Pu and Zheng Tinggui, *Records of Jingdezhen Ceramics*, Quoted in Yu Jiadong, *History of Jiangxi Ceramics* (Zhengzhou: Henan University Press, 1997), 493.

[4] Zhang Zebing, "Historical Experience and Contemporary Practices of Inheriting and Innovating Jingdezhen Ceramic Culture," *Jiangxi Social Sciences*, 2022 (12).

(3) The Social Environment Nurtures the Ceramic Copyright Awareness

The diverse and inclusive social culture that has shaped Jingdezhen ceramics has sustained a thriving porcelain industry for over a thousand years. During the Song Dynasty, widespread warfare prompted a large number of northern craftsmen to migrate south for livelihoods, establishing the social foundation for Jingdezhen's innovative porcelain-making structure. By the Yuan Dynasty, Jingdezhen had nurtured an all-embracing environment that blended various ethnic artistic traditions. The blue-and-white porcelain from this period not only expanded the artistic expressions of high-temperature underglaze painting but also transformed traditional Chinese literary themes—such as "Zhaojun Going Beyond the Frontier Pass"[1] and "Three Visits to the Thatched Cottage"[2]—into creative motifs for Yuan blue-and-white ceramics, giving rise to derivative works that enriched the artistic legacy of the era.

During the Ming and Qing dynasties, with the collaboration between official and private kilns in Jingdezhen, a comprehensive decorative system was established. Supported by guilds and merchant associations, and leveraging its geographical advantages and familial networks, Jingdezhen became a renowned center for ceramic innovation, earning the reputation of "a major town under the jurisdiction of Fuliang in Jiangxi, producing pottery wares that benefit the world. Craftsmen from all directions flock here to earn their livelihood through their skills."[3] Throughout different periods, Jingdezhen's inclusive and open social environment nurtured a diverse ecosystem for ceramic artistic creation. A significant number of ceramic artisans dedicated their time and intellect to enrich

---

[1] "Zhaojun Going Beyond the Frontier Pass" is a popular story in Peking Opera, also known as Beijing Opera. It is based on the historical figure Wang Zhaojun, anoblewoman from the Han Dynasty.

[2] The story originally comes from the *Romance of the Three Kingdoms*, depicting Liu Bei's visit to recruit Zhuge Liang in the late Han Dynasty.

[3] Xiong Liao and Xiong Wei, eds., *Collection of Ancient Chinese Ceramics* (Shanghai: Shanghai Culture Publishing House, 2006), 535.

Small Boats Transporting Porcelain Clay on the Chang River (Image courtesy of the Jingdezhen Archives)

the creative expressions of Jingdezhen ceramics. This intense focus and dedication fueled a continuous flow of innovations, driving the evolution of ceramic craftsmanship across generations. The high degree of creativity and originality in these works also contributed to the growth of a copyright awareness, which evolved and thrived through ongoing innovation and integration.

Section III

The Evolutionary Logic of Jingdezhen's Ceramic Copyright Protection

The ceramic copyright awareness in Jingdezhen has evolved over time alongside institutional and technological advancements. This transformation—from the initial emergence of ideas to private remedies and ultimately to legal protection—follows an evolutionary logic based on which copyright protection gradually aligns with legal norms. Across different historical periods, this progression has been shaped by social changes, technological innovations, and economic development, with each era's distinct characteristics influencing the evolution of copyright practices.

(1) From Social Culture to Legal Norms: Optimizing the Forms of Ceramic Copyright Protection

Before written laws came into existence, copyright protection in Jingdezhen has evolved through mechanisms such as official regulations, merchant guilds, and technical restrictions before the introduction of codified law. These measures introduced protective practices like inscriptions, official patterns, ceramic marks, prohibitions, and trade rules. However, the lack of stability and standardization in their enforcement limited their ability to sustain long-term ceramic innovation. With social changes and the integration of foreign legal concepts, stable legal norms became essential for optimizing copyright protection. During the late

Qing period, the establishment of copyright legal norms—by merging Western copyright protection ideas with China's copyright protection philosophy—marked the first attempt to explore and transform methods of copyright protection via codified law. This development emphasized the central role of creators and initiated efforts to regulate Jingdezhen's ceramic copyright activities through more stable legal frameworks.

(2) From Fragmented to Comprehensive: Expanding the Content of Ceramic Copyright Protection

During the Song and Yuan dynasties, limited by China's legislative and ceramic technological development, the ceramic copyright protection activities in Jingdezhen primarily manifested through the attribution of authorship, with personal rights not yet clearly defined. By the Ming and Qing dynasties, as the personal dependence of ceramic artisans gradually weakened, and the commodity economy grew, copyright awareness expanded towards property rights. As Wang Guangyao pointed out, "Before the Jiajing period of the Ming Dynasty, no fees were paid to artisans. Technical craftsmen were requisitioned by the government, while laborers from Fuliang County and Poyang County were assigned to work in the factories. After the Jiajing period, hired labor became more common, but their wages were likely drawn from the payments made to official craftsmen."[1] This indicates that innovative subjects began to form property relationships around intellectual innovations. In the late Qing period, legislation extended copyright protection from two-dimensional works like books, paintings, and photographs to include three-dimensional works such as sculptures and models, integrating both intellectual and property rights into the legal framework, reflecting the evolving needs of copyright protection.

---

[1] Wang Guangyao, *The Ming Dynasty Palace Ceramic History* (Beijing: The Forbidden City Publishing House, 2010), 148.

(3) From Conservative and Closed to Open and Shared: The Evolution of Concepts of Ceramic Copyright Protection

During the Song and Yuan dynasties, the ceramic copyright awareness emerged from the creators' exclusive mindset toward their intellectual innovations. In the Ming and Qing dynasties, imperial intervention introduced restrictive and conservative measures for protection, while ceramic trade guilds imposed strict industry rules and inheritance systems, limiting the transmission and sharing of innovations and techniques. This led to the risk of creative outcomes being lost and private rights remaining inadequately protected. In the late Qing period, the *Copyright Code of the Great Qing Dynasty* required registration at designated agencies for intellectual works.[1] This move made copyright registration a crucial step for legal protection and progressively clarified the relationship between intellectual achievements and copyright. After the founding of the PRC, ongoing improvements in the copyright registration system and the establishment of a social service framework for copyright further developed the concept. This evolution transformed copyright from an individual, exclusive "private right" to a concept that also embraced "open sharing" as a public right, promoting protection while encouraging broader access and sharing of intellectual achievements.

---

[1]   Zhou Lin and Li Mingshan, eds., *Research Literature on the History of Copyright in China* (Beijing: China Fangzheng Press, 1999), 55.

Section IV

Conclusion

In conclusion, the various forms of ceramic copyright protection in Jingdezhen throughout its different historical stages faithfully reflect the evolution of copyright awareness and innovation governance, vividly demonstrating the crucial role of copyright protection philosophy in advancing ceramic industry development. The foundation of copyright in Jingdezhen has been shaped by the influence of ceramic production and replication techniques driving the development of copyright protection, the flourishing domestic and international ceramic markets accelerating its refinement, and the wealth of creative ideas fostering progress in safeguarding copyright. This diverse and symbiotic "copyright protection" has contributed to Jingdezhen's reputation as a "millennia-old Porcelain Capital" both in China and internationally. In terms of the evolution of Jingdezhen's copyright protection system, it showcases a transition from reliance on private remedies to the adoption of optimized legal regulations, an expansion of copyright protection from limited and fragmented content to a scientifically comprehensive approach, and a shift in copyright philosophy from being conservative and closed to open and shared. This increasingly sophisticated "copyright system" in Jingdezhen continues to sustain the enduring vitality of its thousand-year-old ceramics industry.

Chapter IV

Preserving Jingdezhen Ceramic Heritage: Copyright's Role in the New Era

Leveraging its profound legacy as the "Millennium Porcelain Capital," Jingdezhen has forged a new development paradigm for ceramic cultural and creative industries centered on intellectual property rights. The city has established an end-to-end copyright ecosystem integrating creation, application, protection, administration, and service provisions. This comprehensive mechanism fundamentally ensures enhanced creative quality, optimized resource utilization, rigorous rights protection, scientific management frameworks, and citizen-friendly services, collectively driving the innovative evolution of ceramic cultural industries.

Section Ⅰ

Copyright Development for Jingdezhen Ceramics

Emerging ceramic companies, represented by Jingdezhen Renew Cultural Technology Co., ltd. (hereinafter referred to as Jingdezhen Renew), demonstrate that effective use, protection, management, and service of copyright depend on the continuous creation of high-quality works. Therefore, the development of the Jingdezhen ceramic copyright is anchored in ongoing creativity. Thanks to Jingdezhen's long-standing porcelain-making heritage, current copyright creation activities are supported by the exploration, dissemination, and modernization of traditional ceramic culture. Jingdezhen's approach combines government and market-driven initiatives to concentrate creative entities while also expanding their reach through industry integration. Together, these strategies ensure a steady increase in creators, and the evolution of creative models drives sustained improvements in the quality of their work.

(1) Jingdezhen Renew: A Pioneer in Cultural and Creative Innovation

At the opening ceremony of the 2021 China Jingdezhen International Ceramic Expo, Jingdezhen launched its first city gift to the world: the "Fu Ruyi" tea set. This creation uses innovative design to tell the story of the porcelain capital, promotes a refined lifestyle through ceramic cultural products, and embodies the city's cultural vitality driven by heritage IP. The success of "Fu Ruyi" is rooted in Jingdezhen Renew's steadfast commitment to the ceramic cultural industry. Their philosophy of sustainable copyright-driven development inspires more ceramic creators to preserve and innovate cultural traditions.

The Rising Jingdezhen Renew: Its Founding Vision

Jingdezhen Renew has become a shining jewel in Jingdezhen's ceramic cultural and creative industry. Despite being fraught with challenges throughout its development journey, the company has remained committed to innovation. Originally established as Jingde Xianyunju Ceramic Culture Company Ltd., it had no difference among other ordinary ceramic businesses in the region. Positioning itself as a high-end handcrafted porcelain manufacturer, it found hard to channel its products into everyday life and distinguish itself from competitors. The key challenge was how to incorporate cultural creativity into ceramic manufacturing, making traditional ceramics more relevant to modern lifestyles and enabling the evolution of ceramic cultural and creative production from small workshops into a comprehensive industry, thereby enhancing the company's innovative capabilities. This operational dilemma was not only faced by Xianyunju but also reflected a common challenge for many ceramic enterprises in Jingdezhen.

Extensive market research revealed that while each Jingdezhen ceramic company had its strengths, most found themselves trapped into a vicious cycle of "being unable to grow" or "collapsing when they expanded." Jingdezhen Renew recognized that to find a way out, it needed to redefine its development direction and establish clear goals. Duan Jianping, the chairman of Jingdezhen Jingde Xianyunju Ceramic Culture Company Ltd. believed that to materialize the concept of "original design and artistic lifestyle," the company needed to make breakthroughs in product design, process optimization, and production models. The goal was to integrate Jingdezhen's millennia-old craftsmanship into contemporary living, transitioning personalized ceramic cultural products from individual workshops to scaled and industrialized operations. After more than a year of exploration, a brand-new entrepreneurial project—Renew Cultural and Creative—was launched in February 2019.

The name "瑞牛" (Rui Niu) is derived phonetically from the English word "renew," symbolizing a fresh start and a pioneering spirit. The company creatively blends traditional Chinese culture with millennia-old ceramic craftsmanship, combining customization with scalability to attract market attention through creative design while leveraging production capacity to support limitless creativity.

The design of the "福如意" (*Fu Ruyi*) tea set exemplifies Jingdezhen Renew's vibrant exploration of new development models. Inspired by a precious artifact in the collection of the Jingdezhen China Ceramics Museum—the Qing Dynasty Blue-and-white Gourd-Shaped Vase with a Gourd Motif—it also embodies the Chinese cultural concept of "harmony." The gourd shape phonetically represents "福禄" (*Fu Lu*, wealth and prosperity), symbolizing blessings of fertility and abundance. The rounded and full bottle shape signifies functionality when opened and artistic beauty when closed, resembling the character "吉" (*Ji*, auspicious), which conveys good fortune and harmonious governance. Overall, the piece reflects the extraordinary journey of Jingdezhen's ceramics industry in preserving heritage while fostering innovation. It showcases the innovative charm of contemporary aesthetic lifestyles and represents Jingdezhen's open-heartedness and engagement with the global community.

Breaking Through Barriers to Achieve Customized Mass Production

The success of the "Fu Ruyi" tea set has reinforced Jingdezhen Renew's entrepreneurial vision, emphasizing the necessity to overcome barriers to customization and scalability as they pursue industrial development.

To break through the barriers of customization and scalability, it is essential to integrate resources across creativity, design, R&D, and manufacturing. This approach helps reduce production costs and enhance productivity. When it comes to customization, the goal is to align it with innovation. To address the disconnect between artists, designers, and craftsmen, Jingdezhen Renew has forged collaborations that unit these key players. This collaboration ensures creative ideas to be seamlessly transformed into tangible works, blending design concepts and craftsmanship to achieve near-perfect products. First, Jingdezhen Renew ensures that designers deeply understand the artistic visions behind the works of artists. By close collaboration, designers can gain insight into the artists' creative inspirations, aesthetic goals, and intentions, thereby incorporating these elements into the product design. In this way, the products not only reflect the designers' unique visual style but also convey the deeper cultural meanings and emotional expressions of the artists. Second, Jingdezhen Renew ensures that designers master the artisans' craftsmanship. Through in-depth study of artisans' techniques, designers gain knowledge of the essential skills involved in ceramic production, the characteristics of the materials, and the intricacies of the production process.

Creative Research Center of Jingdezhen Renew (Photo courtesy of Jingdezhen Renew Company)

This allows them to account for the practicality of the products during the design phase. Thus, the designs not only possess artistic and innovative qualities but also fully showcase the artisans' exquisite craftsmanship and quality in the final product. Finally, with designers who understand both the artists' creative concepts and the artisans' traditional craftsmanship, the product creation process flows naturally. Additionally, Jingdezhen Renew employs retired workers from ceramic factories to oversee production, providing valuable job opportunities while ensuring that product quality remains consistently high.

In terms of scalability, the goal is to achieve both scale and efficiency. To address limitations such as inefficient upstream and downstream industrial chains and high material costs during production, Jingdezhen Renew has adopted a "Design + R&D+ Supply Chain" model, innovating the "Ceramics +" industry ecosystem to enhance its core competitiveness. This strategy, leveraging ceramics as a foundation, integrates various elements like "Ceramics + Intangible Heritage," "Ceramics + Craftsmanship," "Ceramics + Copyright," "Ceramics + Artists," "Ceramics + Designers," "Ceramics + IP Derivatives," "Ceramics + Cross-Industry Materials," "Ceramics + Supply Chain," and "Ceramics + Digitalization." This precise alignment allows Jingdezhen Renew to effectively meet customer needs in cultural and creative industries. To cater to the market demand for cultural creativity and transform design and craftsmanship research into tangible, personalized ceramic products, Jingdezhen Renew has integrated its industrial chain resources, employing a "flexible industrial chain" approach. This enables differentiated and scalable production. Following this shift towards mass production, Jingdezhen Renew achieved profitability in 2020, with its revenue doubling for two consecutive years by 2022.

Whether in customization or scalability, Jingdezhen Renew consistently views innovation as the key to making breakthroughs; it believes that both models and creations must be innovative—only through innovation can the company strengthen its position and lead the pack. Fully aware that protecting intellectual property is critical to safeguarding innovation, the company actively ensures its intellectual property rights are protected, which is essential for maintaining long-term competitiveness. As of July 2023, Jingdezhen Renew has signed contracts with 55 artists, 120 designers, and 16 freelance designers. The number of copyright registrations rose from 117 in 2022 to 989 in 2023. For each creation, the company establishes clear agreements with designers to define copyright ownership, streamlining future efforts in intellectual property protection.

Creative Breakthroughs: Jingdezhen Renew Forever Moving Ahead

Jingdezhen Renew has set its long-term strategy on becoming the leading brand in the customized ceramics sector. The company is dedicated to being a model in cultural and creative industries, advancing steadily through strong copyright protection measures. Since its inception, Jingdezhen Renew has received numerous awards, including recognition as a "National Copyright Demonstration Unit," a "Jiangxi Province Specialized and Sophisticated SME," a "Provincial Industrial Design Center of Jiangxi," and a "High-tech Enterprise." Its innovative business model was also ranked among the top 100 outstanding management cases in the 13th National Management Case Elite Competition. In the realm of cultural and creative design, Jingdezhen Renew also stands out. In 2022, it launched the city's first digital collectible—"Qingqing Zijin" (Asure Collar), in collaboration with the Jingdezhen China Ceramics Museum and the Jingdezhen National Ceramic Copyright Trading Center.

The "Furui Dongfang" (Blessed East) digital cultural tourism project launched by Jingdezhen Renew has been included in the fourth batch of VR Application Demonstration Projects by the Jiangxi Provincial Department of Industry and Information Technology. Moreover, Jingdezhen Renew has developed ceramic cultural and creative products for outstanding brands and organizations such as COMAC, China Tower, Alibaba, VIVO, Baidu, Estée Lauder, Zeekr, NIO, China Merchants Bank, Bank of Jiujiang, Peking University, Renmin University of China, and Jiangxi Normal University. Among its notable creations, the "Fu Ruyi" tea set has been designated as the city gift of Jingdezhen, while the ceramic cultural and creative product "Flying Pavilion" tea set, developed by Jingdezhen Renew, has been recognized as a city gift for Nanchang.

Standing at a new historical starting point, Jingdezhen Renew adheres to the guiding principle of "dedication, creation, excellence, and efficiency." By continuing its development strategy centered on elegant design, efficient R&D, and a robust supply chain, it constantly seizes opportunities for growth and innovates product design while enhancing manufacturing capabilities. Jingdezhen Renew injects fresh vitality into the development of Jingdezhen's ceramic cultural and creative industries, showcasing the resilience and ambition of local ceramic enterprises amid market competition and evolving trends. It also underscores the flourishing innovative capacity and vast potential of the ceramics industry centered around copyright.

(2) The Sustainable Model of Ceramic Copyright Creations in Jingdezhen

Access to Resources

The continuous acquisition of resources for ceramic copyright creations in Jingdezhen lays the foundation for its ceramic copyright development. This process represents the initial step in transforming traditional cultural resources into copyright products, ultimately fostering a copyright industry that serves as a significant driving force for the city's development. If the Jingdezhen's ceramic copyright resources diffuse like concentric circles,[①] their acquisition follows a reverse excavation model. First, it involves uncovering creative methods from

---

① Concentric Circle Diffusion: This diffusion pathway is influenced by both the geographical and business scopes of industrialization. It represents a cultural resource diffusion method that starts from its place of origin, initially spreading to a primary diffusion area, and then gradually expanding to a secondary diffusion area. See Wang Zhibiao, "Path Analysis of the Industrialization of Traditional Cultural Resources," *Journal of Henan University* (*Social Sciences Edition*), 2012, 52 (02).

Collections of the Jingdezhen China Ceramics Museum (Photo courtesy of Jingdezhen China Ceramics Museum)

the thriving ceramic cultural resources. Then, these methods are used to trace, explore, and establish the origins of copyright creations. A prime example of this approach is Jingdezhen's in-depth research and exploration of imperial kiln sites. By developing the Imperial Kiln Factory sites, Jingdezhen conducts research and preservation of the unearthed artifacts, gradually recreating lost ceramic copyright resources and providing fresh inspiration for ceramic copyright creations.

Jingdezhen boasts a rich ceramic heritage, with a millennia-long tradition of porcelain-making that has produced countless pieces of blue-and-white porcelain, Linglong porcelain, famille rose porcelain, and colorful glazed ceramics. Thousands of intricate patterns and designs are etched onto these exquisite wares. While some have vanished without a trace, many more lie buried underground, either intact or in shards. Through excavation and preservation efforts, these vessels—embodying centuries of artistic achievements—are being restored to their former glory, becoming valuable resources for modern ceramic copyright creations.

The Jingdezhen China Ceramics Museum, established shortly after the founding of the PRC, is one of the earliest specialized museums dedicated to ceramic art, housing a rich collection of porcelain artifacts. Beyond its role in exhibiting traditional Chinese ceramic culture, the museum holds significance for copyright creations by securing creative resources and serving as a "gene bank" for ceramic copyright works. Jingdezhen's first city gift, the "Fu Ruyi" tea set, was inspired by the museum's Qing Dynasty Blue-and-White Gourd-Shaped Vase with a Gourd Motif. Increasingly, creators are aware that Jingdezhen's vast ceramic culture is an inexhaustible wellspring of inspiration.

Jingdezhen's guiding principle for acquiring ceramic copyright resources is to focus on its geographical range, constantly looking inward to unearth and establish its diverse ceramic traditions as the source for creativity. By doing so, Jingdezhen largely relies on its own rich heritage without overly resorting to external resources. The vision of building Jingdezhen into "the City of Museums" is steadily becoming a reality, as it seeks to secure and solidify these ceramic copyright resources, integrating them into the city's daily life.

The Concentration of Copyright Creators

As Jingdezhen culture contributes more to its economic growth, the city is continually expanding its ceramic copyright industry while refining its structural framework. The clustering effect within the industry has become an inevitable trend. A key characteristic of this clustering is the growing aggregation of copyright creators in Jingdezhen. Unlike more singular market-driven or government-led aggregation models, Jingdezhen employs a hybrid approach that combines both government and market forces, thereby broadening the scope of ceramic copyright creators beyond traditional boundaries.[1]

The Jingdezhen Municipal People's Government attracts creators by reimagining and enhancing existing ceramic copyright resources through comprehensive planning. This new approach includes efforts to establish a model city for copyright, which encompasses improvements in both regulations and infrastructure. The enhancement and transformation of ceramic copyright

---

[1] Researchers have identified three basic models of spatial agglomeration in the cultural industry: market-driven, government-driven, and a hybrid model that combines market with government. Due to differences in the driving factors for agglomeration and the ways in which resources are utilized, these three fundamental aggregation models exhibit distinct characteristics. See Dai Yu, "Research on the Spatial Agglomeration of the Cultural Industry: A Case Study of Hunan Province," Doctoral Thesis, Wuhan University of Technology, 2013, 71.

Cultural Tour in Taoxichuan Ceramic Art Avenue (Photo courtesy of Jingdezhen Municipal Integrated Media Center)

resources are vividly illustrated by initiatives such as renovating old porcelain factory sites into the increasingly popular Taoxichuan Ceramic Art Avenue and upgrading the ceramic trading platform to the International Trading Center at the Ceramic Expo City. To acquire ceramic copyright resources, a city equipped with clear resource planning and timely upgraded platforms is undoubtedly more appealing to creators in the field of ceramics. With government support ensuring resource availability, a vibrant and inclusive market environment also draws together copyright creators with diverse purposes and styles. Whether it's Jingdezhen Renew, which focuses on the industrialization of creativity, or the "Jingdezhen Girl"[①] creator, who specializes in unique patterns and production techniques, all are empowered to transform their ideas into tangible works in this

① The "Jingdezhen Girl," named Xiaofang Momo, draws inspiration for her fragmented paper pattern ceramics from her passion for environmental protection. By combining traditional Jingdezhen ceramic techniques with modern artistic elements, she creates a unique aesthetic. Since their debut, her works have received unanimous praise from both industry professionals and consumers alike. Many have remarked that her pieces embody the richness of traditional culture while also showcasing innovative modern art, offering a refreshing perspective. In Jingdezhen's ceramic market, Momo's creations have become highly sought after, with some even traveling from afar specifically to purchase her work.

dynamic city.

Jingdezhen's attraction to ceramic copyright creators is also evident in the transformation of the creators themselves. The city promotes the integrated development of culture and tourism, leveraging cultural resources such as the Imperial Kiln Ruins to establish new models of cultural tourism. Notable initiatives include Taoxichuan, offering "cultural tours," Gaoling China Village, providing "immersive tours," and Zhushan Mountain Night Tours with events like Porcelain Music and Porcelain Banquet.

Meanwhile, the "Culture + Education" development model has led to the thrive of research and study tours. By leveraging resources of ceramic cultural research and pottery education, and incorporating international artistic concepts and creative thinking, these initiatives provide fresh perspectives for ceramic copyright creation. This integration of cultural, tourism, and education sectors breaks down traditional boundaries among them. Participants are encouraged to move beyond conventional industry mindsets, develop tourism projects that hold cultural value, and design research courses featuring cultural symbols, all while ensuring these projects align with Jingdezhen's unique market dynamics. As such, they evolve beyond mere tourism or education practitioners, becoming an indispensable group within Jingdezhen's ceramic copyright landscape, continually engaging in activities that foster ceramic creations.

Improved Quality of Ceramic Copyright

The internal exploration and acquisition of ceramic copyright creation resources, combined with the aggregation and expansion of copyright creators, have created the conditions necessary for the ultimate enhancement of ceramic copyright quality. Jingdezhen has achieved this goal by rapidly transitioning from a large-scale, one-directional model of copyright creation to one focused on large-scale customized and personalized copyright creation. The era of the "Ten Major Porcelain Factories" represents a typical example of the one-directional copyright creation model, where porcelain manufacturers were the sole copyright creators, while customers acted merely as recipients and users of the products. Although there were breakthroughs in copyright creation during this phase, progress was hindered by the manufacturers' creative habits and relatively conservative business practices. Consequently, while product quality was maintained, the improvement in creative quality was slow.

Influenced by waves of reform, the dominant position of state-owned porcelain enterprises in the ceramics industry gradually weakened, compounded by the depletion of local natural resources. As a result, Jingdezhen could no longer rely on its previous models of creation. During this transition, the city adopted an approach that preserved the essence of traditional ceramic culture while invigorating the market, shifting the focus of ceramic copyright products towards customized and personalized designs. Copyright resources are continuously being explored, and the ongoing activities of the creators are deconstructed into smaller units, allowing for rapid reorganization and renewal during the creative phase. A typical example can be found in traditional ceramic creation processes, where a complete set of patterns must be meticulously applied to corresponding objects for them to be considered as artworks, thereby allowing the process itself to be recognized as ceramic creation. In today's landscape, even a small ceramic fragment can showcase designs that can inspire artists to continuously explore new creative expressions, presenting great market potential. This restructuring of copyright resources provides invaluable support for the customization and personalization of ceramic creations.

A prime example of this is service-oriented creation, where customers play an active role in the copyright works. On one hand, customer demands and preferences shape the direction of a company's creative efforts. In Jingdezhen's open environment, businesses tailor their creations to meet the unique requirements of customers. On the other hand, the growing diversity of customer demands enriches the creative process. As these personalized requests accumulate, companies and artists growingly recognize the inspirations provided by customers, transforming them into copyright products using their professional expertise. Ultimately, it is the buy-side that determines the quality of ceramic copyright works, and Jingdezhen has successfully improved its creative output by adapting its mindset and methods.

Section II

Flexible Utilization of Copyright in Jingdezhen Ceramics

Taoxichuan Ceramic Art Avenue stands as a brilliant example of copyright utilization in Jingdezhen ceramics. In just over a decade, it has evolved from relative obscurity to a vibrant cultural hub. Not only does it embody Jingdezhen's rich ceramic heritage, but its innovative approach to copyright application has also made it a brand calling of this thousand-year-old porcelain capital. Taoxichuan's success demonstrates how Jingdezhen is fostering greater coordination and interaction among stakeholders by refining its copyright utilization system. By innovating copyright utilization, the city has broken down barriers and enabled shared methods for managing intellectual property. Moreover, the revitalization of the ceramic copyright industry has transcended traditional limitations, opening up limitless possibilities for the ongoing expansion of copyright-driven industries.

(1) The Vibrant and Creative Taoxichuan Ceramic Art Avenue

Taoxichuan Ceramic Art Avenue, an internationally renowned open cultural and artistic district, boasts numerous prestigious titles, including a National Cultural Demonstration Zone, a Demonstration Base for Entrepreneurship and Innovation, a National Entrepreneurship Demonstration Base, a Copyright Demonstration Zone, a National Nighttime Cultural and Tourism Consumption Cluster, a National Tourism Technology Demonstration Area, and a Non-material Cultural Heritage Tourism Street. For artists, designers, brand owners, and visitors,

Taoxichuan serves as a vibrant hub for ceramic cultural exchange and a haven for ceramic derivative art. The district has created a powerful synergy of creation and protection through innovative mechanisms for ceramic copyright incentives and services. Here, creativity comes to life, entrepreneurs come to light, and every work is safeguarded by a robust copyright law.

Masterful Craft: Creating a Ceramic Creative Space

What does the name "Taoxichuan" signify? "Tao" refers to ceramics, the very essence of Jingdezhen and the foundation of the former Yuzhou Ceramics Factory. "Xichuan" represents nature and life, embodying the continuous flow and enduring vitality of life itself. Located in the heart of the thousand-year-old porcelain capital, Taoxichuan gets its name from the idea of ceramic creativity flowing together like streams converging into a river, drawing on the rich local heritage to channel this creativity into a dynamic and powerful force.

In 2012, the Jingdezhen Municipal People's Government initiated the transformation of the former site of the state-owned Yuzhou Ceramics Factory, launching the "Taoxichuan International Ceramic Culture Industrial Park" project, with this historic area at its core. With a total investment of 6.8 billion yuan, the project includes a built-up area of 1.5 million square meters. Planned and designed in collaboration with Tsinghua Tongheng Urban Planning & Design Institute

The Large Chimneys in the Taoxichuan Ceramic Art Avenue (Photo courtesy of Jingdezhen Municipal Integrated Media Center)

(THUPDI) and design firms from Japan and the Republic of Korea, the project aims to integrate ceramic cultural resources under a sustainable development philosophy. By revitalizing and utilizing the remnants of the ceramics industry, it seeks to foster cultural creativity, tourism, and modern services, ultimately shaping Taoxichuan Ceramic Art Avenue.

Firstly, through thoughtful and intricate design, some original elements such as the jagged and herringbone factory buildings, 11 towering chimneys, water towers, and old slogans written on the walls are skillfully woven into every corner of the district, turning these once industrial remnants into cherished features treasures. Here, artisans can find a sense of nostalgia and reconnect with memories of the past. Secondly, efforts have been made to protect and restore 22 old factory buildings, coal-burning tunnel kilns, round kilns, and other industrial facilities of Yuzhou Ceramics Factory, all while preserving their original textures and appearances. The former workshops have been repurposed into spaces like Jingdezhen Heritage of Ceramic Industry Museum, the Ceramic Art Avenue Art Gallery, Yikongjian Entrepreneurship and Innovation Incubation Base, Taogongshu Educational and Research Base, and the B&C Design Center. To further advance the cultural and creative industries in Taoxichuan, prestigious institutions such as the Central Academy of Fine Arts, China Academy of Art, People's Daily Online, and Tangying Society have been invited to contribute. Moreover, over 170 well-known cultural and creative brands, including Kungfu Mud, Ceramic 3D Printing, the European Ceramic Workcenter, and Germany's DWH Woodwork Academy, have been brought in to help transform and upgrade the old porcelain factory into a cultural and creative district with international flair and cross-disciplinary operations.

The development of Taoxichuan Ceramic Art Avenue has provided a robust platform for cultural creation. However, in its early stages, the prevalent plagiarism led to the homogenization of works. Despite the presence of thousands of creators in Taoxichuan, the easy access to others' creations and the low costs of infringement bred frequent cases of copying. To address this negative trend, the copyright management departments of Jiangxi Province and Jingdezhen City, along with Taoxichuan's administrators, recognized that establishing a systematic and professional copyright protection framework was essential for ensuring the healthy and sustainable growth of the cultural and creative industries. Therefore, by leveraging the power of copyright as an incentive for cultural innovation, Taoxichuan has established a comprehensive support system that integrates entrepreneurial funding, talent cultivation, platform services, and copyright incentive mechanisms, thereby forming a new model for the growth of the ceramic cultural and creative industry.

First, entrepreneurial funding support. Taoxichuan offers financial assistance to ceramic artists through subsidies for operating incubator bases, entrepreneurship grants, interest-subsidized loans, and one-time startup allowances. These funding policies have helped alleviate the funding pressures faced by ceramic artists at different stages of their entrepreneurial journey.

Second, talent training support. As a national copyright demonstration park (base), Taoxichuan actively raises public awareness of intellectual property protection, regularly inviting copyright experts to conduct public lectures on intellectual property rights for ceramic artists. Forums and lectures featuring internationally acclaimed designers and ceramic artists are also held to provide specialized guidance on managing and leveraging copyright assets. Moreover, through the "72 Young Artists" project and international exchange programs, Taoxichuan encourages collaborative design projects between overseas artists based in Jingdezhen and local talents, inspiring the creation of more globally recognized original works.

Third, platform service support. Taoxichuan assists ceramic artists with services such as individual or business registration, union support, and accounting agency services. Meanwhile, by leveraging the Taoxichuan LIVE streaming base, supply chain selection center, and warehousing logistics center, the site opens up online sales channels, providing ceramic artists with multiple business operation pathways across production, sales, and distribution.

Fourth, brand promotion support. Taoxichuan enhances visibility for ceramic artists by organizing vibrant themed activities, such as copyright exhibitions and contests for outstanding works. These events provide high-quality, diverse platforms for showcasing creations and facilitating product transactions. Taoxichuan leverages official media partnerships and social media to offer comprehensive promotional services, helping ceramic artists reach a broader audience.

Fifth, copyright admission and advancement mechanism. Taoxichuan implements a copyright admission and advancement mechanism through two physical spaces: the stall market and the Yikongjian (creative space). The stall market consists of traditional and creative zones, collectively known as the "ordinary market." This market primarily features stalls run by artists selling handmade crafts, with those in the creative zone required to possess at least one work registration certificate. However, the ordinary market can accommodate only 1,500 stalls per week, while the total monthly applications for stall space up to 4,000—two to three times the available capacity. As a result, the artists occupying the stalls are not fixed, leading to weekly changes. To maximize their visibility, artists must apply for eligibility to occupy a designated stall in Taoxichuan.

In this regard, Taoxichuan requires that the works displayed by artists at stalls must possess a certain level of originality to qualify for entry. To evaluate this originality, the Taoxichuan Copyright Service Station has established a copyright database for comparison and analysis. All items in the ordinary market are incorporated into this resource pool for evaluation. If a work is found to be over 60% similar to another piece, it will be deemed non-original, and its creator will be denied entry into the Taoxichuan stall market.

Yikongjian, on the other hand, offers more stable stall placements, allowing operators to showcase their works for a long period. Almost all ceramic artists aspire to settle in Yikongjian, as it provides a pathway to stable operations within the Taoxichuan night market. However, the entry requirements for Yikongjian are stricter compared to the ordinary market: First, artists must have operated in the ordinary market for at least three months; second, their works must demonstrate strong originality; and third, they should have a certain volume of products and sales. Once these basic conditions are met, final approval for entry is subject to review by a group of professional designers. This designer group consists of about 70 members and operates under a self-management model, wherein existing designers vote amongst themselves to select new members without any external organizational involvement. Since designers may exit the group monthly, artists from the ordinary market can apply to join the designer group each month. In addition to filtering applications for Yikongjian, this designer group also makes decisions regarding entry and exit in the ordinary market, determining which artists will be eligible to run stalls in the upcoming month. Through the expertise of the designer group, Taoxichuan's copyright admission mechanism ensures the originality of works while encouraging artists to innovate continuously and produce higher-quality pieces, enabling them to challenge themselves for advancement to higher levels.

A Flourishing Diversity: Creating a New Ecosystem for Ceramic Creation

The core of an industrial ecosystem is innovation[1]. Taoxichuan centers its development around ceramic cultural creativity, fully stimulating the vitality of copyright creations, expanding avenues for copyright application, and unlocking the copyright value. This has led to a comprehensive ecosystem for ceramic cultural and creative industries that integrates "production support services + sales channel assistance + copyright protection + a full range of service offerings." Based on this industrial ecosystem, Taoxichuan has developed nearly 200,000 ceramic products, established over 2,700 brands, and registered more than 1,000 small and micro enterprises.

First, providing comprehensive production support services to facilitate the transformation of creativity. Taoxichuan has built a standardized factory of 800,000 square meters and a fully integrated ceramic smart manufacturing workshop for makers and artists. By introducing advanced manufacturing equipment from affiliated companies in Germany and Italy, it has built a complete ceramic industry ecosystem that integrates R&D, design, prototyping, and production. By leveraging the advantages of industrial clustering and offering tailored nanny-style services, Taoxichuan provides entrepreneurs with startup spaces, refined raw materials, product sampling, customized production, and e-commerce logistics, positioning itself as an accelerator for ceramic innovation and entrepreneurship.

Second, establishing a digital platform to broaden sales channels for ceramic cultural creative products. To expand its sales channels, in addition to continuously optimize offline sales, Taoxichuan is actively enhancing its online market presence to help businesses precisely reach their target audience. By Collaborating with leading internet platforms like Douyin (TikTok), Kuaishou, WeChat Channels, Taobao, and JD.com, Taoxichuan has launched an online flagship store and established a live-streaming base. Currently, Taoxichuan is recognized as Douyin's first ceramic LIVE streaming base in China and serves as the exclusive cooperative

---

[1] Bronwyn H. Hall and Nathan Rosenberg, *Handbook of the Economics of Innovation*, *Volume 1*, Trans. Shanghai Institute for Science of Science (Shanghai: Shanghai Jiao Tong University Press, 2017).

Jingdezhen Ceramic Smart Manufacturing Workshop (Photo courtesy of Taoxichuan Ceramic Art Avenue)

operator for tea ceramics on Kuaishou in Jiangxi. Through a "host + e-commerce + live streaming" model, Taoxichuan achieves resource integration and fosters synergy between online and offline sales. In 2020, the total online transaction volume at Taoxichuan's live-streaming base reached 350 million yuan. With more e-commerce businesses settling into the live-streaming base, this amount surged to 3.07 billion yuan in 2021, followed by 5.76 billion yuan in 2022. By 2023, it further escalated to 7.14 billion yuan, marking nearly a 20-fold increase in total annual online transactions over the three-year period.

Third, establishing a robust copyright service system to deliver a comprehensive suite of copyright services. Taoxichuan has introduced various copyright service institutions, including the Jiangxi Ceramic Intellectual Property Information Center, the Jiangxi Provincial Rights Protection Assistance Ceramic Workstation, the Jingdezhen Ceramic Copyright Service Station, and the Jingdezhen (Ceramic) IPR Rapid Aid Center, creating a matrix of copyright services. Through a "downstream" copyright registration service, Taoxichuan enables rights holders to obtain copyright certificates without leaving the area, leading to an explosive surge in both the innovative enthusiasm of Taoxichuan artists and their eagerness to register copyrights. Furthermore, Taoxichuan has diversified its copyright consulting services, evolving from initial activities such as copyright lectures and consultations to more advanced brand events like the Taoxichuan Taoran Craft Market, continuously emphasizing the visible role of copyright in the commercialization of ceramic products. Taoxichuan has also developed a one-stop rights protection service that creates a rapid coordination mechanism among cultural law enforcement, public security, and the courts. This gradually constructs a comprehensive copyright protection framework led by judicial safeguards and supported by administrative measures, providing a conducive environment for creative ceramic makers.

Fourth, building a comprehensive support service system to optimize the creative and living environments for creators, designers, and artists. Taoxichuan provides high-quality artists with free access to a full range of services, including entry, training, and learning opportunities, creating an enriching creative atmosphere and comfortable living spaces. By hosting international, high-caliber cultural art events, such as the Taoxichuan Spring & Autumn Art Fair, Taoxichuan invites ceramic artists, designers from around the world, along with students and faculty from renowned art institutions across China, to gather and engage in the exchange of works, ideas, and perspectives. Through observation and mutual learning in these events, creators continually draw artistic inspiration and elevate their creative skills. Taoxichuan also collaborates closely with local art education and training organizations, regularly inviting distinguished artists, designers, and scholars from both domestic and international backgrounds to give free lectures. This initiative, called "Yi Lecture," offers various open courses focused on innovation, entrepreneurship, and aesthetic design, providing young entrepreneurs with the training and marketing support needed to develop their own brands. Moreover, the "Yikongjian" (creative space) operates on a nearly zero-cost model, allowing artists to focus on their work without financial burden. Those running businesses in Yikongjian enjoy certain discounts on rent, utility bills, and taxes. For artists needing accommodations in Jingdezhen, Taoxichuan's sister enterprise, Yishan Workshop, offers elegant rooms at a nominal rent of just 200 yuan per month. Creators staying at Yishan Workshop also receive meal subsidies.

Aromatic Influence: Expanding the Reach of Ceramic Art

Taoxichuan's favorable copyright environment provides comprehensive protection and services for ceramic artists, which not only stimulates more creative breakthroughs but also fosters a growing desire among artists for greater recognition and promotion of their works. In response, Taoxichuan continuously enhances the reach and impact of ceramic pieces through brand incubation, promotional showcases, and the cultivation of a supportive and creative atmosphere.

To boost the influence of ceramic works, Taoxichuan actively aligns with the national initiative for mass entrepreneurship and innovation, with a focus on youth and originality. The platform is committed to providing brand incubation services for ceramic artists, guiding them in areas like ceramic innovation, youth entrepreneurship and innovation, talent cultivation, and brand building.This approach encourages creators to build original, high-quality, and scalable ceramic brands. Currently, Taoxichuan has successfully incubated over 3,000 businesses, and provided services to more than 20,000 artists, generating employment for over 100,000 individuals in the region. By hosting exhibitions of outstanding copyrighted works, Taoxichuan increases the visibility of its makers' newest creations each year. It also organizes copyright achievement competitions, encouraging mutual learning and exchange among artists, which helps elevate their skills and foster fresh creative ideas.

At this stage, Taoxichuan is working to upgrade its "Yikongjian" (creative space) to the next level, termed "Shekongjian" (community space). This effort involves creating a live-streaming base, expanding international artist residency programs, and developing long-term rental housing for foreign artists in Jingdezhen. The goal is to create a more open, shared community for young artists, designers, and craftsmen, thus fostering innovation and entrepreneurship. By addressing practical concerns such as housing, Taoxichuan enables artists to fully immerse themselves into ceramic creations, continually nurturing and developing talent in this field.

(2) Flexible Models for the Utilization of Copyright in Jingdezhen Ceramics

Improving the Copyright Utilization System for Jingdezhen Ceramics

The non-renewable nature of general resources, coupled with absolute ownership, lead to inherent exclusivity in their use. While the intangible and replicable qualities of copyright, to some extent, soften the negative effects of this exclusivity, fierce market competition, along with the constraints imposed by industry players, can still drain resources generated during the copyright utilization process. To tackle these challenges, Jingdezhen has developed a ceramic copyright utilization mechanism based on a model of "Cooperative Entities—Coordinated Application—Value Co-Creation."[1] This approach strengthens the foundational cooperation among stakeholders, leverages each participant's unique advantages, and emphasizes effective collaborative interactions throughout the copyright application process. The ultimate goal is to achieve value co-creation and build a "Jingdezhen Community for Ceramic Copyright Utilization."

Jingdezhen has built its city brand, "The Millennia-old Porcelain Capital," by combining ceramics as its core cultural element with regional industrial strengths and a spirit of innovation. This brand integrates various elements of ceramic copyright—cultural heritage sites, corporate brands, master artists' works, and creator ceramics—alongside the city's development of tourism and education, resulting in a city image rich in copyright value. Whether it's the local government guiding and encouraging ceramic cultural enterprises to develop brand IPs, like the "Blue-and-White Story," which taps the economic potential of ceramic copyright, or Master Xu Guoqin, known as the "Peony Fairy," who carries forward the legacy of "Blue-and-White Kings" Wang Bu and Wang Enhua while creating her own distinctive style by blending modern and traditional techniques, or the film *A Porcelain Vase* (*Ji Hong*), which reignited interest in vermilion glazed ceramics by depicting ceramic artists' struggle to preserve this ancient art—each entity contributes to Jingdezhen's brand as an ambassador of its ceramic heritage. By cultivating a sense of cultural identity and belonging among these participants, Jingdezhen strengthens responsibility, cooperation, and cultural awareness during the copyright utilization process, elevating the city's mission beyond market competition. This shared mission enhances the potential for resource sharing within the industry and cross-industry integration, making industry norms, regional policies, and laws more effective, even without strict enforcement. The core of Jingdezhen's ceramic copyright mechanism lies in the idea that "shared

---

[1] See Feng Weiyi and Li Shimeng, "Research on the Mechanism of Value Co-Creation in Innovation Networks from the Perspective of Intellectual Property Operations," *Information Science*, 2023, 41 (01).

success or failure" binds everyone together. Through this, the city's brand takes shape, and its collective value co-creation effect is realized.

Expanding Copyright Utilization in Jingdezhen Ceramics

Copyright utilization typically takes the form of multi-channel operations, which involve integrating resources across various platforms to manage and capitalize on works within reasonable limits. The greatest challenge of this approach lies in breaking down the barriers between different industries. Disney as the sole controller of numerous well-known IPs, is able to seamlessly apply copyright elements from its original animated works across a range of industries—whether in the development of theme park attractions, the licensing of consumer products, or the adaptation of video games and live-action movies—thus effectively overcoming industrial barriers. In contrast, Jingdezhen faces significant challenges in replicating Disney's model by cultivating a singular, dominant IP and then deploying it in an all-round, cross-industry manner. Jingdezhen's approach to overcoming these barriers lies instead in closely linking ceramic copyright activities with frequent exhibitions and cultural exchange events. This strategy aims to achieve three main objectives: promoting ceramic culture, expanding the market for ceramic copyright transactions, and revitalizing the pathways for ceramic copyright utilization.

The advantage of the "Exhibition + Transaction" model in guiding ceramic copyright utilization lies in the following aspects: First, bridging the gap between copyright utilization and product transactions. One obstacle to effective copyright utilization is the uncertainty surrounding the market value of the final products. Frequent exhibitions and exchange events allow copyright holders to stay in close contact with potential buyers, enabling them to make informed and rational judgments about the scope of their operations. Second, make the use of copyrights transparen. Another barrier to effective copyright application is the lack of clarity across different industries regarding how copyrights are employed. Exhibition events bring together various copyright stakeholders, creating opportunities for mutual learning and inspiration. This fosters a greater diversity of methods within the ceramic copyright industry and lays the groundwork for further innovations in copyright utilization practices.

Innovation in Copyright Utilization of Jingdezhen Ceramics

The copyright utilization process often encounters challenges such as time, geographic, and industry limitations, coupled with tedious procedures that hinder timely and effective alignment between supply and demand. In response, Jingdezhen is embracing modern technology to fully explore the use of information network dissemination rights, developing an industrial model that combines "platform economy + ceramic copyright utilization." By establishing an internet platform specifically designed for the development of Jingdezhen's ceramic copyright industry and facilitating collaborations between ceramic enterprises and major platforms, the city aims to achieve significant innovation within this sector.

The Internet platform takes on various forms to serve different sectors within the industrial economy. Jingdezhen is committed to developing a platform that integrates information consulting and technical services, focusing on the technological aspect to facilitate copyright transactions. By leveraging technologies such as copyright imprinting, timestamps, digital signatures, and blockchain, the city aims to provide a wide range of authentic and reliable data to support the growth of the ceramic copyright digital economy. These technologies will also further assist in verifying copyright ownership, authenticating the identity of rights holders, offering technical proof for copyright protection, and safeguarding both the transaction entities and the process itself. A prime example of this effort is the Ceramic Industry Internet Platform established by the Jingdezhen National Ceramic Copyright Trading Center, along with the comprehensive ceramic copyright trading service platform developed in collaboration with China Telecom.

The core business of copyright utilization in areas such as online sales, social entertainment, and lifestyle services operates through a combination of leveraging internal copyright resources and forging partnerships with external platforms. Jingdezhen is proactively seizing new opportunities to expand the copyright utilization industry by collaborating with e-commerce platforms. The city encourages ceramic enterprises to establish strategic alliances with mainstream e-commerce platforms, incorporating elements of ceramic craftsmanship and intangible cultural heritage into live-stream sales. This approach serves a dual purpose: safeguarding and promoting the preservation of ceramic heritage while unlocking and enhancing the copyright value of ceramic works.

In 2022, the city's online retail reached 12.736 billion yuan, a significant increase from just 806 million yuan in 2012, with an annual growth rate of

Homepage of the Jingdezhen National Ceramic Copyright Trading Center (Photo courtesy of the Jingdezhen National Ceramic Copyright Trading Center)

31.79%. A total of 4,756 enterprises registered and conducted transactions on major third-party trading platforms, leading to the emergence of 32,480 online stores. This expansion not only broadens the market for ceramic goods but also lays the groundwork for new forms of copyright utilization. Besides, in the same year, the State Council approved the establishment of a comprehensive cross-border e-commerce pilot zone in Jingdezhen, marking a significant milestone in the development of cross-border e-commerce and opening up new international markets for ceramic copyright transactions. Additionally, Jingdezhen has leveraged new media to overcome the limitations of the ceramic copyright utilization industry. By capitalizing on the "cultural breakout" opportunities presented by new media, the city has used technology to create avenues for secondary dissemination and transactions in ceramic copyrights. For example, in May 2023, the "Silent Bodhisattva" exhibit at the Jingdezhen China Ceramics Museum went viral online. The museum leveraged this popularity to create a porcelain painting drama titled *Funny Porcelain Painting* (*Ci Hua Zen Jiang*), developing an engaging cartoon IP that also promotes China's rich ceramic culture. Throughout this process, the museum transcended its traditional role as a mere provider of public cultural services, achieving great innovation within the copyright utilization industry.

Section III

Specialized Copyright Protection for Jingdezhen Ceramics

The development of ceramic copyright is closely tied to the protective role of copyright law throughout the phases of creation, utilization, and subsequent management and services. Since the inception of the copyright system, a key challenge has been how to balance the protective function of copyright law in safeguarding rights without hindering creativity. In response, China has taken a series of effective measures, represented by the establishment of a specialized intellectual property court system with concentrated jurisdiction. The Jingdezhen Intellectual Property Right Court, as a vital component of this system, plays an indispensable role. Leveraging this advantage, Jingdezhen has pioneered a specialized judicial protection system for ceramic copyrights tailored to the unique characteristics of ceramic copyright development. First, it established a dedicated judicial protection framework for ceramic copyright, enhancing the efficiency and professionalism by combining specialized protective institutions with a unified protection model. Second, it clarified administrative copyright protection pathways by integrating both personal and public interest approaches, thereby strengthening effectiveness and impact. Finally, it optimized the coordination mechanism between administrative and judicial copyright protection by establishing the Jingdezhen Intellectual Property Protection Center as a central hub, facilitating the efficient operation of collaborative protection mechanisms.

IP and Creative Industry:
Jingdezhen Story

(1) Jingdezhen Intellectual Property Right Court: The Preferred Venue for Resolving Ceramic IP Disputes

The Jingdezhen Intellectual Property Right Court is a specialized court focused on protecting ceramic intellectual property, with cross-regional jurisdiction over copyright, patents, trade secrets, and disputes related to well-known trademarks and monopolies within the areas of Jiujiang, Shangrao, Yingtan, and Jingdezhen. It serves as the preferred venue for resolving ceramic IP disputes.

Adapting to the Ceramics Industry: Tailored Judicial Protection for Ceramic IP

As a globally renowned hub of ceramic culture, Jingdezhen is home to over 100,000 ceramic practitioners. With such a large community, it's challenging for creators to make their works stand out, leading some to take the shortcut of plagiarism for profit. Since the 1980s, rampant infringements of ceramic IP have hindered innovation and healthy growth within Jingdezhen's ceramics industry. Furthermore, inadequate protection capabilities, lengthy enforcement processes, and high costs have made copyright disputes difficult to resolve effectively, leaving copyright holders' legal rights inadequately protected. To maintain order in Jingdezhen's ceramic copyright market and strengthen copyright protection, it is imperative to establish a comprehensive, integrated mechanism for copyright enforcement and judicial protection.

In 2012, The Supreme People's Court has approved a pilot program in which the Intellectual Property Court of Jingdezhen Intermediate People's Court and the Intellectual Property Court of Jingdezhen Zhushan District People's Court will handle civil, administrative, and criminal intellectual property cases uniformly. Over the course of eight years, significant changes have occurred in both the landscape of Jingdezhen's ceramic cultural and creative industries and their judicial protection. To better support the development of these industries and fully leverage judicial protection mechanisms, proposals were put forward during the 2020 China's Two Sessions[1] to the National People's Congress, advocating for the

---

[1] The collective term for the National People's Congress of the People's Republic of China and the Chinese People's Political Consultative Conference.

establishment of the Jingdezhen Intellectual Property Right Court and a dedicated Ceramic Intellectual Property Court. The proposals highlighted the unique ceramic arts ecosystem that has developed in Jingdezhen, emphasizing the importance of protecting its environment for survival and growth. So there's an urgent need for a specialized intellectual property court in Jingdezhen to advance the safeguarding of IPR. In response to these proposals, the Supreme People's Court of the People's Republic of China (hereinafter referred to as "the Supreme People's Court") conducted research and a comprehensive evaluation of the proposal to establish an intellectual property court in Jingdezhen, concluding that setting up such a court aligns with legal regulations and holds great practical significance.

After extensive investigation and research, the Supreme People's Court concluded that establishing the Jingdezhen Intellectual Property Right Court would help unify standards for adjudicating IP cases and improve both the quality and efficiency of IP trials. This court will provide comprehensive judicial protection for ceramic copyrights, trademarks, trade secrets, and other forms of ceramic IP, thereby offering robust judicial support for building Jingdezhen into a pilot zone for ceramic cultural preservation and innovation. In December 2020, the Supreme People's Court officially approved the establishment of the Jingdezhen Intellectual Property Right Court, which was inaugurated on April 26, 2021. Focusing on ceramic IPR protection and operating with cross-regional jurisdiction, this court represents the third intellectual property court in China located outside of provincial capitals.

Two Verticals and Three Horizontals: A Seamless Pathway for Full-Chain Protection

To achieve efficient judicial protection of rights, the Jingdezhen Intellectual Property Right Court has developed a three-dimensional full-chain protection system known as "Two Verticals and Three Horizontals." This framework facilitates effective coordination between litigation and non-litigation methods, including mediation, arbitration, administrative adjudication, and administrative reconsideration, ensuring that various dispute resolution approaches effectively complement one another.

The First Vertical involves establishing IPR circuit trial sites at key industrial parks in Jiujiang, Shangrao, Yingtan, and Jingdezhen. Guided by the judicial principle of serving the people, this initiative further integrates IP judicial resources, enhances the level and effectiveness of IP judicial protection, and promotes unified development in this area. It facilitates nearby litigation for parties involved and improves the relevance of legal education through case examples, thereby strengthening the impact of legal awareness campaigns.

The Second Vertical establishes IP judicial service sites in Jingdezhen, including Mingfang Garden in Changnan New District, Fuliang Ceramic Industrial Park, and the CCTV Ceramic Digital Industry Cultural Base. These sites are designed to offer customized services for ceramic practitioners, addressing the evolving demands and expectations for IPR from businesses. Through one-stop services, these sites ensure "zero distance" in judicial support, enabling companies to invest with confidence, operate securely, and focus on growth. Since 2022, these three judicial service sites have delivered over 200 legal consultations and check-up services, while distributing more than 500 informational and promotional materials on laws and regulations.

The First Horizontal emphasizes the collaboration between judicial protection and administrative law enforcement. The Intermediate People's Court of Jingdezhen, together with the Jingdezhen People's Procuratorate and the Jingdezhen Public Security Bureau, has jointly issued the *Framework Agreement for Intellectual Property Protection Cooperation*. This agreement establishes a regular communication mechanism for criminal IP cases, enhances collaborative efforts in handling IP cases, and improves the efficiency of combating IP violations and crimes.

In addition, the Intermediate People's Court of Jingdezhen, in collaboration with the Jingdezhen Municipal Bureau of Culture, Broadcasting, Television, Press and Publication and the Jingdezhen Market Supervision Bureau, has issued the *Management Measures for Ceramic Technology Investigators in Jingdezhen (Trial)* and the *Notice on Appointing Ceramic Technology Investigators in Jingdezhen*, introducing a pioneering mechanism for IP ceramic technology investigators in the province. The first batch of 18 appointed technology investigators comes from various sectors, including universities, research institutions, enterprises, and social organizations. They all possess over five years of experience in the ceramic sector and hold professional titles of associate senior or above. With their deep understanding of the current technological landscape and development trends in ceramics, these experts are well-equipped to tackle challenges in identifying ceramic IP disputes. Moreover, the court has established a multi-faceted mechanism for clarifying technical facts, integrating technical investigations, consultations, and appraisals. This approach effectively combines technical insights with legal reasoning. The court has also signed a *Cooperation Memorandum on Intellectual Property Dispute Resolution* with seven other entities, including the Jingdezhen Market Supervision Bureau and the Jingdezhen Municipal Bureau of Culture, Broadcasting, Television, Press and Publication. The aim is to facilitate diversified channels for mediating IP disputes. Furthermore, it has entered into a *Cooperative Agreement for Rapid Joint Intellectual Property Protection* with the Jingdezhen Intellectual Property Protection Center, working together to promote a mechanism that integrates judicial confirmation with administrative mediation for more effective dispute resolution.

The Second Horizontal focuses on the mutual enhancement of judicial protection and lawyer mediation. Jingdezhen has established the province's first IPR Lawyer Mediation Center, accelerating the resolution of IPR disputes through diverse means. This center appoints specialized IPR lawyers from Jiujiang, Shangrao, Yingtan, and Jingdezhen to take turns on duty, facilitating pre-litigation mediation efforts.

The Third Horizontal emphasizes collaboration between judicial protection and community autonomy. The court, in partnership with the Jingdezhen Women's Federation, has signed a *Cooperation Agreement on Promoting Intellectual Property Protection for Women*. This initiative incorporates federation staff and people's mediators into the IP mediation framework, guiding parties to resolve disputes in accordance with the law. It aims to combine emotional, rational, and legal considerations in dispute resolution, thereby enhancing the effectiveness of judicial IPR protection. Additionally, in collaboration with the Jingdezhen Federation of Industry and Commerce, the court has streamlined channels for quality complaints and consumer rights protection. Together, they are committed to combating counterfeit and substandard products, thus contributing to creating a favorable legal environment for brand.

Accelerating the Development of a Robust Legal Framework for Ceramic Protection

The Jingdezhen Intellectual Property Right Court is continuously innovating ceramic copyright protection mechanisms, leading to rapid improvements in protection standards. The court has built a collection of exemplary cases and best practices in the judicial protection of ceramic copyrights, fostering a positive legal environment for ceramic copyrights.

First, exemplary judicial cases are selected to provide guidance for resolving ceramic copyright disputes. Notable cases handled by the Jingdezhen Intellectual Property Right Court include the copyright dispute involving Auratic Ceramic and the copyright ownership and infringement case concerning traditional "Two-sided Continuous Pattern" ceramic lidded tea cups, both of which were recognized among the 50 Typical Intellectual Property Cases by Chinese Courts in 2021 and 2022, respectively. The case involving the "Eight Friends of Zhushan" ceramic copyright dispute was included in the Supreme People's Court's *New Rules for Intellectual Property Case Applications*. In addition, several other ceramic copyright cases have been recognized as part of the annual Top Ten Intellectual Property Cases by Jiangxi courts, as well as typical IPR protection cases related to the digital economy and those supporting the development of the private sector in Jiangxi.

★ Auratic Ceramic Copyright Dispute Case[①]

This case represents a typical example of copyright infringement involving an e-commerce operator selling ceramic art pieces that contain generic elements. In this instance, the defendant company, an online store operator, labeled the disputed product as "Madam Porcelain" on its sales page. A comparative analysis revealed substantial similarities between the defendant's products and those owned by the plaintiff in terms of design details, colors, dimensional layering, and overall layout (see Table 4-1). In determining whether the defendant's actions constituted copyright infringement, the court acknowledged the presence of generic elements in the ceramic art pieces but clarified a crucial judgment: Even if a ceramic art piece contains generic elements, it remains eligible for copyright protection, provided it is not a mere copy or repetition of designs or styles traditionally employed in the ceramics industry. The work must demonstrate original expression and possess aesthetic significance in its selection, arrangement, and design, thereby enabling the public to differentiate it from

---

① Civil Judgment No. 4 (2021) Gan 02 Zhi Min Chu of the Intermediate People's Court of Jingdezhen, Jiangxi Province.

existing works. Unauthorized reproduction of such art would constitute copyright infringement. The court's ruling effectively curbed infringement activities related to counterfeit ceramic products sold on e-commerce platforms, safeguarding the rights of copyright holders. This decision has supported the re-creation of ceramic works, fostered significant growth within the ceramics industry, and established guidelines for regulating market order and the conduct of online operators, ultimately contributing to a more favorable legal business environment.

Table 4-1: Comparison of Infringing Product Designs and Plaintiff's Copyrighted Images

Product Types	Infringing Product Image	Plaintiff's Artworks
8-inch Soup Plate (Notarial Certificate Attachment 1, Page 45)		
1 Flower Basket (Notarial Certificate Attachment 1, Pages 16-17)		Guangdong Registration No. 2019-F-00009387 National Registration No. 2018-F-00505619

Auratic Ceramic "Madam Porcelain" Image and Infringing Image (Photo courtesy of Jingdezhen Intellectual Property Right Court)

★ The Copyright Ownership and Infringement Dispute Case of Traditional "Two-sided Continuous Pattern" Ceramic Lidded Tea Cups[①]

This case exemplifies the assessment of originality in traditional ceramic works and the determination of the starting date for copyright protection. In this instance, the plaintiff company registered its artistic work *Blossoming* with the Jiangxi Copyright Protection Center. This piece features a lidded tea cup adorned

---

① Civil Judgment No. 171 (2022) Gan 02 Min Zhong of the Intermediate People's Court of Jingdezhen, Jiangxi Province.

with gourd-shaped lines on the front and a "Ji" (吉, auspicious) character motif inside. The bottom, lid, and saucer are adorned with floral and vine elements in a two-sided continuous pattern. The defendant company, however, sold "Shanyin" ceramic lidded tea cups on Taobao, which also featured gourd-shaped lines on the front and characters "Shan Yin" (山音). The plaintiff argued that the defendant's tea cups infringed upon their copyright and subsequently filed a lawsuit. The court, after reviewing, determined that the designer's adaptation of traditional two-sided continuous patterns, combined with color choices and variations in Chinese characters, resulted in a design with aesthetic significance. While inspired by traditional elements, the overall composition reflected the designer's unique imprint, showcasing distinct intellectual choices that met the copyright law's originality requirements. Hence, the court affirmed that the plaintiff's work deserved legal protection. Nonetheless, the court found insufficient evidence to determine the creation date of the disputed work. Evidence provided by the defendant confirmed that they began selling the allegedly infringing product on Taobao before the plaintiff's registration date. Moreover, while both parties utilized traditional two-sided continuous patterns, the styles and forms of the vines and flowers on the defendant's product were sufficiently different from those in the plaintiff's work. Therefore, the court did not find substantial similarities and ruled that the defendant's product did not constitute infringement. The ruling underscored that innovative applications derived from traditional elements, which showcase a creator's unique design style, possess originality and should be protected under copyright law. This outcome encourages ceramic practitioners to innovatively explore traditional ceramic elements, contributing to a vibrant ceramic market and cultural advancement. Besides, the court's application of high standards and strict criteria in assessing infringement helps prevent the monopolization of traditional ceramic elements and public domain elements, thereby safeguarding the valuable resources generated by ceramic copyright creations.

Second, the court integrates public awareness with judicial review, continuously extending the IPR protection scope. In 2021, the Jingdezhen Intellectual Property Right Court was designated as a "Legal Education and Publicity Base of Jiangxi Province" by the Publicity Department of the CPC Jiangxi Provincial Committee, the Department of Justice of Jiangxi Province, and the Jiangxi Provincial Legal Affairs Office. And each year, on the occasion of World Intellectual Property Day, the court sets up legal awareness booths at People's Square in Jingdezhen, distributing IP brochures, and conducting in-depth legal education within ceramic enterprises to actively promote awareness. Furthermore, the court emphasizes case-based legal education and utilizes new media platforms to enhance awareness of judicial IPR protection. It also prioritizes talent cultivation by establishing a practical training base for the Law School at Jingdezhen Ceramic University, allowing students to engage directly with IPR judicial practices. This hands-on approach is designed to strengthen law students' practical skills and bolster the court's overall efforts in promoting legal awareness.[1]

Third, the court closely integrates academia, industry, and research to strengthen judicial protection. In October 2021, the court hosted a forum on ceramic IPR protection during the 2021 China Jingdezhen International Ceramic Expo. The event gathered over 110 participants, including experts, scholars, seasoned IPR judges, ceramic masters, industry representatives, and relevant administrative departments, to discuss ceramic IPR protection. This forum established a pioneering platform for academic, industrial, and artistic exchanges in the field of ceramic IP. Looking ahead, the court will continue to refine its complementary mechanism of "learning, research, and judgment."They plan to enhance judges' professional competencies through regular internal training, expert lectures, and case discussions. Additionally, the court aims to strengthen exchanges and collaborations with other domestic and international IP courts, jointly promoting innovation and development in copyright adjudication.

(2) Specialized Model for Copyright Protection in Jingdezhen Ceramics

Developing a Judicial Protection System for Jingdezhen Ceramic Copyright

The development of China's IP judicial protection system has undergone two distinct stages. The first stage, known as the "Separation of Three Reviews,"

---

[1] Hu Zhiyong, "Good News! The Jingdezhen Intellectual Property Right Court Selected as a Legal Education Base in Jiangxi Province," January 10, 2022. Accessed December 11, 2023. http://jdzzy.jxfy. gov.cn/article/detail/2022/01/id/6476936.shtml.

began in the 1990s. With the introduction of key IP laws, the number of IP-related cases across various levels of courts started to increase. However, jurisdiction over technically complex first-instance IP cases remained dispersed among numerous intermediate and grassroots courts. While the traditional separation offered advantages such as facilitating litigation for the parties involved, aiding in case hearings and executions, and balancing the workload of courts at different levels, it also gave rise to challenges in the specialized field of intellectual property, including fragmented jurisdiction, jurisdictional conflicts, and a disconnect between judicial and administrative protections. The second stage, referred to as the "Great Protection" phase, commenced in 2014 with the establishment of dedicated IP courts and tribunals. During this period, categories of IP-related cases became increasingly specific, and the hierarchy of adjudicating courts became more systematic. This evolution gradually formed a Great Protection framework that integrates IP court adjudications with a four-tier court system.[1] Building on this framework, discussions about the feasibility of a "Three-in-One"[2] protection model for intellectual property have emerged, leading to its application in judicial practices, most notably with the establishment of the IP Court at the Hainan Free Trade Port in 2020. Implementing the "Three-in-One" protection model requires, on the one hand, a substantial number of IP cases in the region, necessitating centralized jurisdiction across regions for various types of first-instance cases.[3] On the other hand, it demands an optimized staffing structure within these judicial bodies to ensure the professionalism of case rulings.[4]

The challenges in judicial protection of ceramic copyrights are twofold. First, the general lack of specialized knowledge among judges regarding ceramic

---

① Supreme People's Court, *Certain Provisions on the Jurisdiction of First Instance Civil and Administrative Cases Involving Intellectual Property*. Fa Shi (2022) No. 13.

② The "Three-in-One" Trial refers to a unified trial mechanism for IPR civil, criminal, and administrative cases. This approach consolidates all civil, criminal, and administrative cases related to intellectual property to be uniformly heard by the Intellectual Property Tribunal.

③ He Zhen and Wei Dahai, "Reform Exploration and Active Innovation: Summary of the Symposium on 'Three-in-One' Judicial Protection of Intellectual Property," *Journal of Law Application*, 2010 (08).

④ Cui Shanshan, Zhang Weihao and Wang Yanan, "Judicial Protection of Intellectual Property and the Complexity of Enterprises Importing Technologies: A Quasi-Natural Experiment Based on Intellectual Property Cases under the 'Three-in-One' System," *Macroeconomics*, 2023 (05): 85-103.

copyright can negatively affect the quality of judicial protection. Second, difficulties in coordination between corresponding criminal, civil, and administrative cases can hinder the protection efficiency. In response to these issues, Jingdezhen acknowledges that, while the region faces numerous ceramic copyright disputes, it also possesses a robust pool of professionals dedicated to judicial protection. Therefore, the city has opted to establish a two-tier IP adjudication system utilizing a "Three-in-One" model to enhance the judicial protection of ceramic copyrights.

The establishment of two-tier specialized IP adjudication bodies not only leverages the advantages of a clear division of court responsibilities—making litigation easier for parties and enhancing the quality of judgments—but more importantly, it fosters an optimized judicial environment for independent innovation. This encourages investment in creativity within the ceramic industry's copyright sector, reduces losses associated with copyright exploitation, and ultimately promotes innovation throughout the entire Jingdezhen ceramics industry.[1] Moreover, the "Three-in-One" adjudication mechanism, with its unified enforcement standards, lowered litigation costs, and increased efficiency, further alleviates barriers to rights protection for entities in the ceramic copyright industry, allowing them to allocate more resources to the creation, utilization, and management of copyrights. Consequently, the "Three-in-One" mechanism positively impacts innovation within the ceramic copyright sector. This facilitative effect is immediate, as it stems from the innovative mechanisms established, particularly benefiting small-scale ceramic enterprises, startups, and many "Jing Piao" creators that primarily rely on copyright creation rather than extensive resources for rights protection. As previously noted, the rapid revitalization of Jingdezhen in the new era heavily depends on the vitality of copyright creation and the diverse applications of copyright. The specialized adjudication institutions, in conjunction with the "Three-in-One" judicial protection system, serve to accurately address the needs of various stakeholders involved in both copyright creation and utilization. Through more effective judicial protection of copyrights, they provide greater opportunities for innovation within the ceramic copyright landscape.

---

① Zhuang Jiaqiang, Wang Hao and Zhang Wentao, "Does Strengthening Judicial Protection of Intellectual Property Contribute to Enterprise Innovation? — Evidence from the Establishment of Intellectual Property Courts," *Contemporary Finance & Economics*, 2020 (09): 16.

IP and Creative Industry:
Jingdezhen Story

Exploring Administrative Approaches to Rights Protection in Jingdezhen Ceramics

Among the various factors supporting the development of ceramic copyright in Jingdezhen, judicial protection while significant in promoting innovation, is not the sole determining factor. Most rights holders prefer to avoid litigation for resolving copyright disputes and are more inclined to leverage the power of administrative agencies. This inclination is especially pronounced when the Jingdezhen municipal government is actively involved in the entire process of ceramic copyright development, as the proactive efforts of administrative bodies highlight the government's leadership role in safeguarding these copyrights. However, one major drawback of direct enforcement by administrative agencies is that copyright protection is merely a part of broader cultural law enforcement. Compared to special judicial bodies, the enforcement actions of administrative agencies often lack specificity and expertise. Therefore, enhancing the professionalism of copyright administration is becoming a key direction for the development of copyright administration in China. As the primary entity that gathers ceramic copyright creators, enhances the framework for copyright utilization, and builds platforms for copyright application, the Jingdezhen municipal government's comprehensive involvement in the entire process of ceramic copyright development is gradually transforming its role from a singular administrative enforcer. This shift allows administrative agencies to receive copyright-related information from multiple sources, facilitating the accumulation of experience in copyright work and enhancing their professional capabilities during the administrative enforcement phase.

Crucially, Jingdezhen's approach to administrative rights protection is transcending the limitations of a primarily private interest focus, instead integrating both private and public interest protections.[1] Traditionally, efforts were mainly centered around cultural law enforcement. For example, in 2022,

---

[1] Private-interest-oriented administrative protection refers to the statutory rights and maintenance of intellectual property holders, while public-interest-oriented administrative protection primarily aims to promote national and social interests related to intellectual property. See Qi Jiangang, "On the Reform of China's Administrative Protection Model for Intellectual Property," *Wuhan University Journal* (*Philosoply & Social Science*), 2020 (02): 154.

the Jingdezhen Copyright Bureau, in collaboration with the Jingdezhen Market Supervision Bureau and the Public Security Bureau, established a joint task force for inspecting a local ceramic factory and a ceramics company. As a result, they discovered that the company's computers contained floral designs featuring the Beijing Winter Olympics mascots "Bing Dwen Dwen" and "Shuey Rhon Rhon," which were used on ceramic wine bottles produced by the factory. This led to the confiscation of infringing materials and a fine of 20,000 yuan, thereby protecting the legal rights of the Beijing Winter Olympics Organizing Committee. In contrast, the new approach seeks to balance private and public interests, creating innovative pathways for administrative rights protection. In September 2023, the Jingdezhen Market Supervision Bureau and the Jingdezhen Intellectual Property Protection Center participated in the 24th China Ceramics Fair (Tangshan). There, in collaboration with the Tangshan Market Supervision Bureau, they launched an initiative focused on IPR protection and rights assistance and established a dedicated consultation station for copyright-related services. This strategy enables administrative agencies to engage more actively with the market, combining the handling of copyright infringement complaints, rights assistance, and legal advice (private interest protection) with public education and awareness campaigns (public interest protection). This integrated approach has enhanced the overall effectiveness of administrative rights protection in the region.

Integrated Coordination Mechanism for Copyright Protection in Jingdezhen Ceramics

To address the differences between judicial and administrative protections for ceramic copyrights, Jingdezhen has established an integrated coordination mechanism centered around the Jingdezhen Intellectual Property Protection Center. This mechanism connects copyright administrative enforcement agencies, judicial entities, and social management organizations, creating a cohesive "Administrative + Judicial" framework. The primary goal is to provide efficient support for copyright enforcement, judicial rulings, rights protection assistance, and arbitration mediation. The center's primary responsibilities include rapid authorization and swift rights protection through a one-stop service for handling copyright complaints and reports. It is tasked with promptly managing administrative decisions and mediation cases to facilitate the efficient resolution of ceramic copyright disputes. This approach not only safeguards the interests of rights holders but also helps to alleviate the burdens associated with copyright protection work.

To enhance its connection with judicial authorities, the protection center has signed Memorandums of Cooperation, effectively establishing an alternative rights protection pathway for rights holders. In 2021, the protection center entered a memorandum with the People's Court of Zhushan District in Jingdezhen, leveraging judicial authority to reinforce community mediation efforts. This collaboration provides an additional dispute resolution channel within the community mediation system, addressing limitations in the enforceability of mediation agreements. By serving as a coordinating body, the protection center enables judicial authorities to confer binding power to community mediation agreements, ensuring their effective implementation and opening new avenues for ceramic copyright protection.

Additionally, in response to the current rise in copyright infringement cases on e-commerce platforms, the protection center has integrated with the China National Intellectual Property Administration's national e-commerce enforcement system to enhance enforcement efforts online. A dedicated e-commerce task force within the protection center was established to ensure each case is processed within 24 hours, typically by issuing legal opinions and other necessary actions. In 2021 alone, the protection center handled 659 cases across various domestic and international e-commerce platforms like Taobao and Tmall. This rapid rights protection mechanism not only enables rights holders to swiftly safeguard their interests and improve the online business environment but also lays the groundwork for further administrative or judicial actions, offering a dual benefit. The establishment of the Jingdezhen Intellectual Property Protection Center as the central coordinating entity for copyright protection underscores a significant evolution in copyright protection philosophy—from independent protection to collaborative support, from a closed approach to an open framework, and from singular to multi-faceted protection strategies. These initiatives reflect Jingdezhen's practical and impactful measures in the field of copyright protection.

Section IV

Distinctive Copyright Management for Jingdezhen Ceramics

The sustained creation, flexible application, and specialized protection of ceramic copyrights continually drive and support the copyright initiatives in Jingdezhen. To further enhance the efficiency of these efforts and create a streamlined institutional mechanism, a distinctive management model for ceramic copyrights is essential. At the macro level, Jingdezhen has bolstered institutional leadership in administrative management, introducing innovative practices in the administration of ceramic copyrights. Meanwhile, at the micro level, the city encourages various ceramic copyright enterprises to prioritize the development of internal management mechanisms, thereby establishing robust management systems within these companies. This approach—from external to internal, macro to micro—creates a comprehensive management network connecting all stakeholders, continuously optimizing the development path for ceramic copyright initiatives. Representing this model, the Jingdezhen National Ceramic Copyright Trading Center combines administrative and enterprise resources to provide a wide range of ceramic copyright trading services, establishing a unique approach to transaction-level copyright management.

(1) A Specialized Copyright Trading Center

Copyright, as the core asset of the cultural industry, is fundamental to advancing cultural innovation and creativity. The establishment of the Jingdezhen

National Ceramic Copyright Trading Center further solidifies the foundation for the circulation of ceramic cultural works, promoting the rapid growth of the ceramic cultural and creative industry.

A Trailblazer in Advancing the Ceramics Industry

To develop itself into a national ceramic culture inheritance and innovation pilot zone and create a new platform for cultural exchange, Jingdezhen aims to forge a path for the inheritance and innovative development of traditional culture that holds global significance, embodies Chinese values, reflects the characteristics of the new era, and highlights local traits. To this end, the city has conducted extensive research on major domestic culture assets and equity exchanges, as well as copyright trading centers, to guide the establishment of the Jingdezhen National Ceramic Copyright Trading Center. By drawing on advanced experiences from other provinces and cities, Jingdezhen has focused on the distinctive realm of the ceramic cultural and creative industry, formulating what is known as the "Jingdezhen Model" for the establishment of its copyright trading center. This model involves creating a comprehensive regional copyright service platform and a copyright service system centered on transactions. It includes establishing a nationwide copyright pledge and financing platform, as well as blockchain and big data platforms. These initiatives will provide a series of specialized services such as copyright registration, trading, pledging, and financing to ceramic enterprises and individuals across the country. Through these efforts, Jingdezhen aims to unleash the vibrant potential of ceramic copyrights and transform the trading center into a renowned platform that covers the province, extends nationwide, and reaches a global audience.

To accelerate the establishment of the Ceramic Copyright Trading Center project, Jingdezhen has actively promoted the integration of industry, academia, and research. The city has engaged in close collaboration with the Intellectual Property Office of Jiangxi Province, leveraging the talent and resources of its research platforms to jointly develop a copyright protection framework for the trading center. A Copyright Economic Research Institute has also been established, with the goal of utilizing the expertise of renowned domestic and international scholars to create effective copyright trading modules. Furthermore, a comprehensive organizational structure and management system have been put in place, along with scientifically designed workflows and standards, to facilitate efficient copyright transactions. Meanwhile, efforts are being made to forge partnerships with prominent domestic and international enterprises and institutions, enhancing international copyright exchange and cooperation.

In July 2021, the Jingdezhen National Ceramic Copyright Trading Center (hereafter referred to as the "Copyright Trading Center") received approval from the National Copyright Administration for its construction and officially commenced operations on August 28, 2022. As the fifth national copyright trading center nationwide and the only one dedicated to the ceramics industry, it aims to inject new momentum into the in-depth development of the Jingdezhen ceramic culture inheritance and innovation pilot zone.

On the day the Copyright Trading Center was put into operation, it launched three copyright operation services that yielded encouraging results. First, a copyright auction service was initiated via a WeChat Official Account program developed by Weimob Inc. This service allows for diverse auction combinations such as "copyright + physical goods, copyright transfers and partial copyright licensing." Second, a copyright marketplace was opened, showcasing 92 works from inheritors of intangible cultural heritage, all registered for copyright to ensure authenticity and rightful ownership. Lastly, a digital cultural creative platform was unveiled, facilitating digital copyright trading that integrates cultural creativity, digital innovation, and copyright transactions. This initiative has further enriched the digital copyright asset trading models in ceramics through legitimate and compliant pathways.

A Relentless Explorer of Operating Models

The Copyright Trading Center has established four main business sectors: basic copyright services, operational services, trading services, and financial services. Its goal is to create a new model and paradigm for comprehensive copyright development by integrating "copyright + blockchain + digitization + finance" throughout the entire chain, and it has achieved significant progress in this endeavor.

Basic Copyright Services: At its core, the basic copyright services focus on copyright registration and consultation. Copyright registration plays a vital role in protecting the legal rights of creators, ensuring the security of copyright transactions, promoting the effective use of copyrights, facilitating the creation and dissemination of works, and advancing the development of the copyright industry. The Copyright Trading Center has actively engaged in copyright registration, showcasing registered works on the copyright trading platform. This approach helps protect creators' rights and resolve copyright disputes arising from ownership issues. To create more accessible channels for work registration and accumulate original resources for the center, a dedicated team has been formed to proactively engage with creators using targeted strategies. For instance, they focus on engaging university students and young entrepreneurial teams while providing on-site registration services for key enterprises. Additionally, to enhance registration efficiency and prevent the loss of copyright resources from artists outside the province, the Copyright Trading Center applied to the Jiangxi Provincial Copyright Administration (Jiangxi Provincial Copyright Protection Center) to establish a copyright registration processing portal. They have also obtained pilot qualifications for cross-regional copyright work registration in Jiangxi Province, which enhances the authority and reach of copyright registration, leading to a rapid increase in registration volumes. As of January 2024, Jingdezhen has recorded a total of 40,015 copyright registrations, with the Copyright Trading Center accounting for 19,144 of these. During the China Jingdezhen International Ceramic Expo, the center set up a dedicated copyright service station, offering comprehensive services to various ceramic enterprises. In 2023, the center provided copyright registration services to over 1,000 individuals at the Expo and processed intention registrations for more than 810 works from local Jingdezhen companies.

Copyright Operational Services: The Copyright Trading Center has been actively exploring new models and pathways for the creative transformation and innovative advancement of the ceramics industry. By collaborating with various museums and copyright enterprises, the center has revitalized cultural relics through secondary creation, thereby industrializing cultural products and achieving an ingenious integration of copyright and culture. Recognizing that "control over high-quality work copyrights is a core competitive advantage," the Copyright Trading Center has launched the Ceramic Copyright Custodial Database Project. It has already signed agreements with over 200 ceramic enterprises, both within and outside the province, to collaboratively build a digital database of high-quality copyrights.

Copyright Trading Services: The Copyright Trading Center has continually innovated copyright application scenarios by signing contracts with many established, emerging, and young artists, as well as inheritors of intangible cultural heritage in Jingdezhen. Through the secondary creation of artists' original works, the center has facilitated copyright transfer and trading, expanding the scope of copyright transactions beyond merely serving original creators. To ensure the authenticity, reliability, and smoothness of online transactions, the CPC Jingdezhen Municipal Committee and Jingdezhen Municipal People's Government have undertaken an overall planning approach for the Copyright Trading Center. During its initial phase, they invested in acquiring certain copyrighted works or obtaining relevant licenses. This strategy aims to gradually cultivate market awareness and public interest through operational holding and guided trading. Once the market stabilizes, the model will shift to a light-asset operation to lead the physical ceramic sector. The center is also exploring a business model that combines "digital collectibles issuance + physical ceramic manufacturing," alongside synchronous interaction between online and offline commerce. By leveraging the platform capabilities of the Copyright Trading Center, this initiative can offer substantial support to ceramic enterprises from Jingdezhen and across the country participating in exhibitions, effectively addressing long-standing challenges related to low product added value and limited sales channels.

Copyright Financial Services: The Copyright Trading Center is steadily progressing with its application for financial institution operating licenses, laying the groundwork to offer future financial services such as copyright pledges, bonds, and financing.

Specialization and Sophistication: Pioneering the "3+X" Model

The Copyright Trading Center has developed its main business scope using the "3+X" model. The "3" includes comprehensive copyright services, copyright trading venue operations, and copyright industrial park management, while "X" includes all other initiatives that promote copyright trading and protection. This model aims to create a one-stop platform for copyright trading and protection that integrates copyright enforcement and application. It centers around digitalization and financialization, supported by technologies such as blockchain and big data. The platform will incorporate functions such as rights confirmation, protection, trading, IP development, and copyright industrialization services.

The first component of "3" is comprehensive copyright services. This includes establishing a one-stop service system that offers basic services like registration, documentation, rights confirmation, assessment, protection, training, consultation, and promotion. In addition, it provides value-added services such as traceability and authentication, comprehensive online monitoring, rights protection representation, exhibitions, derivative product development, and licensing transactions.

The second component of "3" is copyright trading venue operations. This involves establishing a ceramic copyright capital system and an asset circulation framework, providing services for cultural factor allocation, trading, and financing. Branches are planned to be set up in the Guangdong-Hong Kong-Macao Greater Bay Area, to develop a digital asset circulation model featuring "mainland issuance and Hong Kong trading."

The third component of "3" is copyright industrial park operations. Utilizing the "Big Bowl"[①] and the Pinzi Building as bases, this initiative aims to create a headquarters economy through a copyright-themed town centered around "Culture + Copyright + Digital + Technology." Plans include establishing a cluster of museums, perennial exhibitions, the metaverse, digital art, the Changnan "Bowl" collection, copyright design competitions, training programs, and live streaming bases, gradually evolving into a national demonstration park for the copyright industry economy.

"X" refers to all other businesses that can promote copyright trading and protection. The Trading Center actively hosts or co-hosts various exhibitions, competitions, forums, and lectures to cultivate the intellectual property market, supporting the inheritance and innovation of ceramic culture while balancing economic benefits with social norms. For instance, during the China Jingdezhen International Ceramic Expo, the Changnanli Night Market themed ceramics attracted over 60,000 visitors in just three days. The Arab Arts Festival featured a side event, "Silkroad Ceramics: A Free Exchange of Wisdom," showcasing creative ceramic copyright designs, which collected 958 physical or digital copyright

---

① Jingdezhen Changnanli Cultural and Art Center features a bowl-shaped structure that stands 80 meters tall, with a mouth diameter of 80 meters and a base diameter of 40 meters. The design concept is inspired by the Song Dynasty Shadow Green Bamboo Hat-shaped Bowl, exuding a dignified elegance and symbolizing the "Mother of All Porcelains."

works from over 600 artists across ten countries. Several leaders from Chinese ministries and dignitaries from Arab nations also visited during the exhibition. Additionally, the first National Ceramic Intangible Heritage Copyright Works Competition received 1,132 entries of artistic ceramic works from both domestic and international participants, followed by a nationwide tour exhibition. To provide users with more accessible trading channels, the Copyright Trading Center has launched copyright auction services through its "Copyright Center" WeChat official account and mini-programs, offering diverse auction options, including "Copyright + Physical Goods," "Copyright Transfer," and "Partial Copyright Licensing." Furthermore, the center is expanding its business scope and revenue channels through e-commerce live streaming, educational activities, and IP cultural creation development, focusing on supporting 3,000 ceramic talents in areas such as artistic creation, technology development, and marketing, while promoting and representing the copyright works of 1,000 ceramic enterprises.

In the future, the Copyright Trading Center will maintain its commitment to integrating "digital" and "physical," promoting a development model of "Physical Goods + Digital Collections + Rights + Cross-Industry Collaboration." The center will continually optimize its business offerings and expand its scope, fully leveraging its role in facilitating the creative transformation of ceramic culture and the innovative development of the ceramics industry.

(2) The Distinctive Model for Jingdezhen Ceramic Copyright Management

Innovation in Administrative Management of Copyright in Jingdezhen Ceramics

Jingdezhen has shifted its focus from micro-level copyright management to market-oriented management, reinforcing institutional improvement and systematic management at a macro level. Guided by a robust copyright management system, it has established a diversified organizational management model for ceramic copyright that combines government administrative oversight with enterprise and industry association management. Specifically, on the one hand, the government enhances the management system for ceramic copyrights and oversees the development of the ceramic copyright industry. On the other hand, it creates a distinctive management model for Jingdezhen ceramic copyright through strategic, grid-based, and intelligent administrative practices.

Jingdezhen is enhancing its top-level design for copyright management by improving the regulatory framework for the ceramics industry and fostering a supportive social environment for copyright oversight. At the top level, the Jingdezhen municipal government and the CPC Jingdezhen Municipal Committee have aligned the overall management of the ceramics industry with the national economic and social development agenda, incorporating ceramic copyright management and growth into this larger framework. The Jingdezhen Municipal Bureau of Culture, Broadcasting, Television, Press and Publication is responsible for the specific management and development of ceramic culture, while various departments—such as Reform, Finance, Natural Resources and Planning, Housing and Urban-Rural Development, Market Supervision, and Ceramics Industry Development—each fulfill their roles and work in concert within the broader framework of ceramic copyright administration. This cohesive management approach indicates that ceramic copyright management is no longer a minor component of daily administrative duties of the Culture, Broadcasting, Television, Press and Publication Bureau; rather, it has become an integral aspect to Jingdezhen's broader development strategy, requiring coordinated efforts among various administrative departments.

In its innovative approach to copyright administration, Jingdezhen has first established a high-level, comprehensive copyright promotion organization—the Copyright Work Leading Group, led by the mayor—to manage copyright protection, oversight, and public awareness efforts. This group has introduced a routine supervision mechanism, elevating copyright administration to a strategic level within urban development. Second, a grid-based network of copyright service stations has been implemented across both city and county levels. This network spans multiple districts (such as the Copyright Service Station at the Changjiang District), copyright industrial parks (like the Copyright Service Station at Jingdezhen Ceramic Cultural Development Industrial Park), and key copyright creators (including the Copyright Service Station at Jingdezhen Ceramic University). New stations can be flexibly added to meet various needs, including copyright registration, transaction management, and information management. Furthermore, Jingdezhen's administrative agencies have pioneered a third-party comprehensive management service platform for ceramic copyrights, fostering the development and application of an intelligent copyright management system. A notable example is the 2022 launch of Jingdezhen Changnanli Ceramic Copyright Trading Center Co., Ltd. This company, state-owned but market-oriented, employs blockchain, artificial intelligence, and big data technologies to advance the ceramic copyright industry. Through this technical management system, administrative bodies can monitor the ceramic copyright market in real-time, ensuring precise and responsive governance, thereby creating a favorable market environment for the ceramic copyright industry.

Establishing an Enterprise Management Model for Jingdezhen Ceramic Copyright

Jingdezhen has developed a comprehensive management system for ceramic copyright enterprises, centered on establishing robust internal management mechanisms within the enterprises. This core framework is further complemented by an external management structure, where industry associations and alliances serve as socialized entities for copyright oversight.

To establish an internal management mechanism, Jingdezhen encourages ceramic enterprises to adopt a new management model focused on comprehensive copyright operations, all-media marketing, and full-spectrum self-service capabilities. First, enterprises are guided to cultivate managerial talent with expertise in copyright law, aiming at creating recognizable brands and unlocking their commercial value. To enhance internal management, the national standard *Enterprise Intellectual Property Management* is actively implemented, providing a regulatory framework that supports these efforts. Through this process, ceramic enterprises come to appreciate the significance of copyright management and the economic potential of their copyrighted works, prompting them to establish specialized copyright teams to handle the registration, operation, and protection of their creative assets. Second, enterprises have adopted an all-media marketing strategy to create a new competitive edge. This modern approach extends beyond traditional sales models to include live streaming, social media advertising, film and television promotions, and documentaries, all of which can showcase their offerings. This strategy not only boosts sales of ceramic products but also broadens the market reach of the copyrighted works, making corporate culture and copyright core components of enterprises' competitive advantage.

Lastly, ceramic enterprises have built a full-chain management system to meet both their operational needs and those of their clients. They designate personnel to participate in copyright knowledge training organized by municipal and provincial governments, assign staff to handle copyright registration, appoint legal representatives for copyright enforcement, and foster long-term partnerships with copyright experts. This culminates in a self-service model that supports the entire copyright management chain.

To establish external social management mechanisms, Jingdezhen's ceramic copyright industry has created a management model that combines industry associations with industrial alliances. Given the inherently social nature of the copyright industry, it is essential to unite copyright-related social forces and stakeholders, helping enterprises maximize their copyright benefits. On one hand, Jingdezhen has formed a "Four Centers and One Alliance"[1] structure to standardize industry management for the ceramic copyright sector, serving as a bridge connecting the government, platform providers, other ceramic cultural enterprises, and consumers. It can undertake copyright custodianship for enterprises and assist with daily copyright management. Through this alliance, businesses gain increased opportunities for creative exchanges and copyright transactions, thus invigorating the ceramic copyright trading market. On the other hand, Jingdezhen incorporates various organizations—such as the Leading Group for Non-Public Ownership Rights Protection Service, the Municipal Copyright Association, and the Expert Committee on Ceramic Copyright—into the framework of external management. This collaborative approach effectively protects creators' rights, allowing them to concentrate fully on their artistic endeavors or business operations, while heightening efforts to combat infringement and uphold order in the ceramic copyright trading market.

---

[1] It is the only National Center for Chinese Ceramics Intellectual Property Information, the National Ceramic Copyright Trading Center, the Intellectual Property Protection Center, the Jingdezhen (Ceramic) IPR Rapid Aid Center, and the Ceramic Intellectual Property Alliance.

Section Ⅴ

Normalized Copyright Services in Jingdezhen Ceramics

The final component of the "China Model" for ceramic copyright in Jingdezhen is a normalization of ceramic copyright services. To ensure the sustainability and effectiveness of these services, the focus is on establishing a robust copyright service system, characterized by clear task design and meticulous responsibility assignment, enabling the sustained operation of Jingdezhen's copyright service framework. With this solid foundation, a market-driven copyright service industry can be nurtured, leading to the emergence of new models that complement the copyright service system, thereby achieving a regular positive cycle within the ceramic copyright service ecosystem in Jingdezhen. During the process of establishing new platforms for cultural exchange, the China Jingdezhen International Ceramic Expo serves as a vital link between domestic and international market players and an important venue for showcasing ceramic artistry and culture. Its growing influence has positioned the Expo as a key driving force behind the normalization of ceramic copyright services in Jingdezhen.

(1) An Everlasting International Ceramic Expo

The annual China Jingdezhen International Ceramic Expo (hereinafter referred to as the "Ceramic Expo," or "Expo") continues the grand tradition of the ancient Silk Road, bringing together visitors from all corners of the world to discuss the New Silk Road for the ceramic cultural industry. Jingdezhen positions ceramic exchange and trade as the core focus of the Expo, leveraging a diverse platform to promote mutual blending and learning of international ceramic culture and industry. Anchored in copyright, the Expo employs various approaches to reactivate the rich legacy of ancient ceramic culture. This initiative has crafted a compelling narrative of ceramic copyright that engages in dialogue with the international community, while also charting a distinctive path for the innovative inheritance of fine traditional culture.

Millennium-Old Silk Road: Cultural Techniques Through the Ages

Since the Song Dynasty, Jingdezhen porcelain has journeyed along both the land and maritime Silk Roads, continuously making its mark on the world. This has created a flourishing scene characterized by the saying, "craftsmen come from across China, and their wares traverse the globe." For centuries, exquisite pieces of porcelain have departed from Jingdezhen, crossing vast oceans to illuminate the brilliance of Chinese civilization. Over a millennium, Jingdezhen's ceramic culture and techniques continue to exert a profound influence on the ceramics industry, both domestically and internationally. Before 2004, Jingdezhen hosted regular international ceramic festivals, attracting numerous enthusiasts of ceramic culture over the world, thereby strengthening cultural and trade exchanges. However, as the landscape of the ceramics industry evolved and Jingdezhen experienced rapid development, a purely celebratory festival could no longer reflect the effects of an exhibition economy. Therefore, Jingdezhen shifted its strategy, aiming to create an international professional event that integrates the display of high-quality ceramics, cultural exchanges, and product transactions. In 2004, coinciding with the millennium celebration of Jingdezhen's founding, the China Jingdezhen International Ceramic Expo was officially established. This initiative aimed to promote high-quality development in the ceramic cultural industry and to deepen international exchanges in ceramic culture and trade, thereby recreating the millennium prosperity of Jingdezhen's ceramic. Since then, the Expo has become a platform offering greater opportunities for ceramic manufacturers, creators, distributors, and buyers to showcase, communicate, and transact. It has transformed into a international, national-level, and professional expo that encompasses communication of ceramic information, trade interactions, technical cooperation, and cultural exchange.

In September and October of 2013, President Xi Jinping introduced the initiatives for building the "New Silk Road Economic Belt" and the "21st-Century Maritime Silk Road," marking the official start of national-level cooperative initiatives between China and partner countries involved in the Belt and Road Initiative. In 2014, the 11th China Jingdezhen International Ceramic Expo began to enhance cultural and commercial exchanges and cooperation among relevant countries and regions by hosting exhibitions and trade activities focused on ceramic and tea, closely tied to the Silk Road. This effort aimed to help Jingdezhen actively align with and integrate into the Belt and Road Initiative, expanding the pathways for ceramic enterprises to engage in international trade. Subsequent expos continued to reinforce Jingdezhen's role in the Belt and Road Initiative through various means, including media activities, academic seminars, collaborative ceramic art exhibitions with partner countries, and the signing of agreements for the dissemination of ceramic culture. These efforts have further elevated Jingdezhen's historical influence along the Silk Road.

The ongoing China Jingdezhen International Ceramic Expo bears witness to the continuity and evolution of ceramic culture and techniques while presenting a fresh perspective on this millennia-old tradition. The Expo attracts a plethora of exquisite ceramic artworks, highlighting recent advancements in ceramic design innovation and the contemporary spirit of Chinese ceramic art. It also showcases Jingdezhen's unique cultural charm and artistic excellence. Visitors can explore the remarkable achievements of ceramic culture and trade across different historical periods through the diverse works on display. The successful hosting of this event has provided an endless source of momentum for the sustainable growth of the ceramic culture. Initiatives promoting innovative development in this sector—especially those driven by copyright—have revitalized this ancient craft, allowing its rich heritage to shine anew.

Annual Ceramic Expo: Connecting China and the World

Since its inception in 2004, the China Jingdezhen International Ceramic Expo has been successfully held 20 editions, establishing itself as a crucial platform for industrial investment, trading, and cultural exchanges in the ceramics industry, both in China and globally. It has become a vital bridge for Jiangxi Province and China to strengthen cultural exchange and cooperation with the world. Leveraging the Expo as a platform and adopting a market-oriented approach, Jingdezhen seeks to fully capitalize on the economic value of its ceramic heritage while expanding its international market for ceramic artworks. This has led to the establishment of an operational model for Jingdezhen's ceramic copyright industry that promotes cultural transmission through events and facilitates trade through exchanges. Since its launch, the China Jingdezhen International Ceramic Expo has continually expanded in scale, with its global influence growing steadily. To date, a total of 2,500 overseas enterprises from 49 countries and regions have participated[①]. Both online and offline transaction volumes have risen year on year, now surpassing 10 billion yuan. The exhibitors and buyers represent a wide range of regions, including Europe, North America, the Asia-Pacific region, Africa, and the Middle East, making the Expo's international network of connections, collaborations, and partnerships increasingly expansive.

In recent years, the Ceramic Expo has facilitated better integration of ceramic culture between China and other countries through a variety of cultural exchange

The Grand Occasion of the China Jingdezhen International Ceramic Expo (Photo courtesy of the Taobocheng International Ceramic Trading Center)

---

① Tang Ying, "The 2023 China Jingdezhen International Ceramic Expo Opens with the Theme 'Ceramics Facilitate World Communication; Ceramic Trade Connects the World'." October 18, 2023. Accessed December 15, 2023. https://jx.chinadaily.com.cn/a/202310/18/WS652fd0b1a310d5acd876aa7c. html.

activities and by establishing diverse product trading platforms. This has enabled ceramic culture to reach a wider global audience and enhanced the international connectivity of ceramic trade. The transaction volume during the Expo has shown a significant upward trend year after year. During the fourth Ceramic Expo in 2007, the total domestic trade volume reached 617 million yuan, while the total foreign trade volume exceeded USD 100 million, with on-site transactions totaling 8.182 million yuan. The Expo's effect in boosting ceramic trade was already becoming evident. Fast forward ten years to the 14th Expo, where the cumulative domestic trade volume hit 1.094 billion yuan, and the cumulative foreign trade volume reached USD 186 million, with on-site transactions totaling 74.1946 million yuan (including 50.591 million yuan from auctions). As ceramic trade evolved with the times, online transactions emerged as a major component. During the five-day duration of the 18th Ceramic Expo in 2021, the total transaction volume of ceramics reached 9.145 billion yuan, with online transactions accounting for 7.93 billion yuan and offline transactions remaining robust at 1.215 billion yuan.

In 2022, the 19th Ceramic Expo provided a broader platform for international cultural exchanges in ceramics through impactful cooperative projects. These included the signing of a collaborative agreement between the city's Chamber of International Commerce and Shenzhen Western Post Intelligent Warehouse Technology Co., Ltd. to establish overseas warehouse projects, as well as a trade procurement project signed between Jingdezhen Minghai Ceramics Ltd. and the Imperial Porcelain Factory from Russia. Additionally, cross-border e-commerce buyers and overseas purchasing groups engaged in on-site negotiations with Jingdezhen ceramic enterprises. The deepening and ongoing cooperation in ceramic culture has also driven growth in ceramic trade. For the first time, the total transaction volume at the 19th Ceramic Expo exceeded 10 billion yuan, reaching 10.28 billion yuan, a 12.4% increase year-on-year. This included online transactions amounting to 8.96 billion yuan, up 13%, and offline transactions totaling 1.32 billion yuan, a 9% increase. In 2023, the Ceramic Expo further optimized its approach to cultural exchange and trade discussions by dividing the exhibition into two sections: the Exhibition Center and the Trading Center. The Exhibition Center focused on cultural displays, emphasizing three main areas: cultural exchanges, the inheritance of ceramic culture, and innovations in ceramic culture. This immersive experience allowed visitors from around the world to appreciate

Jingdezhen's rich ceramic heritage and its vibrant contemporary ceramic culture. Over the five-day event, total foot traffic reached 200,000, setting a historical record. Building on the platform effect of the Exhibition Center, the Trading Center achieved a total transaction volume of 12.262 billion yuan, marking a 19.28% increase over the previous year's 10 billion yuan. Of this, online transactions accounted for 10.752 billion yuan, reflecting a 20% year-on-year growth, while offline transactions reached 1.51 billion yuan, up 14%.

Never-Ending Display: The Ongoing Exchange Among Civilizations

Since its inception, the Ceramic Expo has been held for 16 years with the theme "Showcasing World-Class Ceramic Treasures and Promoting the Civilization of the Millennium Porcelain Capital." In 2019, Jingdezhen was designated as a Ceramic Culture Inheritance and Innovation Pilot Zone, with its core mission centered on creating new platforms for international cultural exchange. This initiative strives to forge a path for the inheritance and innovative development of traditional culture that holds global significance, embodies Chinese values, reflects the characteristics of the new era, and highlights Jingdezhen's unique attributes. As a result, the 17th Ceramic Expo in 2020 adopted the theme "Strengthening International Cooperation to Enhance the Industrial Chain," aligning with the core tasks of the Pilot Zone's development. The Expo also proposed the vision of a "Never-Ending Ceramic Expo," emphasizing continuous role in advancing international cooperation and industry upgrading. By adopting a hybrid exhibition model, the event collaborated with Tmall to establish the Tmall "Cloud Ceramic Expo" live broadcasting center, enabling 24-hour live streaming throughout the exhibition.

In 2021, the Ceramic Expo established a year-round themed exhibition area titled "China Jingdezhen International Ceramic Expo Perennial Exhibition" at the Jingdezhen International Exhibition Center. This ensured that all special exhibitors remain on display without closing, allowing for continuous exhibitions 365 days a year, thereby preserving the vibrant atmosphere of the ceramic exhibition. The Expo established a "display + market" approach to create a comprehensive system that incorporates a multi-vendor B2B trading platform, cloud warehouse management, supply chain finance, logistics, live broadcasting operations, and brand building. This has formed a software product matrix and platform services that integrate information, transactions, warehousing, finance, and marketing, ensuring that ceramic trade operates in an orderly manner throughout the year, thus achieving the vision of a "never-ending" trading platform.

In 2022, the Ceramic Expo, themed "World on Porcelain: Sharing the Future," further refined the "Cloud Ceramic Expo." By integrating traditional e-commerce with new media platforms such as Douyin, Kuaishou, and Bilibili, the Expo enhanced online marketing efforts for precise targeting. This approach not only achieved a perennial presence in terms of duration but also ensured that ceramic displays and transactions could continue indefinitely across various spaces.

The 2023 Ceramic Expo, themed "Ceramics Facilitate World Communication,Ceramic Trade Connects the World," continued to upgrade its exhibition and sales models built on past experiences. It adopted a market-oriented and regular exhibition mode featuring "exhibition + trading." Over 500 ceramic merchants have settled into the trading center through an invitation-based approach, achieving regular operations.[1] This Ceramic Expo aimed to create a benchmark ceramic marketplace that integrates exhibition, trade, and investment under the concept of "Buy Globally, Sell Globally."[2]

Reflecting on the history of the Ceramic Expo, the deep-seated reason behind the sustained operation of this thriving and expansive platform for ceramic exchange and trade lies in the relentless innovation and inheritance within ceramic culture, along with the ongoing mutual enrichment between Chinese and foreign civilizations. The enduring, evolving, and creatively innovative spirit embodied in ceramic craftsmanship has become the intrinsic

2024 International Copyright Forum (Photo courtesy of Jingdezhen Municipal Copyright Bureau)

---

①　Public Gazette of Jiangxi Provincial People's Government. "News Conference for the 2023 China Jingdezhen International Ceramic Expo Held in Nanchang." October 9, 2023. Accessed October 15, 2023.

②　Public Gazette of Jiangxi Provincial People's Government. "News Conference for the 2023 China Jingdezhen International Ceramic Expo Held in Nanchang." October 9, 2023. Accessed October 15, 2023.

mechanism that ensures the Ceramic Expo's "never-ending" nature. Jingdezhen has embraced this historical trajectory, recognizing ceramic copyright as a "universal language" for engaging with the world. It understands that copyright is a production factor and resource endowed with cultural, wealth-related, industrial, and high-value attributes, capable of functioning as the "universal currency" for global ceramic exchange and trade. Since the 2020 Ceramic Expo, Jingdezhen has incorporated ceramic copyright into the event to encourage creators to enhance technological research and focus on turning innovative ideas into tangible products. This effort has fostered continuous renewal in the ceramic cultural and creative industry while ensuring its ongoing prosperity.

Beginning in 2020, a copyright workstation was established at the Ceramic Expo, inviting staff from the provincial copyright protection center and industry experts to deliver on-site presentations and address questions regarding copyright knowledge and legal regulations. Comprehensive services were also provided, including copyright explantions of registration process, art registration, and review procedures. Plus, administrative law enforcement personnel were on-site to address any infringement issues.

During the 2022 Ceramic Expo, an International Copyright Forum was held under the theme "Promoting Chinese Culture to the World." This event not only raised national and global awareness of China's copyright initiatives but also highlighted the achievements of Jingdezhen's ceramic culture and its outcomes in protecting ceramic copyrights.

During the 20th Ceramic Expo in 2023, Jingdezhen hosted a Cultural Innovation and Development Forum themed "Cultural Inheritance and Development Through Mutual Learning Among Civilizations." This forum emphasized the integration of ceramic trade and culture while exploring the copyright value of ceramic works. Additionally, Jingdezhen organized the Copyright Promotes High-Quality Urban Development Forum, along with a series of international academic exchanges on copyright. The city also hosted themed exhibitions covering topics such as exemplary cases of copyright protection by the World Intellectual Property Organization (WIPO), grassroots cultural copyright protection, and the implementation of the Marrakesh Treaty. Through these initiatives, Jingdezhen invited industry experts and scholars from both domestic and international backgrounds to discuss copyright-related knowledge and latest trends. Hundreds of representatives from WIPO, copyright authorities from relevant countries, overseas copyright certification agencies, domestic ministries, provincial copyright bureaus, collective copyright management organizations, and academia participated both online and offline, creating a vibrant atmosphere for copyright. This effort aimed to promote high-quality development in the ceramic cultural and creative industry, guided by copyright principles.

From September 8 to 10, 2024, a delegation led by Daren Tang, Director-General of the WIPO, visited Jiangxi to investigate and survey copyright work. They also attended the 2024 International Copyright Forum organized by the National Copyright Administration of China (NCAC) and WIPO in Jingdezhen.

Daren Tang Visited Jiangxi Province and Attended the 2024 International Copyright Forum in Jingdezhen

WIPO Director General Daren Tang visited Jiangxi and undertook a copyright work survey from September 8 to 10, 2024. During his visit, he attended the 2024 International Copyright Forum in Jingdezhen, an event co-organized by the National Copyright Administration of China (NCAC) and WIPO, and co-hosted by the Jiangxi Provincial Copyright Administration and the Jingdezhen Municipal People's Government. This was the second time Jingdezhen has hosted the forum following the 2022 edition, and the first time Director General Daren Tang attended in person.

On September 9, at the opening ceremony of the 2024 International Copyright Forum in Jingdezhen, over 300 participants attended, including representatives from international organizations like WIPO, copyright and cultural officials from over 40 countries, IP and cultural attaches from embassies and consulates in China, delegates from copyright associations and collective management organizations, officials from copyright management departments across various provinces, autonomous regions, and municipalities in China, as well as rights holders, industry leaders, and academics from both domestic and international spheres. The forum centered on the theme "Copyrights and Creative Industries Driving Sustainable Development," with the objectives of implementing innovation-driven development strategies, fostering high-quality growth in the copyright industry, and advancing the construction of a culturally strong nation from a renewed historical vantage point. Furthermore, the forum sought to foster cultural exchanges and promote global cultural prosperity through copyright. The comprehensive agenda featured the following key themes: "Copyright Protection Promoting the Inheritance and Innovation of Traditional Culture: Policies and Measures," "The Application of Artificial Intelligence in Content Creation: Opportunities and Challenges," "Copyright System Ensuring Cultural Access and Participation: Protection and Limitations," "Collective Copyright Management in the Knowledge Economy Era: Current Status and Prospects," and "The Role of Copyright in the Sustainable Development of Creative Industries: Measures and Outcomes."

On the sidelines of the forum, foreign guests toured the Taobocheng International Ceramic Trading Center, the Jingdezhen National Ceramic Copyright Trading Center, the Sanbao International Ceramic Valley, and the Jingdezhen Imperial Kiln Ceramic Art Museum. These visits provided insights into the development of copyright and cultural industries in the city. The guests experienced the enduring charm of Jingdezhen porcelain (china), and witnessed the vibrant spirit of cultural innovation and creation within China.

During his visit to Jingdezhen, Daren Tang explored key cultural sites, including the Jingdezhen Imperial Kiln Museum, Taoyangli Historical and Cultural Tourism District, the Ancient Fuliang County Government Office, the Deng Xiping Color-Glazed Porcelain Art Museum at Mingfang Park, Changnan New District, Master Lai Dequan's Studio (Art Gallery), and the Taoxichuan Ceramic Art Avenue, to conduct research on traditional culture and copyright practices. He also toured historical and cultural sites, engaged in discussions with master ceramic artists, and experienced firsthand the vibrancy and charm of copyright markets.

At the Deng Xiping Color-Glazed Porcelain Art Museum, Daren Tang attentively admired various color-glazed porcelain pieces and had a cordial conversation with Master Deng Xiping. Master Deng provided a comprehensive, multi-faceted overview of his creative insights over the past 50 years, detailing the historical development, craftsmanship, heritage, innovative achievements, and artistic allure of Jingdezhen's color-glazed ceramics. At Master Lai Dequan's Studio, Tang carefully examined Master Lai's ceramic works and held in-depth discussions on ceramic art and copyright protection. Master Lai gifted Tang a hand-painted porcelain plate, expressing a heartfelt warm welcome for his visit to Jiangxi and Jingdezhen. Tang highly praised Jingdezhen's ceramic culture and fully affirmed the city's endeavors in copyright protection.

Daren Tang emphasized that one of the most meaningful aspects of copyright is its close link to culture and history. Jiangxi province boasts a rich cultural legacy, and Jingdezhen ceramics serve as a world-renowned cultural icon. The province is committed to integrating cultural innovation with copyright protection, making full use of its rich historical and cultural heritage to nurture a thriving cultural market that blends tradition with modernity. Openness and innovation are pivotal to the enduring status of Jingdezhen—the millennium porcelain capital—as an international exchange hub. Strong intellectual property protection, including copyright, is essential to the success of the ceramics industry. The successful hosting of the 2024 International Copyright Forum in Jingdezhen demonstrated Jiangxi's spirit of openness, inclusiveness, and innovation, further solidifying its international reputation in the field of copyright.

Daren Tang also affirmed that WIPO stands ready to collaborate with stakeholders to empower creators, culture, and heritage across all countries through intellectual property. WIPO will continue to leverage copyright as a

Lai Dequan Presented a Porcelain Plate to Daren Tang (Photo courtesy of Jingdezhen Municipal Copyright Bureau)

IP and Creative Industry:
Jingdezhen Story

catalyst for sustainable innovation and creativity, deepen cooperation with Jiangxi Province in areas such as intellectual property protection, professional talent exchange, and cultural heritage innovation, and work towards mutual benefit and shared prosperity.

(2) The Normalized Copyright Service Model for Jingdezhen Ceramics

Establishing the Ceramic Copyright Service System in Jingdezhen

Jingdezhen has strategically developed a ceramic copyright service system by clearly delineating roles, responsibilities, and accountability mechanisms. This system is built on a cooperative framework involving the government, market, and society, resulting in a highly integrated, coordinated, and practical "triadic synergy" model for copyright services. It aims to support a diverse range of innovative entities while addressing the entire process of copyright utilization, protection, and management.

In this framework, the Jingdezhen People's Municipal Government acts as the supervisor and guide for copyright services, establishing accountability mechanisms to ensure performance outcomes. Firstly, the government uses the results from copyright service supply evaluations as a basis for assessing and holding service providers accountable. Secondly, performance assessments of IP service provision are utilized as criteria for evaluating the staff involved. Thirdly, these evaluation results help optimize the allocation of resources and the scope of services offered. This approach not only incentivizes the delivery of copyright services but also ensures their quality. Specific copyright services will be carried out by social welfare organizations and market operators, based on a distinction made between those with high business viability and competitive market positioning.

Jingdezhen's core ceramic copyright services encompass both regular services—such as copyright registration, public education, and legal consultation—and specialized services like copyright transactions and pledge financing. For regular services, Jingdezhen has formed a professional team that integrates personnel from government, enterprises, academia, research, and judiciary fields.

329

Each year, this team conducts "Five Into" activities (into government agencies, enterprises, communities, schools, and shopping malls) to share fundamental legal knowledge about ceramic copyright. They also participate in large-scale ceramic culture exchange events, such as the Ceramic Expo, to educate attendees on copyright registration and protection while addressing ceramic copyright legal queries from creators. To resolve complex copyright disputes involving enterprises and artists, the government regularly hosts ceramic copyright symposiums and organizes expert advisory panels to provide guidance for the development of ceramic copyright industry in the city. The Jingdezhen Copyright Association, with over 50 member units, actively assists its members in work registration, copyright transactions, and collaborates with the municipal copyright bureau to raise copyright awareness, organize forums, and hold exhibitions of copyrighted works.

These regular services are primarily initiated and led by the government, with contributions from copyright scholars, judicial experts, ceramic business managers, and ceramic research specialists. Ultimately, the government evaluates the effectiveness of these services and determines the next phase of projects and the relevant service providers. This approach ensures that Jingdezhen consistently delivers high-quality public copyright services. With the established ceramic copyright service system, specialized services will be guided by market forces, fostering the formation of a copyright service industry. The vibrant copyright market in Jingdezhen provides a fertile environment for these specialized services to thrive and flourish.

Development of the Ceramic Copyright Service Industry in Jingdezhen

Jingdezhen has established a robust operational mechanism for its ceramic copyright service industry by enhancing service quality, empowering service platforms, innovating service models, and strengthening regulatory oversight. This comprehensive approach fosters the orderly development of the ceramic copyright market.

First, enhancing the service quality of copyright institutions. The Jingdezhen People's Municipal Government has organized expert-led seminars, such as "Copyright in Enterprises," and provided training for staff at copyright service organizations. These efforts aim to improve the quality of services like agency representation, information dissemination, and consulting, while also encouraging value-added services related to the assessment, custody, and transformation of ceramic works' copyright value. Second, creating a digital copyright operation service platform. Jingdezhen has developed two commercial trading platforms focused on ceramic works, facilitating smooth information flow between supply and demand markets. These platforms offer specialized, international, and legally compliant services for ceramic copyright transactions. Third, encouraging financial institutions to innovate new financing models for ceramic copyrights. The city encourages financial institutions to develop various financing options, such as copyright pledges, loans, and insurance products. This support enables young creators to secure funds by pledging their works, allowing them to continue producing high-quality pieces and further advancing the ceramic copyright industry. Fourth, strengthening regulatory oversight of the copyright service industry. Jingdezhen aims to create a balanced management system that combines incentives with regulation. By utilizing blockchain technology, the city implements dynamic and technical oversight, fostering a fair and transparent environment within the copyright service market.

Section VI

Conclusion

Jingdezhen has established a distinctive full-chain development system for ceramic copyrights, encompassing "Creation-Application-Protection-Management-Service."

Creation. Initially, Jingdezhen's focus was on large-scale production; however, it has gradually shifted towards a more customized and personalized creative model. This transformation not only addresses the increasingly diverse market demands but also fosters innovation and growth in ceramic art, allowing Jingdezhen ceramics to showcase a unique competitive edge in the global marketplace.

Application. Through diversified and industrialized strategies, Jingdezhen has significantly expanded the application scope of ceramic copyrights. A prime example of this innovation is the successful establishment of the Taoxichuan Ceramic Art Avenue, which tightly integrates culture with industry. This initiative breaks away from traditional copyright application models and creates new commercial pathways, allowing for broader recognition and promotion of the value of ceramic copyrights.

Protection. Jingdezhen has established a comprehensive legal framework and oversight mechanism to safeguard the copyright rights of ceramic works. By enhancing law enforcement efforts and conducting extensive public awareness campaigns, the city has effectively protected these rights. These thorough protective measures have not only reduced infringement instances but also raised public awareness about the copyright protection, creating a safer environment for ceramic artists to pursue their creative endeavors.

Management. Jingdezhen employs a scientific and systematic approach to enhance the efficiency and standardization of copyright management. By establishing standardized management processes and utilizing information technology, the city has optimized the allocation of copyright resources, ensuring fair distribution and reasonable use. This solid management foundation is pivotal for the sustainable development of the ceramics industry.

Service. Jingdezhen has integrated the strengths of the government, market, and society to form a comprehensive and regularized copyright service system. This system has elevated the professionalism of copyright services while also providing holistic support for creation, application, and protection. As a result, it has enhanced the global dissemination and influence of Jingdezhen's ceramic culture.

Overall, Jingdezhen's comprehensive innovations in creation, application, protection, management, and service have advanced the inheritance and development of ceramic culture, laying a solid foundation for the continuous prosperity of China's ceramics industry. This highlights the strong vitality and adaptability of traditional Chinese culture within the modern context.

Chapter V

Ceramic Copyright: A Catalyst for Jingdezhen's High-Quality Development

Jingdezhen, a city born from porcelain, has flourished through its thriving porcelain-making industry. Today, its rapid development is fueled by ceaseless innovation in ceramics. In just over a decade, Jingdezhen has undergone a remarkable revival, with copyright playing a pivotal role in this remarkable transformation. Recognizing the importance of ceramic copyright for creation, the city has explored various aspects, establishing a distinctive and replicable model for its development.

Looking ahead, Jingdezhen's high-quality development still depends on ceramic copyright to reach new historical heights. As Jingdezhen moves forward, it is vital to clarify the theoretical foundations of copyright's role in driving high-quality urban growth and to establish a corresponding evaluation system, ensuring precision in planning. With these strategies in place, it is equally important to set specific development goals, further providing a clear path for the future of Jingdezhen.

Section I

The Theoretical Basis for Copyright's Role in Promoting High-Quality Urban Development

Over its 300-year history, copyright has transformed from a private law aimed at protecting copyright holders' rights into a comprehensive system that can actively promote high-quality urban development. Originally a "small rule" for safeguarding publishers, it has now become a "big system" driving development across various sectors. As its impact is increasingly recognized, the booming research findings also underscore copyright's significant contributions to urban industrial transformation, social environment optimization, and urban competitiveness.

(1) Driving Urban Industrial Transformation

First, copyright lays a solid foundation for the cultural industry. As society advances economically and culturally, with productivity and material wealth on the rise, people's expectation for a better life have shifted from purely material gains to a focus on spiritual enrichment. Especially in today's knowledge economy, this trend is reflected in the strong demand for knowledge and cultural products, which emphasizes not only the pursuit of material wealth but also the greater importance of spiritual fulfillment. Driven by this potential, more individuals are engaging in the production and operation of these industries.[①] Market mechanisms further stimulate demand for knowledge and cultural products, thus expanding their production and distribution, and ultimately leading the industrial transformation.

Copyright arises from economic necessity. Economically, copyright system was established due to the economic value and scarcity inherent in cultural products. This value is evident in three main areas: First, cultural products fulfill people's needs for cultural enrichment, generating social benefits; second, when produced, cultural products can be converted into tangible goods that meet material needs, yielding economic benefits; third, consumers can enhance their humanistic quality by absorbing the knowledge within these products, thereby enhancing their strength in market competition.[②] The scarcity of cultural products is primarily due to their long production cycles, complexity, and high costs, making their creation and acquisition challenging. These qualities confer commodity value upon cultural products, which necessitates copyright protection to preserve this value. The copyright system grants authors both moral and economic rights, classifying unauthorized use of their works as infringement. This system helps prevent misuse of original creations, encouraging creators in literature, art, and science to produce more valuable cultural works. Only when the creation and production of cultural products are protected can the cultural industry thrive—making copyright indispensable to its growth.

Second, copyright increases the added value of related industries. According to the 2015 update to *The Economic Contribution of the Copyright Industries* by WIPO, copyright industries are still divided into four categories—core copyright industries, interdependent copyright industries, partial copyright industries, and non-dedicated support industries.[③] The copyright factor for core copyright

---

① Wu Xue'an, "Optimizing and Adjusting Industrial Structure: Actively Developing the Copyright Industry is Beneficial for Eliminating Economic Weaknesses," February 9, 2015, accessed September 14, 2023, http://www.iprchn.com/Index_NewsContent.aspx?newsId=81793.

② Sun Wusheng, "On the Copyright Protection System and the Development of Cultural and Creative Industries," *Law Science Magazine*, 2016 (10): 89.

③ World Intellectual Property Organization, *Guide on Surveying the Economic Contribution of the Copyright-Based Industries*, 2015, accessed October 12, 2023, https://www.wipo.int/edocs/pubdocs/en/copyright/893/wipo_pub_893.pdf.

industries is fixed at 100%, while for the remaining three categories (collectively termed non-core copyright industries), it must be calculated to determine copyright's contribution or each industry's reliance on copyright. Core copyright industries, such as publishing, broadcasting, and performing arts, depend fully on copyright. Interdependent copyright industries encompass sectors that manufacture and sell copyright-related equipment, such as televisions, computers, and photocopiers. Partial copyright industries involve artistic design, like textiles, jewelry, and ceramics. Non-dedicated support industries—like general wholesale and retail, transportation, telecommunications, and the internet—serve as infrastructure that supports the growth of other copyright-based industries.

For core copyright industries, which fully rely on copyright, the role of copyright in boosting their added value is self-evident. Regarding non-core copyright industries, firstly, interdependent copyright industries gain value from products reliant on copyright content, like TV shows, computer software, and music. The quality and quantity of these works directly affect the sales of related products. For example, major gaming console companies like Sony and Microsoft routinely release exclusive games with new consoles to boost sales—a well-established industry practice.[1] Secondly, partial copyright industries have adopted a strategic approach rooted in a broad cultural development perspective during periods of development and transformation, increasingly prioritizing content development and medium integration to cater to people's personalized choices and cultural needs. Unlike traditional methods focused primarily on improving practical value, these industries amid the transition period, recognizing the limitations of this approach, have shifted toward emphasizing creative elements in their products, which heavily depend on copyright. In recent years, copyright's role in adding value to partial copyright industries has become ever more prominent.[2] Lastly, non-dedicated support industries are also undergoing an information-driven transformation driven by the information technology revolution. For example, in the development of Jingdezhen's ceramics industry,

---

① Ni Feng, "Research on the Business Model of Cloud Gaming Platforms: A Case Study of OnLive," *Quality & Market*, 2020 (16).

② Xiang Yong, "Research on the Development Model of China's Cultural Industry during the Transitional Period," *Dongyue Tribune*, 2016 (02): 66.

growth traditionally relied on optimizing human resources and improving manufacturing capabilities. Today, however, even small-scale ceramic enterprises depend on digital office software for internal management, while the Jingdezhen government's annual industry-wide assessments similarly rely on big data-driven computer software tools. These cases demonstrate how the development and application of IT-related works have become integral to the growth of Jingdezhen's ceramics industry.

(2) Optimizing Social Environment

First of all, copyright optimizes talent cultivation models. Its positive impact on employment is primarily seen in its expanding capacity for supporting job creation. This occurs in two ways: Copyright helps sustain existing jobs, stimulating the positive momentum in employment growth positive employment growth; and it also facilitates the emergence of new job opportunities. Amid today's unstoppable knowledge economy and new technological revolution, the copyright industry— underpinned by intellectual achievements and driven by knowledge innovation— faces unprecedented opportunities for growth. With its high profitability, strong growth potential, and added value, the copyright industry has made substantial contributions to regional economies and urban high-quality development. By harnessing the copyright industry, regional economies can establish specialized division of labor and collaborative relationships of numerous independent yet interconnected copyright enterprises and supporting institutions, leading to the formation of industry clusters with local characteristics and aligned with regional development realities.[1] The influx of creative talent to Jingdezhen, known as the "Jing Piao" (Jingdezhen migrants) community, and the expansion of its ceramic copyright industry demonstrated this theory in action. As a vital engine of regional economic development, copyright can thus generate more job opportunities. With the copyright industry's positive growth and rising workforce, its capacity to support employment continues to expand, becoming a powerful driver of social

---

[1] Wang Xingpeng, "Copyright Industry: A New Source of Regional Economic Development," *China Copyright*, 2013 (04): 30.

well-being. Put simply, its contribution to employment lies in its role in promoting the overall job growth. In addition, in an era of widespread creative participation, booming self-media industries, such as short videos and live streaming, offer new career pathways, although they also give rise to infringement issues. Copyright protection thus plays a crucial role in safeguarding original content, fueling the flourishing development of these emerging industries and solidifying copyright's contribution to employment growth as a sustained, normalized dynamic.

The development of copyright can support the exploration of higher-level talent cultivation models, as a skilled workforce forms the foundation of progress in the copyright industry. Amid the transformation of global economic landscape, China is advancing a strategy to strengthen intellectual property, heightening demand for versatile, applied copyright talent. However, traditional training models are increasingly unable to meet industry needs, resulting in a supply-demand gap for copyright talent. Responding to market demand, talent cultivation models are evolving. Fields such as art, engineering, and natural sciences now emphasize not just specialized knowledge but also showing an increasing tendency to integrate intellectual property protection and management knowledge into teaching innovation to students. In parallel, intellectual property programs, traditionally based on law and management, are exploring integration with other related disciplines.

Furthermore, copyright can support the multifaceted development of women, who make up 49.6% of the global population and contribute significantly to social and economic progress. Despite a nearly equal gender ratio, data reveals a pronounced global gender gap[1] across various fields, including intellectual property (IP). Research indicates that women are often discouraged from entering innovation-driven sectors, less told about the advantages of the IP field, and are less frequently introduced to this field. The number of women in IP legislation and

---

[1]   According to the *World Economic Forum's Global Gender Gap Report 2022*, only 68.1% of the gender gap had been closed globally by 2022, and at the current rate of progress, it will take another 132 years to completely close the gender gap. World Economic Forum, *Global Gender Gap Report 2022*, June 2022. Accessed October 18, 2023.

administration remains notably lower than that of men.[①]

Organizations like WIPO are increasingly recognizing the need to eliminate the negative impacts of gender gap within the IP sector. Copyright can play a key role in promoting women's development in two primary ways. First, it can provide more job opportunities. Traditional industries with rigid development models often struggle to reform workforce structures due to long-standing barriers. In contrast, copyright-related industries, which rely on creative content and demand a diverse talent, tend to be more inclusive and easier to reduce gender disparities. Second, copyright expand avenues for female expression. Traditional patriarchal education systems have limited women's access to equal educational opportunities, leaving many unprepared for fields such as literature, art, and music, traditionally governed by copyright. Although countless classics have emerged over time, the vast majority are narrated from male perspectives, underscoring a historical deprivation of female representation.[②]

In today's era of high demand for female expression, an increasing number of women are creating and expressing themselves in the ceramics copyright industry through a female perspective. Cai Wenjuan, a inheritor of Jiangxi Province's Yuan Dynasty blue-and-white porcelain heritage, integrates female perspectives into the establishment and management of her brand, "Qinghua Story." She believes that women are more willing to draw inspiration from daily life with a heightened emotional sensibility, infusing their creations with both practicality and artistry. In business management, her perceptive insights and strong communication skills blend logic with empathy, allowing her to address challenges effectively and foster a workplace culture of respect, encouragement, and mutual support. Under her leadership, Qinghua Story has nearly quadrupled its output over recent years and was among the first batch of companies authorized to use the "Made in Jingdezhen" label. Professor Zhang Jingjing from Jingdezhen Ceramic

---

① Brant, Jennifer, Kaveri Marathe, Jaci McDole and Mark Schultz, "Policy Approaches to Close the Intellectual Property Gender Gap: Practices to Support Access to the Intellectual Property System for Female Innovators, Creators, and Entrepreneurs," 2019, accessed October 18, 2023. https://www.wipo.int/export/sites/www/ip-development/en/agenda/docs/policy_approaches_close_the_ip_gender_gap.pdf.

② Du Ping and Zhou Weigui, "The Female Image from the Perspective of Male Discourse: Venus in Shakespeare's Works," *Journal of Hainan University (Humanities and Social Sciences Edition)*, 2011 (06): 96.

University incorporates feminine grace, elegance, and vitality into her "Wind and Water" series. These pieces harmonize the elements of wind and water, achieving a refined aesthetic while creating contemplative spaces that feel both tangible and ethereal—representing the avant-garde ceramic style of Jingdezhen. As Dean of the International College, Prof. Zhang emphasizes that the key to the future of Jingdezhen ceramics lies in fostering communication and diversity. Ceramics, as a medium for cross-cultural exchange and mutual learning among civilizations, have played a crucial role in deepening interactions between Jingdezhen and the global community, which has, in turn, contributed to the diversity and inclusiveness of the city's ceramics industry. Beyond ceramic practitioners, creatives from other artistic disciplines can also find opportunities in Jingdezhen, helping it grow into a true cultural capital of East Asia.

(3) Enhancing Urban Competitiveness

Firstly, copyright can contribute to urban economic development. The copyright system, by innovating incentive mechanism, positively impacts creative activities and intellectual output, thereby enhancing urban economic growth and competitiveness. This influence functions in three implementation path: First, copyright law incentivizes creativity by clearly defining and protecting intellectual property rights. Second, it sets internal limits on public domain status and protection duration, preventing the overreach of private rights and supporting ongoing creative activities. Third, copyright utilization aligns the interests of creators, distributors, and users, ensuring the optimal economic use of intellectual property and advancing high-quality urban development.

The establishment of the copyright system grants creators exclusive rights, thus incentivizing innovation. Essentially, the emergence of original ideas largely depends on the balance between private benefits and associated costs. If private interests diverge from social benefits, the development of valuable intellectual innovations may be delayed.[1] Innovation brings in knowledge products, and the

---

① Jiang Yuhong and Shan Xiaoguang, "The Impact of Intellectual Property Systems on Urban Competitiveness: An Analysis Based on Innovation Incentives," *Intellectual Property*, 2007(03): 29.

copyright system structures their ownership, ensuring that creators can anticipate and secure private benefits. By conferring private property rights, the copyright system offers creators substantial rewards, establishing a robust, effective, and enduring incentive that fosters continued innovation, and ultimately, fuels economic growth.

Secondly, copyright helps concentrate urban innovation resources. As a driver in urban economic growth, innovation is a key factor in determining urban competitiveness. Innovation activities rely on the support of essential resources such as talent, capital, and information. In the context of the urban economy, competitiveness is reflected in the extent to which production factors are effectively owned, allocated, and utilized in a market-oriented manner.[1] Urban competitiveness stems from a city's capacity to attract and transform resource factors, and the copyright system contributes by confirming ownership to reduce transaction costs associated with property rights. By directing the flow of innovative resources, copyright enables optimal resource allocation, thereby enhancing urban competitiveness.

A well-refined urban copyright protection system can effectively attract resources, particularly innovative ones, through two main pathways: First, copyright protection strengthens a city's ability to attract and allocate resources. Capital, talent, and other assets migrant across regions in pursuit of maximized profits. A robust property rights system ensures the security of economic actors' assets, drawing both domestic and foreign resources into the city. This fosters industrial growth, specialization, and market openness, which in turn enhances the city's clustering effect and competitiveness. Resource elements demonstrate a clear tendency to concentrate within major enterprises and core urban areas. Conversely, inadequate copyright protection can disrupt anticipated returns, hampering resource inflows and potentially resulting in substantial resource outflows from within the city.

If copyright protection is poorly regulated, and intellectual property infringements and abuses are not effectively controlled, the interests of creators

---

[1] Zhou Zhenhua, Chen Wei, Tang Jingbo, Huang Jianfu, Shen Kaiyan, Jing Xueqing and Yang Yaqin, "A Comparative Study of Comprehensive Competitiveness Among Several Major Cities in China," *Shanghai Journal of Economics*, 2001 (01): 17.

and copyright holders will be compromised, diminishing the motivation for innovation. This may impede the development and commercialization of intellectual achievements and even lead to further outflows of key resources, such as talent and technology. Within a single country, disparities in local legislation, public policies, administrative practices, judicial systems, and law enforcement can create varied environments for the creation, utilization, management, and protection of copyrights across cities. Such differences can greatly impact the movement of resources, like technology and capital, between cities.

Second, copyright protection impacts capital mobility and accumulation. Capital is highly sensitive to the state of copyright protection; due to the ease with which intellectual property can be replicated at low cost, it is acutely responsive to unfair competition in this sector. When a city maintains orderly competition and favorable conditions for economic security, it can experience rapid capital growth and efficient capital utilization. Empirical studies have shown, for example, that stronger IPR enforcement at the local level can effectively promote foreign investment, particularly benefiting the service industry and technology-intensive sectors.[1] An exemplary case is Jingdezhen, which has bolstered its urban competitiveness and established a strong city brand by enhancing its copyright system and accumulating copyright resources.

---

[1]　Han Jian and Xu Yayun, "Intellectual Property Protection and the Use of Foreign Capital," *Business and Management Journal*, 2021(04): 18.

Section II

An Evaluation System for the Role of Copyright in Promoting High-Quality Development in Jingdezhen

The theories discussed above provide a multi-faceted perspective on the link between copyright and high-quality urban development, convincingly proving copyright's catalyst role as a powerful driver. Leveraging a robust copyright framework and related resources, Jingdezhen has in recent years advanced its copyright-driven economy. Key initiatives include building ceramic cultural communities, enhancing ceramic art museums, promoting ceramic culture online, and supporting ceramic artists throughout their creative processes. These efforts have propelled Jingdezhen into prominence. To realize the vision of "establishing Jingdezhen as a culturally significant city and a globally influential center for ceramics,"[1] it is crucial to harness copyright's potential to transform the quality, efficiency, and driving forces of local development. However, assessing and even quantifying copyright's impact on Jingdezhen's high-quality development demands further research. Unlike a physical industry whose contribution can be gauged through direct indicators, the institutional nature of copyright calls for a more conceptual approach. By connecting institutional indicators to urban development metrics, we can gain a more objective assessment through data collection and analysis. To evaluate how copyright contributes to Jingdezhen's growth, a comprehensive assessment framework is needed, combining qualitative

---

[1] From the *Implementation Plan for the Ceramic Culture Inheritance and Innovation Pilot Zone*, Issued in August 2019.

and quantitative indicators that align with the city's unique context and goals. By translating relevant indicators into quantifiable data, we can better understand the impact and direction of copyright's influence. This approach—building an evaluation framework, defining indicators, and structuring assessment content—offers a feasible basis for measuring how copyright empowers Jingdezhen's high-quality development.

(1) Establishing an Evaluation System Framework Aligned with the *Outline for Building an Intellectual Property Powerhouse (2021-2035)*

The evaluation system framework should be grounded in the *Outline for Building an Intellectual Property Powerhouse (2021-2035)* (hereinafter referred to as *Outline*), issued by the CPC Central Committee and the State Council on September 22, 2021. This *Outline* sets a 15-year plan to strengthen China's IPR regime, elevating it to a national strategic priority and offering guidance for assessing its development.

The *Outline* contributes to China's IP experience by dividing its development into five key areas: creation, utilization, protection, management, and service. These five areas are further organized into six focal points: 1) Establishing an IP system aligned with socialist modernization; 2) Creating a protection system that fosters a world-class business environment; 3) Developing a market mechanism that encourages innovation; 4) Building a public service system that benefits the people; 5) Cultivating a socio-cultural environment that promotes high-quality IP development; and 6) Actively participating in global IP governance. This structure suggests that evaluating IP development requires assessing its influence across each of these dimensions, highlighting its positive impact. Additionally, the *Outline* clarifies the broad concept of "IP development" by breaking it down into these six areas. When evaluators need to assess IP's impact on a specific sector, they can do so by examining how each of these six aspects influences that sector. Furthermore, the six areas—framework, protection, market operation, public service, socio-cultural environment, and global governance—closely correspond to primary indicators for evaluating high-quality urban development. This alignment shows that the *Outline* offers a valuable theoretical framework for establishing an evaluation system to measure IP's impact on high-quality urban growth.

As copyright is a key IP category, an evaluation system to assess its impact on high-quality development in Jingdezhen can also be formulated around the *Outline* as a theoretical framework. Based on this framework, the recommended primary indicators for the evaluation system include six components: 1) Copyright System Framework; 2) Copyright Protection Mechanism; 3) Copyright Economy; 4) Copyright and Urban Public Services; 5) Copyright and Cultural Environment; and 6) Copyright and International Influence.[1]

(2) Anchoring Evaluation System Indicators Using Four Key Standards

To construct indicators for the evaluation system, it's essential to refer to existing indicators in urban development-related evaluation frameworks. In recent years, various organizations have developed scientific evaluation systems to assess the innovation and comprehensive development of countries or cities. In the realm of national innovation evaluation, WIPO's annual Global Innovation Index provides a comprehensive set of indicators to assess each country's innovation capabilities. Given the close link between copyright and innovation, the Global Innovation Index provides valuable insights for defining specific indicators in a copyright-enabled evaluation system to support Jingdezhen's high-quality development. For comprehensive urban development evaluation, three authoritative indicator systems have been established by the International Organization for Standardization (ISO) and China's Standardization Administration. These include: 1) ISO 37120:2014,[2] developed by ISO's Technical Committee on Sustainable

---

[1]   Considering that participation in global copyright governance activities only occurs at the national level, and acknowledging that one of the ways copyright influences the high-quality development of cities is by gradually enhancing their international influence through this "globally recognized language," the final item in the evaluation system is designed as "Copyright and International Influence."

[2]   The subtitle of this international standard is "Sustainable Cities and Communities—Indicators for City Services and Quality of Life." It aims to assess sustainable cities and communities through a specific set of indicators.

Cities and Communities (ISO/TC 268) in 2014, and revised as ISO 37120:2018 in 2018; 2) the New-type Urbanization: Evaluation Index System of Quality City (GB/T 39497-2020), released by the State Administration for Market Regulation and the Standardization Administration of China on November 19, 2020; and 3) the Evaluation Indicators for Quality of City Development (GB/T 40482-2021), published by the same agencies on August 20, 2021.

Global Innovation Index

This index system comprises seven primary indicators—Institutions, Human Capital and Research, Infrastructure, Market Sophistication, Business Sophistication, Knowledge and Technology Outputs, and Creative Outputs—further divided into 21 secondary and 80 tertiary indicators to evaluate a country's innovation capacity. Unlike comprehensive urban development evaluation systems, which heavily focus on economic, social, ecological, and urban construction factors, this system prioritizes "Institutions" as the foremost criteria. Since the *Outline* also places "Institutions" and "Protection" at the core of its framework, indicators related to copyright policies and regulatory structures are essential in assessing copyright's role in driving Jingdezhen's high-quality development.

ISO 37120:2018

This indicator system assesses urban development through 104 indicators across 19 categories, including Economy, Education, Energy, Environment and Climate Change, Finance, Governance, Health, Housing, Population and Social Conditions, Recreation, Safety, Solid Waste, Sports and Culture, Communication, Transportation, Urban/Local Agriculture and Food Security, Urban Planning, Wastewater, and Water. Of these, 45 are core indicators and 59 are supplementary indicators. Copyright is directly linked to six key areas: economy, education, finance, governance, social conditions, and culture.

New-type Urbanization: Evaluation Index System of Quality City (GB/T 39497-2020)

This system outlines five primary indicators: Economic Development, Social Culture, Ecological Environment, Public Services, and Resident Life. It includes 13 secondary and 76 tertiary indicators (including five extended indicators) to comprehensively evaluate urban development. Of these, four primary indicators—Economic Development, Social Culture, Public Services, and Resident Life are directly related to copyright, with the exception of Ecological Environment.

Evaluation Indicators for Quality of City Development (GB/T 40482-2021)

This index system consists of five primary indicators: Economic Development, Ecological Environment, Urban Construction, Public Services, and Resident Life, with 50 secondary indicators assessing urban development. Among these, three primary indicators—Economic Development, Public Services, and Resident Life—are closely related to copyright, with the exception of Ecological Environment and Urban Construction.

(3) Defining Evaluation System Content Based on Statistical Results

After establishing the six primary indicators for the evaluation system and referencing the structure of relevant indicator frameworks, we further examined the *Outline*'s specific content while incorporating actual data from Jingdezhen's statistical work. Considering Jingdezhen's foundation in copyright development, we propose 15 secondary and 46 tertiary indicators as the detailed components of the evaluation system.

The primary indicator, "Copyright System Framework," includes two secondary indicators: "Local Legislation Related to Copyright," with tertiary indicators that assess the total number and five-year growth rate of relevant current local legislation, and "Copyright-Related Administrative Normative Documents," which evaluates the number and five-year growth rate of current administrative documents.

The primary indicator, "Copyright Protection Mechanism," consists of three secondary indicators: "Judicial Protection of Copyright," measuring the number of copyright cases per 100,000 people, case closure rate, mediation rate, and average compensation; "Administrative Protection of Copyright," focusing on the number of copyright administrative penalties per 100,000 people and the total fines and confiscations; and "Coordinated Protection of Copyright," assessing the sustained operations of intellectual property protection centers, the number of copyright cases handled by these centers per 100,000 people, and mediation rate at the center.

The primary indicator "Copyright Economy" encompasses three secondary indicators: 1) Copyright Industry—measured by six tertiary indicators, including

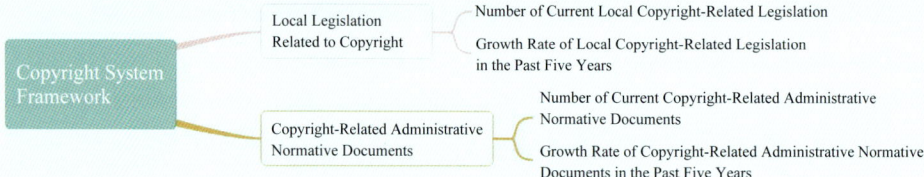

Diagram of Primary Indicator "Copyright System Framework"

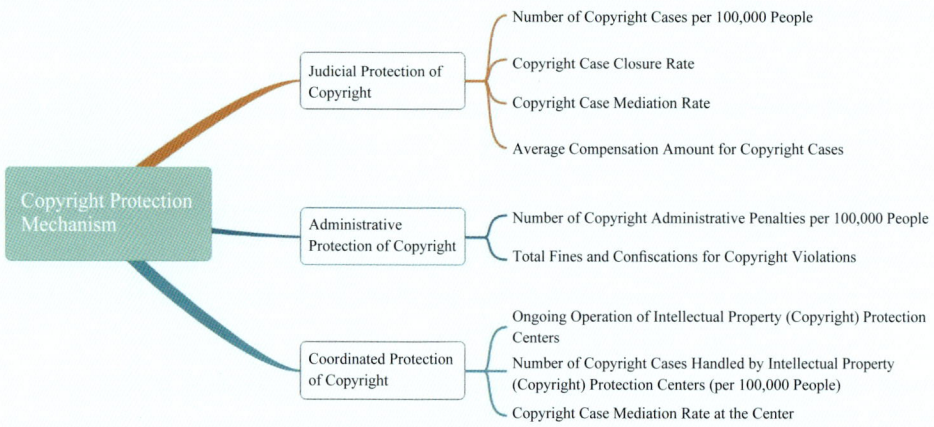

Diagram of Primary Indicator "Copyright Protection Mechanism"

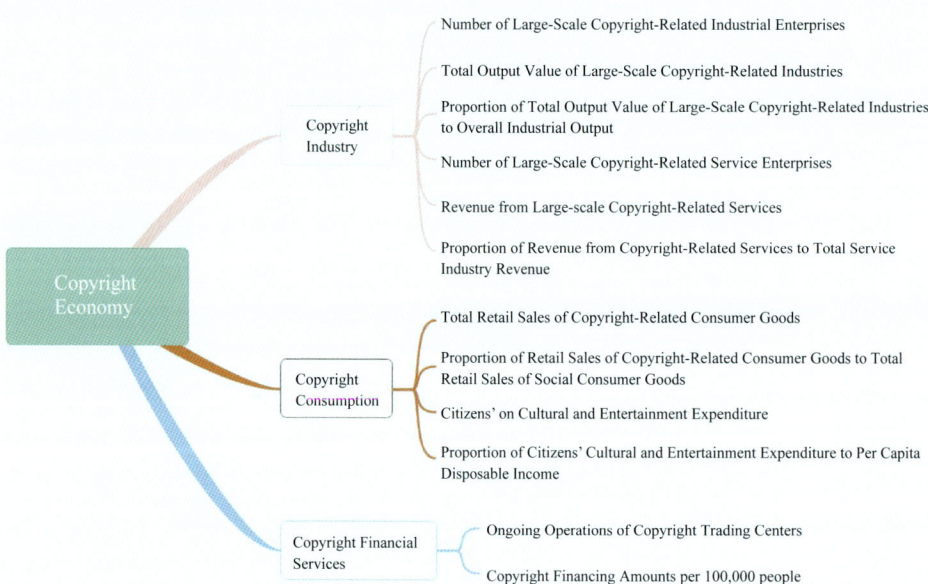

Diagram of Primary Indicator "Copyright Economy"

the number of large-scale copyright-related industrial enterprises, total output value of these industries and its share of overall industrial output, the number and revenue of large-scale copyright-related service enterprises, and the proportion of this revenue within total service industry revenue; 2) Copyright Consumption—evaluated by four tertiary indicators like the total retail sales of copyright-related consumer goods, their proportion of total retail sales, citizens' cultural and entertainment expenditure, and the ratio of this expenditure to per capita disposable income; 3) Copyright Financial Services—assessing the ongoing operations of Copyright Trading Centers and copyright financing amounts per 100,000 people.

The primary indicator "Copyright and Urban Public Services" consists of three secondary indicators: 1) Copyright Registration—which includes the number of copyright registrations per 100,000 people as a tertiary indicator; 2) Copyright Finance, encompassing two tertiary indicators—financial expenditure on cultural and sporting media per 100,000 people and the proportion of this expenditure to total fiscal spending; 3) Copyright Facilities, which consists of six tertiary indicators—the number of art galleries, participation in cultural activities per 100,000 people, the number of visitors to exhibitions per 100,000 people, the number of libraries, collection volume per 100,000 people, and library circulation per 100,000 people.

The primary indicator "Copyright and Urban Cultural Environment" comprises two secondary indicators: 1) Copyright Education, which includes tertiary

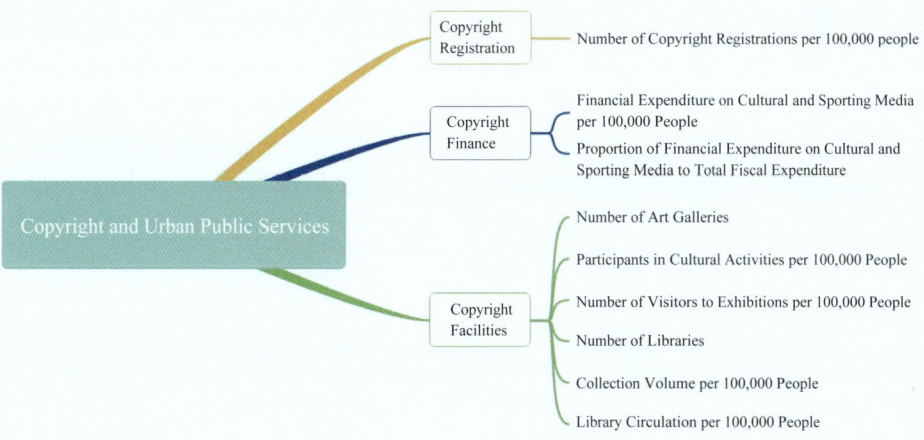

Diagram of Primary Indicator "Copyright and Urban Public Services"

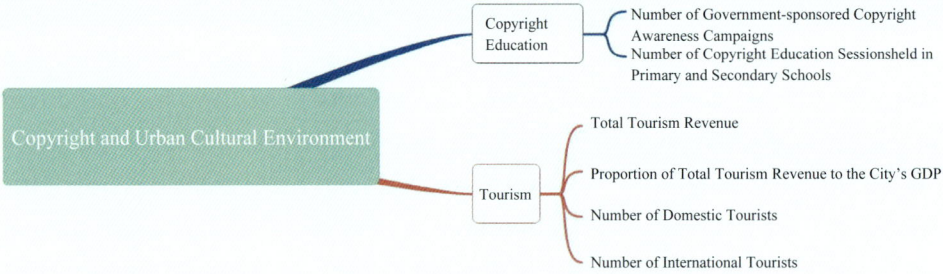

Diagram of Primary Indicator "Copyright and Urban Cultural Environment"

Diagram of Primary Indicator "Copyright and International Influence"

indicators such as the number of government-sponsored copyright awareness campaigns and the number of copyright education sessions held in primary and secondary schools; 2) Tourism, featuring four tertiary indicators: total tourism revenue, the proportion of total tourism revenue to the city's GDP, the number of domestic tourists, and the number of international tourists.

The primary indicator "Copyright and International Influence" consists of two secondary indicators: 1) Copyright International Exchange, which includes tertiary indicators such as the number of copyright international exchange events held annually, the number of participants in copyright international exchange activities per 100,000 people, the number of foreign tourists, and the number of local foreign artists; 2) International Copyright Trade, which encompasses tertiary indicators including the total volume of international copyright trade and the number of international copyright trade collaborations, based on contracts and agreements.

Section III

The Tangible Effects of Copyright in Promoting Jingdezhen's High-Quality Development

By synthesizing and analyzing relevant data from various local agencies—including the Jingdezhen Municipal Bureau of Culture, Broadcasting, Television, Press and Publication, the Jingdezhen Municipal Bureau of Statistics, the Jingdezhen Intellectual Property Court, the People's Court of the Zhushan District, and the Jingdezhen Intellectual Property Protection Center—we can illustrate the role of copyright in promoting Jingdezhen's high-quality development from five key aspects: its impact on institutional frameworks, judicial and administrative protection, market economy, public services, and socio-cultural environment.

(1) Contributing to the Development of Jingdezhen's Institutional Framework

Given Jingdezhen's relatively small urban size and population, along with the presence of numerous top-level regulations, the legislative work of the Jingdezhen People's Congress is not particularly active. Since 2016, only ten local regulations have been released on the official website of the Jingdezhen Municipal People's Government, most of which are related to public health management or the protection of drinking water sources, directly linked to residents' well-being. Among these ten regulations, two specifically pertain to copyright: *the Regulations on the Protection and Management of the Site of the Imperial Kiln Factory in*

353

Jingdezhen, effective from May 1, 2018, and *the Regulations on the Inheritance and Innovation of Ceramic Culture in Jingdezhen*, effective from January 1, 2022. Although the sample size is small, the fact that copyright-related regulations account for one-fifth of all new local regulations since 2016 highlights that copyright legislation has become an integral part of Jingdezhen's local regulatory framework.

According to the *Notice of the Jingdezhen Municipal People's Government on the Results of the Review of Administrative Normative Documents* released in July 2023, the city has currently 102 effective normative documents, along with 23 amended documents and 17 scheduled for future amendment. This brings the total number of normative documents to 142, creating a relatively complete system of government normative documents. Apart from the *Notice on the Pilot Program for Tax Collection Management of Art Ceramic Practitioners in Jingdezhen* (originally issued in 2015 and amended in 2018), no other copyright-related normative documents exist. Nevertheless, in 2021, the Jingdezhen Municipal Government and relevant departments released three pilot normative documents directly related to copyright,[①] bridging this gap and marking an important shift from having none to establishing an initial framework.

(2) Enhancing Jingdezhen's Rights Protection Mechanism

Copyright's impact on Jingdezhen's rights protection mechanism is evident in three key areas: judicial copyright protection, administrative copyright protection, and coordinated copyright protection.

Regarding judicial copyright protection, an analysis of copyright case handling by the People's Court of Zhushan District, Jingdezhen, from 2016 onward reveals two notable trends.[②] First, the number of copyright cases shows a marked increase. In 2016, the court received no copyright cases, but this number grew progressively

---

① These include the *Guidelines for Copyright Innovation and Creation in Jingdezhen (For Trial Implementation)*, *Measures to Support the Copyright Industry in Jingdezhen (For Trial Implementation)*, and *Selection Measures for Outstanding Copyright Works in Jingdezhen (For Trial Implementation)*, all released on July 11, 2021.

② Copyright cases at the first instance level in Jingdezhen are primarily concentrated in the People's Court of Zhushan District. Therefore, this study focuses on analyzing the copyright cases handled by this court.

over the next six years: 1 case in 2017, 2 in 2018, 6 in 2019, 25 in 2020, and a dramatic surge to 253 cases in 2022—more than three times the total of the prior six years combined. Second, mediation has become the primary method of case resolution. From 2016 to 2021, the court handled a total of 76 copyright cases, with only three handled through mediation, accounting for around 4% of all cases. However, in 2022, in response to the sharp rise in case volume, the court enhanced its dispute resolution mechanisms, settling 156 cases via mediation, representing over 60% of the total that year. These statistics highlight two key developments in Jingdezhen's judicial protection of copyright: First, rights holders are increasingly opting for judicial protection, indicating growing public trust in Jingdezhen's judicial mechanisms. Second, as copyright cases multiply, courts are favoring mediation, suggesting the growing effectiveness of diversified dispute resolution approaches, which balance both judicial efficiency and the rights of all parties involved.

In administrative copyright protection, the number of copyright administrative penalty cases has fluctuated from 2016 to the present, with annual totals as follows: 1, 4, 0, 1, 6, 4, 2, and 14 cases (as of September 2023). The proportion of copyright-related administrative penalty cases to the total number of comprehensive enforcement cases in the cultural sector has also increased, from an initial range of 5%-15% to approximately 35% in 2023. Likewise, the total amount of fines for copyright violations has correspondingly increased since 2016, with amounts reported as 1,000 yuan, 50,400 yuan, 0 yuan, 3,000 yuan, 11,050 yuan, 26,000 yuan, 20,000 yuan, and 147,020 yuan. Additionally, in 2021, Jingdezhen introduced an administrative mediation system for copyright, resulting in 3, 13, and 4 cases mediated over the past three years. These data reflect two key efforts by Jingdezhen in enhancing administrative copyright protection: First, comprehensive law enforcement in the cultural sector is gradually prioritizing copyright cases to better support the administrative protection needs of creators. Second, the copyright administrative mediation system should be implemented, and the frequency of copyright administrative mediations should be increased, reducing the costs associated with copyright enforcement.

Regarding coordinated copyright protection, the Jingdezhen Intellectual Property Protection Center was officially established in 2022. Currently, the center's primary focus remains on coordinated protection of patents and trademarks. Looking ahead, the center plans to incorporate copyright protection into its agenda, leveraging its accumulated experience in intellectual property collaboration to develop more effective mechanisms for copyright protection.

(3) Promoting Economic Restructuring in Jingdezhen

During the economic structural transformation, the impact of copyright on Jingdezhen's economy can be illustrated through statistical data related to the total industrial output value above designated size, operating income in the service industry above designated size, and retail sales of consumer goods.

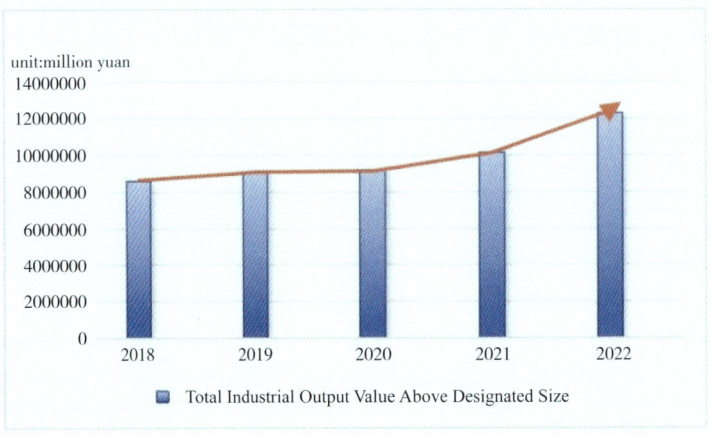

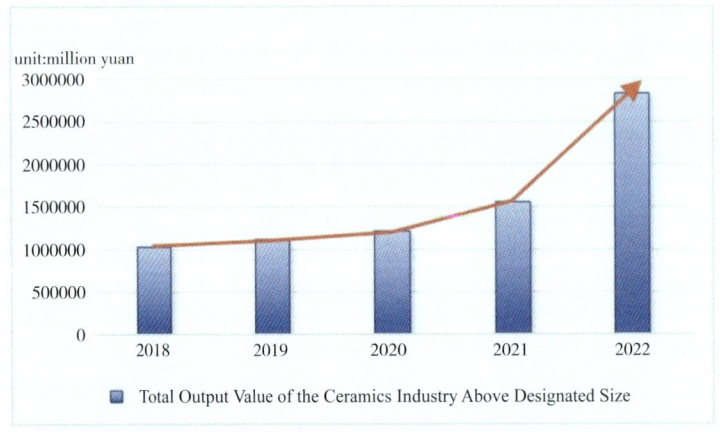

Comparison of Total Industrial Output Value Above Designated Size and Total Output Value of the Ceramics Industry Above Designated Size in Jingdezhen

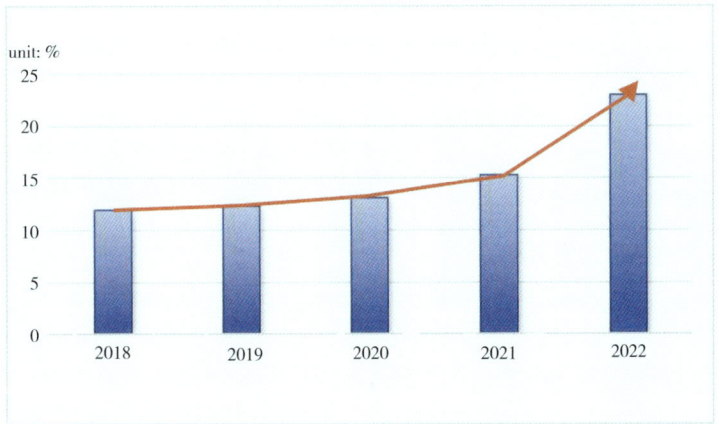

unit: %

Changes in the Proportion of Total Output Value of Ceramics Manufacturing Above
Designated Size to Total Industrial Output Value Above Designated Size in Jingdezhen

From 2018 to 2022, Jingdezhen's total industrial output value above designated size rose from 86.117 billion yuan to 122.995 billion yuan, reflecting a growth rate of 42.82%. In the same period, the total output value of ceramics manufacturing above designated size—most representative of copyright-related industries—surged from 10.306 billion yuan to 28.282 billion yuan, marking an impressive increase of 174.43%, or four times the growth rate of the overall industrial output value.

The contribution of copyright-related industries can also be visually manifested by the proportion of their total output value as a percentage of overall industrial output value. Between 2018 and 2022, the total output value of Jingdezhen's ceramics manufacturing above designated size rose from 11.97% to 22.99% of total industrial output. This indicates that the impact of copyright-related industries on Jingdezhen's overall industrial level effectively doubled during this five-year period. Furthermore, it showcases the significant role copyright has played in driving output value and leading transformation within the secondary industry in Jingdezhen.

The impact of copyright in the service industry, representing the tertiary sector, cannot be overlooked. From 2018 to 2022, Jingdezhen's revenue from the services above designated size grew rapidly, increasing from approximately 6.964 billion yuan to around 12.748 billion yuan—an increase of 83.07%—despite challenges posed by the pandemic and other factors. In comparison, from 2018

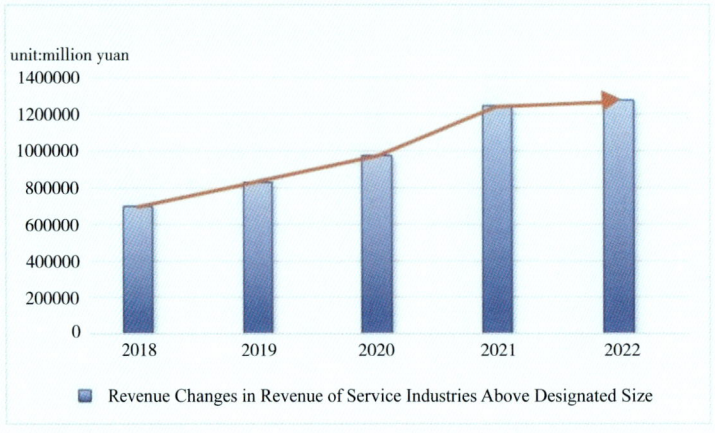

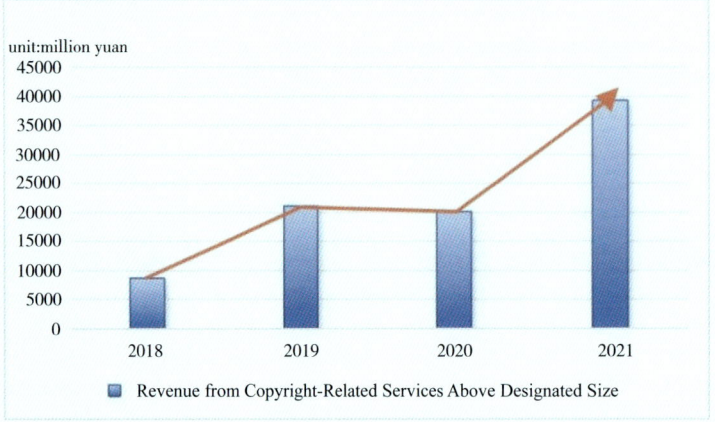

Comparison of Revenue Changes in Revenue of Service Industries Above Designated Size and Revenue from Copyright-Related Services Above Designated Size in Jingdezhen

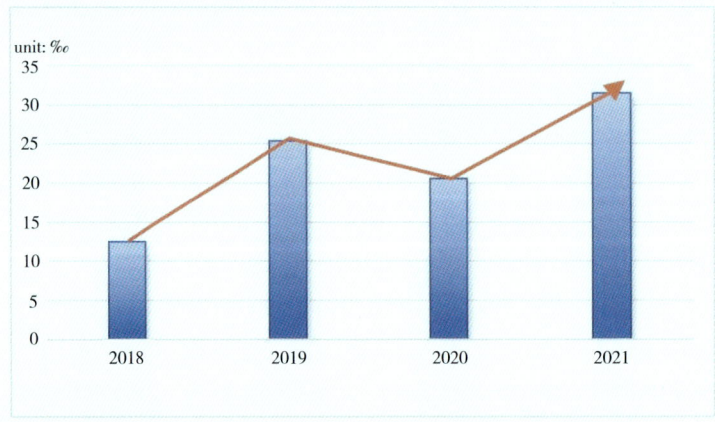

Changes in the Proportion of Revenue from Copyright-Related Services to Total Revenue of Service Industries Above Designated Size in Jingdezhen

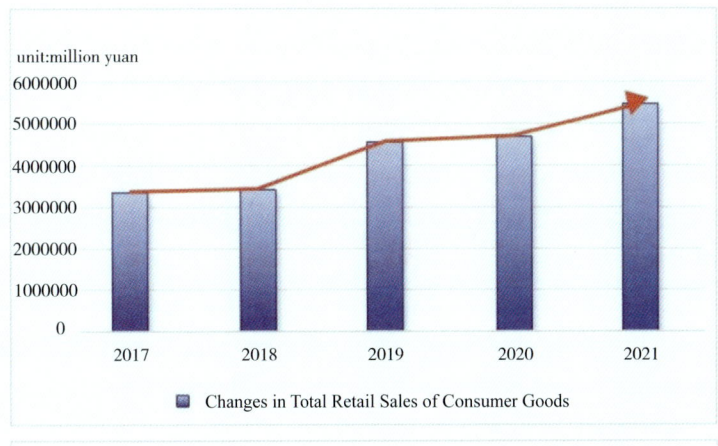

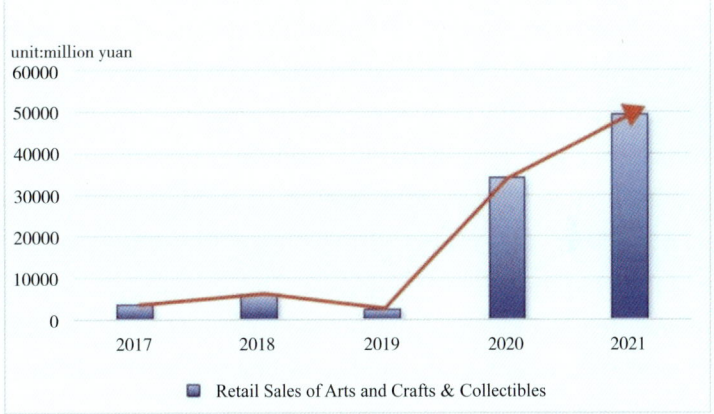

Comparison of Changes in Total Retail Sales of Consumer Goods and Retail Sales of Arts and Crafts & Collectibles in Jingdezhen

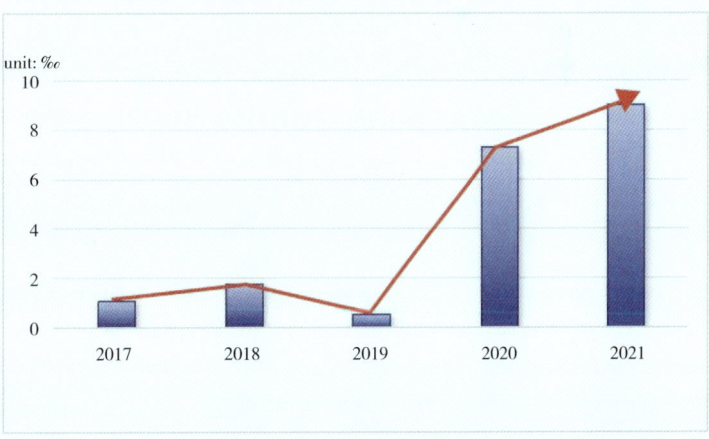

Changes in the Proportion of Retail Sales of Arts and Crafts & Collectibles to Total Retail Sales of Consumer Goods in Jingdezhen

to 2021 (with 2022 data still pending), revenue from copyright-related services[1] surged from 87.09 million yuan to 392.64 million yuan, marking an impressive increase of 350.84%. Although the sample size is relatively small, this trend still demonstrates robust growth in revenue for copyright-related services.

The proportion of revenue from copyright-related services to the overall revenue of the service industry serves as an important indicator of copyright's influence on this sector. Between 2018 and 2021, this proportion in Jingdezhen's copyright-related services above designated size increased from 12.5‰ to 31.5‰. Although there was a slight decline in 2020, the overall trend shows a steady upward trajectory.

Changes in public consumption of copyright-related products and services also reflect the impact of copyright on the overall economic structure. In Jingdezhen, total retail sales increased from 33.593 billion yuan in 2017 to 54.817 billion yuan in 2021, marking an impressive growth rate of 63.18% despite pandemic challenges. Notably, retail sales of arts and crafts and collectibles—representative of copyright-related consumer goods—surged from a modest 35.65 million yuan to 493.58 million yuan over the same timeframe, achieving a staggering increase of 1,284.52%. This growth was driven by a marked rise in market demand for copyright-related consumer goods, resulting in the proportion of retail sales of arts, crafts, and collectibles to total retail sales of consumer goods to skyrocket from 1.06‰ in 2017 to 9‰ in 2021.

Analyzing the impact of copyright on Jingdezhen's industry, services, and consumer goods market in recent years reveals three key facts: First, Jingdezhen's overall economy has shown a relatively stable growth trajectory;[2] second, copyright-related economic indicators have demonstrated explosive growth; and third, the share of copyright-related economics is becoming increasingly significant. Undoubtedly, copyright not only boosts Jingdezhen's economic growth but also subtly optimizes its economic structure, helping the city rise from the

---

[1] According to the annual *Jingdezhen Statistical Yearbook* published by the Jingdezhen Statistics Bureau, copyright-related services can be classified as the sum of five categories of service industries: software and information technology services; news and publishing; broadcasting, television, film and recording production; cultural arts; and entertainment.

[2] This fact is also supported by the changes in Jingdezhen's Gross Regional Product (GRP), which increased from 84,957,140,000 yuan in 2016 to 119,218,930,000 yuan in 2022, indicating a steady economic growth trajectory.

quagmire of resource depletion and becoming a vital driver in its transformation into an innovative city.

(4) Enhancing Jingdezhen's Public Services

The improvement of public services can be reflected through visualized aspects such as the construction of public facilities and service delivery, as well as less tangible areas like the replenishment of social insurance funds and the distribution of related subsidies. To illustrate government investment in enhancing public services with clear and direct data, we can analyze general public budget

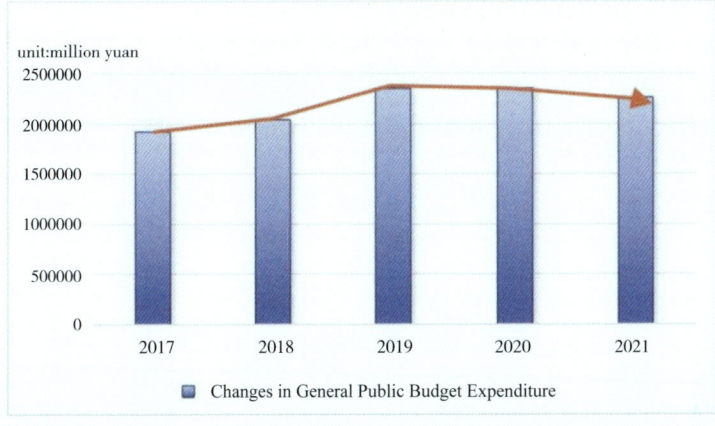

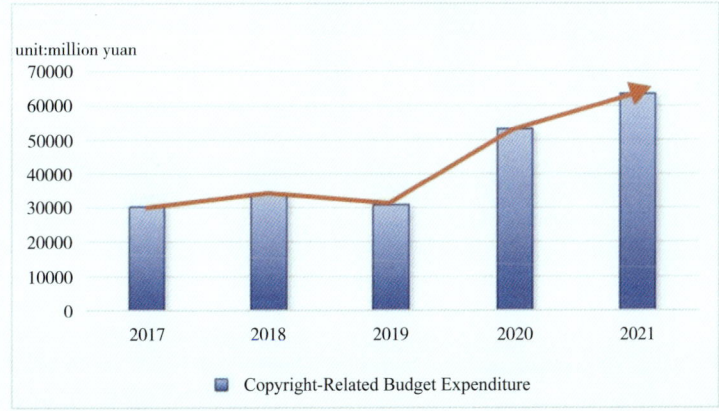

Comparison of Changes in General Public Budget Expenditure and Copyright-Related Budget Expenditure in Jingdezhen

expenditure. Typically, there is a positive correlation between public budget spending and the quality of social public services. A comparative analysis of Jingdezhen's general public budget expenditure from 2017 to 2021 reveals a slight increase from 19.212 billion yuan to 22.652 billion yuan. In 2019 and 2020, public budget expenditure exceeded 23 billion yuan due to the pandemic, but returned to a more typical level in 2021. During this period, the growth rate for this expenditure was 17.90%, indicating steady progress that aligns with the national trend of increasing public budget spending.[1] In contrast, copyright-related public budget expenditure in Jingdezhen—covering cultural, sports, and media spending—rose significantly from 30.217 million yuan to 53.473 million yuan during the same period, marking an overall increase of 76.96%. This growth far surpasses the normal increase in the city's general public budget expenditure, with particularly noticeable growth between 2019 and 2020.

The proportion of copyright-related public budget expenditure increased from 15.73‰ in 2017 to 23.61‰ in 2021. Although this change might not seem dramatic, it's important to recognize that fluctuations in various general

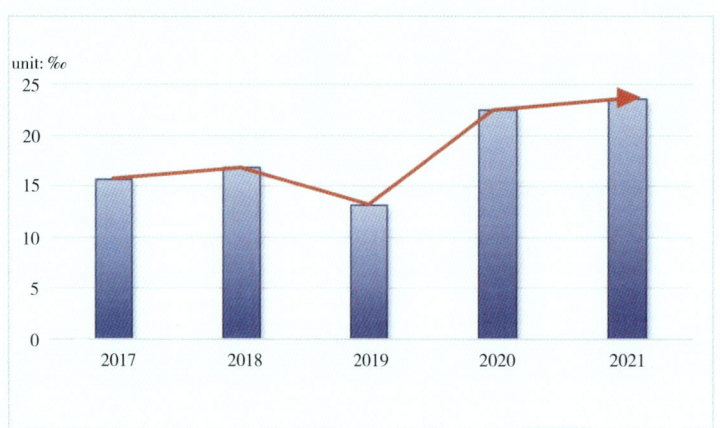

Changes in the Proportion of Copyright-Related Budget Expenditure to Total Public Budget Expenditure in Jingdezhen

---

[1] National general public budget expenditure increased from 20,333 billion yuan in 2017 to 24,632.2 billion yuan in 2021, representing a growth rate of 21.14% over five years. Considering that the items in the national public budget differ from those in urban public budget, it can be inferred that the increase in Jingdezhen's general public budget expenditure during this period is comparable to the national level.

public budget expenditures are typically minimal during periods of steady urban development. Jingdezhen's decision to consistently increase the share of copyright-related public budget spending—especially amid a slight overall decline in total expenditure—underscores the city's commitment to enhancing public service quality through greater investment in copyright-related initiatives.

(5) Enhancing Jingdezhen's Cultural Environment

Jingdezhen is renowned worldwide as the "Porcelain Capital", attracting countless domestic and international visitors. As a Top Tourist City of China and a National Garden City, Jingdezhen has long used its rich ceramic culture as its calling card, continuously enhancing its cultural environment. In recent years, the total number of tourists visiting Jingdezhen peaked in 2018 and 2019, reaching 49.543 million and 55.2305 million, respectively—more than 30 times the city's total population.

Meanwhile, tourism revenue hit 61.437 billion yuan in 2018 and 71.857 billion yuan in 2019, accounting for 71.71% and 77.97% of the city's GDP, respectively. Yet, due to the pandemic, visitor numbers dropped to 22.4745 million in 2020. Fortunately, in the following two years, this figure rebounded to a normal scale of 40 million to 50 million, with 55.3165 million in 2021 and 44.6669 million in 2022. Although post-pandemic tourism revenue fell to about half of 2019's figures, it still contributed over 40% to the region's GDP. Unlike other prominent tourist cities in the province that often rely on historical, natural, or revolutionary resources to shape their cultural environments, Jingdezhen consistently highlights its unique cultural landscape centered on ceramics. To create a harmonious blend of being a Millennium Porcelain Capital and a Creative City, Jingdezhen must not only preserve its ceramic heritage but also innovate within that tradition. The city's ceramic culture is vibrant; people's recognition of Jingdezhen stems not just from its long history in ceramics but also from its status as a thriving hub for ceramic artists and their works. From the architectural charm of the Imperial Kiln Museum to the diverse ceramic trinkets found at the Night Market on Taoxichuan Ceramic Art Avenue, every element that enriches Jingdezhen's cultural environment ultimately relies on copyright support.

Section IV

Future Outlook on Copyright's Role in Promoting Jingdezhen's High-Quality Development

Looking ahead to the future achievements of high-quality development in Jingdezhen, copyright will increasingly play a vital role in transforming industries, shaping a new cultural city, and establishing a center for ceramic culture. Firstly, copyright will continue to drive innovation within the ceramics industry and foster the integration of multiple sectors. Secondly, it will support urban planning and the cultivation of the city's spirit. Finally, copyright will energize the creation of a ceramic cultural ecosystem and facilitate external exchanges of ceramic culture.

(1) Driving Jingdezhen's Industrial Transformation

To continuously advance Jingdezhen's high-quality development, industrial transformation is essential. The *14th Five-Year Plan of Jingdezhen City for Economic and Social Development and the Long-Range Objectives Through 2035* (hereinafter referred to as the *14th Five-Year Plan of Jingdezhen,* or simply *Plan*) identifies the "development of a modern industrial system with Jingdezhen characteristics" as a key task for the city's future. Many components of the Plan are closely tied to industrial transformation, in which copyright will play a significant role.

In the future, Jingdezhen will continue to focus on the ceramics industry, aiming to establish it as a trillion-yuan industrial cluster. In addition to traditional sectors like daily-use ceramics, accelerating the development of high-tech

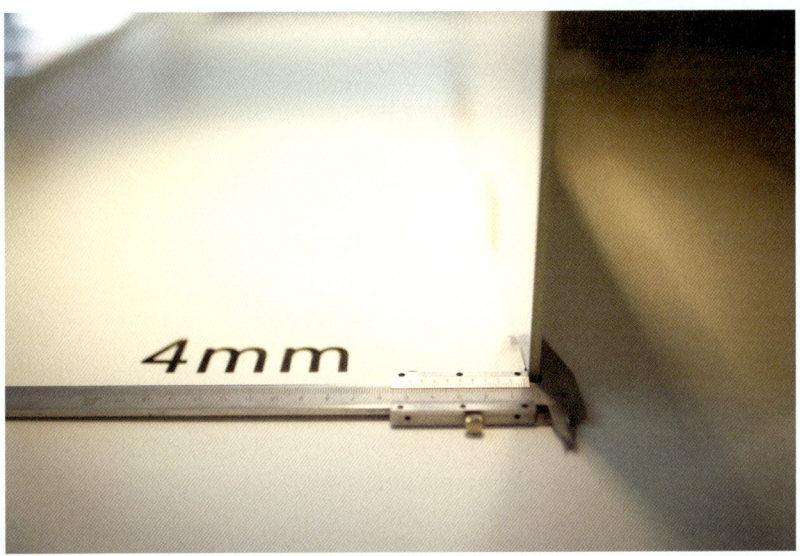

Advanced Ceramic Materials with a Thickness of Only 4 Millimeters [Photo courtesy of Chianvre Ceramic Art (JINGDEZHEN) Co., Ltd]

ceramics and creative ceramics is crucial for cementing the industrial chain. Copyright not only facilitates the continuous innovation of creative elements within daily-use ceramics, adding value to the industry, but also serves as a core component of both high-tech and creative ceramics, directly influencing their survival and growth.

Jingdezhen will continue to vigorously develop the digital economy, promoting a deep integration of digital and real economies. Whether merging big data, artificial intelligence, and blockchain with the ceramics and cultural tourism sectors, or accelerating R&D in cloud computing, the Internet of Things, e-commerce, and digital audio-visual industries, copyright plays a crucial role throughout this process. The "tools" utilized for industry development—such as computer software—and the final "products" created—including artwork and audiovisual works—are all closely tied to copyright which provides essential protection.

Furthermore, Jingdezhen needs to enhance and expand its services. In the new era, both productive and lifestyle service industries collectively require the creation of information platforms and the provision of cloud services. At their core, these rely on the development of computer software and various artistic and audiovisual works to deliver visual services to clients—all of which are protected by copyright. Thus, copyright will be essential for supporting the growth of the service industry in this new era.

(2) Driving Jingdezhen's Transformation into a New Cultural City

Looking ahead to 2035, Jingdezhen envisions growing into a new cultural city of national significance. To achieve this goal, the *14th Five-Year Plan of Jingdezhen* emphasizes the need to enhance urban functionality and quality, fully showcasing the unique charm of "beautiful scenery, ample virtue, and vibrant town life".

To showcase its beautiful scenery, Jingdezhen must prioritize meticulous urban design and effective management of its natural and cultural landscape. Building on a solid framework of overall urban planning, the city needs to undertake a series of design and construction initiatives to enhance its structural quality. Beyond strengthening infrastructure and public services in new districts, and advancing the protection of the old town and modern industrial heritage—efforts that largely rely on engineering—projects such as repurposing old factories, developing industrial heritage sites, constructing the Changjiang Scenic Belt, and creating a cohesive ecological landscape will depend greatly on artistic design. These endeavors will require numerous architectural and artistic works to enrich every corner of Jingdezhen, all of which hinge on robust copyright support and protection.

To embody Jingdezhen's ample virtue, it is crucial to continue promoting the construction of a civilized city, embedding virtuous values deeply within the community. This involves actively cultivating and practicing the core socialist values while thoroughly exploring the ideas, cultural spirit, and moral standards inherent in the city's rich ceramic history. The profundity of these ideas requires rich forms of expression. Efforts to nurture and convey these virtues—including the creation of themed neighborhoods, campuses, and squares centered on socialist core values, as well as organizing cultural activities and crafting slogans— will rely on works that reflect both socialist values and exceptional ceramic culture, all supported by robust copyright protection.

(3) Propelling Jingdezhen's New Platforms for Cultural Exchange

"Creating new platforms for cultural exchange" is a significant mandate entrusted by the state for Jingdezhen's development. With its rich historical heritage and unique artistic charm, Jingdezhen's ceramic culture holds a distinct advantage in fulfilling this national mission. Known as the "Millennium Porcelain Capital", Jingdezhen bears the responsibility of creating innovative avenues for cultural exchange with the world, further enhancing the international influence of Chinese ceramic culture.

To that end, one of the key goals outlined in the *14th Five-Year Plan of Jingdezhen* is to establish a culturally impactful platform for external exchanges. This process seeks not only to preserve and promote Jingdezhen's ceramic culture but also to encourage its innovative transformation and creative development. The goal is to forge a path for the transmission and innovation of outstanding

Foreign Ceramic Artists Exhibit at the Spring and Autumn Art Fair, Taoxichuan Ceramic Art Avenue (Photo courtesy of Taoxichuan Ceramic Art Avenue)

traditional culture that is globally relevant, aligns with Chinese values, reflects the new era, and highlights Jingdezhen's unique characteristics.

By improving the legal framework for the protection of ceramic artifacts and implementing the Jingdezhen Major Site Protection Plan, the foundation for protecting ceramic culture is being solidified. As part of these efforts, Jingdezhen plans to create an ecological protection zone for ceramic culture, improve training of representatives of intangible cultural heritage in traditional craftsmanship, and elevate the development level of local museums. Innovations in exhibition formats, the establishment of digital museums, and online museum activities are also essential to transforming Jingdezhen into a City of Museums. Additionally, a comprehensive media promotion plan for ceramic culture will leverage a multitude of outstanding cultural creations for broader dissemination. In this process, artisans will continually draw inspiration from traditional ceramic culture to produce new works, while museums will innovate cultural display platforms rooted in this tradition. Jingdezhen will also promote captivating artistic productions based on its ceramic heritage. Ultimately, the success of these initiatives lies in the creation, application, protection, management, and service of copyright.

Using ceramics as a medium, Jingdezhen's ceramic culture undoubtedly serves as the best calling card in its exchanges and collaborations with foreign cultural institutions. The city's ceramic art—whether showcasing traditional craftsmanship or innovative modern creations—embodies the dedication and wisdom of its creators. These works are not only artistic displays but also vital vehicles for the preservation and promotion of Chinese culture. Cultural exchange in Jingdezhen occurs through the dissemination of various ceramic-related works, with the influence of copyright being undeniable. For foreign friends, Jingdezhen is more than just a pilgrimage site for ceramic art; it is also a hub for in-depth study of ceramic techniques and a platform for significant international cultural exchange. Here, they can appreciate the profound depth of Chinese culture while engaging in artistic creation and cross-cultural dialogue. Copyright plays a crucial role in the creation, application, protection, and management of their works, profoundly impacting their artistic endeavors. Thus, an important task for Jingdezhen's high-quality development is to enhance the overall quality of its copyright system to meet the diverse demands arising from its efforts to establish new platforms for external cultural exchange.

The evolution of copyright systems has occurred through the interplay of various international conventions and domestic legal frameworks, which in turn influences China's engagement on the global stage. Amid shifting international political and economic dynamics, China is steadily enhancing its international reputation, reflected in its growing influence in global copyright discourse. Simultaneously, the historic Jingdezhen City in northeastern Jiangxi is undergoing urban transformation, with its ceramic culture shining even brighter under copyright protection. Undoubtedly, copyright will be pivotal in realizing Jingdezhen's vision for the future.

Section V

Conclusion

This chapter offers an in-depth analysis of the positive impact of copyright plays in on Jingdezhen's ceramics industry across multiple dimensions, exploring four major areas: theoretical foundation, evaluation system, practical outcomes, and future prospects. It lays a solid theoretical and practical groundwork for Jingdezhen's pursuit of high-quality development.

On the theoretical level, this analysis reveals the strategic significance of the copyright system in Jingdezhen's pursuit of high-quality growth. Copyright, as a powerful legal instrument, establishes a robust defense for creators' rights while also acting as a key driver of innovation and advancement in the cultural industry. By providing legal protection for intellectual achievements, the copyright system fully unleashes society's creative potential to the fullest, enabling Jingdezhen to thrive amid the currents of cultural creativity and high technology, thereby solidifying its status as a global ceramic capital.

The construction of an evaluation system presets a scientific framework for Jingdezhen's sustainable development. This chapter innovatively develops a city development assessment framework centered around the copyright system, integrating multiple dimensions such as the completeness of the copyright system, the flourishing state of the copyright economy, and the far-reaching impact of copyright service. This framework offers Jingdezhen with precise metrics to measure the copyright-driven effects. With this tool, Jingdezhen can effectively identify the strengths and weaknesses of its copyright efforts, adjust its development strategy accordingly, and take more solid steps in enhancing copyright protection and increasing the city's overall competitiveness.

The presentation of practical outcomes vividly illustrates the achievements of Jingdezhen's copyright system in action. The robust implementation of copyright protection has invigorated innovation within the ceramics industry, allowing Jingdezhen's products to stand out in the global market, while also fostering the overall prosperity of the cultural and creative industries. From traditional ceramic arts to emerging fields like cultural tourism and creative products, Jingdezhen has made remarkable strides. These impressive accomplishments provide clear evidence of the indispensable role that the copyright system has played in driving the city's economic transformation and upgrading.

Looking ahead, Jingdezhen will continue to explore and advance its journey in copyright protection and utilization. In the face of new challenges and opportunities, the city is dedicated to strengthening its copyright system while embracing innovation with an open mindset. It aims to deepen the integration of copyright with technology, culture, and the economy, continuously enhancing its international visibility and influence. With copyright as its driving force, Jingdezhen will fully commit to promoting high-quality development throughout the city, ensuring it maintains a leading position in the global ceramics and cultural and creative industries, paving the way for an even more brilliant future.

In summary, this chapter provides a comprehensive overview of the profound impact of the copyright system on Jingdezhen's multifaceted development, achieved through an in-depth analysis of its theoretical foundation, evaluation framework, practical results, and future prospects. The effective application of copyright has injected robust momentum into Jingdezhen's economic and cultural prosperity, enhancing its recognition on the global stage, while establishing a solid foundation for sustainable development in the future.

Conclusion: Experience and Insights

Through a series of plans, deployments, and measures in the process of high-quality urban development, Jingdezhen has built a comprehensive copyright system, structure, and mechanism. The continuously optimized and improved system for copyright creation, utilization, protection, management, and services has provided valuable reference experience for other cities in China and even around the world on how to promote high-quality urban development through copyright. Jingdezhen has thus become a "Model of the times," presenting a replicable and scalable approach that leverages copyright for high-quality development in urban, cultural, and industrial spheres.

Experience 1: Innovating and Advancing—Developing a Comprehensive Copyright System

With the advantages of traditional production factors waning, institutional support has become a key competitive edge. Jingdezhen has centered its efforts on copyright as a core asset, developing a well-defined and effective policy framework that includes local regulations, government rules, and normative documents related to copyright protection, creation, incentives, public services, and industry. This framework has been continuously refined and modernized to align with contemporary needs and local distinctiveness, optimizing the copyright protection environment, stimulating innovation and creativity, and advancing the modernization of the copyright governance system and its capabilities.

Introducing a series of local regulations. In May 2018, Jingdezhen launched the *Regulations on the Protection and Management of the Imperial Kiln Factory Site*, its first local law aimed at preserving historical and cultural heritage, marking a big step toward legal management. In January 2022, the *Regulations on the Inheritance and Innovation of Ceramic Culture* came into effect, providing essential legal backing for the development of the pilot zone. This regulation has been instrumental in preserving and leveraging Jingdezhen's rich ceramic culture, while also giving full play to the positive role of culture in industrial transformation and upgrading and regional high-quality growth. Moreover, the *Measures for the Intellectual Property Rights Protection in Jingdezhen Ceramics*, first formulated in 2008, is set for revision to better address the current needs of ceramic IP protection in this new era.

Establishing a series of copyright rules and regulations. The *Jingdezhen Copyright Development Strategy (2020-2025)* and the *Three-Year Action Plan* for

Jingdezhen Copyright Protection and Operation (2021-2023) were released to enhance top-level design, strengthen IP protection, invigorate various copyright creators, and refine the city's public copyright service management system, creating a vibrant copyright ecosystem that drives the robust growth of the copyright industry. Additional regulations include the *Measures for Recognizing Jingdezhen Copyright Demonstration Units and Parks*, *Guidelines for Copyright Innovation and Creation in Jingdezhen*, *Reward System for Outstanding Copyright Works in Jingdezhen*, *Measures for Supporting Jingdezhen's Copyright Industry*, and the *Trial Measures for Tax Collection Management of Artistic Ceramics Practitioners in Jingdezhen*. These initiatives are designed to innovate IP management and services, enhance the quality of IP creation, maximize the benefits of IP utilization, and support all-round innovation. These distinctive incentive measures also aim to align industry and financial policies with copyright-related industries to foster both copyright creation and utilization. To advance copyright protection, Jingdezhen has also introduced the *Measures for the Protection of Intellectual Property Rights in Jingdezhen Ceramics* and the *Management Measures for Intellectual Property Investigators in Jingdezhen*. These regulations aim to promote a favorable policy environment for copyright protection, safeguard the city's renowned ceramic brand, establish distinctive judicial protections for ceramic copyright, and address practical challenges in combating copyright infringement, effectively supporting rights holders in their protection efforts.

Issuing a series of normative documents. The *Key Points for the Construction of the Ceramic Culture Inheritance and Innovation Pilot Zone*, introduced by the leadership group office for this endeavor, aims to promote the inheritance and innovation of ceramic culture. It highlights the important role of copyright in supporting the sustainable and healthy development of the ceramics industry and in guiding economic growth and urban modernization. Furthermore, the Jingdezhen Municipal People's Government and the CPC Jingdezhen Municipal Committee have formulated the *Four-Year Action Plan for the Ceramic Culture Inheritance and Innovation Pilot Zone (2022-2025)*. This plan focuses on preserving and revitalizing culture, fostering innovation to strengthen the industry, promoting integrated development to boost tourism, and cultivating talent to attract skilled professionals. In 2021, the Jingdezhen Municipal Bureau of Culture,

Broadcasting, Television, Press and Publication released the *Guide for Copyright Protection*, providing detailed and clear guidance on copyright protection actions and rights enforcement for ceramic enterprises, artists, studios, and other market participants.

Experience 2: Revitalizing Tradition Through Innovation—Copyright as a Catalyst for Industrial Transformation and Upgrading

Jingdezhen is committed to establishing itself as a "National Copyright Demonstration City" by leveraging the guiding role of copyright demonstration enterprises, parks, and bases. Through measures like copyright research and development, fostering new business models, and providing financial support, the city is driving high-quality development in the copyright industry.

First, enhancing the quality of the ceramic culture industry. As part of effort to build a copyright demonstration city, over 70 ceramic enterprises across Jingdezhen have established R&D centers, greatly strengthening their research and development capabilities and boosting the core competitiveness of the ceramic culture industry.

Second, driving innovation in the ceramic culture industry. The Jingdezhen Municipal Bureau of Commerce has established strategic partnerships with platforms like Douyin, JD.com, Kuaishou, Taobao, and Tmall, securing exclusive rights to operate ceramic live-streaming sales. New business models combing "short videos + e-commerce + live streaming" has developed rapidly, showing notable growth. Additionally, Jingdezhen has organized various copyright trading events to promote the transformation and application of copyright assets, laying a solid foundation for the flourishing of the copyright industry. The 2023 Changnan Bowl Fair, hosted by the Jingdezhen Urban Investment Group and organized by the Jingdezhen National Ceramic Copyright Trading Center, offered visitors a vibrant night-life experience while promoting copyright awareness and showcasing copyright achievements through an integrated "art + music + market" approach. As a leading force in the ceramics industry and copyright economy, the Jingdezhen National Ceramic Copyright Trading Center is committed to fostering a favorable environment for copyright innovation and protection, actively exploring new models and pathways for the creative transformation and innovative development of the ceramics industry

Third, optimizing operations within the ceramic cultural industry. In 2023, the

People's Bank of China Jingdezhen City Branch, using copyright as the basis for audit and loan review, in collaboration with copyright authorities, launched the innovative "IP Pledge Loan" product, providing 53.02 million yuan in credit support to 36 growth-stage "Jing Piao" (Jingdezhen migrants) with established operations. Plus, based on ceramic technical qualifications, the bank introduced the "Porcelain Capital Ceramic Art Loan," granting an additional 56.75 million yuan in credit to 73 seasoned "Jing Piao" who hold professional titles or honors in ceramic arts, or positions in university art programs. Since 2020, Jingdezhen Rural Commercial Bank has developed a comprehensive suite of over 30 ceramic financial products, including the "Bai Fu Ceramic Copyright Loan," "Bai Fu Ceramic Artist & Jingpiao Loan," and "Bai Fu Microcredit Loan," catering to the diverse financing needs of clients across customer tiers. The bank has established fast-track channels for risk assessment, known as "5+2" and "white + black,"[1] to streamline loan approvals for advanced ceramic enterprises. Furthermore, the bank has advanced copyright pledge financing through the Jingdezhen National Ceramic Copyright Trading Center, offering tailored "Ceramic Copyright Loans" for ceramic businesses and professionals. This initiative aims to build a technology-enabled, convenient, and efficient copyright financial service ecosystem, with both online and offline channels.

Experience 3: Legal Channels: Establishing an Efficient Copyright Protection Mechanism

Jingdezhen has made ceramic cultural copyright protection a focal point, continually innovating its protection methods and establishing a comprehensive protection system that integrates administrative oversight, judicial adjudication, and social services. Specifically, Jingdezhen has launched an Intellectual Property Court, an Intellectual Property Protection Center, Jingdezhen (Ceramic) IPR Rapid Aid Center, and various copyright service stations. Through the rapid coordination of cultural law enforcement, public security, and other departments, the city has established a copyright protection system covering verification and registration, complaint handling, enforcement, and infringement resolution. By enhancing collaborative protection efforts among multiple stakeholders, Jingdezhen has further reinforced ceramic copyright protection and enhanced the effectiveness of

---

① 24 × 7, twenty–four by seven.

Chapter VI
Conclusion: Experience and Insights

rights enforcement.

First, administrative copyright protection has advanced steadily, with effective implementation of administrative mediation and judicial confirmation mechanisms, as well as cross-regional enforcement cooperation. Since Jingdezhen began its journey to become a national copyright demonstration city, Jingdezhen's Cultural Market Comprehensive Law Enforcement Brigade has prioritized tackling cases of copyright infringement and piracy to meet ceramic creators' needs for administrative protection. Ongoing initiatives such as the Sword Network Campaign against online infringement and piracy, the copyright protection efforts for the 2022 Beijing Winter Olympics, and youth copyright protection projects have all delivered tangible results.

Between 2021 and 2022, Jingdezhen conducted 698 inspections across various locations as part of special enforcement operations, mobilizing over 1,400 law enforcement personnel. The cultural market enforcement brigade successfully mediated 15 copyright disputes through administrative means, issued penalties in five cases, and transferred three cases for further action. Since 2016, Jingdezhen's Cultural Market Comprehensive Law Enforcement Brigade has continuously intensified efforts to combat copyright infringement, reinforcing copyright protection within the broader cultural law enforcement framework. Effective measures have also been implemented to enhance the effectiveness and targeting of administrative copyright enforcement. In 2022, Jingdezhen introduced a system for judicial confirmation of administrative mediation in copyright disputes. This "administrative mediation + judicial confirmation" model allows courts to formally validate the mediation agreements reached between parties, facilitating the resolution of intellectual property (copyright) disputes. This approach effectively links administrative and judicial efforts, significantly improving the multi-tiered mediation mechanism for intellectual property disputes and enhancing the efficiency of copyright mediation. Additionally, given the cross-regional nature of online piracy and infringement cases, Jingdezhen has established cooperative enforcement partnerships with neighboring regions, jointly cracking down on piracy and infringement, thereby fostering a robust copyright ecosystem.

Second, judicial efforts in copyright protection have been continuously strengthened, with a focus on resolving ceramic copyright disputes. From 2021 to 2023, the Jingdezhen Intellectual Property Court and the Zhushan District

People's Court, both with jurisdiction over intellectual property cases, handled 237, 276, and 392 copyright dispute cases, respectively. This robust judicial protection benefits various ceramic sectors, including those under the "Jingdezhen Made" geographical indication, advanced industrial ceramics, cultural and artistic ceramics, and high-end daily-use porcelain. This effort has contributed to the development of a distinctive judicial protection mechanism tailored to the ceramic IPR protection needs in Jingdezhen.

The Jingdezhen Intellectual Property Court, rooted in the city's unique context, has prioritized the protection of ceramic intellectual property, drawing deeply from ceramic culture. It has actively promoted the specialized, standardized, and streamlined handling of ceramic-related cases, ensuring protection that is strict, comprehensive, swift, and consistent.

Third, Jingdezhen has fostered a collaborative approach to copyright protection across multiple stakeholders, cultivating a positive social atmosphere. The city embraces the philosophy that "Protection cultural heritage is not about locking it away or hiding it in a vault. The best protection is to integrate culture into people's daily lives and enrich their spiritual world."[1] The Jingdezhen Copyright Association, taking a standardized group approach, has established new standards for the copyright service system. In partnership with government and businesses, the established Taoxichuan copyright service station advances copyright registration and management, supporting enterprise incubation and operations, thus creating new possibilities for the copyright service landscape. Institutions like the Jingdezhen Imperial Kiln Ceramic Art Museum are enhancing this system through youth educational programs. Additionally, local female ceramic entrepreneurs have brought unique insights to copyright advocacy, injecting new vitality into the system. In Jingdezhen, from large entities like associations and public welfare organizations to small businesses and individual market players, all are contributing to integrating copyright protection into their respective domains. Notably, the Jingdezhen Intellectual Property Protection Center, officially established in 2022, currently focuses on collaborative protection

---

[1] "Transforming Cultural Resources into Development Advantages (Live Commentator · Promoting High-Quality Development of the Yangtze River Economic Belt IV)," *People's Daily Online*. Accessed on December 11, 2023.

for patents and trademarks. Looking forward, the center plans to incorporate copyright into its collaborative protection efforts, applying its accumulated experience to explore more effective mechanisms for cooperative copyright protection.

Experience 4: Cultivating Cultural Brilliance: Enhancing the Social Environment Through Copyright Empowerment

Jingdezhen is continually enhancing its healthy copyright ecosystem, centered on its vibrant ceramic heritage that defines the city's unique cultural identity. In crafting a harmonious fusion of its "thousand-year porcelain capital" legacy with its aspirations as a "creative city," Jingdezhen not only preserves ceramic traditions but also drives their innovation. Jingdezhen's identity is a living one, with its renown stemming not just from a long ceramic history but also from its dynamic role as an enduring home for ceramic artists and creations. This progress is grounded in establishing copyright ecosystem embraced by the public, and raising awareness of copyright across society. For years, Jingdezhen has worked toward cultivating a intellectual property culture that respects knowledge, values innovation, upholds integrity and fairness, and supports lawful, fair competition. This approach has created a positive atmosphere for innovation and a thriving ecosystem for creative endeavors, igniting a creative enthusiasm city-wide. As a result, Jingdezhen continually attracts talented ceramic entrepreneurs, artists, and "Jing Piao," whose presence has fueled its dynamic and creative growth.

Jingdezhen has established an innovative and multifaceted framework for promoting copyright, featuring fresh content and diverse, integrated communication channels. By adopting varied mass media approaches, the city facilitates the swift and precise spread of IP culture, allowing the public to subtly absorb and embrace it.[1] By fully leveraging public outreach resources, Jingdezhen has made copyright promotion both innovative and targeted, with campaigns tailored for different groups. This strategy has made copyright knowledge more widely accessible, fostering a culture where all are encouraged to engage with and care about copyright matters. First, Jingdezhen promotes copyright awareness through a variety of channels, cultivating a supportive cultural

---

[1]   Cai Ying, "Creating a Cultural and Civilized Environment for High-Quality Development," *China Intellectual Property News*, December 15, 2021.

environment. During the 2022 Jingdezhen Copyright Awareness Week, the city hosted a series of promotional activities. The organizers not only arranged the 2022 Copyright Works Exhibition and Copyright Market for citizens and guests to visit, but also held the "Vibrancy, Passion, Innovation, Development" Copyright Exchange Forum and an NFT Digital Promotion Demonstration event. At the same time, the Jingdezhen Cultural Market Comprehensive Law Enforcement Team created a copyright knowledge pamphlet and display panels, compiling relevant copyright information into a booklet for distribution to citizens. They also set up a consultation service desk on-site to provide answers and clarifications for the public.[①] On-site consultation desks were set up to address citizens' inquires, while outreach efforts extended to parks, enterprises, and campuses to deepen public understanding of copyright. Second, Jingdezhen capitalizes on platforms such as the "China International Copyright Expo," the "China Jingdezhen International Ceramic Expo," and various copyright-themed activities—like WeChat articles, writing contests, and public speaking events—to expand its copyright promotion. Through media channels such as radio, television, newspapers, magazines, and online platforms, copyright advocacy is integrated into broader public initiatives, including campaigns for a "National Health City" and a "National Civilized City"— all highlighting the role of copyright in supporting industrial development. Furthermore, Jingdezhen has also promoted copyright through seminars, public interest documentaries on copyright achievements, and by recruiting university students in IP-related majors as volunteers or ambassadors. These efforts broaden the reach of copyright promotion, fostering a broader societal understanding of IP's importance.

Jingdezhen is creating a more open, proactive, and vibrant environment for copyright talent. First, the city has launched comprehensive, inclusive talent training programs, offering sessions for copyright management personnel, IP seminars for businesses, and specialized training for enforcement officers. Copyright education has been woven into the city's civil servant and local official training programs, empowering leaders to champion copyright respect and protection. Special emphasis has been also placed on youth education,

---

① Creating the East Asia Culture Capital—Jingdezhen Cultural Market Comprehensive Law Enforcement Team Participates in the 2022 Jingdezhen Copyright Awareness Week Event.

with lectures, quizzes, and other activities designed to foster early awareness of copyright issues. Second, Jingdezhen has implemented diverse measures to attract talent specializing in copyright creation, utilization, protection, services, and management. By listing copyright professionals as highly needed specialists, the city has strengthened its efforts to recruit top talent. Jingdezhen encourages leading copyright-focused enterprises to bring in talent from within and outside the province through flexible arrangements such as position transfers, project-based hiring, guest and part-time roles, regular consulting, and collaborative projects. Key enterprises play a central role in this talent-pooling. Favorable policies, including support for housing, healthcare, and education have been introduced, to streamline the pathways for high-level professionals and build a robust hub for copyright talent. Third, Jingdezhen has established a multi-level incentive mechanism to motivate and reward talent. Key measures include promoting role models in dedicated columns, holding regular talent selection and evaluation events, and providing increased rewards, all of which help foster an environment that encourages, supports, and celebrates the contributions of professionals, thus driving a culture of excellence.

Jingdezhen, in the pursuit of excellence and the drive for high-quality urban development, has implemented a series of key strategies focused on meticulously designing and refining its copyright framework to foster innovation and prosperity within the ceramic culture industry. By thoroughly enforcing distinctive local regulations and establishing an efficient, collaborative copyright protection system across various sectors, Jingdezhen has not only built a solid copyright protection barrier for its ceramics industry but also nurtured a vibrant, creativity-driven copyright ecosystem.

Fueled by the dual engines of protection and innovation, Jingdezhen's ceramics industry has been revitalized, radiating unprecedented brilliance. Each piece of ceramic art embodies both profound cultural heritage and unique creative spirit. This successful model drives the city's sustained prosperity while also standing as an exemplary reference for cities nationwide and around the globe. Like a time-polished ceramic artwork, this invaluable experience grows even more radiant, lighting Jingdezhen's development path and setting a visionary course for the future of cultural industries—shining as a beacon that leads the trends of our era.

Appendix I

Directory of Ceramic Companies for Research

Jingdezhen Ceramic Culture Tourism Group

Jingdezhen Towyi Cultural Development Co., Ltd.

Jingdezhen Renew Culture & Technology Company

Jingdezhen Red Leaf Ceramics Co., Ltd.

Jingdezhen Fuyu Blue-and-white Linglong Ceramics Co. Ltd.

China Yong Feng Yuan (Auratic) Co., Ltd., Jingdezhen Branch

Jingdezhen Yubo Ceramics Co., Ltd.

Jingdezhen Chinastory Ceramic Culture Develop Co., Ltd.

Jingdezhen Huangyao Ceramics Co., Ltd.

Jingdezhen Jiajia CERAMIC Co., Ltd.

Qinghe Ceramics (Jingdezhen) Co., Ltd.

Jingdezhen Huadeleku Ceramics Co., Ltd.

Jingdezhen Yuqiu Ceramics Co., Ltd.

Jingdezhen Evergreen Homegarden Arts & Crafts Co., Ltd.

etc.

Appendix II

Selected Excerpts from the Research Record

I. Research Record of Jingdezhen Renew Culture & Technology Company

Interview Date: August 2023

Interview Location: Jingdezhen Renew Culture & Technology Company

Interviewee: Duan Jianping, Head of Jingdezhen Renew Culture & Technology Company

(1) Q: You have more than ten years of experience in the media industry and gained a solid reputation in the field. What motivated you to change your career path? What inspired you to start a ceramic company?

A: Jingdezhen has a ceramic legacy that spans over two thousand years— It's truly a city of ceramics, where everyone shares a deep, almost inseparable bond with the craft. Previously, I served as the editor-in-chief of the Cidu Evening News in Jingdezhen. My role often brought me into close contact with artists, designers, and ceramic artisans. In Jingdezhen's media industry, the primary mission was to tell the story of ceramics. So, when I decided to venture out on my own, it felt only natural to focus on ceramics. Ceramics are woven into the very DNA of Jingdezhen, and they've left an indelible impression on me as well.

(2) Q: The ceramic industry in Jingdezhen is highly competitive. How do you stand out and build a thriving business among so many ceramic companies?

A: With over 10,000 businesses and workshop-style studios in Jingdezhen, the path we choose becomes crucial amid such fierce competition. In 2015, I launched Jingdezhen Jingdexianyunju CERAMIC Culture Company Ltd. From 2015 to 2019, Xianyunju focused on handcrafted ceramics—mid- to high-end, finely crafted pieces. Our brand philosophy was "Original Design, Artistic Life," aiming to bring art into everyday life, and integrate design into people's routines. We wanted to make Jingdezhen ceramics more accessible, ensuring more people could enjoy refined ceramics. Our teapots, for instance, have a scholarly, elegant vibe, averaging over 4,000 yuan each. To be honest, during that period, our approach at Xianyunju overlapped with that of other competitors. Lacking a strong design team, we struggled to create products with a unique identity. So in 2019, we decided to embark on a new direction and launched a new subsidiary—Jingdezhen Renew Culture & Technology Company.

The primary mission of Renew Company is customization, integrating key elements of Jingdezhen—artists, designers, and ceramic craftsmen—into our work. Artists contribute a refined aesthetic vision and deep understanding of art, defining Renew's brand aesthetic standards. Designers help us realize customization. We currently have 16 freelance designers (one-third of our team), along with contracted designers, including an upcoming partnership with a Royal Designer from the UK. These designers are deeply versed in Jingdezhen's ceramic-making techniques. Our ceramic craftsmen, rooted in the city's heritage of excellence, push the limits of traditional skills, aiming for mastery and honoring intangible cultural heritage. With a focus on innovation and creative design, we provide creative, service-oriented products tailored to our clients' needs. Our goals are to build strong design capabilities, make R&D highly efficient, and create a robust and streamlined supply chain. As a cultural startup, our core competitive edge lies in our flexible supply chain—anchored in Jingdezhen, extending across region and reaching nationwide. Every product category has a specialized, highly efficient supply chain model, fostering a healthy and productive ecosystem. Our collaborations with other Jingdezhen companies have secure them numerous orders and opportunities. For example, we helped a ceramic trade company formerly dedicated to exports transition to a balanced model with both export and domestic scales. Our customized approach provided this company targeted insights, positioning them for successful entry into the domestic market. All in all, Renew's corporate philosophy centers on creative design, establishing ourselves as a truly creative, service-driven (service manufacturing) enterprise.

(3) Q: What sparked the inspiration for the concept of City Gift? Given its wide

recognition, have there been any infringement or plagiarism cases? How has your company handled this? Or have you encountered any infringement issues, and how do you protect your rights? Do you have a specific department responsible for this?

A: The City Gift concept originated from a global call for submissions we launched in 2021, which became a highlight of that year's China Jingdezhen International Ceramic Expo. Through City Gift, we intend to deepen global understanding of Jingdezhen, and its success reflects our unique approach to connecting creativity and culture with the city's identity. Actually, around six months before this initiative, we had already started developing a feature product called "Fu Ruyi," a piece symbolizing good fortune. The intersection of "Fu Ruyi" with City Gift presented a great opportunity for our business. "Fu Ruyi" represents the fusion of traditional Chinese culture with innovation in ceramics, allowing Chinese museum collections and artifacts to be re-imagined and revitalized. This concept captures the spirit of "innovation while preserving tradition" and embraces modern design trends, breathing new life into cultural relics.

As of today, we haven't handled a single intellectual property lawsuit. We don't have the energy or resources to engage in long, drawn-out legal battles. Instead, our focus has been on continuous innovation, because we believe innovation is the core edge of our business. We only resort to legal action when infringement threatens our survival or growth. Currently, we have a dedicated legal team and have signed with copyright lawyers from Guangdong province to manage our IP, especially in the copyright protection. To date, we hold over 1,000 copyrights and more than 100 patents.

(4) Q: Your company has been recognized as a National Copyright Demonstration Unit. Could you share your experiences in copyright management?

A: Our company was recognized as a provincial-level Copyright Demonstration Unit in 2021 and a National Copyright Demonstration Unit in 2022. First, we would like to thank the regulatory authorities for their keen recognition. Second, copyright management has become an integral part of our daily operations. Copyright protection closely aligns with our company's development philosophy and management approach. With the protection and benchmarking of copyrights, it has empowered our company a competitive edge. Today, our company's direction is highly compatible with the national strategies and policies, creating a perfect synergy.

(5) Q: Your company primarily focuses on creative research and development. Have you encountered any bottlenecks during your growth? How did you navigate through these challenging periods?

A: The uncertainty in economic development and the downward dynamic in the economy have posed severe challenges for the real economy, so it's inevitable for us to encounter some resistance. My primary concern is maintaining the supply chain ecosystem with our partners, which I expect to achieve a stable development, thus ensuring mutual benefit and deeper collaboration. This is also the path to support our goal of achieving competitive differentiation and truly scalable customization. At Renew, our philosophy is to preserve ancient artistry while creating contemporary brilliance. We provide customized ceramic cultural products that use Chinese cultural symbols to serve globally recognized brands. We have already forged partnerships with renowned brands such as La Mer, Estée Lauder, Baidu, Alibaba, Geely, and Zeekr.

II. Research Record of the Taoxichuan Ceramic Art Avenue

1. University Student Entrepreneur Group

Research Date: November 2022

Research Location: Taoxichuan Ceramic Art Avenue

Target Group: University Student Entrepreneur Group

(1) Q: Are all the works you produce your own original designs?

A: Yes, everything is designed in-house, including the inscriptions on the ceramics.

(2) Q: Are you familiar with copyright? How did you learn about it?

A: Yes, we do. We gained an understanding of copyright when we exhibited some of our works at the recent Arab Knowledge Exhibition.

(3) Q: Have your current works been registered copyright, and if not, do you plan to consider it in the future?

A: We haven't registered copyright yet, as this is our first time setting up a stall at Taoxichuan Ceramic Art Avenue. In the future, we will certainly consider it, as it provides a form of protection for our work.

(4) Q: Have you experienced any copyright infringement incidents around you, and how do you protect your rights?

A: Yes, there have been some. Some would make minor changes to our designs and quickly mass-produce and sell the items. We now mainly use social media platforms like rednote to raise awareness and voice our concerns. We generally avoid litigation, because the process is too long, and not cost-effective.

(5) Q: Has using media outlets helped resolve these issues?

A: Not entirely. It hasn't been fully resolved, but it does help raise public awareness and conveys the idea that "those who are innocent will clear their name".

(6) Q: What's your impression of Jingdezhen? (The respondent is not a local)

A: Jingdezhen is a city full of young people and with great potential for development. Ceramics here are really appealing to the young generation. The wide variety of ceramic forms offers creators ample space to explore and experiment. There's sufficient creative freedom, allowing creators to go beyond traditional, ancient styles. Even with the same type of piece, like a simple covered bowl, there are countless ways to add unique creative touches. This diversity of ideas has offered us much inspiration and new insights.

2. Operator of "Jingdezhen He Qi"

Research Date: November 2022

Research Location: Taoxichuan Ceramic Art Avenue

Target Group: Operator of "Jingdezhen He Qi"

(1) Q: Are all the works you produce your own original designs?

A: Some of them are replicas of ancient designs. For example, this set of ancient kiln pieces is made to a 1:1 scale. Despite lacking any decorations, they still exude a timeless beauty. While some more elaborate pieces might seem grand, they can't compare to the understated elegance of these monochrome-glazed items. There's a unique beauty in simplicity. The production cycle for ancient kiln pieces is very short, and only 67 pieces are documented. The rest are designs created by us.

(2) Q: Have you registered your current works for copyright?

A: We have applied for a design patent for this piece, but we haven't registered any copyright yet.

(3) Q: Have you encountered any counterfeits of your works in the market?

A: I don't really pay much attention to that issue or worry about it. Of course, imitation does happen, but it's unavoidable.

(4) Q: Will you consider registering your works for copyright in the future?

A: We are more inclined to apply for design patents rather than register copyrights.

3. Ms. Zhao, Studio Entrepreneur

Research Date: August 2023

Research Location: Taoxichuan Ceramic Art Avenue

Target Group: Ms. Zhao, Studio Entrepreneur at Taoxichuan Ceramic Art Avenue

(1) Q: Are you from Jingdezhen? Why did you choose to come to Jingdezhen?

A: No, I'm not born here. I came here for university, where I studied ceramics at Jingdezhen Ceramic University. I've always had a passion for ceramics, so after graduation, I decided to stay here and start my own business.

(2) Q: Why did you choose Jingdezhen over other ceramic cities, like Dehua?

A: I'm more familiar with Jingdezhen, and the cost of starting a business here is relatively lower. Plus, Jingdezhen has a strong reputation in ceramics, which gives it a big advantage.

(3) Q: Do you currently have any copyright registration certificates? Have you applied for all your works?

A: Some pieces do have certificates, but I haven't registered all of them because there are simply too many. I've only applied for copyrights for the ones I feel most passionate about.

(4) Q: Did you choose ceramics as your major because someone in your family is involved in the field?

A: No, it was my personal choice, driven by my passion for ceramics. Some of my friends have also stayed in Jingdezhen to start their own businesses, as we share a love for ceramics and expertise in the field, though there are also friends who have pursued careers in other industries.

(5) Q: Where do you draw your creative inspiration from?

A: Every piece has its own inspiration, which often comes from life. For example, when summer arrives, I may design works based on this year's trending colors or themes of the season.

(6) Q: Do you design and fire the ceramics yourself?

A: Yes, we do everything ourselves.

(7) Q: In Jingdezhen, if you have your own creative ideas, you can find specialists to help you bring your ceramics to life, right?

A: Yes, that's correct. In Jingdezhen, the ceramics industry is highly specialized. You can focus on just one aspect of the process and still complete the creation. For example, if you're skilled at drawing, you can work as a designer and hand over the design to someone else for production.

(8) Q: Did you take the initiative to register your copyrights, or was it something the ceramic service station required you to do? Are you familiar with the services the station provides?

A: The staff from the copyright service station come over to promote copyright registration and guide us in completing the process. I registered with their help. If you want to register, you can share your images in the group chat to contact them. Once they see your submission, they'll explain the steps, inform you of the required documents, and help you with the submission. From submitting the materials to receiving the certificate, the process typically takes less than a month.

(9) Q: Do the staff from the copyright service station regularly visit to inspect or manage activities? Do they monitor every booth?

A: Yes, they do. They mainly come to check in, see if you need help, assist with copyright registration, and promote awareness. It's more like a monitoring role. If they notice that you haven't registered yet, they'll come over and remind you. I moved from an outside booth to the Yikongjian Entrepreneurship and Innovation Incubation Base, where more materials are required than outdoor booths. Now, you need to prove that you're under 35 years old or a university student, show your studio, and provide a registration certificate to confirm that your work is original. They'll come to your studio for verification. If you just apply for an outdoor booth, you only need to submit product images and a photo of your graduation certificate, with the focus being mainly on the products.

(10) Q: When you were selling at the outdoor booth, did you spend all your time in your studio expect when you were at the booth? How long have you been running your studio? How long did it take you to transition from the outdoor booth to the Yikongjian Entrepreneurship and Innovation Incubation Base?

A: I've been working on this since 2020. The transition from the outdoor booth to the Base took just over a year, which is relatively fast. In the beginning, I spent most of my time at the studio making crafts and updating designs, aside from the time spent at the booth. Once I built a stable customer base, I proactively applied for the Dase. It's been an active application process on my part. If the staff at the copyright service station notice that your products are well-received and selling well, they may step in and ask if you'd like to set up a shop at the Base.

(11) Q: Do you think joining Taoxichuan Ceramic Art Avenue has had an impact on your entrepreneurial career?

A: Yes, it has. My income has increased, and I've attracted more customers.

(12) Q: Are there any copyright infringement concerns regarding the earrings you've designed?

A: Not at the moment. I don't actively search for infringements, but as an original creator, I do pay attention if someone brings it to my attention. So far, I haven't taken any legal action because I'm concerned that the process would be time-consuming and costly. It just feels too much of an effort. I haven't explored the Jingdezhen (Ceramic) IPR Rapid Aid Center yet. I believe the pace at which others might copy my designs can't keep up with how quickly I update my work. I've had a few instances of copying in the past, but I didn't pursue legal steps. First, it's a hassle; second, I'm not too bothered by it because I have the ability to keep updating and improving my designs.

(13) Q: How do you assess your competitiveness? Do you have any kind of screening mechanism in place?

A: The competition here is quite intense. It depends on the situation. Sometimes they do a screening process once a month. The person in charge of Taoxichuan Ceramic Art Avenue conducts the screening based on factors like sales, how committed you are to the store, and how often you update your products. Since this is a startup environment, there's always a need for fresh offerings, and turnover is high. If you don't keep improving, it's easy to get filtered out. We receive a 60% subsidy here, with no additional fees. The monthly rent for the shop is 1,000 yuan, but with the subsidy, we only pay 400 yuan. Our stall changes location every three months, with a fee of 400 yuan. Utility costs are also included, with discounts available. It's a very favorable subsidy program.

(14) Q: After you received your copyright registration certificate, did they offer any subsidies or rewards? Was the process of submitting materials complicated?

A: No, there were no subsidies or rewards. Therewas no application fee for the registration process either. The submission of materials wasn't complex—everything required is clearly specified in advance. When I first started, I provided my materials to the service station staff, and they helped me submit them online. As the volume increased, it became more of a consultative process.

(15) Q: You mentioned earlier that the cost of starting a business in Jingdezhen is relatively low. Did you come to this conclusion based on comparisons you made?

A: Yes, I lived in Beijing and worked in other cities for a while. From a production cost perspective, Jingdezhen is very affordable because it's a major hub for raw materials. In other cities, I'd also have to factor in transportation costs. The industrial chain here is well-developed. Plus, rent and living costs are low, making it very convenient. For example, if I need a design made, I can just go straight to the factory, or find a painter who sells pigments. I can simply provide them with a sketch, and they'll be able to make it for me. The communication costs are minimal as well.

4. Mr. Lai, Taoxichuan Entrepreneur

Research Date: August 2023

Research Location: Yikongjian Entrepreneurship and Innovation Incubation Base in Taoxichuan Ceramic Art Avenue

Interviewee: Mr. Lai, Taoxichuan Entrepreneur

(1) Q: Are all these pieces made by you?

A: Yes. From the clay to the finished products, we handle everything ourselves. It all starts with a sketch on paper.

(2) Q: Why did you choose Jingdezhen for your career?

A: I've always been drawn to ceramics because of its endless possibilities. You can paint, sculpt, make functional wares, or even create purely decorative pieces. It allows for both traditional and contemporary artistic expression. What makes Jingdezhen so appealing is the boundless potential this city offers in the ceramic field.

(3) Q: Is the cost of starting a business in Jingdezhen lower than elsewhere?

A: The cost of direct creation is quite high. Many people think clay is cheap, but the production process involves multiple steps, each adding to the overall cost. Also, for younger people, understanding ceramics or appreciating its aesthetic value can be challenging. However, the cost of living here is low, and the ceramics industry in Jingdezhen has already become highly industrialized.

(4) Q: Do you have your own studio now? Was the copyright registration something you applied for on your own initiative?

A: Yes, I have my own studio. I proactively applied for the copyright registration myself.

(5) Q: Are you worried about copyright infringement?

A: Not entirely. There are several reasons why I registered my works. First, I'm determined to become a designer, and registering my works helps build recognition. Plus, the data from the copyright registration help raise public awareness about the importance of protecting original work. Personally, I support the copyright registration system because it makes our work easier. It encourages and inspires creativity, and it also enables us to legally protect our rights.

(6) Q: Have you been focusing on cat-themed creations in recent years?

A: Not exactly. Cats are just one small subset of my work, part of a series of products. I create a lot more than that, which is why I have many copyright certificates.

(7) Q: Before you had your own studio, did you sell at a booth outside?

A: Yes, before I moved into my independent studio, I had a booth. I sold there for two years, and the approval process was pretty lengthy.

(8) Q: How would you compare your experience before and after moving into your own studio here?

A: Of course, there's a notable difference. Moving from an outdoor booth to a studio is essentially a shift in mindset. When you showcase your work here, the key is to have something worth seeing. I hold myself to a high standard, ensuring that the work I bring to the table is solid, tangible, and something people can truly appreciate. This is what sets you apart from others, and being unique is precisely what makes it possible to apply for copyright. If your work is just like everyone else's, you won't be eligible for copyright. And if it's just a random mishmash of copied material, it won't pass the review process.

(9) Q: Do the staff at the copyright service station communicate with you about your work on a regular basis?

A: I go to them when I need to apply. Here's how it works: Any author with a need can approach the copyright staff, and they'll guide you through the whole process step by step. Once you are familiar with the procedure, you can simply take photos of your work and upload them yourself. The review process is quite fast now. One time, I uploaded my work in the morning, and by noon, it had already been reviewed—it's really quick and efficient. Nowadays, even older masters are starting to apply for copyrights, paying much more attention to copyright protection.

(10) Q: Over the years, have you ever been inspired by other people's works? Where do you typically find your inspiration?

A: Creation is inseparable from our lives. For example, a friend of mine has a cat, which inspired the very first cat I made. Over the past three years, I've been able to craft cats purely from imagination. Each piece I create is unique, and my inspiration is always closely intertwined with my everyday experiences.

(11) Q: In your career, what significance do ceramics and Jingdezhen hold for you?

A: My perspective on ceramics has shifted over time, with each phase of my career bringing a new focus. At times, I concentrate on painting; at others, I delve into materials. This suggests the vast potential for growth in ceramics, which spans both material science and artistic exploration. In art, ceramics cover the ancient, contemporary, and even the future, while in material science, Jingdezhen's heritage has blended techniques and materials from across the country. Both fields—art and material science—offer a lifetime of study, and ceramics stands as the fusion of these two realms. This combination is part of why porcelain is so highly valued. Yet it raises a question: Is porcelain expensive because of the cost of its materials, or because of its artistic value? The research potential here is immense. Our generation faces two major challenges—and a heavy responsibility—in combining both art and materials, a true mark of a ceramic artist.

(12) Q: When we interview stall owners outside, many of them mention feeling stuck in a creative bottleneck. Do you have any advice for them?

A: This is a common challenge for many creators, but there's no simple solution— I can only say it's something they must explore on their own. It's deeply connected to their knowledge, perspective, and dedication to learning in the arts. Everyone's artistic pursuit is unique, which is why they ultimately reach different levels.

III. Research Record on the Jingdezhen Intellectual Property Right (IPR) Court

Interview Date: August 2023

Interview Location: Jingdezhen Intellectual Property Right Court

Interviewees: Judge Lin, Head of the Intellectual Property Right Court, and Judge Dan, Intellectual Property Right Court

(1) Q: Since the establishment of the IPR Court, are there data available on overall IPR cases, as well as those specifically involving ceramics and ceramics-related copyright cases?

A: I will send the data on overall IPR cases, ceramic-related IPR cases, and ceramic copyright cases to you shortly in electronic form. In fact, the number of ceramic-related cases here is not high. First, the awareness of IPR protection among the people in Jingdezhen is still developing. Second, jurisdiction rules often require cases to be filed in the court where the defendant resides or where the infringement occurs. As a result, most cases heard in our court are initiated by external parties against residents of Jingdezhen. This also highlights that the people here have a strong sense of originality, focusing primarily on creating unique works rather than on defending against infringement. (We handle first-instance cases involving amounts over one million yuan, as well as second-instance cases.)

(2) Q: From the perspective of collaborative protection through judicial measures and administrative enforcement, and specifically from the viewpoint of the Jingdezhen (Ceramic) IPR Rapid Aid Center, what responsibilities does the court assume?

A: The court collaborates with the IPR Protection Center through a formal partnership. It handles cases involving patents, trademarks, and software copyrights—which often present technical complexities. In such cases, legal expertise alone may not be sufficient, so the role of the technical investigator is essential to bridge the gap between law and technology. For technically complex cases, the court commissions the IPR Center to provide technical reports as a reference. The center also acts as a mediation body, facilitating case resolution, and the IPR Court can then formally confirm these mediation results, ensuring efficient protection. The court also holds regular joint meetings with the Market Supervision Bureau and the Jingdezhen Municipal Bureau of Culture, Broadcasting, Television, Press and Publication, fostering an exchange of experience on intellectual property issues among various. Additionally, during Intellectual Property Awareness Week, these organizations unite to hold joint events, further expanding the reach and impact of IPR awareness efforts.

(3) Q: What are the advantages of the approach to judicial and administrative coordination?

A: We mainly invite technical investigators, who are experts from universities, government agencies, and ceramic research institutes. The initial group of technical investigators primarily specializes in ceramics. Our goal is to establish ceramics as a premium brand, with a strong focus on protecting local brands. Every year, we conduct large-scale visits and surveys as part of our judicial activities. During these, we often uncover issues such as malicious litigation. When such cases arise, we typically implement appropriate countermeasures and conduct public awareness campaigns.

(4) Q: Can you discuss the advantages and prospects of the independent establishment of the IPR Court?

A: We aim to use ceramics as a starting point to create a nationwide model for IPR Courts, positioning it as a demonstration hub for judicial protection with a focus on ceramics.

IV. Research Record on the Taoxichuan Copyright Service Station

Interview Date: August 2023

Interview Location: Taoxichuan Copyright Service Station

Interviewees: Ms. Xu and Ms. Yuan, staff members of the Copyright Service Station

(1) Q: Could you provide an overview of the Taoxichuan Copyright Service Station?

A: The Taoxichuan Copyright Service Station was established in 2019, initiated by the Taoxichuan Management Authority. In that same year, we received an instruction from the city to collaborate with the local Copyright Center to assist entrepreneurs with copyright applications and registrations. The Center provides a green channel for these services. The facilities and personnel are managed by the Jingdezhen Municipal Bureau of Culture, Broadcasting, Television, Press and Publication, with approval from the Publicity Department of the CPC Jiangxi Provincial Committee. The service station scope covers areas such as Taoran Craft Market, Yikongjian Entrepreneurship and Innovation Incubation Base, Yi Gallery, and the Creative Market. Copyright service stations in other parts of Jingdezhen are not managed by the Jingdezhen Municipal Bureau of Culture, Broadcasting, Television, Press and Publication.

The Taoxichuan Copyright Service Station began preparations in 2015 and officially started hosting entrepreneurs in 2016. From 2016 to 2019, even before the service station was formally established, we had already provided copyright services. It wasn't until 2019 that we obtained the qualification to offer intermediary services. Prior to 2019, there was no green channel, so the process was slower. The provincial review of related documents typically took about a month. Now, the Taoxichuan station can complete reviews on the same day, and at most, it takes about a week.

(2) Q: Why do you think it was necessary to establish a copyright service station at Taoxichuan Ceramic Art Avenue?

A: There are both internal needs and a directive from higher authorities. Our market is divided into traditional and creative zones, and because the market turnover is fast, we aim to protect creative products effectively. We also seek to provide a strong platform and better services to support young entrepreneurs and foster innovation.

(3) Q: What are the key areas of focus for your copyright service center?

A: Our key services include copyright consultation and registration, along with registration applications, where the service station conducts the initial review and the provincial bureau handles the final review. We also focus on copyright protection. For copyright disputes, we provide a rights protection channel as part of the IPR Rapid Aid Center. We've also established a local point at Taoxichuan, where any leads would be forwarded to the cultural law enforcement team. We also engage in public awareness efforts, such as holding seminars. Enterprises that settle in Taoxichuan are included in the management scope of the copyright service station. Businesses in the surrounding area also come to us for copyright registration, making it a routine service with a wide reach. The attendance and revenue at the copyright service station are significant, with a high number of applications, which indicates the considerable workload during the initial setup phase.

(4) Q: Are there any specific standards for setting up a stall at the Taoxichuan Night Market?

A: The focus is on handmade crafts, with the goal of creating a nurturing base for young entrepreneurs. Applicants must be under 35 years old and engaged in craftsmanship to apply for a spot.

(5) Q: Could you provide an overview of the Taoxichuan Night Market?

A: The Taoxichuan Night Market is divided into three main sections: the stall market, the Yikongjian Entrepreneurship and Innovation Incubation Base, and Yi Gallery, as well as the workshops. There is a promotion system in place for progression from stalls to the Base and Gallery. Vendors must first operate at the market stalls for at least three months, demonstrating good product quality and a certain level of sales before being eligible to move into the Yikongjian. The specific criteria are as follows:

The market stalls are divided into two sections: the Traditional Zone and the Creative Zone. Stalls are reviewed once a month, with around 1,500 spots available each week, and the stall operators can change every week. Each month, about 4,000 applications for stalls are reviewed, with only 1,500 spots approved. There are no fast-track options for those who have applied before. Before 2019, applications were paper-based and processed offline, but now they are handled online. Designers are responsible for reviewing the applications, and the volume of applications is typically two to three times the available spots. First, Traditional Zone: This zone is for handmade products, mostly focused on works that imitate or replicate existing designs. If the similarity to another product exceeds 60%-80%, the application will not be approved. The copyright service station has its own comparison database, including a local one for Jiangxi Province, as well as the ability to cross-check through platforms like Taobao. Second, Creative Zone: This zone is for original designs. New applicants can have a trial stall for one month, but after that, they must have at least one copyright certificate to continue. Once approved, their work will undergo a quality check for further validation. Stalls in this area are distinguished by either red or yellow umbrellas, depending on the approval status. Third, Creative Zone Advanced—Designer's Collection: This area is curated for a select group of designers. The selection process is roughly as follows: About 70 designers in the Creative Zone Advanced will vote independently. Designers who are not selected may choose not to reapply. These designer stalls are marked with larger white umbrellas and are more spacious than regular stalls. Finally, the Yikongjian Entrepreneurship and Innovation Incubation Base has a fixed number of available spots for new businesses. There are 106 spots on the first floor, and every three months, some businesses are eliminated based on a selection process. This area is more dynamic, with designers managing the space and making decisions through a voting system.

(6) Q: Could you provide more details about the self-management model you mentioned earlier?

A: The copyright service station itself carries an administrative management function, so we don't directly handle the review process to ensure fairness. Instead, the review responsibility is entrusted to the Designer's Collection, where members meet professional standards and can learn from each other, a practice that entrepreneurs highly appreciate. Designers join by application, and any vendor can apply to move from the regular market to the Designer's Collection after one month. The application volume is usually two to three times the available spots. As for Yikongjian Entrepreneurship and Innovation Incubation Base, a management committee is established and rotates every three months.

(7) Q: How has the intellectual property protection work progressed?

A: IPR protection is not a frequent task for us. When stall owners file complaints, we usually resolve them through offline negotiations, which often lead to successful mediation. If there are reports of actual plagiarism, we immediately order the removal of the infringing products. Cases requiring compensation are rare, and if they do arise, they are handled by the enforcement team.

(8) Q: Could you share the process and the number of copyright registrations?

A: Sure. For traditional categories, consultation registrations are relatively few. For creative categories, when the management committee or copyright service station staff encounters a promising vendor, they proactively suggest registering and applying for a copyright certificate. Last month (July), we processed over 4,000 copyright registrations.

(9) Q: What is the target audience for the research and study activities you

organize, and what is the format of these activities?

A: Our main audience consists of students from local universities, such as Jingdezhen Ceramic University and others. The activities we organize typically include internships, lectures, and seasonal markets (held every July and October, featuring both domestic and international artists, including participants from the top eight art academies and local artists). Nearby colleges often send volunteers to assist with these events. Additionally, we run an international residency program called the International Studio, which invites foreign artists to work with us. There is always a rotating group of international artists at the studio, with each cycle lasting either three or six months, and we provide financial support for their stay. The program includes product development, lectures, and cross-cultural exchanges, with dedicated studios for each activity.

V. Research Interview Record of "Yang Jing Piao" (foreign potters in Jingdezhen)

Interview Date: August 2023

Interview Location: Taoxichuan Yikongjian Entrepreneurship and Innovation Incubation Base

Interviewee: Nelson Lim Sang Choon, Singaporean Ceramic Artist

(1) Q: What does Jingdezhen porcelain represent to you?

A: It represents the continuation of history and the essence of Chinese culture as a whole. I have a keen interest in Chinese philosophy, such as the ideas of Laozi, and I've done some research on the subject.

(2) Q: Have any of your well-known works been involved in copyright infringement cases?

A: No, the types of works I create are quite unique, and none of my existing pieces have been registered for copyright protection. However, there have been instances of others copying my work. As an artist, once a piece is completed and exhibited, any imitation within the industry can usually be recognized. I have considered registering my works for copyright protection in the future.

(3) Q: Having visited so many countries, do you feel that China, and Jingdezhen in particular, differs from other countries?

A: The porcelain culture in Jingdezhen is deeply rooted and closely connected to ceramics. The atmosphere in artist residencies here is distinct from other countries, where the focus is often just on the residency itself, without as much emphasis on the creative process. I hope to have more time to explore Jingdezhen more thoroughly.

(4) Q: Are you familiar with Jingdezhen's porcelain culture? What inspired you to choose ceramics as your profession?

A: I bought a book about the local customs of Jingdezhen to gain some insights. When I was in art school, I initially majored in multimedia. In my first year, I had to take all the courses offered by the art department. During a ceramics class, I asked the teacher for more time to complete my projects, and as I spent more time with my mentor, my interest in ceramics grew stronger. By my second year, I switched my major to ceramics. After graduation, I've continued engaging in ceramics education.

(5) Q: What direction do you think the future of Jingdezhen and its ceramics will take?

A: Preserving tradition while embracing continuous innovation is key. The city should be more inclusive in understanding foreign cultures, while also maintaining the essence of its own heritage. Traditional ceramics will always have a market, but their success depends on the overall quality and appeal of the products. As for my own creative direction, I am still in the process of exploration.

(6) Q: What is your opinion on the tradition of passing down craftsmanship in Jingdezhen, such as masters mentoring apprentices or children inheriting their family's craft legacy?

A: There's a big difference between making craftsmanship public and keeping it a secret. In foreign countries, glaze formulas are often shared online, which allows more people to make steady progress. A conservative approach is not conducive to innovation; so I prefer a more open and inclusive attitude towards craftsmanship.

(7) Q: What is your opinion on the lack of interest in ceramic culture and traditional craftsmanship among young people?

A: It's crucial to continuously document and preserve traditional techniques. The guidance of mentors plays a vital role in this process. We should encourage young people and inspire them by sharing our own experiences.

Appendix III

Milestones in Jingdezhen's Efforts to
Build a National Copyright Demonstration City

November 2019: Jingdezhen City received approval from the National Copyright Administration to establish a National Copyright Demonstration City.

April 2020: Jingdezhen Rapid Ceramic Copyright Protection Center was established.

September 2020: The 2020 National Copyright Demonstration Work Training Workshop was held in Jingdezhen by the National Copyright Administration.

November 2020: The Taoxichuan Ceramic Art Avenue in Jingdezhen was granted the "WIPO-NCAC Copyright Award for Copyright Utilization."

April 2021: The Jingdezhen Copyright Association was founded.

July 2021: The Jingdezhen National Ceramic Copyright Trading Center was approved for its establishment.

September 2021: Jingdezhen was granted the title of "National Copyright Demonstration City", marking a significant breakthrough as the first city in Central China to achieve this designation.

January 2022: The Jingdezhen News Media Group Co., Ltd. was approved as a pilot unit for the national "Blockchain + Copyright" initiative.

June 2022: The Jingdezhen Changnanli Ceramic Copyright Trading Center Co., Ltd. was officially launched.

July 2022: "The Silk Road, the Birthplace of Ceramics, an Unhindered Exchange of Wisdom" Ceramics Creative Design (Copyright) Competition was held.

October 2022: Jingdezhen was approved to carry out a World Intellectual Property Organization (WIPO) Research Project on the case study of best practices in copyright utilization and protection, titled "IP and Creative Industry: Jingdezhen Story."

November 2022: The National Copyright Administration and WIPO jointly hosted the 2022 International Copyright Forum and the International Risk Management Training for the Copyright Industry in Jingdezhen.

December 2022: The 5th "Arab Arts Festival" was held in Jingdezhen.

April 2023: Jingdezhen Taoyi Cultural Development Co., Ltd. was honored as one of the "Top 10 Copyright Holders of 2022."

April 2023: The Jingdezhen Copyright Bureau won the "WIPO-NCAC Copyright Awards for Copyright Administration & Management."

October 2023: During the China Jingdezhen International Ceramic Expo, the 2023 Jingdezhen Cultural Innovation and Development Forum and the Copyright Promoting High-Quality Urban Development Forum were held.

December 2023: The "Journey of Ceramics: 2023 Jingdezhen International Ceramic Art Biennale" was held.

Appendix IV

Survey on the Impact of Copyright on the Development of the Jingdezhen's Ceramics Industry

Dear Sir/Madam,

Greetings!

You are about to participate in a survey for the World Intellectual Property Organization (WIPO) Research Project on the Case Study of Best Practice in Copyright Utilization and Protection, titled "IP and Creative Industry: Jingdezhen Story." This research aims to explore copyright protection's impact on impact on the development of Jingdezhen's ceramics industry, support the ongoing improvement of the city's ceramic copyright protection system, and share Jingdezhen's best practices in copyright protection on a global scale. Please note that this survey is not specifically targeted at businesses. Thank you for your participation!

Instructions for Completing the Survey:

1.All information collected in this survey will be used exclusively for academic research purposes. We will ensure that your responses remain strictly confidential.

2.Please select the most appropriate option based on your situation (you can either check the box or enter the corresponding number). For open-ended questions, kindly provide the required text or numbers.

I. Basic Information

Company Name:_____ Registered Capital:_____

1. Your Role: [Single choice]

A. Independent Maker

B. Researcher

C. Manager

D. Company Executive

2. Your age: [Single choice]

A. Under 18

B. 18-35

C. 36-45

D. Over 46

3. How long have you been working in the ceramics industry? [Single choice]

A. Less than 1 year

B. 1-5 years

C. 6-10 years

D. Over 10 years

4. What is the organizational structure of the company or organization you work for in the ceramics industry? [Single choice]

(Note: "Studio" is not a legal term, but rather an operational model. A "studio" can take the form of either an individual business or a company. Please select the option that best reflects your situation.)

A. Joint-stock company (a. Listed company; b. Unlisted company)

B. Limited liability company

C. Sole proprietorship

D. Partnership

E. Individual business

F. Other: _____

5. What is the size of the ceramic company you work for? [Single choice]

A. Fewer than 10 employees

B. 10-50 employees

C. 51-100 employees

D. More than 100 employees

II. Ceramic Copyright Creation and Protection

6. Have you participated in ceramic copyright creation activities? [Single choice]

A. Yes

B. No

7. How many ceramic copyright registrations has your company made in the past five years? [Fill in the blanks]

A. 2023: _____

B. 2022: _____

C. 2021: _____

D. 2020: _____

E. 2019: _____

8. Does your company have a special incentive mechanism for ceramic copyright creation? [Single choice]

A. Yes

B. No

9. How do you think copyright protection impacts ceramic innovation? [Single choice]

A. Promotes innovation

B. No impact

C. Hinders innovation

10. Has your company ever been involved in legal disputes over ceramic copyrights? [Single choice]

A. Yes, there have been international copyright disputes (occurred _____ times)

B. Yes, there have been domestic copyright disputes (the largest amount involved: RMB _____)

C. No

11. When your company encounters ceramic copyright infringement, what methods have you used to resolve the issue? [Multiple choice with variable options]

A. Resolved through third-party mediation

B. Negotiated directly with the infringer

C. Requested arbitration

D. Filed a lawsuit

E. Sought government protection

F. Ignored it

G. Other (please specify): _____

12. What factors do you think contribute to ceramic copyright infringement? [Multiple choice]

A. Weak legal awareness

B. Ineffective market regulation

C. Intense market competition

D. High enforcement costs

E. Profit-driven motives

13. What do you think are the main challenges ceramic companies face in copyright protection? [Multiple choice]

A. Lack of awareness about copyright protection

B. High enforcement costs and insufficient funds

C. Lack of specialized personnel and difficulty in gathering evidence of infringement

D. Ineffective market regulation

E. Other

14. Which departments do you think should be involved in copyright protection for the ceramics industry? [Multiple choice]

A. Government

B. Enterprises

C. Industry associations

D. Legal institutions

E. Educational institutions

15. What specific measures do you think ceramic companies should take for copyright protection? [Multiple choice]

A. Copyright registration

B. Strengthening internal management

C. Raising employee awareness of copyright

D. Initiating copyright enforcement

E. Other

16. What measures do you think can improve copyright protection in the ceramics industry? [Multiple choice]

A. Improve laws and regulations

B. Raise copyright awareness within companies

C. Increase copyright protection training

D. Strengthen market oversight

E. Increase penalties for infringement

F. Develop a diversified copyright dispute resolution mechanism

17. Do you support government agencies strengthening policies for ceramic copyright protection? [Single choice]

A. Yes

B. No

18. In terms of ceramic copyright protection, in which areas would you like relevant departments to strengthen their efforts in the future? [Multiple choice with variableoptions]

A. Take the lead in establishing a ceramic copyright protection fund and provide subsidies for rights protection

B. Build an "administrative + judicial" protection mechanism for ceramic copyrights

C. Enhance consultation services and talent development in ceramic copyright protection

D. Increase penalties for copyright infringement

E. Other (please specify): _____

19. How do you think copyright protection affects the market competitiveness of ceramic products? [Single choice]

A. Enhances competitiveness

B. Has no impact

C. Weakens competitiveness

20. How do you think copyright protection affects the brand value of ceramic products? [Single choice]

A. Increases brand value and strengthens company competitiveness

B. Has no impact

C. Reduces brand value and hinders company development

21. What impact do you think copyright protection in the ceramics industry has on international markets? [Multiple choice]

A. Increases international competitiveness

B. Promotes exports

C. Increases the burden on enterprises

D. Has no significant impact

III. Ceramic Copyright Utilization and Management

22. Has your company ever had the copyright value of its ceramic works assessed by a professional organization? [Multiple choice with variable options]

A. Yes (a. The intangible asset value has been recorded; b. The intangible asset value has not been recorded)

B. No, and currently there are no plans to do so

23. Compared to products without copyright registration, do products with copyright registration tend to have higher prices and higher sales volumes? [Single choice]

A. Yes, both price and sales volume are higher

B. No, neither price nor sales volume is higher

C. Price is higher, but sales volume is not higher

D. Sales volume is higher, but price is not higher

E. Not necessarily (please explain why): _____

24. What methods of copyright utilization has your company explored for ceramic works? [Multiple choice]

A. Ceramic copyright licensing transactions

B. Ceramic copyright transfer or licensing transactions

C. Ceramic copyright pledge, loans, and insurance, etc. (please specify the work name and amount: _____)

25. What challenges do you think the ceramics industry currently faces in copyright utilization? [Multiple choice]

A. Poor transaction transparency

B. Ineffective market regulation

C. Outdated transaction methods

D. Lack of high-quality works

E. Other (please specify): _____

26. In the past five years, what is the highest amount your company has received from ceramic copyright transactions? [Single choice]

A. Less than 100,000 yuan

B. Between 100,000 yuan and 500,000 yuan

C. Between 500,000 yuan and 1,000,000 yuan

D. Over 1,000,000 yuan (please specify the work name and specific amount: __
_____)

27. In the past five years, what has been the average proportion of your company's ceramic copyright transaction amount to its annual revenue? [Single choice]

A. 5% or below

B. Between 6% and 10%

C. Between 11% and 15%

D. Above 15%

28. What do you consider to be the key factors in the process of copyright utilization? [Multiple-choice with variable options]

A. Sufficient financial support

B. A high-quality intellectual property team

C. Supportive policies and incentives

D. Transparent information channels

E. Effective internal incentives

F. A well-established ceramic copyright management system

G. Other (please specify): _____

29. Does your company have a dedicated ceramic copyright management department or specialized personnel? Do you think it is necessary to implement "specialized management" for ceramic copyrights? [Single choice]

A. Yes, it is professionally managed

B. No, and it is necessary to implement it

30. Have you participated in any professional training related to ceramic copyrights? [Single choice]

A. Yes

B. No

31. Does your company have a written intellectual property management system? [Single choice]

A. No written regulations

B. Yes, with written regulations, including (multiple choices): a. Ceramic intellectual property rights ownership system; b. Intellectual property management procedures; c. Intellectual property professional training system; d. Intellectual property evaluation system

32. In your opinion, what areas should be prioritized to improve copyright management in the ceramics industry? [Multiple choice]

A. The government should strengthen the top-level design for copyright management and improve the copyright regulatory system in the ceramics industry

B. Guide ceramic copyright companies to establish internal management mechanisms and improve internal intellectual property regulations

C. Leverage the external management role of industry associations and industrial alliances

D. Increase investment in intellectual property management

33. Which model do you think is more effective in terms of copyright management? [Multiple choice]

A. Managed solely by administrative authorities

B. Strengthen self-management by ceramic copyright companies

C. Government regulatory oversight + Government promotion of company and industry association management

D. Let the market develop freely

IV. Suggestions for Improving Copyright Services

34. Which stages in the ceramics industry do you think are most prone to copyright disputes? [Multiple choice]

A. Design

B. Production

C. Sales

D. Promotion

E. Logistics

35. Which of the following copyright services do you think are beneficial for the development of the ceramics industry? [Multiple choice]

A. Basic ceramic copyright services (such as copyright registration, consulting, etc.)

B. Ceramic copyright operation services (such as ceramic copyright management, etc.)

C. Ceramic copyright transaction services (such as offline transaction centers, online trading platforms, etc.)

D. Ceramic copyright financial services (such as copyright pledging, bonds, financing, etc.)

36. Do you think the current ceramic copyright policies are sufficient? [Single choice]

A. Sufficient

B. Insufficient, need improvements in the following areas (multiple choices): a. Creation; b. Operation; c. Protection

37. What are your suggestions and opinions on how copyright can drive the development of the ceramics industry? [Open-ended question]

_____

Survey completed! Thank you once again for your participation! We wish you a joyful life and continued success in your work!

Appendix V

Survey on the Impact of Copyright on the High-Quality Development of Jingdezhen

Dear Sir/Madam,

Greetings!

You are about to participate in a survey for the World Intellectual Property Organization (WIPO) Research Project on the Case Study of Best Practice in Copyright Protection, titled "IP and Creative Industry: Jingdezhen Story". This research aims to explore the impact of copyright protection on the high-quality development of Jingdezhen, promote the ongoing development of a complete system for copyright creation, utilization, protection, management, and services in the city, and share its experience of using copyright to support high-quality urban development globally. Thank you for your participation!

Instructions for Completing the Survey:

1. All information collected in this survey will be used solely for research purposes, and we will ensure that your responses are kept strictly confidential.

2. Please select the corresponding option based on your actual situation (you can tick the box or directly enter the corresponding number); for questions requiring written answers, please provide the requested text or numbers.

I. Basic Information

1. Your age: [Single choice]
A. Under 18
B. 18-35
C. 36-45
D. Over 46

2. How long have you lived in Jingdezhen? [Single choice]
A. Less than 1 year
B. 1-3 years
C. 4-10 years
D. Over 10 years

3. What is your current profession? [Single choice]
A. Related to the ceramics industry
B. Not related to the ceramics industry
C. Administrative, legal, or public service
D. Other

II. Copyright System

4. Does your profession involve dealing with copyright? [Single choice]
A. Yes, I deal with it regularly
B. Yes, but only occasionally
C. No, I don't deal with it
D. Not sure

5. Have you or your organization ever registered the copyright for your works? [Single choice]

A. Yes, we have registered it

B. No, we haven't registered it

C. Not sure

6. During the process of applying for copyright registration, did you or your organization receive any official services, such as promotional materials, training, or platform support related to the application? [Single choice]

A. Yes, we received these services

B. No, we did not receive these services

C. Not sure

7. Have any of the copyrighted works you or your organization registered been counterfeited or copied? If so, how was the issue typically resolved? [Single choice]

A. Yes, but I don't know how to handle it

B. Yes, we chose to resolve it privately

C. Yes, we resolved it through official mediation, enforcement, or legal action

D. No

E. Other (please specify): _____

8. Have you or your organization ever infringed on someone else's copyrighted works? If so, how was the issue typically resolved? [Single choice]

A. Yes, we chose to resolve it privately

B. Yes, we resolved it through official mediation, enforcement, or legal action

C. No

D. Other (please specify): _____

9. Do you or your organization have any contact with official copyright departments, such as the Jingdezhen Municipal Bureau of Culture, Broadcasting, Television, Press and Publication (Copyright Bureau), Intellectual Property Court, Intellectual Property Protection Center, Cultural Law Enforcement Teams, in your daily life or business operations? [Single choice]

A. Frequent contact

B. Some contact, but not often

C. No contact

D. Not sure

10. In your daily life or business operations, have you or your organization ever received any official copyright-related support, such as copyright funding, training, sales platforms, or other public services provided by the government? [Single choice]

A. Yes, we have received such support

B. No, we have not received such support

C. Not sure

11. Have you heard of the copyright service stations in your area or received any copyright-related services from them (such as copyright knowledge seminars, copyright registration guidance, etc.)? [Single choice]

A. Yes, I have heard of them and received copyright-related services

B. Yes, I have heard of them but have not received any copyright-related services

C. No, I have not heard of them

D. Not sure

12. Do you think official copyright-related actions, such as the green channel for copyright registration, copyright awareness campaigns, and copyright law enforcement, have had any impact on your daily life or your organization's business operations? [Single choice]

A. Yes, the impact is noticeable

B. Yes, but the impact is not obvious

C. No impact

D. Not sure

13. How satisfied are you with the current copyright service system in Jingdezhen? [Single choice]

A. Quite satisfied, it meets the needs of the cultural product market

B. Mostly satisfied, but there are areas that need improvement

C. Not very satisfied, there is significant room for improvement

D. Not sure

14. In your opinion, what areas could Jingdezhen further improve in its copyright service system? [Open-ended question]

III. Socioeconomic Aspects

15. In your personal experience, do you believe registering a work's copyright has economic value? [Single choice]

A. Yes, it can enhance consumer recognition or increase the work's added value

B. It has some value, but the impact is not significant

C. No, it doesn't lead to any noticeable change

D. Not sure

16. In your personal experience, do you think registering a work's copyright can help reduce infringement and piracy in the market? [Single choice]

A. Yes, for example, the registration certificate can be used to demand that infringers cease their activities or pay compensation

B. No, even with copyright registration, it is still difficult to detect infringement in a timely manner

C. Not sure

17. Have you or your organization ever leveraged copyrighted works for conversion or other purposes (such as copyright pledge financing, using copyright as capital for equity, etc.)? [Single choice]

A. Frequently

B. Occasionally

C. Never

18. What is your general attitude towards copyright? [Single choice]

A. I fully recognize the value of copyright and actively register every work

B. I don't have strong opinions, and occasionally register my works

C. I do not recognize the value of copyright and never register my works

D. Other (please specify): _____

19. Has your annual income increased over the past five years? [Single choice]

A. It has grown steadily

B. It has generally increased

C. No increase

D. It has decreased

20. Has your company's annual revenue increased over the past five years? [Single choice]

A. It has grown steadily

B. It has generally increased

C. No increase

D. It has decreased

21. Compared to the past, how do you think the situation of counterfeiting and imitation in the Jingdezhen ceramic market has changed? [Single choice]

A. Much improved, with a significantly greater awareness of authentic products in the market

B. Somewhat improved, but counterfeiting and imitation are still relatively serious issues

C. No significant change

D. Counterfeiting and imitation have worsened

E. Not sure

22. Do you think the current local market competition environment in Jingdezhen can support business development? [Single choice]

A. The market environment is fully competitive and supports business growth

B. The market environment is relatively fair, but there is room for improvement

C. The market environment is average, and many areas need improvement

D. Not sure

23. Compared to the past, how do you perceive the overall development of the Jingdezhen ceramic market? [Single choice]

A. It is more vibrant and has more growth potential than before

B. There has been little change compared to the past

C. It is less dynamic and has less growth potential than before

D. Not sure

24. Do you have any suggestions for optimizing the business environment in Jingdezhen? [Open-ended question]

IV. Innovation Atmosphere

25. In your opinion, which of the following factors is the most crucial for a

product to gain a competitive advantage in the current Jingdezhen market? [Single choice]

A. Creative and aesthetically appealing designs, with a focus on quality (Quality is King)

B. A well-developed upstream and downstream marketing network, with a focus on channels (Channels are King)

C. Thoughtful and convenient after-sales service (Service is King)

D. Low product price (Price is King)

26. In recent years, do you think creative designers in Jingdezhen have been given sufficient recognition within their companies (based on factors such as salary levels or position ranks compared to regular employees)? [Single choice]

A. They are highly valued and hold senior positions in the company

B. They are somewhat valued and hold mid-level positions in the company

C. They are not valued and hold average positions in the company

D. They are undervalued and hold low positions in the company

E. Not sure

27. Does your company or organization take any measures (e.g., specifying copyright matters in contracts with clients) to avoid infringing on others' copyrights during business operations? [Single choice]

A. Yes, we actively take various measures to avoid infringing on others' copyrights

B. Occasionally, we take limited measures to avoid infringing on others' copyrights

C. We don't pay much attention to whether we infringe on others' copyrights

28. Does your company or organization pay attention to protecting its own copyrights during business operations? [Single choice]

A. We proactively take preventive measures and, if infringement occurs, take various actions, including legal actions, to defend our rights

B. We proactively prevent infringement, but cannot or do not effectively protect our rights if infringement occurs

C. We do not proactively prevent infringement, but we will take action to protect our rights if infringement occurs

D. We do not prioritize protecting our copyrights

29. Do you think a culture of "respecting and valuing innovation" has been

established in Jingdezhen? [Single choice]

A. Yes, it has been well-established, and every industry highly values innovative development

B. It has mostly been established, but there are still some issues with infringement and piracy in certain industries

C. No, it has not been established yet, and there is still a long way to go

V. Sustainable Development

30. Has your organization ever experimented with green and eco-friendly creative designs in urban architecture, ceramic production, or other areas? [Single choice]

A. Yes, we have tried

B. No, we haven't

31. Has your organization ever experimented with using new eco-friendly materials or developed new production processes with lower energy consumption and pollution in ceramic manufacturing? [Single choice]

A. We have tried both

B. We have used new eco-friendly materials in ceramic production

C. We have developed new production processes with lower energy consumption and pollution in ceramic production

D. No, we haven't

32. How does your organization handle the industrial waste generated from firing ceramics? [Single choice]

A. It is disposed of as regular waste

B. It is processed using specialized equipment for harmless treatment

C. It is recycled and reused

D. Other (please specify): _____

VI. Social and Cultural Aspects

33. During your time operating a business or living in Jingdezhen, how

convenient have the public services (e.g., public infrastructure, business registration, etc.) been? [Single choice]

A. Both business operations and personal life have been quite convenient

B. Business operations are convenient, but personal life is fairly average

C. Personal life is comfortable, but business services are average

D. Both business operations and personal life are quite average.

E. Not sure

34. Compared to the past, how do you think the appearance of Jingdezhen has changed? [Single choice]

A. It has changed significantly, and the living experience has improved

B. There have been some changes, but the living experience remains average

C. There has been little change

D. Not sure

35. Do you think Jingdezhen is a livable city today? [Single choice]

A. Yes, it is very suitable for living and settling

B. It is generally livable, but there are areas that still need improvement

C. No, there are many areas that need significant improvement

D. Not sure

36. Do you think Jingdezhen today supports personal creativity and talent development? [Single choice]

A. Yes, it fully supports personal creativity and talent development

B. It generally supports it, but there are areas that still need improvement

C. No, both the city's infrastructure and services need significant improvements

D. Not sure

37. How well do you think Jingdezhen preserving and inheriting traditional culture today? [Single choice]

A. The preservation and inheritance are excellent, with a strong cultural atmosphere where traditional culture is frequently experienced

B. The preservation and inheritance are average, and traditional culture can be occasionally felt

C. The preservation and inheritance are poor, with traditional culture almost replaced by modern civilization

D. Not sure

38. From your personal experience, how would you rate Jingdezhen's current

level of economic and cultural exchange with the outside world? [Single choice]

A. It is more open and inclusive, with the number of domestic and international tourists continuing to grow, and more cultural exchanges

B. There has been little change compared to before

C. There are fewer foreign visitors, with a decrease in cultural exchanges

D. Not sure

39. Do you plan to live in Jingdezhen long-term in the future? [Single choice]

A. Yes

B. No

C. Not sure

40. What do you think are the main factors that might attract people to live in Jingdezhen? [Multiple choice]

A. Natural factors, such as climate and geography

B. Economic factors, such as a fair market environment and industry clustering

C. Cultural factors, such as a strong cultural and artistic atmosphere

D. Urban development factors, such as convenient public services and well-developed infrastructure

41. In your opinion, which areas still need improvement in Jingdezhen? [Open-ended question]

_____

Survey Complete!

Thank you again for your participation. We wish you a joyful life and continued success in your work!

References

Chapter II

Monographs

Qiao Yanxiu and He Xiling, eds., *Fuliang County Annals: Food, Goods and Pottery Administration*, Volume Eight, Engraved Edition of the Third Year of the Emperor Daoguang's Reign of the Qing Dynasty.

Xiong Liao and Xiong Wei, eds., *Collection of Ancient Chinese Ceramic Texts* (Shanghai: Shanghai Culture Publishing House, 2006).

The Publicity Department of the CPC Jingdezhen Municipal Committee, ed., *A Brief History of Jingdezhen Ceramics* (Nanchang: Jiangxi Education Publishing House, 2023).

Song Lian, *The History of the Yuan*, Volume 88 (Beijing:Zhonghua Book Company, 1976), 2227.

Jingdezhen Municipal Local Chronicles Office, eds., *The Porcelain Capital of China: Jingdezhen Ceramics Chronicle, Volume II* (Beijing: China Local Records Publishing House, 2004).

Newspaper or journal articles

"Embrace Innovation, Make Strides, Leverage Strengths, Address Weaknesses, Strengthen the Foundation, Promote Renewal, and Strive to Write a New Chapter of Chinese-style Modernization in Jiangxi," *People's Daily*, October 14, 2023.

Feng Hefa, "Current Status and Trade Conditions of China's Ceramics Industry," International Trade Newspaper, 1932(03).

"Fostering Cultural Vitality Through a New Intangible Cultural Heritage Ecosystem: Highlights and Achievements of Jingdezhen's Intangible Cultural Heritage Protection Work," *Jingdezhen Ceramics*, 2022(03).

Zhang Long, "Jingdezhen, Jiangxi: Using Porcelain as a Medium to Strike a Strong Punch in Online International Communication," *China Cybersecurity Review*, 2024(07).

Chapter III

Monographs

Qiao Yanxiu and He Xiling, eds., *Fuliang County Annals: Food, Goods and Pottery Administration*, Volume Eight, Engraved Edition of the Third Year of the Emperor Daoguang's Reign of the Qing Dynasty.

Hong Yanzu, wrote, Hong Zai, ed., *Excerpts from the Apricot Garden*, Siku Quanshu Edition.

Zhang Bai and Yao Jing, eds., *The Grand View: A Collection of Essays on the Blue-and-White Porcelain Pilgrimage During the Late Yuan and Early Ming Dynasties* (Nanchang: Jiangxi Fine Arts Publishing House, 2017).

Xu Pu et al. wrote, and Li Dongyang et al. Revised the *"Ming Hui Dian"* (*The Ming Code*), Volume 157, in the Siku Quanshu edition.

Tie Yuan and Xi Ming, *A History of Qing Dynasty Imperial Kiln Porcelain II* (Beijing: China Pictorial Press, 2012).

Xiong Liao and Xiong Wei, eds., *Collection of Ancient Chinese Ceramic Texts* (Shanghai: Shanghai Culture Publishing House, 2006).

Jingdezhen Municipal Local Chronicles Office, ed., *The Porcelain Capital of China: Jingdezhen Ceramics Chronicle Volume II* (Beijing: China Local Records Publishing House, 2004).

Lan Pu and Zheng Tinggui, wrote, Yu Zhuqing. ed., *A New Reading of Classical Jingdezhen Porcelain Records* (Hefei: Huangshan Publishing House, 2015).

Zhou Lin and Li Mingshan, eds., *Research Literature on the History of Copyright in China* (Beijing: China Fangzheng Press, 1999).

Tie Yuan and Xi Ming, *Identification of Republican Era Porcelain: Body Glaze, Colored Decoration, and Shape* (Beijing: Hualing Publishing House, 2004).

Jingdezhen City Chronicles Compilation Committee, ed., *Outline of Jingdezhen City Chronicles*(Shanghai: Chinese Dictionary Publishing House, 1989).

Robert Finley, *The Pilgrim Art: Cultures of Porcelain in World History*, Trans. Zheng Mingxuan (Haikou: Hainan Publishing House, 2015).

Lothar Ledderose, *Ten Thousand Things: Module and Mass Production in Chinese Art*, Trans. Zhang Zong et al. (Beijing: SDX Joint Publishing Company, 2005).

Yu Jiadong, *History of Jiangxi Ceramics* (Zhengzhou: Henan University Press, 1997).

Wang Guangyao, *The Ming Dynasty Palace Ceramic History* (Beijing: The Forbidden City Publishing House, 2010).

Newspaper or journal articles

Jiangxi Provincial Institute of Cultural Relics and Archaeology, Leping Museum, Jingdezhen Ceramic Archaeological Institute, Jingdezhen Folk Kiln Museum, "Report on the Survey of the Nanyao Kiln Site in Leping, Jiangxi," *Journal of National Museum of China*, 2013 (10).

Guo Jianhui, "The Contemporary Value and Practical Path of Cultural Heritage Protection and Transmission—Based on the Investigation of the Jingdezhen Qingbai Porcelain Site Cluster," *Jiangxi Social Sciences*, 2023, 43 (01).

Xu Changqing and Yu Jiang'an, "New Archaeological Discoveries at Hutian Kiln," *Palace Museum Journal*, 2004 (02).

Weng Yanjun, Jiang Jianxin, Qin Dashu, and Jiang Xiaomin, "Excavation Brief Report of the SongYuan Remains at Luomaqiao Kiln Site in Jingdezhen, Jiangxi,"

Cultural Relics, 2017 (05).

Zhan Jia, Zhao Chuanyu and Yuan Shenggen, "The Evolution of Ceramic Culture Landscape in Jingdezhen Throughout Historical Periods," *Agricultural Archaeology*, 2009 (06).

Chen Chaoyun, "Archaeological Observations on Porcelain Manufacturing Techniques during the Song Dynasty," *Acta Archaeologica Sinica*, 2017 (04).

Xu Xiangyu, "Classification and Verification of Some Textual Records on Song Jingdezhen Qingbai Porcelain," Master's Thesis, Jingdezhen Ceramic University, 2022.

Zhao Yan, "Examination of the Inscription on the Blue-and-White Cloud Dragon Pattern Elephant Ear Vase from the 11th Year of Zhizheng Reign of the Yuan Dynasty," *New Arts*, 2013, 34 (04).

Wang Guangyao, "Observations on the Ancient Official Sample System in China from the Palace Museum's Collection of Qing Dynasty Porcelain Samples: A Study of the Qing Imperial Kiln Factory, Part Two," *Palace Museum Journal*, 2006 (06).

School of Archaeology and Museology at Peking University, Jiangxi Provincial Institute of Cultural Relics and Archaeology, Jingdezhen Ceramic Archaeological Research Institute, "Excavation Report on the Ming and Qing Imperial Kiln Site in Jingdezhen, Jiangxi," *Cultural Relics*, 2007 (05).

"Jingdezhen City Strengthens Protection of Copyright for Ceramic Works," *Jiangxi Daily*, Mar. 22, 2010.

"The Water Mill Construction Technique of Jingdezhen Ceramics (Fifth Batch of National Intangible Cultural Heritage Representative Projects in 2021)," Jingdezhen Ceramics , 2022(03).

Zhang Wenjiang, "Significant Discoveries from the Archaeological Excavation of the Nanyao Site in Jingdezhen," *Cultural Relics of the East*, 2014 (02).

Cheng Renfa, "A Study on the Decorative Techniques of Qingbai Porcelain in Jingdezhen during the Song Dynasty," *China Ceramic*, 2015, 51 (12).

Zhou Juemin, "A Brief Discussion on the Rise of Ceramic Decal Paper in China," *Jingdezhen Ceramics*, 1982 (03).

Li Yiping, "The Hutian Kiln during the Song Dynasty," *Southern Cultural Relics*, 2003 (01).

Ye Wencheng, "Export of Qingbai Porcelain Kiln System in Jingdezhen during the Song and Yuan Dynasties," *Jingdezhen Ceramics*, 1989 (03, 04).

Zhou Sizhong, "The Historical and Cultural Characteristics, Porcelain Production System, and Development Strategy of Jingdezhen," *China Ports*, 2020(S2).

Weng Yanjun, "Estimation of the Scale of Ceramic Exports from Jingdezhen in the 16th to 18th Centuries," *China Ceramics*, 2021, 57 (10).

Zhang Zebing, "Historical Experience and Contemporary Practices of Inheriting and Innovating Jingdezhen Ceramic Culture," *Jiangxi Social Sciences*, 2022 (12).

Chapter IV

Monographs

Bronwyn H. Hall and Nathan Rosenberg, *Handbook of the Economics of Innovation, Volume 1*, Trans. Shanghai Institute for Science of Science (Shanghai: Shanghai Jiao Tong University Press, 2017).

Newspaper or journal articles

Wang Zhibiao, "Path Analysis of the Industrialization of Traditional Cultural Resources," *Journal of Henan University* (*Social Sciences Edition*),2012, 52 (02).

Dai Yu, "Research on the Spatial Agglomeration of the Cultural Industry: A Case Study of Hunan Province," Doctoral Thesis, Wuhan University of Technology, 2013.

Feng Weiyi and Li Shimeng, "Research on the Mechanism of Value Co-Creation in Innovation Networks from the Perspective of Intellectual Property Operations," *Information Science*, 2023, 41 (01).

He Zhen and Wei Dahai, "Reform Exploration and Active Innovation: A Summary of the Symposium on 'Three-in-One' Judicial Protection of Intellectual Property," *Journal of Law Application*, 2010 (08).

Cui Shanshan, Zhang Weihao and Wang Yanan, "Judicial Protection of Intellectual Property and the Complexity of Enterprises Importing Technologies: A Quasi-Natural Experiment Based on Intellectual Property Cases under the 'Three-in-One' System," *Macroeconomics*, 2023 (05).

Zhuang Jiaqiang, Wang Hao and Zhang Wentao, "Does Strengthening Judicial Protection of Intellectual Property Contribute to Enterprise Innovation? — Evidence from the Establishment of Intellectual Property Courts," *Contemporary Finance & Economics*, 2020 (09).

Qi Jiangang, "On the Reform of China's Administrative Protection Model for Intellectual Property," *Wuhan University Journal (Philosoply & Social Science)*, 2020 (02).

Chapter V

Newspaper or journal articles

Sun Wusheng, "On the Copyright Protection System and the Development of Cultural and Creative Industries," *Law Science Magazine*, 2016 (10).

Ni Feng, "Research on the Business Model of Cloud Gaming Platforms: A Case Study of OnLive," *Quality & Market*, 2020 (16).

Xiang Yong, "Research on the Development Model of China's Cultural Industry during the Transitional Period," *Dongyue Tribune*, 2016 (02).

Wang Xingpeng, "Copyright Industry: A New Source of Regional Economic Development," *China Copyright*, 2013 (04).

Du Ping and Zhou Weigui, "The Female Image from the Perspective of Male Discourse: Venus in Shakespeare's Works," *Journal of Hainan University (Humanities and Social Sciences Edition)*, 2011 (06).

Jiang Yuhong and Shan Xiaoguang, "The Impact of *Intellectual Property* Systems on Urban Competitiveness: An Analysis Based on Innovation Incentives," Intellectual Property, 2007 (03).

Zhou Zhenhua, Chen Wei, Tang Jingbo, Huang Jianfu, Shen Kaiyan, Jing Xueqing and Yang Yaqin, "A Comparative Study of Comprehensive Competitiveness Among Several Major Cities in China," *Shanghai Journal of Economics*, 2001 (01).

Han Jian and Xu Yayun, "Intellectual Property Protection and the Use of Foreign Capital," *Business and Management Journal*, 2021 (04).

Chapter VI

Newspaper or journal articles

Cai Ying, "Creating a Cultural and Civilized Environment for High-Quality Development," *China Intellectual Property News*, December 15, 2021.

图书在版编目（CIP）数据

IP与创意产业：景德镇故事：汉英对照 / 中国国
家版权局, 世界知识产权组织编著. –– 南昌：江西人民
出版社, 2025. 7. –– ISBN 978-7-210-16117-2

Ⅰ. G239.275.63

中国国家版本馆CIP数据核字第202547T3S7号

IP与创意产业：景德镇故事
IP YU CHUANGYI CHANYE：JINGDEZHEN GUSHI

中国国家版权局　世界知识产权组织　编著

出版人：梁　菁　组稿编辑：李月华　书籍设计：章　雷

责任编辑：（汉）章　雷　李鉴和　万莲花

　　　　　（英）吴丽红　陈　茜

出版发行：江西人民出版社　　地址：江西省南昌市东湖区三经路47号附1号

编辑部电话：0791-86898860　　发行部电话：0791-86898815　　邮编：330006

网址：www.jxpph.com　E-mail：120708658@qq.com

经销：各地新华书店

版次：2025年7月第1版　　印次：2025年7月第1次印刷

开本：720毫米 × 1000毫米　1/16　印张：28.25　字数：（汉）182千字　（英）228千字

书号：ISBN 978-7-210-16117-2　　赣版权登字-01-2025-235

定价：128.00元

承印厂：浙江海虹彩色印务有限公司